British Business in the Formative Years of European Integration, 1945–1973

This book questions conventional accounts of the history of European integration and British business. Integration accounts conventionally focus on the nation-state, while Neil Rollings focuses on business and its role in the development of European integration, which business historians have overlooked to this point. Business provided a key link between economic integration, political integration, and the process of Europeanization. British businessmen perceived early on that European integration meant much more than the removal of tariffs and access to new markets. Indeed, British entry into the European community would alter the whole landscape of the European working environment. Consideration of European integration was revealed as a complex, relative, and dynamic issue, covering many issues such as competition policy, taxation, and company law. Based on extensive archival research, this book uses the case of business to emphasize the need to blend national histories with the history of European integration.

Neil Rollings (b. 1961) is currently Head of Department and Senior Lecturer in the Department of Economic and Social History at the University of Glasgow. Rollings previously held posts at the University of Leeds and the University of Bristol. In 2000–2001 he was Associate Professor in the Institute of Economic Research at Hitotsubashi University, Tokyo. Rollings is currently joint chair of the University of Glasgow Business School Strategic Advisory Board and on the Council of the Economic History Society. He is the immediate past treasurer of the Association of Business Historians. Rollings is the joint author of *Economic Planning 1943–51* (1992) and *Economic Policy under the Conservatives 1951–64* (2004) and joint editor of *Labour Governments and Private Industry* (1992).

CAMBRIDGE STUDIES IN THE EMERGENCE
OF GLOBAL ENTERPRISE

Editors

Louis Galambos, *The Johns Hopkins University*

Geoffrey Jones, *Harvard Business School*

Other books in the series

National Cultures and International Competition: The Experience of Schering AG, 1851–1950, by Christopher Kobrak, ESCP-EAP, European School of Management

The World's Newest Profession: Management Consulting in the Twentieth Century, by Christopher D. McKenna

Knowledge and Competitive Advantage: The Coevolution of Firms, Technology, and National Institutions, by Johann Peter Murmann, Australian Graduate School of Management

Global Brands: The Evolution of Multinationals in Alcoholic Beverages, by Teresa da Silva Lopes

Banking on Global Markets: Deutsche Bank and the United States, 1870 to the Present, by Christopher Kobrak, ESCP-EAP, European School of Management

British Business in the Formative Years of European Integration, 1945–1973

NEIL ROLLINGS

University of Glasgow

CAMBRIDGE
UNIVERSITY PRESS

CAMBRIDGE UNIVERSITY PRESS
Cambridge, New York, Melbourne, Madrid, Cape Town, Singapore, São Paulo, Delhi

Cambridge University Press
32 Avenue of the Americas, New York, NY 10013-2473, USA

www.cambridge.org
Information on this title: www.cambridge.org/9780521888110

First published 2007

Printed in the United States of America

A catalog record for this publication is available from the British Library.

Library of Congress Cataloging in Publication Data
Rollings, Neil.
British business in the formative years of European integration : 1945–1973 / Neil Rollings.
p.   cm. – (Cambridge studies in the emergence of global enterprise)
Includes bibliographical references and index.
ISBN 978-0-521-88811-0 (hardback)
1. Europe – Economic integration.   2. Great Britain – Economic integration – History.
3. European Economic Community countries – Foreign economic relations.
I. Title.   II. Series.
HC241.R585   2008
338.094109′045–dc22   2007029413

ISBN   978-0-521-88811-0 hardback

To Sue, Emma, and Beth

Contents

List of Tables and Figure

TABLES

FIGURE

Series Editors' Preface

The story of business history within European integration has just begun to be written amidst a shift in the literature identifying the importance of business and economic interests rather than political ones in the process. There has been until now no reliable historical study of the policies of British business towards European integration. Given the importance of British business in the global economy and the new European system, we welcome this addition to the literature and to our series, Cambridge Studies in the Emergence of Global Enterprise.

Here you will find an account based on rich research in the extensive British government records held in that country's National Archives and the records of the key peak association, the FBI. Professor Rollings uses these and other archives to develop the first serious account of how, exactly, British business adapted to the challenges of integration. The book presents much information that is new and integrates the archival evidence with the relevant secondary literature in English and several other languages in history, political science, management, and economics. The coverage is indeed comprehensive. This is an authoritative economic and business history that helps us understand the twists and turns of political economy in an era when a new European system was emerging.

Geoffrey Jones
Harvard Business School

Louis Galambos
The Johns Hopkins University

Acknowledgements

This book has a very long history, and, as a result, a large number of personal and institutional debts have been built up. The book has also changed so enormously in that time that those with an early input may not recognize it. These early contributions came from Jim Smyth and Alan McKinlay, with whom the original ideas were developed, as well as Helen Mercer and Robbie Wilson who carried out a lot of the original research. My colleagues in the Department of Economic and Social History at the University of Glasgow have shown remarkable patience and support over the years, and each indirectly, if not directly, has played a key role in the completion of the project. I believe I am extremely fortunate to work with such a talented and collegial group of individuals. In particular, I must mention Mike French, Duncan Ross, Catherine Schenk, Tony Slaven, and Ray Stokes for commenting on early drafts of the work. The last two have also offered financial support as Directors of the Centre for Business History in Scotland, based in the Department, which allowed me to present papers related to the research at various conferences and to visit archives. Special mention must also go to the Centre's support of a symposium to discuss the manuscript in June 2006. For Ray Stokes and the Centre to show that degree of belief and support in the project, in addition to the valuable comments received, was enormously appreciated. During the years 2000–1, I was also an associate professor at the Institute of Economic Research, Hitotsubashi University in Tokyo. This was a richly rewarding experience with superb research facilities, and I would like to thank all my colleagues there during that year, and in particular, Tamotsu Nishizawa, who arranged the invitation and acted as my mentor.

Financial support for the project came from the Leverhulme Trust, the Arts and Humanities Research Board (now Council), the British Academy, the University of Glasgow, and, as already mentioned, the Centre for Business History in Scotland. All are gratefully acknowledged. Funding from the Economic and Social Research Council as part of the Whitehall Programme and for the handbook *Economic Policy under the Conservatives, 1951–64* was not directly relevant to the project but was also important in widening and deepening my understanding of business–government relations in Britain. Similarly, the support and assistance of many archives and archivists are also acknowledged with gratitude, as is their willingness to let me use this archive material. Particular thanks should be made to the National Archives, the Modern Records Centre at the University of Warwick, the Glasgow University Archives Business Record Centre, the Guildhall Library, the Conservative Party Archives at the Bodleian Library in Oxford, the Courtaulds Archive, and many other local repositories around Britain. I must also thank P.I.E. Peter Lang for permission to use copyrighted material in Chapter 10 previously published in Marine Moguen-Toursel (ed), *Firm strategies and public policy in integrated Europe* (1950–1980); the Confederation of British Industry, for permission to use and cite the CBI Predecessor Archive at Warwick; and Akzo Nobel UK Ltd for permission to use and cite material from the Courtaulds Archive. Finally, in this respect I would like to thank Mrs Marjorie Hollowood, widow of Bernard Hollowood, for kind permission to reproduce the cartoon used on the cover, and Jane Hollowood, her daughter, for her efforts in arranging this.

Many other individuals need to be thanked too. They include Katie Barclay, Sue Bowden, Ted Bromund, Werner Bührer, Martin Chick, Duncan Connors, Anne Crowther, Teresa da Silva Lopes, Anne Deighton, Eleanor Gordon, Matthias Kipping, Rodney Lowe, Roger Middleton, Marine Moguen-Toursel, George Peden, Astrid Ringe, Janette Rutterford, Stephen Sambrook, Harm Schröter, Jim Tomlinson, and Alasdair Young. Here I must also thank the series editors, Geoff Jones and Lou Galambos, for their interest in and support of the project. Frank Smith at Cambridge University Press in New York has been a very accommodating and helpful editor supported by a very efficient production team.

Finally, I must thank Sue and my two daughters, Emma and Beth, for their enormous patience, support, and encouragement. As this project was nearing completion, one of my daughters asked if it would take as long to read this book as it has taken to write. I hope not!

Abbreviations

ABCC	Association of British Chambers of Commerce
AFBEE	Association for Franco-British Economic Expansion
BDI	Bundesverband der Deutschen Industrie
BEC	British Employers' Confederation
BISF	British Iron and Steel Federation
BPBMA	British Paper and Board Makers' Association
CAP	Common Agricultural Policy
CBI	Confederation of British Industry
CCI	Consultative Committee for Industry
CDEIF	Council of Directors of European Industrial Federations
CEIF/CIFE	Council of European Industrial Federations
CIA	Commonwealth Industries Association
CIFEFTA	Council of the Industrial Federations of the Outer Seven
CNPF	Conseil National du Patronat Français
CPA	Conservative Party Archives
DTI	Department of Trade and Industry
EC	European Community
ECE	Export Council for Europe
ECOSOC	UN's Economic and Social Committee
ECSC	European Coal and Steel Community
EEC	European Economic Community
EFTA	European Free Trade Association
EIU	Economist Intelligence Unit
ELEC	European League for Economic Co-operation
ERP	European Recovery Program
EU	European Union
FBI	Federation of British Industries
FCO	Foreign and Commonwealth Office
FDI	Foreign Direct Investment
FTA	Free Trade Area
GATT	General Agreement on Trade and Tariffs
GLA	Guildhall Library Archive
GUABRC	Glasgow University Archives Business Records Centre
HMG	His/Her Majesty's Government

ICC	International Chamber of Commerce
ICI	Imperial Chemical Industries
ISB	Iron and Steel Board
MRC	Modern Record Centre, University of Warwick
NABM	National Association of British Manufacturers
NCB	National Coal Board
NEDC	National Economic Development Council
NEDO	National Economic Development Office
NFU	National Farmers' Union
NUM	National Union of Manufacturers
OEEC	Organisation for European Economic Co-operation
OTP	Overseas Trade Policy
PEP	Political and Economic Planning
SE	Societas Europaea
SMMT	Society of Motor Manufacturers and Traders
TNA	The National Archives, London
TUC	Trade Unions Congress
UN	United Nations
UNICE	Union des Industries de la Communauté Européenne

1

Introduction

In March 1957, six countries – Belgium, France, West Germany, Italy, Luxemburg, and the Netherlands – signed the Treaty of Rome that created the European Community (EC).[1] Half a century later, the European Union (EU), as it is now known, consisting of twenty-seven countries with a total population of more than 450 million, covers Central and Eastern Europe as well as Western Europe and is likely to grow even larger in the near future. In 2004, if one includes intra-EU trade, the then twenty-five-member EU constituted 42 percent of the world's merchandise exports and 52 percent of the world's commercial services exports. It is no understatement to say that European integration has changed the lives of millions of people, and not just those in Europe. It is the largest trading partner for many nations in the world, including the newly industrialized economies of China and India, and is the source of half of the foreign profits of corporate America.[2] Indeed, it is popularly presented as a competitor or alternative model to the United States.[3] That it is common to refer to "Europe" in this context as a single entity well illustrates the impact of European integration. There are many regional free trade areas in the world today, but none have taken the extra step of creating supranational institutions to which national governments have handed over sovereignty, as has happened in the EC.

Few would have envisaged this future in the early 1950s when the Six, as the group of the six member states was commonly known, originally came together to sign the Treaty of Paris in 1951, which created the European Coal

---

[1] For the purposes of consistency and simplicity the term European Community (EC) is used wherever feasible throughout this book. Technically, there were three European Communities until 1967. These were the European Coal and Steel Community (ECSC); the European Economic Community (EEC), which was also often called the Common Market; and Euratom. The European Union (EU) came into existence in the early 1990s with the ratification of the Treaty of European Union.

[2] Dieter Zetsche, president and CEO, Chrysler Group, "Managing the Global Firm: Lessons of a Transatlantic Merger," talk at the University of Michigan, 8 March 2005.

[3] T. R. Reid, *The United States of Europe: The New Superpower and the End of American Hegemony* (London: Penguin, 2004); Jeremy Rifkin, *The European Dream: How Europe's Vision of the Future is Quietly Eclipsing the American Dream* (Cambridge: Polity, 2004); Rockwell Schnabel, *The Next Superpower? The Rise of Europe and Its Challenge to the United States* (Lanham, MD: Rowman & Littlefield, 2005).

and Steel Community (ECSC), the forerunner of the European Community. Its novelty, therefore, stands out and has provoked debate about what wider lessons can be learned about regional integration given the uniqueness of the experiment. Nor has the history of European integration been straightforward and predictable. Many explanations and theories of European integration have been developed only for events to highlight their flaws.[4] These aspects alone make the history of European integration a fascinating subject. There is much more than this to the subject. Its development has posed all sorts of questions about issues that normally are taken for granted: It offers an alternative lens to provide new insights on topics across the social science and historical disciplines and, as a result, it has been a fertile area for new theoretical advances in the social sciences.[5] It is a boom subject on both sides of the Atlantic, and a vast and ever-growing literature on the subject has emerged, with many disciplines – economics, politics, legal studies, sociology, social anthropology, geography, and history among others – offering their insights on the course of European integration.[6]

HISTORIOGRAPHY

Despite this plethora of approaches, in many respects the study of European integration remains disappointing and unfulfilled. Much work remains discipline specific or at best multidisciplinary and there is a tendency for these disciplines to talk past each other. Yet, on paper at least, the study of European integration is admirably suited for truly interdisciplinary analysis.[7] In part this problem goes back to the roots of the subject when there was a very clear divide between the economic and political aspects of European integration. Few would deny that European integration is both an economic process *and* a political process.[8] Yet the two are often separated for theoretical clarity. Thus, market integration has its roots in the economic theory of international trade, while the origins of the theory of political integration lie in the study of international relations. More than twenty–five years ago, this

4 Alan S. Milward, *The European Rescue of the Nation-State* (London: Routledge, 2nd edn., 2000), 1–20; Andrew Moravcsik, *The Choice for Europe: Social Purpose and State Power from Messina to Maastricht* (London: UCL Press, 1999), 18–85.
5 Michelle Cini and Angela Bourne (eds.), *Palgrave Advances in European Union Studies* (Basingstoke: Palgrave, 2006); and Antje Wiener and Thomas Dietz (eds.), *Theories of European Integration: Past, Present and Future* (Oxford: Oxford University Press, 2003).
6 John T. S. Keeler, "Mapping EU Studies: The Evolution from Boutique to Boom Field 1960–2001," *Journal of Common Market Studies*, Vol. 43, No. 3 (2005) 551–82.
7 Angela Bourne and Michelle Cini, "Introduction: Defining Boundaries and Identifying Trends in European Union Studies," in Cini and Bourne (eds.), *Palgrave Advances*, 7; and Erik Jones and Amy Verdun, "Introduction," in Erik Jones and Amy Verdun (eds.), *The Political Economy of European Integration: Theory and Analysis* (London: Routledge, 2005), 3.
8 Amy Verdun, "Political Economy and European Integration," in Cini and Bourne (eds.), *Palgrave Advances*, 175–89.

point was made in relation to market integration and political integration: These two forms of integration interact with each other and in many ways are interdependent but are still often studied in isolation from one another.[9] Indeed, to magnify the difference, market integration is associated with what is often referred to as negative integration, that is, the removal of barriers to trade, while political integration is presented as positive integration in the form of harmonization or common policies.[10] To the extent that there is a link acknowledged it is often in the form of presenting economic processes and economic issues – the customs union, the single market initiative, and economic and monetary union are cases – as means to political ends.

Another feature of the existing literature is the focus on the nation-state. In many ways, it is inevitable and understandable that the nation-state is the key unit of analysis and the key actor in European integration studies. However, making the nation-state the center of attention does have important consequences. There has been a tendency for nonstate actors to be marginalized in mainstream accounts of European integration, although there are some signs that this is changing.[11] Explicitly assumed away or just ignored, actors like businesses are usually accorded a secondary supporting role or, if given greater prominence, attention does not move beyond consideration of the elite peak of business representatives. This book takes a different perspective by making business the key point of analysis. What are the justifications for taking this different approach? First, approaching subjects with different perspectives illuminates aspects of the subject that otherwise remain in the dark. Although it is common to refer to European integration as a process, most work is only interested in the process as it most directly affects the formal political outcomes. Thus, the wider economic and social forces of integration remain in the background. This "hidden integration" is nevertheless part of the broad process of European integration.[12] Business plays an important role in this process via corporate strategy: The strategies that firms adopt

[9] J. Pelkmans, "Economic Theories of Integration Revisited," *Journal of Common Market Studies*, Vol. 18, No. 4 (1980), 333–54.

[10] For a focus on the market-freeing nature of European integration see J. Gillingham, *European Integration 1950–2003: Superstate or New Market Economy?* (Cambridge: Cambridge University Press, 2003). See also Éric Bussierè, Michel Dumoulin and Sylvain Schirmann (eds.), *Europe Organisée, Europe du Libre-échange? Fin XIXe Siècle – Années 1960* (Brussels: P.I.E. Peter Lang, 2006).

[11] Maria Green Cowles, "Non-state Actors and False Dichotomies: Reviewing IR/IPE Approaches to European Integration," in Jones and Verdun (eds.), *Political Economy*, 25–38; Wolfram Kaiser and Peter Starie (eds.), *Transnational European Union: Towards a Common Political Space* (Abingdon: Routledge, 2005); and Neil Rollings and Matthias Kipping, "Private Transnational Governance in the Heyday of the Nation-State: The Council of European Industrial Federations (CEIF)," *Economic History Review*, Vol. 61 (2008), forthcoming.

[12] Thomas Misa and Johan Schot, "Inventing Europe: Technology and the Hidden Integration of Europe," *History and Technology*, Vol. 21, No. 1 (2005), 1–19; and Jytte Klausen and Louise Tilly, "European Integration in a Social and Historical Perspective," in Jytte Klausen

impact upon European integration at the political level.[13] The single market program of the 1980s is a prime example of this. This marked a renewed effort to create a single market in the EC as part of a relaunching of European integration. It was quickly recognized that however successful the removal of barriers was, the very success of the initiative in terms of improving growth performance and the competitiveness of European business was dependent on the response of business to the opportunities and threats created by the legislation.[14] The European Commission regarded it as sufficiently important to carry out its own research as part of the assessment of the "costs of non-Europe," that is, of not establishing a single market. The third volume of the sixteen-volume study consisted of the results of a questionnaire of European business on their expectations and intentions in the light of the single market initiative, to which 11,000 firms responded.[15] Further work followed on the effect of the single market at the sectoral level, and in 1996, a retrospective survey to test business perceptions of the impact of the single market program was also undertaken.[16] The extent of such efforts is some indication of the recognition of the intertwined, interdependent, and coterminous relationship between business strategy and policy in the context of European integration. In the 1960s, Charles Kindleberger made clear the importance of business in this sense: "If European integration is really to be achieved, there must develop European corporations."[17]

Business can also play a role in the initiation of political integration. Again, the single market program provides a good case study. The role of business

and Louise Tilly (eds.), *European Integration in Social and Historical Perspective: 1850 to the Present* (Lanham, MD: Rowman and Littlefield, 1997), 3–21.

[13] On corporate responses to European integration see Geoffrey Jones and Peter Miskell, "European Integration and Corporate Restructuring: The Strategy of Unilever 1957–1990," *Economic History Review*, Vol. 58, No. 1 (2005), 113–30.

[14] Pierre Buiges and Alexis Jacquemin, "Strategies of Firms and Structural Environments in the Large Internal Market," *Journal of Common Market Studies*, Vol. 28, No. 1 (1989), 53–67; Andrew Pettigrew and Richard Whipp, "Managing Change and Corporate Performance," in Karel Cool, Damien Neven and Ingo Walter (eds.), *European Industrial Restructuring in the 1990s* (Basingstoke: Macmillan, 1992), 227–65; Alexis Jacquemin and D. Wright, "Corporate Strategies and European Challenges Post 1992," in Simon Bulmer and Andrew Scott (eds.), *Economic and Political Integration in Europe: Internal Dynamics and Global Context* (Oxford: Blackwell, 1994), 219–31; and A. Millington and Bryan Bayliss, "Corporate Integration and Market Liberalisation in the EU," *European Management Journal*, Vol. 14, No. 2 (1996), 139–50.

[15] G. Nerb, *The Completion of the Internal Market: A Survey of European Industry's Perception of the Likely Effects* (Luxemburg: CEC, 1988).

[16] Pierre Buiges, F. Ilkovitz, and J. F. Lebrun, "The Impact of the Internal Market by Industrial Sector: The Challenge for the Member States," *European Economy* (special edition, 1990); and Commission of the EC, *The Single Market Review: Results of the Business Survey* (Luxemburg: CEC, 1997).

[17] C. Kindleberger, "European Integration and the International Corporation," *Columbia Journal of World Business*, Vol. 1, No. 1 (1966), 68.

has been disputed but all parties to this debate agree that business attitudes played some role in the creation of policy.[18] At a bare minimum, the idea of the single market was swimming with the tide of European business opinion and many go much further.[19] Studying European integration from the perspective of business provides a bridge between these wider economic and societal forces and the more specific political pressures relating to European integration. It also allows one to see the ways in which European integration impacted upon society and the economy.

Although the current literature focuses on the nation-state as the key actor, the role of business is considered, if sometimes in a rather perfunctory manner. With a few notable exceptions, the same cannot be said of the existing historiography. As Alan Milward, probably the most influential historian of European integration and the official historian of Britain's applications to join the Community, has noted in exasperation, "Virtually every book that exists about the history of the European Community is to all intents and purposes a history of diplomacy."[20] Discussions and correspondence between a small group of politicians and civil servants form the underlying basis of these accounts.[21] The two most important exceptions to this trend are Milward and Moravcsik, both of whom play up the significance of economic considerations more than hitherto. Moravcsik, indeed, goes further, stressing the role of commercial advantage as crucial. Business, therefore, is a cardinal element in his account: "Pressure from economic interest groups generally imposed tighter constraints on policy than did security concerns and the ideological visions of politicians and public opinion."[22] However, both focus on the role of the nation-state and their consideration of business remains a secondary concern and, despite his emphasis of business, Moravcsik does not go beyond existing accounts of peak-level associations.

To be fair, when business has been studied in relation to European integration it has tended to focus on the peak-level representative organiza-

[18] W. Sandholtz and J. Zysman, "Recasting the European Bargain," *World Politics*, Vol. 42, No. 1 (1989), 95–128; Andrew Moravcsik, "Negotiating the Single European Act: National Interests and Conventional Statecraft in the European Community," *International Organization*, Vol. 45, No. 1 (1991), 19–56; and Maria Green Cowles, "Setting the Agenda for a New Europe: The ERT and EC 1992," *Journal of Common Market Studies*, Vol. 33, No. 4 (1995), 501–26.

[19] D. G. Mayes, "Introduction," in D. G. Mayes (ed.), *The European Challenge: Industry's Response to the 1992 Programme* (London: Harvester Wheatsheaf, 1991), 16; and A. Silbertson and C. P. Raymond, *The Changing Industrial Map of Europe* (Basingstoke: Macmillan, 1996), 181–2.

[20] Milward, *European Rescue*, x–xi; similarly, Alan S. Milward, *Politics and Economics in the History of the European Union* (Abingdon: Routledge, 2005), x.

[21] Laurence Badel, Stanislas Jeannesson and Piers Ludlow (eds.), *Les Administrations Nationals et la Construction Européenne* (Brussels: P.I.E. Peter Lang, 2005).

[22] Moravcsik, *Choice for Europe*, 7.

tions, in particular the main national federations.[23] There is a need to go below the peak-level organizations because relationships between business and government were multilayered and complex and often, as will be shown in this book, the peak-level associations' views were not always representative of wider business opinion. This is certainly the accepted view of business–government relations in Britain: "In order to understand the nature and scope of business political activity in Britain the focus must be at the firm level, as well as at the industry level or the business-wide peak organization level."[24] Others have found that it is misleading to depict these relations in Britain in any general way and certainly to focus on the relationship of government–peak-level organizations was unrepresentative.[25] Rather, there was a diverse range of relationships at the micro- and meso-levels between government and industry as well as at the peak level.[26]

This has not been a problem for the historiography on Britain and European integration, which has been even more dominated by diplomatic historians than on the continent. Jacqueline Tratt's study of the Macmillan government's move toward the first application to join the EC in 1961 is a prime example of the genre. Having asserted on the first page that the reasons for Britain's application for EC membership in 1961 were political/strategic she continues, "it was the impact of particular civil service personalities that directly affected the development of policy."[27] Later she dismisses pressure group politics out of hand:

Since the advent of what has become known as pressure or interest group politics it has been all too easy to characterise the development of government policy in terms of government sensitivity to the demands and activities of such groups even though the demands of these groups have their roots as often or not in the changes that were already calling forth a response from government.[28]

---

[23] Michel Dumoulin, René Girault and Gilbert Trausch (eds.), *L'Europe du Patronat: de la Guerre Froide aux Années Soixante* (Berne: Peter Lang, 1993); and T. Rhenisch, *Europäische Integration und Industrielles Interesse: die Deutsche Industrie und die Gründung der Europäischen Wirtschaftsgemeinshaft* (Stuttgart: Steiner Verlag, 1999).

[24] Neil Mitchell, *The Conspicuous Corporation: Business, Public Policy and Representative Democracy* (Ann Arbor: University of Michigan Press, 1997), 110.

[25] Andrew Gamble, "The New Political Economy," *Political Studies*, Vol. 43, No. 3 (1995), 516–30; Martin Smith, *Pressure, Power and Policy* (Hemel Hempstead: Harvester Wheatsheaf, 1993), 233.

[26] S. Wilks, "Government–Industry Relations: Progress and Findings of the ESRC Research Initiative," *Public Administration*, Vol. 67, No. 3 (1989), 329–39; and S. Wilks and Maurice Wright (eds.), *Comparative Government–Industry Relations: Western Europe, United States and Japan* (Oxford: Clarendon Press, 1987).

[27] Jacqueline Tratt, *The Macmillan Government and Europe: A Study in the Process of Policy Development* (Basingstoke: Macmillan, 1996), 4.

[28] Ibid., 43.

Similarly, Daddow's study of the historiography on Britain and Europe refers to the recent opening out of the subject, by which he means the increasing use of the papers of the economic departments of government as well as the Foreign Office.[29] That British business and European integration remains an underresearched area is shown by the way in which historians use Robert Lieber's 1970 account of the subject as their main source.[30] The first task of this book is to update Lieber's account as an initial step toward addressing this gap in the historiography. It also extends the analysis of British business, as Lieber's study again does not go below the peak-level organizations.

BRITAIN AND EUROPE

Britain's position in the development of European integration has also been particularly striking.[31] Britain declined to participate in the discussions about the Schuman Plan in 1950 from which the European Coal and Steel Community emerged. It similarly declined to join the European Community in the mid-1950s but was sufficiently worried to make alternative (later supplementary) proposals for a free trade area covering most of Western Europe. This differed from the EC in being limited to industrial goods and did not include a common external tariff in order to maintain the preferential trading relationship with the Commonwealth. When these proposals failed, Britain formed the European Free Trade Association (EFTA) consisting of Britain and six other countries, which for various reasons were also unwilling to join the EC. Yet only two years later, in 1961, Britain opened negotiations about applying for membership of the EC only to be knocked back by General de Gaulle's veto in January 1963. The French President repeated his veto when Britain applied again in 1967; it was only after his fall from power that Britain was finally able to join the EC in 1973, the same time as Denmark and Ireland became members. This was not the end of the story. Only two years after joining, a new Labour government called a referendum on EC membership and thereafter Britain's relationship with its other member states and the EC Commission has not been easy.

Often characterized as "reluctant Europeans" or "grudging Europeans" Britain has famously been described as "an awkward partner" in Europe, such has been its ambivalence to European integration.[32] Enthusiasts for

---

[29] Oliver Daddow, *Britain and Europe since 1945: Historiographical Perspectives on Integration* (Manchester: Manchester University Press, 2004), 164–9.

[30] Robert Lieber, *British Politics and European Unity: Parties, Elites and Pressure Groups* (Berkeley: University of California Press, 1970).

[31] Recent textbooks include D. Gowland and A. Turner, *Reluctant Europeans: Britain and European Integration 1945–1998* (Harlow: Longman, 2000); and J. W. Young, *Britain and European Unity 1945–1999* (Basingstoke: Macmillan, 2nd edn., 2000).

[32] Gowland and Turner, *Reluctant Europeans*; Roger Jowell and James Spence, *The Grudging Europeans: A Study of British Attitudes towards the EEC* (London: Social

European integration point to Britain's postwar history as one of missed opportunities, particularly in rejecting the initial steps toward European integration in the 1950s. As Prime Minister Tony Blair put it in 2001: "The tragedy for British politics – for Britain – has been that politicians of both parties have consistently failed, not just in the 1950s but on up to the present day, to appreciate the emerging reality of European integration. And in doing so, they have failed Britain's interests."[33]

In contrast, Hugh Gaitskell, the Labour Party leader in the early 1960s, referred to Britain's first application to join the EC as "the end of one thousand years of history," continuing, "How can one seriously suppose if the mother country, the centre of the Commonwealth, is a province of Europe, which is what federation means, it could continue to exist as the mother country of a series of independent nations?"[34] In part rhetoric to appeal to a party conference, this claim nonetheless highlights the historical magnitude of the change that involvement in European integration entailed. Britain had traditionally had a worldwide perspective based on its global empire built up through the course of the eighteenth and nineteenth centuries. Britain traded and invested around the world at that time, and reflecting its economic dominance in the world, moved away from mercantilism toward free trade during the nineteenth century. Although the figure was declining, Britain was still responsible for over 30 percent of internationally traded manufactures in 1913.[35] However, its export sales were becoming increasingly focused on markets in the British Empire, a trend which was only exacerbated by the First World War and the Great Depression. With the contraction in world trade and growth of protection in the other industrialized nations, Britain also turned its back on free trade. Protection of strategic industries had been introduced during the war, but in 1931, it was extended and then made general by the 1932 Import Duties Act which imposed an import duty on manufactured goods of 10 percent, soon increased to 20 percent, but which gave preferential treatment to imports from the Empire. The Ottawa Agreement that summer put in place the system of Imperial Preference whereby imports from the Empire were given preference in Britain in return for

---

and Community Planning Research, 1975); and S. George, *An Awkward Partner: Britain in the European Community* (Oxford: Oxford University Press, various editions).

[33] Tony Blair, 23 November 2001 on opening the European Research Institute, University of Birmingham, *http://www.eri.bham.ac.uk/eriopening.htm* [accessed 15 June 2003].

[34] Quoted in Hugo Young, *This Blessed Plot: Britain and Europe from Churchill to Blair* (London: Macmillan, 1998), 163.

[35] Knick Harley, "Trade, 1870–1939: From Globalisation to Fragmentation," in Roderick Floud and Paul Johnson (eds.), *The Cambridge Economic History of Modern Britain, Vol. 2: Economic Maturity, 1860–1939* (Cambridge: Cambridge University Press, 2004), 171. See Peter T. Marsh, *Bargaining on Europe: Britain and the First Common Market, 1860–1892* (New Haven: Yale University Press, 1999).

preferential treatment of British exports in Empire markets.[36] After the Second World War, this trading relationship was initially strengthened: In 1948, just after the Second World War, the six countries which were to form the EC constituted less than 10 percent of British exports while the Commonwealth made up more than 50 percent. However, the economic relationship changed rapidly. By 1970, Britain's exports to the six member states of the European Community (EC) exceeded those to the Commonwealth for the first time in the twentieth century. By 1973, the year that Britain itself joined the EC, that share of Britain's exports had risen to 25 percent and more than 50 percent of its exports went to Western Europe as a whole. A similar shift from the Commonwealth to Western Europe and the Six happened to British foreign direct investment (FDI).

This economic relationship with the Commonwealth after 1945 was supplemented by moral and cultural ties, particularly with the Dominion countries of Australia, Canada, New Zealand, and South Africa and by the experience of fighting side by side in the First and Second World Wars. There was an unquestioned assumption that the Commonwealth relationship was a key component of Britain's postwar world. Any commitment to Europe was therefore heavily circumscribed by this relationship: If engaging in European integration harmed the Commonwealth relationship then there was a strong presumption held by the general public that the Commonwealth would be put first. It was to this feeling that Hugh Gaitskell was appealing and which must temper the "missed opportunity" school of thinking about Britain's relationship with European integration as one imbued with hindsight.

However, there is a second aspect to Britain's relationship with the Commonwealth and to the "missed opportunity" argument. It is argued that these were less competitive markets and that the increasing share of British exports going to these markets reflected reluctance or an inability to be competitive. British industry remained protected at home during the 1950s as well.[37] This anticompetitive bias was also visible in the cartelization of British industry and the re-establishment of these cartels after 1945.[38] This anticompetitive stance, it has been argued, was a key factor in explaining Britain's relative economic decline after 1945 and the competitive shock of joining the EC in 1973 helped to improve the competitiveness of British business. As one commentator has put it:

British industrial performance between 1945 and 1979 might have been better if governments had pursued different policies. The biggest single mistake was to opt

---

[36] See Tim Rooth, *British Protectionism and the International Economy: Overseas Commercial Policy in the 1930s* (Cambridge: Cambridge University Press, 1992).

[37] Alan S. Milward and George Brennan, *Britain's Place in the World: A Historical Enquiry into Import Controls 1945–60* (London: Routledge, 1996).

[38] H. Mercer, *Constructing a Competitive Order: The Hidden History of British Antitrust Policies* (Cambridge: Cambridge University Press, 1995).

out of European integration in the 1950s. A second error was to give insufficient priority to competition as the main driver of higher productivity.

This is not to say that British industrial performance would have been transformed if there had been a full-blooded attack on cartels after 1945, or if Britain had joined the Common Market in 1958 rather than 1973, or if industrial policy in the 1960s and 1970s had been geared to the promotion of competition rather than the creation of national champions and the preservation of jobs. But a more consistently pro-competitive and pro-European stance on the part of successive governments might have brought forward some of the changes in industry which took place in the 1980s.[39]

BUSINESS AND GOVERNMENT IN BRITAIN

This argument is not just about government policy. It is also a critique of business that promoted this protectionist and anticompetitive stance with the rise of business lobbying. It is common to explain the stance of business on protection and trade liberalization in relation to economic interests: If a sector is competitive then it should support liberalization, if it is weak then it will call for protection.[40] Given Britain's declining share of world trade and apparent lack of competitiveness, one would expect this to be evidenced in growing calls for protection. The attitude of manufacturing industry in Britain was inclining toward protection at the beginning of the twentieth century. The First World War allowed these views to be aired publicly and more vocally and the return of peace saw little change. By the second half of the 1920s "unmodified Free Trade opinion had become a minor force in business circles; in manufacturing, believers in the old orthodoxy were increasingly isolated, whilst the cosmopolitan merchant community . . . had few great names to weigh against the great industrialists who were latent protectionists or active members of the EIA [Empire Industries Association]."[41]

Before 1914, the most significant representative body of business nationally was the Associated Chambers of Commerce of the United Kingdom. It

---

[39] Geoffrey Owen, *From Empire to Europe: The Decline and Revival of British Industry since the Second World War* (London: Harper Collins, 1999), 460. See Stephen Broadberry and Nicholas Crafts, "UK Productivity Performance from 1950 to 1979: A Restatement of the Broadberry–Crafts View," *Economic History Review*, Vol. 56, No. 4 (2003), 718–35.

[40] F. Capie, *Tariffs and Growth: Some Insights from the World Economy, 1850–1940* (Manchester: Manchester University Press, 1994), 17–22; T. J. McKeown, "Firms and Tariff Regime Change: Explaining the Demand for Protection," *World Politics*, Vol. 36, No. 2 (1984), 215–33; H. V. Milner, *Resisting Protectionism: Global Industries and the Politics of International Trade* (Princeton, NJ: Princeton University Press, 1988). For variants of the model see M. J. Gabel, *Interests and Integration: Market Liberalisation, Public Opinion and European Union* (Ann Arbor: University of Michigan Press, 1998); and C. Parsons, "Domestic Interests, Ideas and Integration: The French Case," *Journal of Common Market Studies*, Vol. 38, No. 1 (2000), 45–70.

[41] Andrew Marrison, *British Business and Protection 1903–1932* (Oxford: Oxford University Press, 1996), 433.

was to become the Association of British Chambers of Commerce (ABCC) and was made up of the various regional chambers of commerce.[42] The First World War and its aftermath marked the emergence of a number of new business representative bodies, all of which to varying degrees were sympathetic to protection at this time. Of the many pressure groups to emerge, four were to have a long history. The Empire Industries Association, which after the Second World War renamed itself as the Commonwealth Industries Association (CIA), was as its name suggests, a long-standing supporter of imperial preference.[43] A second body, also overtly protectionist, was the National Union of Manufacturers (NUM). A third organization to emerge was the British Employers Confederation (BEC), which restricted its activities to industrial relations issues and, finally, and most importantly the Federation of British Industries (FBI), which was to become the largest representative industrial organization in Britain, was created.[44] Its membership consisted of both trade associations and individual firms and it was to become the voice of British industry. By the 1930s business was involved in the operation of tariff protection (via membership of the Import Duties Advisory Committee) and the FBI was negotiating with its German counterpart on the division of world markets for their members.[45] The Second World War only reinforced these tendencies, first by drawing many businessmen into government, and secondly, by doing little to dispel ideas about the need for protection and cartelization.

Through the 1950s the FBI was the main voice of business on issues relating to Europe. The National Farmers' Union was a member but by and large, the FBI reflected the interests of manufacturing industry.[46] The FBI's staff was headed by a director-general; for twenty years after 1945 Sir Norman Kipping filled this post. He became hugely influential and had strong links with Whitehall and his counterparts on the continent. A leading businessman was elected president for a two-year term, while the FBI's committees were chaired by businessmen and serviced by the federation's staff. The key committee in relation to European integration was the Overseas Trade Policy Committee, which was chaired from 1950 until 1965 by Lincoln Steel, a director of Imperial Chemical Industries (ICI). Kipping and

---

[42] A. R. Ilersic, *Parliament of Commerce: The Story of the Association of British Chambers of Commerce, 1860–1960* (London, 1960); and Marrison, *British Business*, 79–116.

[43] Marrison, *British Business*, 357–86.

[44] Stephen Blank, *Industry and Government in Britain: The Federation of British Industries in Politics, 1945–65* (Farnborough: Saxon House, 1973), 11–31; and R. Davenport-Hines, *Dudley Docker: The Life and Times of a Trade Warrior* (Cambridge: Cambridge University Press, 1984).

[45] See Sir Herbert Hutchinson, *Tariff-Making and Industrial Reconstruction* (London: Harrap, 1965); and C. C. S. Newton, *Profits of Peace: The Political Economy of Anglo-German Appeasement* (Oxford: Oxford University Press, 1996).

[46] Blank, *Industry and Government*.

Steel, aided by the overseas director, were key individuals. The ABCC, the other main voice of business at this time, better represented the interests of commerce, particularly through its influential London Chamber of Commerce. The ABCC's staff was much less prominent with the president and the chairmen of its committees playing the central roles, in addition to the input received from the regional chambers of commerce. For much of the period when the ABCC was active in this field, the most influential individual was Richard Wills, managing director of the tobacco firm George Wills & Sons Ltd., who chaired the Overseas Policy Committee and the European Panel. The NUM, a smaller body, was regarded as more representative of small business. In 1965 the NUM, by then called the National Association of British Manufacturers (NABM), the BEC and the FBI all merged to create the Confederation of British Industry (CBI) as a truly single voice of industry.[47] The ABCC continued to exist but became less prominent. The CBI adopted a structure based on that of the FBI's, with a director-general: John Davies, the first director-general, went on to become a minister in the 1970 Conservative government and was replaced by Campbell Adamson. CBI presidents were appointed, and a broadly similar committee structure was used. The two main committees dealing with European integration were the Overseas Committee and the Europe Steering Committee.

The main point of contact with the government was the Board of Trade, later renamed the Department of Trade and Industry, but there were also contacts with the other economic departments and the Foreign Office. Indeed, it was contacts with the Foreign Office in the 1960s that were often regarded as the most helpful, in part because they were informal. Generally, although there were frequently voiced concerns about a lack of access to ministers, the organizations seem to have been reasonably content with their ability to talk with government departments. Other important links were maintained by the FBI, CBI, and ABCC with each of their counterparts on the continent. These were a mixture of bilateral and multilateral arrangements that often proved to be helpful sources of information and useful mechanisms for business and the government in testing opinion on the continent.[48]

Given its largely protectionist roots, the apparent anticompetitive stance of business and the problem of relative economic decline, it might be expected that business via their representative organizations would have been opposed to European integration because it would expose business to greater competition even if it also increased the opportunities for British business on the continent. Some trade associations were clearly protectionist but the peak-level associations were not and neither, in general, was the wider business

---

[47] Wyn Grant and David Marsh, *The Confederation of British Industry* (London: Hodder and Stoughton, 1977); and W. P. Grant, "British Employers' Associations and the Enlarged Community," *Journal of Common Market Studies*, Vol. 11, No. 4 (1973), 276–86.

[48] Rollings and Kipping, "Private Transnational Governance."

community. Why was this the case? What factors help explain British business attitudes to European integration? In addition, what impact did these views have? Answering these questions is the main aim of this book.

STRUCTURE OF THE BOOK

It has been intimated that British business was involved with European integration on two levels. It was engaged on one level in the economic realities of trade and investment patterns, of shifting these economic relationships from the Commonwealth to Western Europe and the European Community. These relations are examined in Part I of the book. Chapter 2 examines the position in relation to trade while Chapter 3 considers overseas direct investment. In Part II attention turns to business perceptions of European integration. Chapters 4–8 track the opinion of British business toward European integration from the end of the Second World War to the time of Britain's entry into the EC in January 1973, how it became engaged with the subject, how its attitudes changed, and the reasons for these changes. Part III then elaborates on the second part by showing that business opinion was formed from the consideration of a wide range of factors. Attitudes were not related simply to tariffs and trade but were much more encompassing. Three case studies are presented to illustrate this argument, covering competition policy, taxation, and company law.

PART I

ECONOMIC REALITIES

2

Trade and Protection

According to one leading European economist, the foundation of European integration is internal trade liberalization.[1] Indeed the whole theory of economic integration has developed in the postwar period out of international trade theory.[2] It therefore seems the obvious starting point for a consideration of British business and European integration. The two questions lying at the heart of this chapter are: How did Britain's trading relations with the rest of Europe develop after the Second World War until Britain joined the European Community (EC) in 1973 and, reflecting this, was British business slow to move into European markets? What is clear is that the period marked an enormous turnaround in Britain's trading relations but there has been a school of thought that this happened too slowly and that British business preferred the relatively protected markets of the Commonwealth to the more open and competitive markets of the EC and that EC membership came as a severe competitive shock in 1973. Broadberry is the chief proponent of this view: Interwar concentration on the Empire and imperial preference left an "unfortunate legacy" after the Second World War. The need for a reorientation of export markets was "hampered by the anti-competitive culture of much of British industry at this time. After decades of avoiding head-to-head competition with producers from other industrialized countries through international cartels, British firms were reluctant to break with the old market-sharing agreements."[3] This argument has been summed up:

The thinking that lay behind the abstention from the Schuman Plan was thus part of a mistake by which the UK tied itself to inappropriate markets; to trading partners that British manufacturers could too easily dominate with outdated product lines, rather than markets of increasingly prosperous and critical consumers who

---

[1] A. Sapir, "Regional Integration in Europe," *Economic Journal*, Vol. 102, No. 415 (1992), 1491–506.

[2] F. Machlup, *A History of Thought on Economic Integration* (London: Macmillan, 1977).

[3] Most recently Stephen Broadberry and N. F. R. Crafts, "UK Productivity Performance from 1950 to 1979: A Restatement of the Broadberry–Crafts View," *Economic History Review*, Vol. 56, No. 4 (2003), 718–35. See also Howard Jones, "The Political Economy of Protectionism: Britain in the 1950s and 60s: "Taking the Plunge," Unpublished M. Phil. dissertation, University of Cambridge, 2001.

would put continuous pressure on the UK to modernise its labour and capital, to sort out the sociology of its workplaces and, above all, to embed the latest information on consumer tastes in a continuous striving for product innovation and improvement.[4]

In other words, this is a variant of the "missed opportunity" view of European integration discussed in Chapter 1: Had Britain joined earlier, its economic performance would have been better. Having examined these arguments the chapter concludes by suggesting that important though trade and tariffs were, focusing on these aspects leads to a partial and misleading perception of European integration as perceived by business, even at this early date.

BRITAIN'S TRADING POSITION

At the end of the Second World War, Britain's trading position was, on the one hand, desperate, while on the other hand, offering opportunities. The severity of Britain's balance of payments problem in 1945 has been well documented.[5] During the Second World War, Britain had accrued the largest external debt in history and even if imports were held down below the prewar level, a balance of payments deficit was expected to continue for at least three years, making the problem even worse. "Export or die" was one of the most infamous slogans of the time. More promising was the position of Britain compared to the rest of Western Europe. British exports and industrial production vastly exceeded that of any other country there, including the arch economic rival Germany.[6] At this time, business was faced with a dilemma: It was a seller's market, but in which market was it best to sell? If German industry was to be allowed to recover, was there any point in trying to win new markets in Western Europe when German competition was lacking and risk any successes being short-lived once Germany was in a position to serve these markets again? The *Report of the Board of Trade's Working Party on Carpets* summed up the position succinctly in 1947:

We have examined the position in other countries previously supplied by Germany, notably South America, Scandanavia, Holland, Denmark and Switzerland, where there should be opportunities for developing and holding promising markets . . . .
    The industry, however, faces a dilemma. Old customers, even in countries which are starting their own factories, are clamouring for supplies and are rationed by

---

[4] Christopher Lord, *Absent at the Creation: Britain and the Formation of the European Community, 1950–2* (Dartmouth: Aldershot, 1996), 159.

[5] A. K. Cairncross, *Years of Recovery: British Economic Policy 1945–1951* (London: Methuen, 1985); and Catherine Schenk, *Britain and the Sterling Area: From Devaluation to Convertibility in the 1950s* (London: Routledge, 1994).

[6] Sidney Pollard, *The Wasting of the British Economy: British Economic Policy 1945 to the Present* (London: Croom Helm, 1982).

exporters. The home market is badly starved.... The industry should seriously consider its position. Should it continue supplying old markets which it may lose to local manufacture, or is it to withdraw from these markets and build up new ones which are capable of retention?[7]

The home market was the initial draw.[8] For those exporting, traditional markets in the Commonwealth offered opportunities for saving dollars and were encouraged by the government, as were exports to the United States to earn dollars. Certainly, the significance of Commonwealth markets cannot be denied. As Table 2.1 illustrates, British exports to the Dominions (Australia, New Zealand, South Africa and Canada) and former colonies (together approximating to the Commonwealth) remained at around 50 percent of total exports until the 1960s. It was only then that there was a marked decline in the export share taken by the Commonwealth and exports to Western Europe showed a marked leap in importance. This section now considers trade developments in three subperiods: the first ten years or so after the war, the late 1950s and early 1960s, and, finally from 1963 to 1973. These coincide with the pre-EC era, the period from around the time of the Treaty of Rome to De Gaulle's first veto of Britain's application to join the EC, and the period until Britain finally entered the EC in 1973. In the 1950s the share of total British exports to the six member states of the European Community (EC) was on a scale similar to that to the USA and Canada, or to Australia and New Zealand.[9] Indeed, over the first half of the twentieth century the share of British exports to Commonwealth countries rose, while that to what became the Six became less significant (see Table 2.2). The share of British exports to France was lower in 1953 than that in any year in the period 1854–1938.[10] On this basis British exporters were not simply re-establishing themselves in their traditional markets but were actually increasing their concentration there.

A different way of addressing the issue is to consider Britain's largest export markets. The ten largest national markets for Britain during the interwar and postwar years are set out in Table 2.3. The sustained importance of the Dominions until the 1960s stands out. Of the six EC member states only the Netherlands featured in 1950 and by 1955 West Germany is the sole addition. France, Belgium–Luxemburg, and Italy were respectively Britain's fourteenth, fifteenth, and sixteenth largest export markets behind Norway (eleventh) and Denmark (twelfth) in 1955. If one discounts Ireland, there

[7] *Report of the Board of Trade Working Party on Carpets* (London: HMSO, 1947), 29.

[8] Alan McKinlay, H. Mercer, and Neil Rollings, "Reluctant Europeans? The Federation of British Industries and European Integration, 1945–63," *Business History*, Vol. 42, No. 4 (2000), 98–9.

[9] Alan S. Milward, *The European Rescue of the Nation-State* (London: Routledge, 2000), 353.

[10] F. V. Meyer, *United Kingdom Trade with Europe* (London: Bowes and Bowes, 1957), 128.

Table 2.1. *Direction of British Exports by Region, 1935–1975 (%)*

	Western Europe (1)	USA (2)	Old Dominions (3)	Former Colonies (4)	Columns (3) + (4) (5)
1935–1938	27	5	29	19	48
1950–1954	26	6	30	23	53
1955–1959	27	8	26	23	49
1960–1964	35	9	22	17	39
1965–1969	39	12	20	12	32
1970–1973	43	12	17	10	27

Source: Charles Feinstein, "The End of Empire and the Golden Age," in Peter Clarke and Clive Trebilcock, (eds.), *Understanding Decline* (Cambridge, UK: Cambridge University Press, 1997), 229.

Table 2.2. *Shares of British Exports to "British Countries" and EC6 (%)*

	British Countries	EC6
1907	32.2	24.8
1912	36.0	22.7
1924	42.1	18.7
1930	43.5	18.3
1935	48.0	14.7
1948	52.7	9.8
1951	55.0	10.4
1954	53.0	13.0
1958	49.3	13.1
1963	37.5	20.3
1968	31.2	19.3
1970	25.1	21.7

Note: "British countries" include the Irish Republic, and the Republic of South Africa as well as the Commonwealth.
Source: Broadberry, *Productivity Race*, 96.

were consistently no more than three European countries in Britain's "top 10" until 1965 but thereafter there was a rapid turnaround. In contrast, France had a growing preponderance of European nations among its major export markets – five of the ten largest by 1950, while Germany's trade was dominated both before and after the war by trade with the rest of Europe, the USA being the only non-European country in Germany's ten largest export markets in either 1950 or 1955.

Table 2.3. *Ten Leading Export Markets for Britain in Selected Years 1924–1973, in Terms of Value*

	1924	1932	1938	1950	1955	1960	1965	1970	1973
1	India & Burma	India & Burma	South Africa	Australia	Australia	USA	USA	USA	USA
2	Australia	Ireland	Australia	Canada	USA	Australia	W. Germany	W. Germany	W. Germany
3	USA	Australia	India	South Africa	South Africa	Canada	Australia	Ireland	France
4	Ireland	France	Canada	USA	Canada	W. Germany	South Africa	Netherlands	Ireland
5	Germany	South Africa	USA	India^a	New Zealand	South Africa	Sweden	Sweden	Belgium & Luxemburg
6	France	Canada	Germany	Ireland	India^a	India^a	Canada	Australia	Netherlands
7	South Africa	USA	Ireland	New Zealand	Ireland	Sweden	Netherlands	France	Switzerland
8	Canada	Germany	Argentina	Sweden	Netherlands	New Zealand	France	South Africa	Sweden
9	Argentina	Netherlands	New Zealand	Netherlands	Sweden	Netherlands	Ireland	Belgium & Luxemburg	Canada
10	Japan	Argentina	Denmark	Denmark	W. Germany	Ireland	Belgium & Luxemburg	Canada	Australia

^a The decline in India's share is in part a consequence of partition. Adding Pakistan would rank India second in 1950 and fourth in 1955.

Source: 1924 and 1932 *Statistical Abstract for the United Kingdom* 83, 1924–38; UN, *Yearbook of International Trade Statistics* 1952 and 1955; thereafter *Annual Abstract of Statistics* (various years).

A second contrast between Britain, on the one hand, and France and Germany on the other emerges if one considers the share of the three countries' total exports taken by their ten largest markets in the early postwar years. In the case of Britain, the share of the ten largest markets remained fairly constant in 1948, 1950, and 1955 at about 50 percent. The share of Germany's exports taken by the ten largest was over 60 percent in each of these three years as was the case for France in 1950 and 1955 despite trade with its ex-colonies remaining significant. There was a cost, therefore, in Britain's export pattern.[11] However, it is a simplification to associate this solely with a focus on Commonwealth markets, as is often suggested. The problem was rather the dispersion of markets, to which exporting to the Commonwealth countries may have been a contributory factor, but not the explanation per se.

A further aspect of Britain's export position relates to its commodity composition.[12] The declining significance of textiles is a well-known story but less well known was the rise in engineering exports.[13] Textiles, which contributed more than 30 percent of British exports in the second half of the 1930s, accounted for only a little more than 10 percent by 1957. The rise in the share of engineering exports matched the decline in the share of textiles and crept steadily up during the 1950s to nearly 50 percent by 1957. The scale and nature of these changes need to be examined more closely. The first point to make is that this shift toward engineering exports from textiles brought the commodity pattern of British exports of manufactures closer to that of the USA and West Germany than had been the case in the interwar period.[14] Comparing the commodity composition of exports to the Commonwealth with those to Western Europe (the non-Sterling OEEC countries), a number of further points emerge. Table 2.4 compares the share of exports to both regions by main commodity category in the 1950s. It shows the greater importance of exports of basic materials, mineral fuels, and lubricants from Britain to the OEEC countries than to the Commonwealth and the resulting lower significance of manufactures to that trade. The shares taken by particular categories of exports also shifted in different ways, notably in relation to engineering.

Alan Milward has suggested, "Not until the comparative sluggishness of Sterling Area markets became unmistakable, dramatically so in 1956, did

---

[11] J. Zeitlin, "Americanizing British Engineering? Strategic Debate, Selective Adaptation, and Hybrid Innovation in Postwar Reconstruction, 1945–1960," in J. Zeitlin and G. Herrigel (eds.), *Americanization and Its Limits: Reworking US Technology and Management in Postwar Europe and Japan* (Oxford: Oxford University Press, 2000), 134.

[12] Lynden Moore, *Britain's Trade and Economic Structure: The Impact of the European Union* (London: Routledge, 1999).

[13] See John Singleton, *Lancashire on the Scrapheap: The Cotton Industry 1945–1970* (Oxford: Oxford University Press, 1991).

[14] TNA CAB130/89, GEN444/8 (Final), 16 September 1953, Appendix, 8–9.

Table 2.4. *British Exports by Main Categories to the Commonwealth and Non-Sterling OEEC (%)*

	1952	1953	1954	1955	1956	1957
Commonwealth						
Food, beverages and tobacco	5.7	5.4	5.8	6.0	5.6	5.4
Basic materials	1.3	1.7	1.6	1.8	1.6	1.7
Mineral fuels and lubricants	1.8	2.4	2.1	1.0	1.1	1.0
Manufactured goods	87.9	86.6	86.5	87.4	88.3	88.9
Metals	13.7	13.2	12.8	13.3	14.5	15.1
Engineering products	39.0	39.7	39.6	41.1	43.0	43.6
Textiles (excluding clothing)	15.0	14.9	14.4	12.3	10.7	10.3
Other	20.1	18.8	19.8	20.7	20.2	19.9
Engineering as a percentage of all manufactures	44.4	45.8	45.7	47.1	48.7	49.1
Non-Sterling OEEC Countries and Dependencies						
Food, beverages and tobacco	4.8	3.9	4.0	3.6	4.8	5.1
Basic materials	6.0	6.0	6.1	5.8	5.8	6.0
Mineral fuels and lubricants	10.7	12.4	12.9	12.8	13.7	12.4
Manufactured goods	76.2	75.5	74.9	75.7	73.7	74.7
Metals	10.1	14.3	13.2	14.0	12.8	12.4
Engineering products	39.4	35.7	36.3	36.3	36.4	36.6
Textiles (excluding clothing)	9.3	9.2	8.8	8.1	7.5	8.1
Other	17.4	16.4	16.6	17.3	16.9	17.5
Engineering as a percentage of all manufactures	51.7	47.2	48.5	48.0	49.5	49.1

Source: HM Customs and Excise, *Annual Statement of the Trade of the United Kingdom* (various issues).

British exporters redirect their efforts toward Europe."[15] As Table 2.5 shows, exports to the Sterling Area and the Commonwealth did stagnate in 1956 but what was more important was that this was the start of a period of poor export performance rather than one bad year; British exports to other regions had years of poor performance too, like 1958, but these were temporary. What also stood out in the late 1950s most was the rise in the share of exports to the USA. There were no such clear trends in relation to exports to Western Europe. It would not have been hard on the basis of trade patterns for exporters to have recognized the problems with the Commonwealth/Sterling Area, but it was less obvious that the solution lay in joining the EC: Exports to Western Europe as a whole did not exceed exports to the Commonwealth until 1962, and Western Europe's share of British exports changed little

[15] Milward, *European Rescue*, 365.

Table 2.5. *British Exports by Region, 1953–1963*

	1953	1954	1955	1956	1957	1958	1959	1960	1961	1962	1963
Value (£m.)											
USA	159	150.4	183.1	243.1	244.3	272.7	360.8	325.5	280.4	327	340.3
Sterling Area	1203	1284.5	1379.5	1388.1	1436.2	1393	1341.7	1428.9	1400.5	1341.5	1452.3
Commonwealth	1234.4	1280.9	1376.7	1431.1	1493.6	1235.7	1240.6	1328.1	1286.9	1190.3	1214.6
EC6	334.9	348.1	374.5	427.9	459.5	418.9	465.8	519.8	613.3	720	826.3
EFTA countries	304	329.5	343.7	376.1	377.1	350.5	383.7	430.1	481.6	516.8	555
Western Europe	702.3	736.6	788.4	877.9	908.6	837.7	918	1030	1192.3	1359.5	1520.3
Total	2558	2649.9	2876.7	3143.3	3295	3176.2	3330.1	3554.8	3681.5	3791.1	4080.1
Share (%)											
USA	6.2	5.7	6.4	7.7	7.4	8.6	10.8	9.2	7.6	8.6	8.3
Sterling Area	47.0	48.5	48.0	44.2	43.6	43.9	40.3	40.2	38.0	35.4	35.6
Commonwealth	48.3	48.3	47.9	45.5	45.3	38.9	37.3	37.4	35.0	31.4	29.8
EC6	13.1	13.1	13.0	13.6	13.9	13.2	14.0	14.6	16.7	19.0	20.3
EFTA countries	11.9	12.4	11.9	12.0	11.4	11.0	11.5	12.1	13.1	13.6	13.6
Western Europe	27.5	27.8	27.4	27.9	27.6	26.4	27.6	29.0	32.4	35.9	37.3
Annual Growth (%)											
USA		−5.4	21.7	32.8	0.5	11.6	32.3	−9.8	−13.9	16.6	4.1
Sterling Area		6.8	7.4	0.6	3.5	−3.0	−3.7	6.5	−2.0	−4.2	8.3
Commonwealth		3.8	7.5	4.0	4.4	−17.3	0.4	7.1	−3.1	−7.5	2.0
EC6		3.9	7.6	14.3	7.4	−8.8	11.2	11.6	18.0	17.4	14.8
EFTA countries		8.4	4.3	9.4	0.3	−7.1	9.5	12.1	12.0	7.3	7.4
Western Europe		4.9	7.0	11.4	3.5	−7.8	9.6	12.2	15.8	14.0	11.8

Source: Annual Abstract of Statistics (various issues).

over the 1950s, with the EC member states' share growing only by a small amount.

It was only in the early 1960s that the sustained growth in export share to Western Europe occurred, virtually all due to the increasing share of exports to the EC, along with a similar decline in exports to the Commonwealth. It is common, therefore, to view the early 1960s as marking the culmination of the changes in Britain's economic relationship with the Commonwealth: Britain's main export market was no longer the countries of the Commonwealth. As a result, one of the main economic arguments against closer association with Western Europe and the EC became less important.[16] However, for much of the rest of the 1960s the export share taken by the EC remained static before surging again in the early 1970s (see Table 2.6). Exports to EFTA did not match this growth, but even in 1961, the year Britain first applied to join the EC and potentially turned its back on the Commonwealth and EFTA, these exports represented nearly 80 percent of the value of exports to the EC. EFTA was not, therefore, an insignificant market for Britain, and, combined with the Commonwealth, they together still constituted 43 percent of total British exports in 1963. Some of the EFTA countries did apply to join the EC at the same time as Britain, but even so, any preferential advantage in these two groups would have been lost with EC membership.

Yet the importance of EFTA varied across products with some industries seeing little benefit in EFTA in its own right. The chemical industry is an obvious example here. As Table 2.7 shows, British exports of chemicals to the EC far outweighed those to EFTA and, clearly, this helps explain the ambivalence of the chemical industry to EFTA membership (see Chapter 6). However, EFTA was a more important export market for some other industries. Exports of ships and boats from Britain fluctuated widely from year to year but in every year between 1959 and 1962, the value of exports to EFTA countries was more than four times that to the EC. Nevertheless, during the course of the 1960s, even with the EC's common external tariff in place and trade liberalization within EFTA, British exports to the EC6 remained significantly larger than to EFTA countries. With a final spurt of export growth in preparation for EC entry, British membership in 1973 came not a moment too soon from this perspective.

To sum up, there was a growing commercial imperative favoring closer relations first with Western Europe than with the Commonwealth and secondly with the EC than with EFTA. Britain's trading pattern changed significantly over this period. However, as far as British exports to the EC were concerned, there were two particular bursts of growth of export share – in the early 1960s and in the early 1970s – both just prior to the expected EC entry. This would suggest that the prospect of entry was driving these

[16] Nigel Lawson, "The New Pattern of Trade," *FBI Review* (July 1962), 25–7.

Table 2.6. *Share of British Exports, 1962–1973* (%)

	1962	1963	1964	1965	1966	1967	1968	1969	1970	1971	1972	1973
EFTA	13.6	13.6	14.0	14.0	14.5	15.0	13.8	14.7	15.8	15.2	16.3	16.7
EC6	19.0	20.3	21.1	20.0	19.9	20.0	20.1	20.9	21.7	21.0	22.9	24.7
W. Germany	5.6	5.5	5.4	5.8	5.5	5.3	5.7	5.7	6.2	5.8	6.0	6.3
Netherlands	4.0	4.1	4.5	4.1	3.9	3.9	4.0	4.1	4.7	4.5	4.6	4.8
Belgium & Luxemburg	3.4	3.4	3.7	3.6	3.6	3.5	3.8	4.0	3.6	3.7	4.1	5.0
France	3.8	4.5	4.5	3.9	4.1	4.2	3.9	4.3	4.2	4.3	5.2	5.4
Italy	3.7	4.0	3.1	2.5	2.8	3.0	2.8	2.9	3.0	2.7	2.9	3.1

Source: Annual Abstract of Statistics (various years).

Table 2.7. *British Exports of Chemicals to EC and EFTA Countries, 1959–1962 (£m.)*

	1959	1960	1961	1962
Norway	5.2	5.5	5.4	5.7
Sweden	9.5	10.8	11.5	12.7
Denmark	5.6	6.1	6.8	7.6
Switzerland	3.8	4.3	5.1	6.1
Austria	1.3	1.4	1.8	1.6
Portugal	1.5	1.7	2.0	1.9
EFTA	26.8	29.9	32.5	35.6
W. Germany	11.1	13.2	11.4	13.6
Netherlands	11.9	15.8	15.3	16.9
Belgium	6.8	7.5	7.6	8.1
France	7.0	8.6	9.2	9.3
Italy	9.4	10.3	10.6	14.4
EC	46.1	55.3	54.0	62.4

Source: *Annual Statement of Overseas Trade, Vol. 4 (1963).*

changes: The prospect of political integration was also leading to closer economic integration. As for the timing of this change, it is clear that it was only in the 1960s that clear changes in Britain's main export markets occurred.

BRITAIN'S EXPORT COMPETITIVENESS

To what extent does this trade pattern illustrate a lack of export competitiveness? Export performance was one of the first indicators of these fears: Britain's share of world exports of manufactures fell from 25 percent in 1950 to less than 11 percent in 1970. This was not because of any absolute decline in British exports; it was just that British exports did not grow as fast as those from other industrialized nations. As has been shown, one suggested explanation for these developments was the destination of British exports: For too long they concentrated on Commonwealth markets where demand did not grow as fast, for example, as it did in Western Europe. Milward has shown the defeatism and pessimism of British industry and civil servants about competing with German industry after the war.[17] There were many complaints about German competition from business, often arguing that there must be an unfair advantage for the Germans.[18] To keep a watch on the situation the FBI established a German Panel of the Overseas Trade

[17] Milward, *European Rescue*, 357–67.
[18] N. Tiratsoo and Jim Tomlinson, *The Conservatives and Industrial Efficiency, 1951–64: Thirteen Wasted Years?* (London: Routledge, 1998), 89.

Policy Committee at the end of 1948, consisting of representatives of those industries most likely to be affected by German competition.[19]

Similarly, in the early 1950s when the Conservative government became concerned about the weak progress of British exports, the issue of German competition underpinned much of the discussion. One government initiative was the establishment of the Working Party on UK Export Trends in July 1953. Originally set up to complete a factual analysis of Britain's export position in comparison with its main competitors, the working party continued to operate throughout the 1950s.[20] The working party produced a vast array of papers setting out the export position in various sectors, quarterly reports on the developing export position, as well as reports for ministers. It was not until 1954 that it produced a paper on German competition, but from the beginning, its work was framed in terms of the threat of German competition.[21] These studies found only limited support for business complaints about unfair competition.[22] The 1954 report on German competition concluded in categorical fashion: "Contrary to popular assertions, German industry gains little if anything from more favourable treatment than that accorded to industry in this country."[23] As one government ministry put it:

Manufacturers frequently attempt to justify (or excuse) their inability to compete with German firms by reference to lower German wages, longer German working hours, cheaper German materials, German government export incentive schemes, and so on. UK manufacturers frequently have but a vague, but unfortunately usually an exaggerated, idea of those factors which are to the advantage of German manufacturers, but the impressions that they have frequently seem to induce a somewhat hopeless attitude of mind; an attitude of "how can I do anything when my German competitor has so much in his favour?" The fact the German manufacturers may equally have adverse factors to contend with is rarely recognised.[24]

German competition remained a bugbear for British industry, provoking a continuing litany of complaints of unfair competition into the second half of the 1950s. Yet, when the government's Working Party on United Kingdom Export Trends reexamined the topic in 1956 it again found no evidence to support such "popular assertions."[25]

---

[19] MRC MSS200/F/1/1/189, Kipping at Grand Council meeting, 8 December 1948; and *FBI Annual Report for 1948*, 29.

[20] See TNA CAB130/88–93 and CAB134/2555–7.

[21] See for example TNA CAB130/89, GEN.441/3, 19 August 1953, 3.

[22] TNA CAB130/89, GEN441/8 (Final), 16 September 1953, 12–3.

[23] TNA CAB130/91, GEN441/39 (Final), 6 October 1954.

[24] TNA CAB130/90, GEN441/26, 3 May 1954.

[25] TNA CAB130/93, GEN441/88(Final), May 1956, 17. See Martin Schaad, "Plan G–A 'Counterblast'? British Policy towards the Messina Countries, 1956," *Contemporary European History*, Vol. 7, No. 1 (1998), 39–60; and Alan S. Milward and George Brennan, *Britain's Place in the World: A Historical Inquiry into Import Controls* (London: Routledge, 1996).

However, in other respects the issue was developing and changing. First, the seriousness and long-term implications of the situation were being more fully appreciated. It was no longer possible to explain the differences in relative export performance in terms of Germany's low starting point.[26] Added to that, contemporary analysis suggested that Britain's poor performance could not be explained in terms of the commodity composition of its exports or the nature of its export markets. The working party consistently found that British exporters were doing badly in all markets, including Sterling Area countries, when faced by German competition.[27] There were no "soft" markets in this sense.[28] Worse still, where there were area and commodity dimensions to the problem, it related to exports to OEEC countries, the fastest growing market, and for consumer durables, one of the fastest growing commodity groups.[29]

All these factors pointed to the stark conclusion that there was a fundamental problem with British economic performance: Britain's lack of export competitiveness was a symptom of a wider malaise, relative economic decline, rather than the problem itself. It was increasingly believed that the export problem was understood. The government's Working Party on UK Export Trends, which had tracked export performance since 1953, was wound up at the end of 1959 in part because it seemed unlikely that any further report would reveal any new insights on Britain's export problems.[30] Solving these problems was increasingly viewed from the perspective of how to improve Britain's growth performance rather than simply to increase exports: An NEDC report on export trends in the early 1960s was part of its consideration of the role of exports in improving Britain's growth performance, as set out in its earlier report, *Growth of the United Kingdom Economy to 1966*.[31] As such, this fed into the wider debate about the state that Britain was in and the growing critique of a range of British institutions.[32]

The government responded with a range of policy initiatives as part of its "Great Reappraisal."[33] Membership of the EC became one element of this attempt to modernize Britain. The perceived superior growth record of

[26] TNA CAB130/93, GEN441/88(Final), May 1956, 3.

[27] TNA CAB130/93, GEN441/77(Final), 9–10; CAB134/2555, UK(E)(56)12(Final), January 1957, 4–5; CAB134/2555, UK(E)(56)17(Final), 14–6; CAB134/2556, UK(E)(58)7, 9 June 1958; and CAB134/2556, UK(E)(58)8(Final), 2.

[28] Schenk, *Britain and the Sterling Area*, 80–1.

[29] TNA CAB130/93, GEN441/76, 13 February 1956; and CAB134/2555, UK(E)(56)17(final), 17 and UK(E)(57)7(final).

[30] TNA CAB134/2557, UK(E)(59)7, 23 December 1959; and NEDC, *Export Trends* (London: HMSO, 1963), 22–3.

[31] NEDC, *Growth of the United Kingdom Economy to 1966* (London: HMSO, 1963).

[32] Jim Tomlinson, *The Politics of Decline: Understanding Post-War Britain* (Harlow: Longman, 2000).

[33] The term was coined by Sam Brittan, *Steering the Economy: The Role of the Treasury* (London: Secker and Warburg, 1969).

the Six was seen as, in part, the consequence of EC membership. To some, therefore, EC membership offered a route to modernization through the "cold shower of competition."[34] However, those more pessimistic turned the issue on its head: Britain needed to take action to improve its competitiveness to survive in the EC.[35] Integration with the rest of Europe was, therefore, a double-edged sword as far as improving British economic competitiveness was concerned. A close link was perceived between EC entry and improved competitiveness but the precise nature of that link was more open to dispute.

PROTECTION OF BRITISH BUSINESS

How cold the shower of competition would be from EC entry depended on how protected and anticompetitive was British business.[36] There were two aspects to this: the level of protection and the extent to which business was a keen supporter of the maintenance of protection. Protection itself took two forms: tariffs and quotas to protect domestic industry and Commonwealth preference – the preference offered to British business in the Commonwealth compared to Britain's competitors from outside the Commonwealth.[37] It was possible to maintain Commonwealth preferences in a free trade area (FTA) but entry into the EC would have required their surrender. Preferences were given to a wide range of goods exported to the Commonwealth. The margin of preference on such exports varied from country to country in the Commonwealth, but in 1961, the highest margins were from Australia, New Zealand, and Canada, all major recipients of British exports, where, in the first two countries, more than 80 percent of British goods imported received a preference (see Table 2.8). It was also believed that these preferences in 1961 were worth not much less than they had been in 1948.[38] Moreover, it has been estimated that the UK's share of Commonwealth trade was larger than it would otherwise have been for around a quarter to a half of UK exports to the Commonwealth.[39]

---

[34] *Parliamentary Debates (House of Commons)* 5th ser., Vol. 645, Col. 1605, 2 August 1961; MRC MSS 200/F/3/S2/213, Hirst and Le Mare, Grand Council meeting, 12 July 1961; and Conservative Party Central Office, *Leaders of Industry and the Common Market* (London, 1962).

[35] TNA CAB129/110, C(62)107, "Economic Growth," appendix, 6 July 1962.

[36] See Francisco Rodríguez and Dani Rodrik, "Trade Policy and Economic Growth: A Skeptic's Guide to the Cross-national Evidence," *Macroeconomics Annual*, Vol. 15, No. 1 (2000), 261–325.

[37] Francine McKenzie, *Redefining the Bonds of Commonwealth, 1939–1948: The Politics of Preference* (Basingstoke: Palgrave, 2002).

[38] S. J. Wells, *Trade Policies for Britain* (London: Oxford University Press, 1966), 24.

[39] EIU, *The Commonwealth and Europe* (London, 1960), 20; PEP, *Commonwealth Preference in the United Kingdom* (London, 1960).

Table 2.8. *Margins in the Commonwealth Preference Area, 1961*

	Percentage of Imports from UK Duty Free	Percentage of Imports Receiving Preference	Average Margin of Preference (Inc. Duty)	
			On All Imports from UK	On All Imports from UK Receiving Preference
Canada	67	67	8	12
Australia	66	85	9	11
India	4	18–23	1	6
South Africa	39–62	16–23	1–2	4–5
New Zealand	55–57	83–87	14–16	17–19

Source: Sidney Wells, *Trade Policies for Britain* (London, UK: Oxford University Press, 1966), 129.

Protection of the home market was also considerable, though hard to measure, given the range of different tools – tariffs, quotas, taxes, and subsidies – available to governments.[40] There is agreement that Britain was highly protected until the late 1950s.[41] There is also agreement that liberalization occurred through the removal of quotas (largely achieved in the 1950s), the creation of EFTA (with its liberalization program from 1960 to 1967) and in the 1960s the Dillon (completed by 1962 and estimated to have reduced import duties by 7–11 percent) and Kennedy rounds of trade negotiations in GATT (agreed in 1967 and implemented by 1972 such that the average tariffs on manufactures were cut by 35–40 percent). Nevertheless, it would appear that in Britain, the average tariff was higher than the EC's common external tariff throughout this process.[42]

The disagreement is over how much competition British industry faced as a result of these changes: Broadberry views Britain's EC entry in 1973 as "a severe competitive shock" whereas Tomlinson and Tiratsoo dispute this, pointing to competition in export markets and at home from American multinationals which opened plants in the UK.[43] No measures of effective protection in postwar Britain have been made since the 1970s and more modern measures such as Anderson and Neary's trade restrictiveness index have not been used either.[44] Lack of knowledge about some quotas makes any such measurement conditional in any case and there have been problems in applying such methods to historical cases.[45] There seems to be a tendency to use simpler measures once more, that is, the ratio of import duty revenue to the value of imports. Broadberry used this measure to illustrate the degree of protection afforded to British business and to highlight the extent of changes around 1973, as shown in Table 2.9. In his calculations, not only was the ratio markedly higher for Britain than Germany or the United States, but there

[40] J. E. Anderson and J. P. Neary, "Measuring the Restrictiveness of Trade Policy," *World Bank Economic Review*, Vol. 8, No. 2 (1994), 151–89.

[41] A. D. Morgan, "Commercial Policy," in F. Blackaby (ed.), *British Economic Policy 1960–74* (Cambridge: Cambridge University Press, 1978), 515–6.

[42] Wells, *Trade Policies*, 123; and Simon Young, *Terms of Entry: Britain's Negotiations with the European Community 1970–1972* (London: Heinemann, 1973), 108.

[43] Stephen Broadberry, *The Productivity Race* (Cambridge: Cambridge University Press, 1997), 293; and Jim Tomlinson and N. Tiratsoo, "'An Old Story, Freshly Told'? A Comment on Broadberry and Crafts' Approach to Britain's Early Post-war Economic Performance," *Business History*, Vol. 40, No. 2 (1998), 63–4.

[44] N. Oulton, "Effective Protection of British industry," in W. M. Corden and Gerhard Fels (eds.), *Public Assistance to Industry: Protection and Subsidies in Britain and Europe* (London: Macmillan for the Trade Policy Research Centre and the Institut für Weltwirtschaft, 1976), 46–90; and J. E. Anderson and J. P. Neary, "A New Approach to Evaluating Trade Policy," *Review of Economic Studies*, Vol. 63, No. 1 (1996), 107–25.

[45] Milward and Brennan, *Britain's Place*, 130–1; and K. O'Rourke, "Measuring Protection: A Precautionary Tale," *Journal of Development Economics*, Vol. 53, No. 1 (1997), 169–83.

Table 2.9. *Tariff Rates in the UK, USA,
and Germany, 1950–1980 (%)*

	Ratio of Duties to Total Imports		
	UK	USA	Germany
1945	38.2	9.3	31.3[a]
1950	31.2	6.0	5.4
1960	30.2	7.4	6.5
1970	34.3	6.5	2.6
1980	12.7	3.1	1.3

[a] 1948.
Source: Broadberry, *Productivity Race*, 139–41.

was also little significant decline until the 1970s. Broadberry admits the need for caution with these figures mentioning the issue of oil duties as a potential distortion.[46] As Table 2.10 illustrates, duties on oil were an increasingly important source of British customs revenue, but until the 1970s tobacco was a far bigger distortion. The focus should be on "protective duties."[47] This still covers nonmanufactured goods but ignores duty on tobacco and oil. These were the third largest source of revenue, but when we compare the level of these duties with the value of imports, the results are consistently around 2–3 percent.[48] This is much more in line with the experience of other countries, although we should note that this is not exactly comparing like with like, for example, duty on oil significantly distorts the French figures. In other words, the revenue ratio does not illustrate any tendency for Britain to have been more protected on the scale suggested by Broadberry.

From 1967 to 1980, the government published its own figures of Britain's ratio of protective duties to total imports and total dutiable imports. These are given in Table 2.11. The situation with regard to total imports does offer some support for Broadberry – there is a steady decline in the ratio from 3 percent in 1972 to 1.8 percent in 1978, that is, EC entry did lead to further trade liberalization on this measure but whether this represents a severe competitive shock is less certain.

[46] Broadberry, *Productivity Race*, 139–42.
[47] For example, Neil Rollings, "British Industry and European Integration 1961–73: From First Application to Final Membership," *Business and Economic History*, Vol. 27 No. 2 (1998), 444–54; and P. H. Lindert, *International Economics* (Homewood, IL: Irwin, 1991).
[48] J. Foreman-Peck, "Trade and the Balance of Payments," in N. F. R. Crafts and N. Woodward (eds.), *The British Economy since 1945* (Oxford: Oxford University Press, 1991), 159; and US Tariff Commission, *Trade Barriers, Part 1: An Overview: Chapter 5* (Washington, DC: US Tariff Commission, 1974), 20.

Table 2.10. *Main Items in Net Receipts of British Customs Duties, 1938/1939 to 1970/1971 (%)*

	1938/1939	1945/1946	1950/1951	1955/1956	1960/1961	1965/1966	1970/1971
Tobacco	37	73	67	58	56	46	45
Hydrocarbon oils	26	11	15	27	27	36	54
Protective duties[a]	20	4	8	8	11	8	10

[a] Protective duties as defined by Customs and Excise. Prior to 1958 this covers the Import Duties Act, 1932, the key industries duties, the Ottawa duties (excluding wine and dried fruits), beef and veal, silk and artificial silk and dried or preserved fruit. After 1958 it covers items under the Import Duties Act, 1958, which pulled the existing duties together under one piece of legislation. It does not cover the 1964–66 temporary charge on imports. Inclusion of this item for 1965, the highest year of revenue collection, would change the percentage for protective duties for that year to 16%.
Source: Reports of Commissioners of HM Customs and Excise (various years).

Table 2.11. *UK Ratio of Protective Duties to Total Imports and Total Dutiable Imports, 1966–1979 (%)*

	Total Imports	Total Dutiable Imports
1966	3.2	12.2
1967	3.3	13.6
1968	2.8	12.4
1969	2.8	11.5
1970	2.8	10.7
1971	2.8	9.1
1972	3.0	9.0
1973	2.6	8.2
1974	2.2	7.5
1975	2.1	7.0
1976	2.0	5.9
1977	1.9	7.1
1978	1.8	10.1
1979	1.8	10.1

Source: *Reports of Commissioners of HM Customs and Excise* (various years).

UNDERLYING COMPLEXITIES

So far, this chapter has outlined the broad picture in terms of Britain's trading patterns, growing concerns about the competitiveness of British exports and the degree of protection afforded to British business in the Commonwealth and domestic markets. At this level, it would appear that British exports did not move toward Western Europe and especially the EC6 as quickly as they might have, that there were problems with export competitiveness, and that there was protection of British industry, if not on the scale sometimes suggested. The rest of the chapter will illustrate why it is important to comprehend that this hides considerable diversity and complexity. First, Britain was not alone in Europe in having a strong trading relationship with its ex-Empire territories: In 1952 over 42 percent of French exports still went to former French colonies.[49] Secondly, although there were clear topographical and climatic differences within the Commonwealth, neither Western Europe nor the countries that became the Six could be considered as a single market. Even in the motor vehicle industry, an obvious candidate for Fordist mass production, domestically manufactured cars continued to dominate sales in

[49] W. J. Adams, *Restructuring the French Economy: Government and the Rise of Market Competition Since World War Two* (Washington, DC: Brookings Institute, 1989).

each of the main continental European countries.[50] Analysis of the commodity pattern of British exports to individual European nations illustrates a wide variety of commodity trade patterns in the 1950s. In particular, there is a distinct difference in Britain's exports to France and Germany. After the Second World War, the shares taken by engineering exports to both countries rose while those taken by textiles declined but a clear difference remained, as is shown in Table 2.12. Textile exports to Germany continued to make up over 20 percent of all manufactured exports in every year until 1957 (except 1948), while they constituted less than 8 percent of British manufactured exports to France in each of the postwar sample years. Similarly, while engineering exports to France made up more than 60 percent of British manufactured exports there in 1953, 1955, and 1958, this category constituted less than a third of manufactured exports to West Germany until 1957, although the share rose sharply in 1958.

Other European countries tended to fall somewhere in between these two extremes, but equally the commodity structure of Britain's exports to each was unique. British industry performed very differently in each member state. Table 2.13 sets out the change in import share held by Britain in various manufactured goods over the period 1953–61 in the member states and in the EC, and EFTA. There were some general trends: Loss in market share was pretty general and, in a majority of sectors, the loss in market share was higher in EFTA than in the EC. However, there were significant exceptions and the range of difference between the best and worst performance across industries and across countries is striking. At the extreme, there is the case of Germany where there was a 62.7 percentage point difference in performance between the best and worst sectors: While Britain gained a 34.5 percentage point improvement in import share of power machinery, its import share for pottery fell by 28.2 percentage points. Sectoral performance also varied markedly; power machinery improved its import market share most in Germany, as noted above, but it also improved its market share in the Netherlands, France, and Italy, but experienced nearly a ten-percentage point decline in Belgium.

It is important to remember that aggregate trade figures are the product of thousands, perhaps millions, of individual export sales. From the perspective of individual companies producing a range of particular commodities at this time, this was not a single decision to favor the Commonwealth over Western Europe. Instead, each firm was faced with a set of national markets; which mix offered the greatest, or easiest opportunities differed in every case. There were factors such as imperial preference, a common language, and

---

[50] Sigfrido Ramirez, "Antitrust ou Anti US? L'industrie Automobile Européenne et les Origines de la Politique de la Concurrence de la CEE," in Éric Bussière, Michel Dumoulin and Sylvain Schirmann (eds.), *Europe Organisée, Europe du Libre-échange?: Fin XIXe Siècle – Années 1960* (Brussels: P.I.E. Peter Lang, 2006), 203–28.

Table 2.12. *Percentage of Total Manufactured British Exports and of Total Exports to France and Germany for Selected Commodities, 1932–1958*

	France							Germany						
	1932	1936	1948	1950	1953	1955	1958	1932	1936	1948	1950	1953	1955	1958
	Total manufactured exports (%)													
Textiles	16.4	18.2	2.6	7.1	4.2	5.6	4.0	71.1	61.0	11.2	37.4	25.6	23.7	16.4
Metals	13.0	15.9	9.3	9.2	15.0	10.5	10.8	7.0	9.5	9.5	17.7	19.0	17.9	15.9
Engineering	35.5	30.4	68.8	56.6	61.4	60.3	60.4	9.2	6.0	22.4	22.0	28.2	29.0	42.7
Chemicals	11.0	10.8	9.9	5.1	9.2	11.5	13.9	2.8	2.8	18.7	2.4	8.7	11.1	10.9
	Total exports (%)													
Textiles	7.0	8.1	2.0	5.3	3.4	4.5	3.0	42.0	34.7	3.3	19.1	14.8	15.8	12.7
Metals	5.5	7.1	7.2	6.9	12.4	8.5	8.3	4.1	5.4	2.8	9.0	11.0	11.9	12.4
Engineering	15.1	13.5	53.3	42.3	50.5	48.5	46.5	5.4	3.4	6.5	11.2	16.3	19.3	33.2
Chemicals	4.7	4.8	7.7	3.8	7.5	9.3	10.7	1.7	1.6	5.5	1.2	5.0	7.4	8.5
Coal	42.4	38.4	7.2	11.0	3.6	6.5	5.5	11.0	12.8	1.9	2.2	8.1	5.7	0.7
Manufactures as percentage total exports	42.6	44.4	77.5	74.6	82.2	80.5	77.0	59.1	56.9	29.3	51.0	57.7	66.6	77.7

Source: HM Customs and Excise, *Annual Statement of the Trade of the United Kingdom* (various issues).

Table 2.13. *Changes in Import Share Held by the UK from 1953 to 1961 (in Percentage Points)*

	Belgium–Luxemburg	France	Germany	Italy	Netherlands	Maximum	Minimum	Range	EC	EFTA
All manufactures	-6.3	-7.8	-2.8	-3.7	-8.2	-2.8	-8.2	5.4	-6.1	-8.3
Inorganic chemicals	-9.1	-11.5	-11.1	-15.6	-2.0	-2.0	-15.6	13.6	-8.5	-7.4
Drugs, etc.	2.7	4.3	0.9	-3.9	-11.4	4.3	-11.4	15.7	-0.4	-1.0
Yarn thread	-5.2	-0.7	-7.6	-11.6	-2.6	-0.7	-11.6	10.9	-4.1	-28.1
Cotton fabrics	-6.3	-1.3	-1.8	-15.3	-8.9	-1.3	-15.3	14	-6.6	-19.8
Noncotton fabrics	-2.5	-10.8	-9.7	-22.3	-5.3	-2.5	-22.3	19.8	-8.8	-7.8
Made-up textiles	-11.3	-9.4	-19.1	-18.8	-16.9	-9.4	-19.1	9.7	-15.3	-4.7
Iron and steel	-3.2	-8.3	2.4	-10.2	-5.0	2.4	-10.2	12.6	-5.0	-4.2
Power machinery	-9.7	14.6	34.5	23.6	5.7	34.5	-9.7	44.2	14.2	2.3
Office machinery	-1.3	-0.5	-2.3	-1.8	-9.0	-0.5	-9.0	8.5	-3.2	-4.7
Metal making machinery	4.5	-1.1	-6.4	1.3	1.6	4.5	-6.4	10.9	0.2	-1.8
Electrical machinery and equipment	-6.2	-0.2	0.2	0.2	-8.9	0.2	-8.9	9.1	-3.5	-17.9
Road motor vehicles	-9.1	-13.7	-16.8	4.9	-15.6	4.9	-16.8	21.7	-9.7	-13.3
Rubber manufactures	-11.4	-10.1	-9.0	-12.9	-8.7	-8.7	-12.9	4.2	-9.7	-15.8
Pottery	-1.6	-4.8	-28.2	4.3	1.0	4.3	-28.2	32.5	2.2	-6.4
Clothes (not fur)	-0.5	-24.0	-9.8	10.6	-4.3	10.6	-24	34.6	-6.6	-18.2
Scientific instruments	-4.7	-7.0	2.7	-0.2	-6.1	2.7	-7.0	9.7	-3.2	-3.4
Maximum	4.5	14.6	34.5	23.6	5.7					
Minimum	-11.4	-24	-28.2	-22.3	-16.9					
Range	15.9	38.6	62.7	45.9	22.6					

Source: NEDC, *Export Trends*, 8–9.

market-sharing agreements that encouraged exporters to look to the Commonwealth countries but this did not mean that all exporters favored these markets above others. For example, France was the third largest export market, after Australia and New Zealand, for grinding machine tools, averaging sales over the period 1951–54.[51] This is just one example of the many differences and apparent anomalies. It is important to remember this microperspective when thinking about corporate strategy and business attitudes toward Western Europe and European integration.

Similarly, there are many examples of British business being successful in Western Europe. The picture was one of diversity rather than outright failure. When considering the competitive position of the British engineering industry in the Swedish market, it was found that because the subject was so diverse and fluctuating between different parts of the industry, the number of common discernible patterns was limited.[52] The FBI's German Panel found that while German competition was growing rapidly in 1950 and 1951, it was clear that such competition "varied greatly from industry to industry and between one export market and another."[53] This is not to argue that there was not a problem but that the picture was not all bleak. Just as British industrialists found it easy to complain about German competition, so also has there been a tendency to dismiss the performance of British exporters at this time. As the Working Party on UK Export Trends noticed, virtually all the information received on export performance related to failures – lost contracts, complaints about delivery dates, being too expensive, and so on – with hardly any reports of less colorful successes sent to the Board of Trade from overseas posts. Who would comment on a contract successfully delivered on time, for example? Foreign buyers were also likely to exaggerate their criticisms. The tone of such information was bound to be gloomier than the reality.[54]

Again, it is easy to illustrate the unending complaints of British industry about "unfair competition" as evidence of a defensive mentality. However, while some voices in industry demanded reciprocal action from the British government, the majority refused to countenance such a step, for example, in relation to export subsidies.[55] When the Chancellor of the Exchequer met both sides of industry to discuss the export situation in December 1952, the ABCC and the FBI both submitted statements firmly

---

[51] *Annual Statement of the Trade of the United Kingdom with Commonwealth Countries and Foreign Countries 1954, Vol. 3* (London: HMSO, 1955), 590.

[52] TNA CAB130/92, GEN441/55, 20 December 1954.

[53] FBI, *Annual Report for 1951*, 18; and *Annual Report for 1950*, 30.

[54] TNA CAB130/90, GEN441/25, 26 April 1954; and TNA CAB130/92, GEN441/64, 27 May 1955.

[55] "The Shadow of Foreign Competition," *The Birmingham Chamber of Commerce Journal* No. 51 (1952), 969–70.

rejecting the use of export subsidies, not wanting to enter an export subsidy race and this remained the view in business into the 1960s. Instead, both organizations urged the government to take international action to ban such schemes.[56] Indeed, the FBI felt so strongly on the issue that, faced by what it perceived as the failure of national governments to achieve any progress, it embarked on a series of negotiations with its counterparts across Europe from which eventually a standstill agreement emerged: No new schemes would be introduced during which time it was hoped governments could make progress in their own discussions. As the ABCC's Overseas Trade Committee put it, "The export trade should shoulder its own responsibilities."[57]

It is also easy to exaggerate the importance of protection to business. On Commonwealth preference one contemporary study noted, "Categorical statements based on statistical analysis tend to overstate the importance and effectiveness of Commonwealth Preference. Its economic significance is less than it appears to be."[58] Although bodies such as the Commonwealth Industries Association called for the retention of Commonwealth preference, industry in general raised few complaints by the late 1950s about the prospect of these preferences disappearing.[59] This leads into a more general issue. Despite being characterized as anticompetitive in behavior and having been protected relatively heavily, it is clear that, apart from sectors such as textiles calling for protection, business in general was explicitly committed to trade liberalization. A good example here is the efforts made by the Commonwealth Industries Association and a few others to get Britain to pull out of the General Agreement on Trade and Tariffs (GATT) so that Commonwealth preference could be extended. The FBI's Working Party on GATT concluded:

The development of international trade on a multilateral basis, with due regard for the preservation of existing Commonwealth preferences, is the declared object of United Kingdom commercial policy. . . .

No other country in the world is so dependent on international trade as the United Kingdom. None has so much to gain from its expansion; none stands to be so damaged by its contraction. In reality therefore we have no choice but continually to seek to open up all possible markets.[60]

---

[56] TNA T236/3486, "The Export Situation: Proposed Informal Discussions with Industry," undated, Annex A and Annex B; and TNA T236/3487, "The Export Drive: Informal Meeting with Both Sides of Industry," 17 December 1952.

[57] GLA MS14487/6, Overseas Trade Committee meeting, 3 September 1952.

[58] EIU, *Commonwealth and Europe*, 20.

[59] FBI, *The British Commonwealth, Commonwealth Preference and the Sterling Area* (London, 1958); and Wells, *Trade Policies*, 26.

[60] MRC MSS200F/3/D2/1/8, D/3507, "Report of Working Party on the GATT to Overseas Trade Policy Committee," 16 July 1954.

This is important because it helps to untangle the position with regard to European integration. If business was anticompetitive in its outlook and preferences why did it favor a free trade area covering the whole of Western Europe in the mid-1950s and why was it content to join the EC a few years later? In the first case, while British business would have retained Commonwealth preference it would have removed protection from competitors across Western Europe for domestic business, while EC membership only involved increased competition from the six member states but would have involved the ending of Commonwealth preference. As is shown in later chapters, one of the main reasons was a fear of exclusion and the resulting consequences in terms of weaker competitiveness in third markets. Secondly, and often neglected, the creation of the EC did raise tariffs for Britain to key export markets. The common external tariff was formed from the average of the tariffs of France, Italy, Germany, and a fourth combined tariff covering Belgium, the Netherlands, and Luxemburg. France and Italy were high tariff countries while the others tended to be low tariff; so the creation of the common external tariff raised tariffs for these low tariff countries. As Table 2.3 shows, W. Germany and the Netherlands were both among the ten largest export markets in 1955 and 1960 so there was considerable concern in British business at this rise in protection for these markets. German business would benefit three-fold from the creation of the EC: It would have preferential access to the markets of the Six, it would have greater protection in the home market, and it would be able to exploit these advantages to be more competitive in third markets.[61]

A second factor to explain British business' position is that exports and tariffs are only part of the story. As shown in Chapter 3, investment is also an important, and increasingly more important, consideration as firms began to internationalize. By the end of the 1960s, a large part of ICI's output never appeared in British trade figures as it was produced and sold on the continent. As the rest of the book argues, this and other considerations need to be incorporated. First, there was a gap between economic realities and perceptions. The perceptions of British business were often partial or at odds with the economic information available but attitudes in the wider business community were often slow to change. Also, it is inevitable that industrialists are likely to blame anything other than themselves for any problems. They believed that they could compete as long as they had a level playing field. That they did not was blamed largely on government policy, not their own inadequacies. This relates to a second point. Having such a view of the world made businessmen acutely aware of the political dimensions to their working environment. In looking at the European Community, they were as interested in aspects of political integration as in economic integration. It

[61] S. Dell, *Trade Blocs and Common Markets* (London: Constable, 1963), 86–7.

was common after the Kennedy Round to talk about European integration as being more than just about tariffs. To British business this seemed the case from the beginning. Thus, there was interest in developments in many areas other than tariffs and exports. These issues are developed in the coming chapters.

3

Overseas Investment, Corporate Strategy, and European Integration

Trading patterns provide a clear picture of economic relationships between countries but this is an incomplete picture because such relationships can also exist in the form of overseas investment. Incorporation of this part of the story is particularly important for the years after the Second World War as it marked a clear and extensive period of internationalization of production and of growth in multinational enterprise. Much of this is associated with the internationalization of American business, particularly its growing role in Western Europe, but Britain remained a heavy overseas investor too. In order to understand how Britain's economic relationship with the EC was developing, the pattern and form of its overseas investment needs to be considered. Traditionally Britain was a global investor but this became increasingly concentrated on the Commonwealth countries, much like the story of exports. With regard to European integration, it has been conventional to highlight the resulting shift in US foreign direct investment (FDI) away from Britain to the six European Community member states from the late 1950s. It has also been suggested that British overseas investment was slow to shift away from the Commonwealth countries to Western Europe and the United States, which were growing faster. As British firms were more concentrated and more internationalized than their continental European counterparts, this was a missed opportunity, it has been claimed, to follow the example of American multinationals and exploit the advantages of European integration. This type of argument has direct parallels with the wider literature that presents Britain's failure to be involved in European integration earlier as a "missed opportunity." After a brief section on multinationals and European integration, the first part of this chapter attempts to assess the scale and form of British FDI in Western Europe, and in particular, when British business began investing there.

The British case is also interesting because Britain was on the edge of European integration. While it did not become part of the EC until 1973, it first applied to join in 1961 and there was at that time an expectation that entry would occur. This made the formulation of business strategy less certain than it might otherwise have been. More importantly, it illustrated the conflict between European economic integration in the form of the Europeanization of business and national governments' concerns with national

43

Table 3.1. US Direct Investment in Manufacturing, 1950, 1955–1970 (Book Value in Million Dollars)

	Europe	Europe (%)	UK	UK (%)	EC	EC (%)	Canada	Canada (%)	Total
1950	932	24.3	542	14.1	317	8.3	1879	49.0	3831
1955	1640	25.8	946	14.9	563	8.9	2841	44.7	6349
1956	1816	25.4	1052	14.7	659	9.2	3196	44.7	7152
1957	2195	27.4	1238	15.5	831	10.4	3924	49.0	8009
1958	2475	28.5	1361	15.7	970	11.2	4164	48.0	8673
1959	2927	30.2	1607	16.6	1135	11.7	4558	47.0	9692
1960	3804	34.4	2164	19.6	1436	13.0	4827	43.7	11051
1961	4255	35.5	2305	19.2	1659	13.8	5076	42.3	11997
1962	4883	36.9	2512	19.0	2063	15.6	5312	40.1	13250
1963	5634	37.7	2739	18.3	2528	16.9	5761	38.6	14937
1964	6587	38.9	3010	17.8	3139	18.5	6197	36.6	16935
1965	7606	39.3	3306	17.1	3725	19.3	6872	35.5	19339
1966	8876	40.2	3716	16.8	4401	20.0	7675	34.8	22058
1967	9798	40.5	3878	16.0	4976	20.6	8095	33.5	24172
1968	10798	40.9	4243	16.1	5399	20.4	8568	32.4	26414
1969	12280	41.6	4567	15.5	6382	21.6	9406	31.9	29527
1970	13706	42.5	4977	15.4	7177	22.2	10059	31.2	32261

Source: Adapted from Mira Wilkins, The Maturing of Multinational Enterprise: American Business Abroad from 1914–1970 (Cambridge MA: Harvard University Press, 1974), 331.

economic indicators, in this case, the balance of payments and economic growth. Analysis of this issue forms the second part of the chapter.

MULTINATIONALS AND EUROPEAN INTEGRATION

The post-Second World War years mark the coming of age of multinational enterprise.[1] Just as merger waves were not new phenomena, so also multinationals have a long history.[2] Nevertheless, the scale of FDI in the decades after the war was unprecedented, and concentrated far more than previously on American enterprises establishing subsidiaries in other developed economies. It has been estimated that in the two decades after 1945, possibly 85 percent of all new FDI flows came from the United States. What most caught people's attention was the spread of American manufacturing enterprise to Western Europe, as shown in Table 3.1. This growth is often related to the much-debated postwar process of Americanization with the spread of American business methods and American technology to Europe.[3]

The rise of US FDI to Western Europe is usually linked to European integration. American business was not only aware of the creation of the EC from an early date but also considered the implications of European integration for it.[4] Whether this FDI was driven by the desire to jump the EC's tariff wall or by recognition of European market expansion is disputed, but it is commonly agreed that American business was quicker to exploit the opportunities offered by European integration than European businesses.[5]

---

[1] J. Cantwell, "The Changing Form of Multinational Enterprise in the Twentieth Century," in A. Teichova, M. Lévy-Leboyer, and H. Nussbaum (eds.), *Historical Studies in International Corporate Business* (Cambridge: Cambridge University Press, 1989), 15–28.

[2] See M. Wilkins, "Multinational Enterprise to 1930," in A. Chandler and B. Mazlich (eds.), *Leviathans: Multinational Corporations and the New Global History* (Cambridge: Cambridge University Press, 2005), 45–79; A. Teichova, M. Lévy-Leboyer, and H. Nussbaum (eds.), *Multinational Enterprise in Historical Perspective* (Cambridge: Cambridge University Press, 1986); and G. Jones (ed.), *The Making of Global Enterprise* (London: Cass, 1994).

[3] On Americanization see, H. G. Schröter, *Americanization of the European Economy: A Compact Survey of American Economic Influence in Europe Since the 1880s* (Dordrecht: Springer, 2005); Matthias Kipping and Ove Bjarnar (eds.), *The Americanisation of European Business: The Marshall Plan and the Transfer of US Management Models* (London: Routledge, 1998); and J. Zeitlin and G. Herrigel (eds.), *Americanization and Its Limits: Reworking US Technology and Management on Post-War Europe and Japan* (Oxford: Oxford University Press, 2000).

[4] R. E. Mangan (ed.), *American Business Looks Abroad: Proceedings of the Nineteenth Annual Stanford Business Conference September 1960* (Stanford, CA: Graduate School of Business, Stanford University, 1961); American Management Association, *The European Common Market: New Frontier for American Business* (New York: AMA, 1958); and L. P. Dowd (ed.), *The European Economic Community: Implications for Michigan Business* (Ann Arbor: Bureau of Business Research, University of Michigan, 1961).

[5] For a survey see G. Yannopoulos, "Foreign Direct Investment and European Integration: The Evidence from the Formative Years of the European Community," *Journal of Common*

Indeed, it has been suggested that "American companies have integrated the European economies."[6] Jean-Jacques Servan-Schreiber's seminal work *Le défi américain*, or *The American Challenge* hinted at where this process was heading:

Fifteen years from now the world's third greatest industrial power, just after the United States and Russia, might not be Europe, but *American industry in Europe*. Already, in the ninth year of the Common Market, this European market is basically American in organization [emphasis in the original].[7]

It was not just that American enterprises were investing in Europe that was seen as the problem. Much of the investment took the form of mergers or acquisitions. About a third of US entries into European markets were joint ventures between 1960 and 1967. Of these, 35 percent ended in divorce, usually in the form of a takeover by the American partner or a shift to the American company taking a majority shareholding. As *Business Week* put it, "Many a European company has taken in American partners only to regret it after the warm Yankee embrace became a crushing bear hug."[8] It appeared like a takeover rather than just an invasion. More than this, a study of transnational mergers in the EC found that in the period 1961–69 there were only 257 involving companies based in two EC countries but 820 between a company of an EC member state and a company of a non-member state, mainly from the United States.[9] Domestic mergers remained the most popular form of corporate fusion but European companies were more will-ing, it appeared, to join with a non-EC company rather than another EC company. To some at least, it seemed that European companies were not only being slower than their American counterparts to exploit the oppor-tunities of the common market but also were reluctant to create European transnational companies.[10]

Servan-Schreiber saw the solution to this issue in the creation of "Eurochampions." Only a few transnational mergers of major companies

Market Studies, Vol. 28, No. 3 (1990), 235–59. See also G. Jones, "Multinationals from the 1930s to the 1980s," in Chandler and Mazlish (eds.), *Leviathans*, 97.

[6] J. Behrman, "Industrial Integration and the Multinational Enterprise," *Annals of the Amer-ican Academy of Politics and Social Science*, No. 403 (September 1972), 50; and M. Wilkins, "US Multinationals and the Unification of Europe," in F. Heller and J. Gillingham (eds.), *The United States and the Integration of Europe: Legacies of the Postwar Era* (Basingstoke: Macmillan, 1996), 341–63.

[7] J. J. Servan-Schreiber, *Le Défi Américain* (Denoel, 1967); and J. J. Servan-Schreiber, *The American Challenge* (London: Hamish Hamilton, 1968), 3.

[8] Quoted in M. Brooke and H. L. Remmers, *The Multinational Company in Europe: Some Key Problems* (London: Longman, 1972), 67.

[9] R. Mazzolini, *European Transnational Concentrations: Top Management's Perspective on the Obstacles to Corporate Unions in the EEC* (London: McGraw-Hill, 1974), 1.

[10] R. Vernon, "Enterprise and Government in Western Europe," in R. Vernon (ed.), *Big Business and the State: Changing Relations in Western Europe* (London: Macmillan, 1974), 3–24.

occurred in the 1960s, Agfa-Gevaert being one of the earliest.[11] It was only through this route, he believed, that the technology gap could be closed and European companies would be able to compete with their American counterparts in being able to exploit a European market fully. This was only one aspect of the potential impact of the creation of European transnational companies. As Charles Kindleberger wrote at the time:

Economic integration cannot be achieved by customs unions alone . . . . Ideally in the European integration contemplated by the Treaty of Rome, it would be a European corporation, reconstituted under European charter, or resulting from mergers that transcended national lines to create a truly European, not a national, decision-making entity.[12]

Or, putting it even more strongly, "it is the industrial leaders who will build Europe."[13] Foreign direct investment within Europe would be a key element in creating these European companies and breaking down national barriers to business activity.

BRITISH DIRECT INVESTMENT IN EUROPE

The British case is significant and illuminating in this respect as it raised tensions about Britain's position in Europe. British business was, in theory, ideally placed to play a leading role in the economic integration of Europe. The postwar period marked the consummation of a longer process of change towards Britain's emergence as a corporate economy.[14] The transformation in the postwar years was marked.[15] Underlying this was a sharp increase in concentration. Table 3.2 illustrates the trend in aggregate concentration (the share of the hundred largest enterprises in manufacturing net output) in Britain. The sharp increase in aggregate concentration in the 1950s and 1960s is clear and the same is true for market concentration, whichever measure is used, as shown in Table 3.3. From the late 1950s till 1973, Britain experienced a major merger wave, and it is estimated that mergers accounted for approximately half of the increased concentration of the 1960s and that

[11] On Agfa-Gevaert see G. Devos, "Agfa-Gevaert and Belgian Multinational Enterprise," in G. Jones and H. Schröter (eds.), *The Rise of Multinationals in Continental Europe* (Aldershot: Edward Elgar, 1993), 201–12.

[12] C. Kindleberger, "European Integration and the International Corporation," *Columbia Journal of World Business*, Vol. 1, No. 1 (Winter 1966), 65.

[13] P. Reuter, quoted in W. Feld, *Transnational Business Collaboration Among Common Market Countries: Its Implications for Political Integration* (New York: Praeger, 1970), 24.

[14] L. Hannah, *The Rise of the Corporate Economy* (London: Methuen, 2nd Ed. 1983), 1; and M. Kirby, "The Corporate Economy in Britain: Its Rise and Achievements since 1900," in M. Kirby and M. Rose (eds.), *Business Enterprise in Modern Britain: From the Eighteenth to the Twentieth Century* (London: Routledge, 1994), 156.

[15] G. Jones, *Merchants to Multinationals: British Trading Companies in the Nineteenth and Twentieth Centuries* (Oxford: Oxford University Press, 2000), 118.

Table 3.2. *Trends in UK Aggregate and*
Plant Concentration (%)

	Aggregate Concentration (1)	Aggregate Plant Concentration (2)
1909	16	
1924	22	
1930		10.8
1935	24	11.2
1948		9.0
1949	22	
1951		9.4
1953	27	
1954		10.1
1958	32	10.5
1963	37	11.1
1968	41	10.8
1970	40/41	

Notes: (1) Share of the largest enterprises in manufacturing net output, UK. Early years are approximations;
upper figure for 1970 includes steel and lower excludes
it. (2) Share of the hundred largest manufacturing
establishments in net output, UK. The figure for 1930
is an approximation; that for 1958 is based on sales
rather than net output.
Source: J. G. Walshe, "Industrial Organization and
Competition Policy," in N. F. R. Crafts and N. Woodward (eds.), *The British Economy since 1945* (Oxford:
Oxford University Press, 1991), 341.

had there been no mergers, concentration would not have risen much, if
at all.[16] There are considerable difficulties in making precise comparisons
with continental Europe.[17] While concentration in EC member states rose,
it is generally believed that concentration levels in Britain were significantly
higher.[18] British companies were more internationalized than those on the
continent and tended to be larger: Based on sales, seventeen British firms

[16] Hannah, *Rise of the Corporate Economy*, 145; and L. Hannah and J. Kay, *Concentration
in Modern Industry: Theory, Measurement and the UK Experience* (London: Macmillan,
1977), 86–8.

[17] K. D. George and T. S. Ward, *The Structure of Industry in the EEC: An International Comparison* (Cambridge: Cambridge University Press, 1975), 1; and S. J. Prais, *The Evolution of
Giant Firms in Britain: A Study of the Growth of Concentration in Manufacturing Industry
in Britain, 1909–1970* (Cambridge: Cambridge University Press, 1976), 138–9.

[18] George and Ward, *Structure of Industry in the EEC*, 25; Hannah and Kay, *Concentration in
Modern Industry*, 2; A. Jacquemin, "Size, Structure and Performance of the Largest European
Firms," *Three Banks Review* No. 102 (June 1974), 64; and A. Jacquemin and M. Cardon de

Table 3.3. *Changes in Market Concentration in the UK (%)*

	(1)	(2)	(3)	(4)
1935	26.3			
1951	29.3			
1958	32.4	55.4	56.5	52.3
1963	37.4	58.6	60.1	55.4
1968	41.0	63.4	64.8	58.8
1975			65.0	56.4
1977			64.8	54.8

Notes: (1) Average unweighted 3-firm employment concentration ratios for 3-digit industries ($N = 42$). (2) Average unweighted 5-firm sales concentration ratios for 4-digit industries ($N = 144$). (3) Average unweighted 5-firm sales concentration ratios for 4-digit industries ($N = 121$). (4) Column (3) adjusted for imports.
Source: Walshe, "Industrial Organization," 340.

appeared in the *Fortune* list of the fifty largest European firms in 1965, as against fifteen German companies and only eight French.[19] Moreover, five of the top six had a British input (the top two, Shell and Unilever, were Anglo-Dutch), the top German company, Volkswagen was fifth and the top French company, Renault, was only seventeenth.

Despite these potential advantages, much like the argument in relation to exports (see Chapter 2), it has been argued that British business maintained direct investment in the Commonwealth for too long. Geoffrey Jones concluded in the mid-1980s that while British direct investment in the Commonwealth was not a sign of a lack of international competitiveness in British business in the interwar period, "a clearer case can be made for British companies hugging the safe haven of the smaller, less dynamic Commonwealth markets" in the postwar period.[20] He continued, "It would seem that many British companies were a decade too late in recognizing that the United States and Europe in the 1950s and 1960s offered opportunities which needed to be taken." In reaching this conclusion, he seems to have been strongly influenced by Stopford and Turner's *Britain and the Multinationals*, then just published.[21] Their analysis has a very clear resonance with the "missed

Lichtbuer, "Size, Structure, Stability and Performance of the Largest British and EEC Firms," *European Economic Review* No. 4, (1973), 396.

[19] Christopher Layton, *Trans-Atlantic Investments* (Boulogne-sur-Seine: Atlantic Institute, 2nd ed. 1968), Table X. Shell and Unilever were both counted as part of a British company.

[20] G. Jones, "Origins, Management and Performance," in Geoffrey Jones (ed.), *British Multinationals: Origins, Management and Performance* (Aldershot: Gower, 1986), 18.

[21] J. Stopford and L. Turner, *Britain and the Multinationals* (Chichester: John Wiley, 1985).

opportunities" historiography, which argues that Britain should have partic-ipated in European integration from an earlier date.[22] Two quotes from the book illustrate their argument: "British multinational corporations were late in taking the EEC seriously and it was only in 1971 that investment flows to Western Europe moved ahead of those to the Commonwealth countries. There was a short-lived burst of investment in the immediate aftermath of Britain's entry, but by 1978 attention had shifted to the USA."[23] And again:

The diversification away from the Empire was played out at funereal speed. The need to change direction was only slowly perceived, and, when recognised, often resisted.... As latecomers to Western Europe and North America, the British would be faced with premium entry costs.[24]

Not only was the shift slow but it was only with entry into the EC in the early 1970s that managers' views about direct investment in Western Europe became positive and, even then, this was short-lived, according to Stopford and Turner.

Judging the validity of this argument is not straightforward. The initial difficulty is the lack of data. As has been noted, "a good part of *le defi américain* lies in *les statistiques americaines*."[25] American data on FDI for this period was so much more complete than that of any other industrialized economy that it was easy to highlight the scale and growth of American direct investment. Data for other countries did improve over time but differences in definition and methodology abound.[26] In the case of Britain, the Bank of England collected data on direct investment flows in and out of Britain, but this was not a guide to the stock of direct investment overseas or even the scale of net investment, given that much was funded from sources outside of Britain. The first comprehensive official study of the stock of UK investment abroad was only carried out in 1962, with some data going back to 1958.[27] Even after this date, the data remained partial, and even reliable FDI data still says little about the impact of the direct investment; like all aggregated data it also fails to reflect the complexity and diversity of business.[28]

---

[22] For example Roy Denman, *Missed Chances: Britain and Europe in the Twentieth Century* (London: Cassell, 1996); and Edmund Dell, *The Schuman Plan and the British Abdication of Leadership in Europe* (Oxford: Oxford University Press, 1995).

[23] Stopford and Turner, *Britain and the Multinationals*, 12.

[24] Ibid., 46.

[25] S. Rolfe, "The International Corporation in Perspective," in S. Rolfe and W. Damm (eds.), *The Multinational Corporation in the World Economy: Direct Investment in Perspective* (New York: Praeger, 1970), 9.

[26] G. Jones and H. G. Schröter, "Continental European Multinationals, 1850–1992," in G. Jones and H. G. Schröter (eds.), *Rise of Multinationals*, 10–11.

[27] D. Shepherd, A. Silberston and R. Strange, *British Manufacturing Investment Overseas* (London: Methuen, 1985), 9.

[28] G. Jones, "The Making of Global Enterprise," in Jones, *Making*, 5; Y. Cassis, "Divergence and Convergence in British and French Business in the Nineteenth and Twentieth Centuries,"

A further problem in relation to this study is that like *le defi américain* being in part driven by the availability of data, so that might be the case too with interpretations of the development of British FDI patterns. The standard account of the development of British FDI after the Second World War is of a heavy focus on the Commonwealth: 55 percent of the stock of British FDI was in the Commonwealth by 1962, only 13 percent in Western Europe and less than 10 percent in the United States, with an estimated 80 percent of new FDI going to the Commonwealth between 1946 and 1960. Thereafter, it is suggested, there was a switch first to Western Europe and later to the United States.[29] However, much of the data and many of the resulting tables are only able to track the shift from 1962 onwards and hence there is a tendency to date the shift from that year or from the early 1960s.[30] Yet, we cannot be sure about this. When it comes to considering the timing of British industry's response to European integration, this uncertainty is a problem. Moreover, contrary to Stopford and Turner's argument, others, using macro- and microdata have discovered no sign of a significant shift in UK outward investment around the time Britain became a member of the EC in 1973, with the biggest number of transnational links actually being created in the period 1963–70.[31] Thus, Geoffrey Jones has suggested that it was the French veto in January 1963 of Britain's first application to join the EC that was the trigger for the growth in British FDI to Western Europe.[32]

The obvious starting point for examining this issue is the official data on the stock of overseas capital. Even here annual data does not begin until 1965 supplemented with figures for 1962, as illustrated in Table 3.4. The table makes clear the dominance of the Commonwealth into the 1970s with the stock of assets in Australia still exceeding that in the EC6 in 1974. However, to get a better idea of the way in which British companies may have begun to shift their focus towards Europe, we need to consider investment flows (Table 3.5). This shows a jump in net FDI to the EC in 1971 and again in 1973.[33] It is also clear that the level of net investment to the EFTA countries was on a much smaller scale than that to the EC countries throughout the period. This data can also be broken down to a national level, allowing a

in Y. Cassis, F. Crouzet and T. Gourvish (eds.), *Management and Business in Britain and France: The Age of the Corporate Economy* (Oxford: Oxford University Press, 1995), 8.

[29] G. Jones, *The Evolution of International Business: An Introduction* (London: Routledge, 1996).

[30] M. Panić, "International Direct Investment in Conditions of Structural Disequilibrium: UK Experience since the 1960s," in J. Black and J. Dunning (eds.), *International Capital Movements* (London: Macmillan, 1982), 140–71.

[31] G. Ietto-Gillies, "European Community Integration and Geographical Spread of International Production," in H. Cox, J. Clegg and G. Ietto-Gillies (eds.), *The Growth of Global Business* (London: Routledge, 1993), 180–203.

[32] G. Jones, "British Multinationals and British Business since 1850," in Kirby and Rose (eds.), *Business Enterprise*, 191.

[33] Board of Trade/Department of Industry FDI figures exclude oil, banking and insurance.

Table 3.4. *Values of Direct Outward Investment by Area and Country, 1962–1971: Book Values of Net Assets Attributable to the UK at Year End (Million Pounds)*

	1962	1965	1966	1967	1968	1969	1970	1971	1972	1973	1974
Commonwealth	2048.9	2427.8	2451.1	2836.6	3013	3242.3	3369.2	3364.3	3601.9	4123.7	4500.7
Australia	520.4	712.9	761.1	894.4	966.4	1077.2	1114.8	1137.5	1293.2	1499.4	1747.2
S. Africa	290	391.7	429.8	545.3	585.6	640.8	626.7	644.1	713.7	821.1	997.2
New Zealand	108.5	137.1	144.3	135.1	139.7	147.7	159.3	155.7	163	175.7	184
India	259.7	304	207.7	261.9	277.2	286.7	297.4	289.8	279	274.8	275.3
Malaysia	126.7	144	144.4	174.5	172.6	172.6	182.8	195.9	221	246.9	271.5
Canada	484	531.4	549.1	661	686	722	715.9	671	716.8	846.6	941.2
USA	301.3	387.6	422.1	530	600	646.5	762.2	794.7	790.7	1038.9	1273.3
W. Europe inc. Ireland	451.8	641.9	730.8	864.6	975.3	1131.6	1229.9	1449.3	1755.6[a]	2308.3	2781.1
EC6	272.9	392.2	445.7	550.7	628.9	738.3	808	985.2	1191.4	1548.9	1812.2
EFTA	82.8	114.5	126.9	134.7	152.7	165.4	181.7	192.2	249.3	298.3	377.2
World	3405	4210	4401.6	5186.9	5585.3	6063.2	6404.1	6666.9	7269.7	8685.3	10017.8

[a] Inconsistent with previous years.

Source: Department of Industry, *Business Monitor M4 part I 1972: Overseas Transactions* (HMSO, London, 1974), table 35, and *ibid.*, 1974, Table I.

Table 3.5. *UK Net Outward Investment by Area, 1960–1974 (Million Pounds)*

	1960	1961	1962	1964	1965	1966	1967	1968	1969	1970	1971	1972	1973	1974
Overseas Sterling Area	159.9	123.6	122.3	161	186	118.8	142.2	176.8	313.2	229.6	187.3	227.2	420.3	526
Commonwealth						113	128	100	139	216	175	213	475	441
Non-Sterling Area	90.1	102.4	86.7	102.4	122.4	157.3	138.6	232.9	235.8	316.2	487.9	506	1207.8	1069.3
N. America	44.5	40.1	18.4	34.8	41.3	61.1	85	113.9	89.1	184.6	155.9	161.3	512.8	488.4
W. Europe	25.9	40.2	49.4	45.7	53.1	63.6	24.9	93.5	124.8	105.6	268	275.4	580.6	433.9
EC	21.5	26.4	29.2	36.7	32.1	50.5	29.9	72.8	104.5	77.8	262.5	223.4	518.8	367.1
EFTA	4.1	11.9	19.2	5.2	14.7	11	−8.4	18.8	14	27.5	4.7	51.7	61.8	66.8
Total	250	226	209	263	308	276	281	410	549	546	676	737	1628	1595

Source: 1960–1962: *Board of Trade Journal* 19 July 1969; other years: Department of Industry, *Business Monitor* M4, part 1; 1972: *Overseas Transactions* (HMSO, London, 1974), Table 1.

closer insight to the shifts in British overseas investment to individual countries within the EC and EFTA. This is shown in Table 3.6, which illustrates the growth in net investment to EC countries, especially West Germany from the late 1960s, but no such similar trend for EFTA countries with the exception of Switzerland, also a popular European base for US companies, and some growth in Sweden. There is a jump in net FDI to the EC in 1963, the year of the first veto, but it had been preceded by a steadily rising level of net investment in the years before. One other point worth noting is that in these early years it is West Germany and France which were the two most important recipients of this direct investment.

An earlier official series of private direct investment (excluding oil and insurance) does exist for the period from 1958 to 1962 and is shown in Table 3.7, but it is not directly comparable to the net investment figures. The data for overlapping years are reasonably consistent and so it provides a useful extension of the series and a guide to developments at this key stage of European integration.[34] Four points emerge. First, net investment in the EC was at least the equivalent of that to the USA, net investment to Canada was falling, but, as would be expected from the data on the 1960s, Australia was the largest recipient of British FDI. Secondly, within Western Europe, the EC was consistently the dominant host recipient group of countries compared to EFTA. Thirdly, net direct investment to the EC was rising prior to Britain's first application to join in 1961, while EFTA experienced a small upward movement in the years of the 1961–63 EC negotiations over Britain's application. Fourthly, while West Germany was the main recipient within the EC, in 1958 the situation appears more even. On the basis of this data Houston and Dunning concluded that: "The initial movement to the continent was made between 1959 and 1963. Expenditure in EEC and EFTA rose while investment in the United States remained static. Then, following de Gaulle's 'Non,' investment in the US moved upwards, surpassing the flow of capital to EEC in 1967, 1968 and 1970."[35]

To build on this picture, it is necessary to use a mixture of other data sources. An obvious starting point is the work of the Reddaway Committee. This was appointed by the FBI to consider the economic effects of overseas direct investment on the British economy, notably on the balance of payments. As part of this study it gathered together some data on overseas investment from 1955 to 1964, as shown in Table 3.8. What is significant in this table is the level of growth. Obviously faster growth is easier from a lower base but it is clear that the addition to net operating assets to the European countries were all above the average for the fifteen countries (102.3 percent), if only marginally in the case of France. While assets in Australia and Canada continued to dominate and still grew rapidly, the fastest growth

---

[34] See J. Dunning and D. C. Rowan, "British Direct Investment in Western Europe," *Banca Nazionale del Lavoro Quarterly Review*, No. 18, (1965), 127–56.

[35] T. Houston and J. Dunning, *UK Industry Abroad* (London, 1976), 117.

Table 3.6. *UK Net Outward Investment to EC and EFTA, 1960–1974 (Million Pounds)*

	1960	1961	1962	1963	1964	1965	1966	1967	1968	1969	1970	1971	1972	1973	1974
EC	21.5	26.4	29.2	39.9	36.7	32.1	50.5	29.9	72.8	104.5	77.8	262.5	223.4	518.8	367.1
Belgium & Luxemburg	4.7	1.7	9.2	3.5	-3.1	1.5	5.8	5.4	24.9	22.5	13.3	57.7	30.8	64.2	49.4
France	5.5	10	5.3	12.3	15.6	4	16.5	11.2	8.5	18	26.5	34.9	61.7	118.8	74
Italy	4.1	2.8	-5.5	3.1	3.1	1.2	2.3	2.4	2.6	8.9	8.1	13.9	24.4	26.5	25.6
Netherlands	2.1	2	6	7.5	5.4	9.4	9.3	9.8	14.6	14	9.8	52.9	42.3	105.1	35.4
W. Germany	5.2	9.8	14.2	13.5	15.7	16	16.6	1.2	22.2	41	20.1	103.1	64.1	149.2	109.1
EFTA	4.1	11.9	19.2	16.3	5.2	14.7	11	-8.4	18.8	14	27.5	4.7	51.7	61.8	66.8
Austria							0.4	0.3	0.6	0.2	3.7	4.3	5.6	8.9	4.1
Denmark	0.7	1	1.6	1.3	1.8	2.6	-0.1	1.6	1.1	0.8	1.7	3.8	9.3	9.5[a]	24.9
Finland							0.6	0.1	0.4	0.5	0.6	1.6	2.1	1	4.7
Norway							0.8	0.3	0.4	0.7	-4.2	2.5	2.3	2.1	4.3
Portugal	-0.1	0.6	1.4	2.6	0.8	1.5	1.8	-14.8	3.7	3	3.5	2.4	0.8	6.2	10.3
Sweden	1	3.3	1.5	1.4	-0.8	5.2	5.1	0.2	3.8	5.5	4.8	3.1	15.8	6.4	20.5
Switzerland	1.6	4.7	13.7	8.3	0.9	2.5	2.4	4	8.8	3.2	17.4	-13	15.8	37.1	22.9

[a] Denmark became a member of the EC in 1973.

Source: 1960–1962: *Board of Trade Journal* 19 July 1969; other years: Department of Industry, *Business Monitor* M4, part; 1972: *Overseas Transactions* (HMSO, London, 1974).

Table 3.7. *UK Private Direct Investment (Excluding Oil and Insurance) by Area and Countries, 1958–1962 (Million Pounds)*

	1958	1959	1960	1961	1962
USA	10.6	16	15.7	19.8	9.5
Canada	27.5	36.3	28.1	17.8	7.6
S. Africa	19.9	11.3	18.9	8	12.9
Australia	19.4	27.3	59.6	32.6	44.9
W. Europe	13.8	19.9	25.2	37.7	45.8
EC	8.4	16.1	20.8	24.8	27.1
W. Germany	6.7	6.7	5	9.2	13.2
Netherlands	0.3	−0.1	2	1.9	5.6
Belgium	1.5	3.3	4.6	1.6	8.5
France	−0.4	4.4	5.3	9.4	4.9
Italy	0.1	1.8	4	2.6	−5.2
EFTA	2.9	0.7	3.9	10.7	17.5
Portugal	1.3	0.2	−0.1	0.6	1.3
Switzerland	0.6	0.1	1.6	4.4	12.7
Denmark	0.4	0.3	0.7	0.9	1.5
Total	143.5	190.5	242.1	211.9	193.8

Source: Board of Trade Journal, 14 September 1962 and 7 August 1964.

was by some margin that in operating assets in West Germany.[36] This tells us nothing about when in the period 1955–64 this occurred, but does at least provide further support of the growth of UK investment to Europe in the late 1950s and early 1960s.

The strongest expression of the belief in an early shift in UK direct investment towards Western Europe comes in a rarely cited piece by Houston, the author with John Dunning of *UK Industry Abroad*. Here he notes the substantial shift in the flow of UK funds into the region between 1958 and 1959, adding "but it was widely held that UK companies had been slow to grasp European opportunities before that date and that the principal motive for investment after signature of the Rome Treaty was 'defensive,' investments being made to maintain markets jeopardized by the common tariff."[37] He

[36] B. L. Johns, "Private Overseas Investment in Australia: Profitability and Motivation," *Economic Record*, Vol. 43, No. 102 (1967) 233–61; W. P. Hogan, "British Investment in Australian Manufacturing: The Technical Connection," *Manchester School* No. 35, (1967), 133–66; and J. Dunning, *Studies in International Investment* (London: Allen & Unwin, 1970), 190–232.

[37] T. Houston, "Formation and Scale of UK Direct Investment on the Continent," in D. Tookey (ed.), *Harmonization of Business Practice in the Common Market: A Guide to Essential Changes in UK Procedures and Training* (Epping: Gower, 1973), 133.

Table 3.8. *UK Net Operating Assets 1955 and 1964 for Various Countries (Million Pounds)*

	Addition to assets 1955–1964	Col. 1 as a percentage of 1955 assets	1955 (derived from cols 1 & 2)	1964 (derived from cols 3 & 1)
W. Germany	44.8	302.1	14.8	59.6
Italy	8	162.9	4.9	12.9
France	16.6	104.3	15.9	32.5
Denmark	6.3	218.2	2.9	9.2
USA	103.4	57.7	179.2	282.6
Argentina	14.5	136.5	10.6	25.1
Canada	207.1	136.6	151.6	358.7
Brazil	8.9	43.2	20.6	29.5
Malaysia	13.5	113.8	11.9	25.4
India	70.8	114.2	62.0	132.8
Ghana	−0.1	−0.8	12.5	12.4
Jamaica	7	115.9	6.0	13.0
Nigeria	14.5	44.7	32.4	46.9
Australia	172.2	179.2	96.1	268.3
S. Africa	35.1	43.7	80.3	115.4

Source: Derived from W. B. Reddaway, *Effect of UK Direct Investment Overseas: Final Report*, table IV.6.

continues, "This opinion may understate the significance of the movements into Europe that were made between 1953 and 1959." The basis for his view was the very high levels of exported capital in the 1950s, an increasing share of which was used for direct investment. Even if the share going to Europe represented only a small fraction of the total figure, it could still be significant in historical terms. He adds that it was not so much the scale of the investment but the number of them that was significant: "The new investments in Europe were generally small in volume. The majority of investments were made to establish sales companies or to acquire relatively small producing facilities . . . . It seems the general motive, notably for firms that held a dominant share of their domestic market, was sales growth by participation in rapidly expanding continental markets."[38]

This is one of the main problems with investigating the shifting pattern of investment simply in terms of the flow of funds. It says nothing about the number of such investments. For this we need to look at the actions of individual firms. Unsurprisingly, many examples can be found of companies

[38] Ibid., 134.

concentrating their subsidiaries in the Commonwealth.[39] Houston also notes that there were only a small group of UK companies who controlled several subsidiaries on the continent prior to the Treaty of Rome.[40] He names BP, BAT, Liebigs, Courtaulds, Dunlop, Reckitt and Colman, J & P Coats and the two Anglo-Dutch companies, Unilever and Shell, as companies that controlled affiliated operations in four or more European countries before the mid-1950s. However, he adds that by the end of the 1950s, 42 of the 165 company groups in his sample study controlled subsidiaries in at least four West European countries.[41] Among those that strengthened their position in West European markets were Bowater, Reed, Beecham, Storey Bros, Marley, Ready Mixed Concrete, Clarkson, Dexion, GKN, Gestetner, Mather & Platt, Lines Bros, Lamson Industries, Johnson Matthey, Morgan Crucible, Rank Organization, Simon Engineering, and EMI. From press reports it is clear that these companies were not alone in investing in Europe prior to Britain's first application.[42] Similarly, *The Director* set out a list of sixteen companies with recent UK investments in the EC: ICI, Fisons, Associated Commercial Vehicles, Metal Industries, Metal Box, British Motor Corporation, Leyland Motors, Bowater, Courtaulds, General Electric, British Plaster Board (Holdings), Elliott-Automation, Lines Bros, EK Cole, Exco Electronics, and Head Wrightson.[43] About half of them were investing there for the first time. As one contemporary commentator noted, British companies "have been extremely active in deploying themselves by means of branches, subsidiaries, licenses, or participations with continental firms to find a means of producing or distributing within the Community territory."[44] Another noted, "the number of British companies which carried through such operations in advance of the opening of the negotiations between Britain and the Common Market is very large."[45] Clearly then, there is significant evidence of UK companies making a move towards investment in Western Europe, especially the EC, prior to Britain's first application in 1961. In this light, this investment does not seem to have been delayed, nor one limited to only a few global companies. British business seems to have been more alive to the

---

[39] J. Stopford, "The Origins of British-Based Multinational Manufacturing Enterprises," *Business History Review*, Vol. 43, No. 3 (1974), 303–5; G. Jones (ed.), *British Multinationals: Origins, Management and Performance* (Aldershot: Gower, 1986); and Shepherd, Silbertson, and Strange, *British Manufacturing Investment*.

[40] Houston, "Formation and Scale," 133.

[41] Ibid., 134. This sample of 165 is very close to the 168 groups used by Houston and Dunning in *UK Industry Abroad*, the data for which Houston collected.

[42] For example, "Metal Industries Limited," *The Times*, 8 July 1959, 10; and "The Plessey Company Limited," *The Times*, 30 Dec 1960, 13.

[43] "One Foot in Europe," *The Director*, Vol. 13, No. 2 (August 1960), 273–5.

[44] D. Thompson, "The Project for a Commercial Company of European Type," *International and Comparative Law Quarterly*, Vol. 10, No. 4 (1961), 852.

[45] William Mennell, *Takeover: The Growth of Monopoly in Britain, 1951–1961* (London: Lawrence and Wishart, 1962), 126.

opportunities available in the EC than conventionally believed. *The Director* summed up the position well, pointing to the role of business in European integration:

British industry has decided that it is going into Europe whether or not it leaves the government waving goodbye from the dock. British investment in Europe is now running at about £50 million a year and scarcely a day passes without the announcement of a new British venture on the continent, whether by way of association, purchase of a company, or the establishment of a new subsidiary . . . .

When the whole matter can be seen in historical perspective it may be found that the way in which British industry has moved is more important than any specific phase of the big and complex negotiations between governments. After all, in the creation of the common market itself the desire of European industry for wider markets led the way for the politicians to follow. One does not have to be a determinist to believe that it is very hard for politicians to resist basic economic forces.[46]

OBSTACLES TO INVESTING IN EUROPE

This argument becomes even stronger once other factors are taken into consideration. As the article in *The Director* noted, the split between the Six and the Seven was a source of uncertainty for those companies wishing to embark on a five- or seven-year investment program. Direct investment is also path-dependent. It has been estimated that between 1938 and 1956, the UK lost 40 percent of its overseas business assets through sequestration, wartime destruction and obligatory sales.[47] Many of these losses were in continental Europe. Faced with building businesses from scratch in Europe or developing existing subsidiary businesses in the Commonwealth, there was an inevitable tendency to take the latter course. Once that decision was made further investment inevitably followed, as most investment tends to take the form of expansion of existing facilities, rather than completely new ventures. The historical evolution of firms therefore has an important impact on the pattern of overseas investment.[48]

Path dependence was not the only obstacle in the way of firms shifting their direct investment to Western Europe. There were barriers to entry as well. British Rollmakers, GKN, United Biscuits, Thorn-EMI, and Lucas Industries were all frustrated over the course of the 1960s and 1970s in their efforts to acquire firms.[49] This was usually because of government veto but threats from consumers to refuse to continue purchasing could have the same effect. General Electric, for example, was blocked from buying BMW in 1960 by

---

[46] "Commentary," *The Director*, Vol. 13, No. 3 (September 1960), 419.

[47] Jones, *Evolution*, 211.

[48] Shepherd, Silberston and Strange, *British Manufacturing Investment*, 35; and Stopford, "Origins," 333.

[49] Stopford and Turner, *Britain and the Multinationals*, 84–5.

the Bavarian government.[50] Even without government interference, plans for direct investment in the EC could stall, as illustrated by the case of the Standard Motor Company. Standard had made an agreement with Hotchkiss-Brandt in 1954 for a F new company, Standard-Hotchkiss, to manufacture Massey-Ferguson tractors under license for sale in France.[51] In 1958, Standard investigated the possibility of manufacturing its Triumph sports cars at the Standard-Hotchkiss plant in France, with a second wholly owned Standard subsidiary distributing the cars from Paris "within the framework of the European Common Market."[52] French legal advice suggested that it would be very difficult to get permission from the French authorities to build the cars.[53] Although this proved mistaken, the company then had to negotiate with the Bank of England for permission to make the investment because of exchange control. There was a range of difficulties faced by Standard before it was able to manufacture sports cars in France. Such obstacles were not insuperable but must have deterred many firms who thought about investing in Europe.

The experience of Standard introduces another potentially major obstacle to direct investment in Western Europe. Exchange control prevented large sums of currency leaving the Sterling Area without government, or more precisely the Bank of England's, sanction. This was seen as a way of protecting the balance of payments. In terms of company overseas investment this steered it towards the Commonwealth countries, the vast majority of which were members of the Sterling Area. This has been presented as one factor, but only one factor, in the unprecedented postwar concentration of direct investment in the Commonwealth.[54] However, a survey of European (including British) and American businessmen at the time did list it as a key factor in deciding the location of overseas investment.[55] Exchange control had been applied rigorously immediately after the war but the policy had gradually been liberalized from 1954. By the late 1950s the Bank of England was delegated to deal with any applications by firms wanting to invest less than £100,000. All other cases went to a governmental committee for decision. By the late 1950s it was clear that few applications over £100,000 were being refused (five out of seventy-nine applications in 1958–59) and so at

[50] D. Bailey, G. Harte and R. Sugden, *Transnationals and Governments: Recent Policies in Japan, France, Germany, the United States and Britain* (London: Routledge, 1994), 84.

[51] MRC MSS226/ST/3/HB/1/1, Thomas (Standard Triumph International solicitor) to Ellis, Leyland Motors, 29 March 1962.

[52] MRC MSS226/ST/3/O/F/1, Letter to Perrichon (Standard-Hotchkiss), 7 May 1958.

[53] Ibid., Letter from Sarrut to Société Standard-Hotchkiss, 31 May 1958.

[54] Houston and Dunning, *UK Industry Abroad*, 114; and Bailey, Harte and Sugden, *Transnationals and Governments*, 150–6.

[55] J. Kitching, *Acquisitions in Europe: Causes of Corporate Successes and Failures* (Geneva: Business International, 1973), 94.

the end of 1959, the Bank asked for its delegated powers to be used in cases up to £500,000 (sixty-four of the seventy-nine applications).[56]

Then in the summer of 1961, two weeks before it was announced that Britain intended to apply to join the EEC, a series of emergency measures were introduced to alleviate Britain's balance of payments problems. As a result, two criteria for judging applications for direct investment in the non-Sterling Area were adopted: "clear and commensurate benefits in UK export earnings" within 18 months, or the development of a demand for British exports unrelated to the original investment.[57] In addition, the earnings of overseas subsidiaries had to be remitted back to the UK parent as far as possible. In practice the eighteen-month period was operated flexibly, soon raised to two years, and within a year, the policy was being applied more liberally.[58] Any "reasonable" application for less than £25,000 of foreign exchange was also always approved. Further relaxations followed on the proceeds of the sale or liquidation of post-1939 direct investments in the non-Sterling Area: in 1963 less than 5 percent of applications were refused, amounting to only 1.6 percent of the applications' total value. Even when restrictions were tightened in the 1965 budget very few applications were refused.[59] It seems hard to argue that on the basis of this evidence that exchange control was a strong deterrent to overseas investment in Western Europe, even in the period before 1965 when investment in Western Europe was controlled but that to the Sterling Area was not.

What is clear, however, is that despite the low level of refusals, overseas investment, including direct investment in Western Europe, would have been higher without exchange control. The Treasury estimated in 1964 that overseas investment, that is non-Sterling Area investment, was being reduced by the order of £100 m.[60] In other words, net direct investment in the non-Sterling Area would have been doubled. Having to use the dollar switch market also meant getting foreign currency at a higher exchange rate, adding a premium to overseas direct investment.[61] The size of the premium depended on the demand for currency from the dollar switch market and the resulting difference between that exchange rate and the lower official exchange rate. With official exchange not available for overseas investment from 1965, this premium rose. When the restrictions were originally introduced in 1961, the premium was about 3 percent but by April 1966 the premium stood at 20

---

[56] TNA T318/918, Tansley to Glaves-Smith, 12 November 1959.

[57] MRC MSS200/F/3/E3/32/4, E.252C.61, "The Present Attitude of the Treasury Towards New Investment in the Non-Sterling Area," late 1961.

[58] Ibid., Meetings of the FBI Overseas Investment Committee, 14 December 1961 (E.263.61) and 4 June 1962 (E.96.62); and MRC MSS200/F/3/E3/32/9, "Note of a Meeting at the Treasury on Wednesday October 30th 1963," November 1963.

[59] TNA T295/524, OIG (66)2, 9 February 1966.

[60] MRC MSS200/F/3/E3/32/10, E.219.64, 26 June 1964.

[61] Ibid., E.382.64, undated, but 1964.

percent and had been as high as 25 percent, a potentially hefty increase in the cost of overseas investment. There was also an argument that smaller and medium-sized firms were being deterred from seriously considering overseas investment.[62]

The FBI's Overseas Investment Committee considered only a few individual cases of this sort. One concerning Beckett, Laycock & Watkinson Ltd., related to this very issue.[63] It planned to take a controlling interest in an Italian company as a means of gaining access to that market. The company was turned down for official exchange but given permission for the investment to take place via the switch dollar market. However, the company was unhappy at the premium it would have to pay to obtain the necessary currency to make the investment. Direct investment in Western Europe was held down by exchange control below the level it would otherwise have been, although it is hard to quantify by how much. In this respect, it was not so much the number of refused applications that mattered as the premium paid for using the switch dollar market and the broader climate of discouraging overseas investment.

One further factor strengthens this case. There is clear evidence that European integration was a factor behind some domestic mergers in Britain at this time. For example, as early as April 1957 the issue was presented as central to the proposed merger between Courtaulds and British Celanese.[64] Similarly, in 1961 three of Britain's largest button manufacturers merged in preparation for British entry into the EC.[65] Most significant in this respect, however, was the failed merger between ICI and Courtaulds. This was at that time the largest UK merger ever proposed.[66] Donald Coleman's account of this episode makes no mention of the EC, focusing on its global implications.[67] However, contemporaries certainly saw it from this perspective. In the Six, industrialists saw it as evidence of the potentially harmful impact on their profits and the danger of overproduction if Britain was allowed to join the EEC.[68] In Britain too, some highlighted the European aspect to the proposed merger. Avison Wormald, the managing director of Fisons Ltd, who had previously been the commercial manager of British Nylon Spinners (which was jointly owned by ICI and Courtaulds), wrote to *The Times* about the merger, setting out two strategic aims of ICI's actions which

---

[62] TNA FCO70/1, Rooke to Preston, 28 March 1969.

[63] MRC MSS200/F/3/E3/32/6, unknown to Johnson, 2 November 1962; Johnson to Sir Henry Wilson-Smith, 5 November 1962.

[64] "Courtaulds and Celanese to Merge," *The Times*, 12 April 1957, 16. See also D. C. Coleman, *Courtaulds: An Economic and Social History* (Oxford: Oxford University Press, 1980), 151.

[65] "Three Firms in Button Merger," *The Times*, 22 December 1961, 13.

[66] G. Turner, *Business in Britain* (Harmondsworth: Pelican, revised edn. 1971), 59.

[67] Coleman, *Courtaulds*, 201–37.

[68] "How Continent Sees ICI Bid," *The Times*, 20 December 1961, 14.

"have not attracted the attention they deserve." The second is relevant here:

> To acquire Courtaulds' massive interests in both the Common Market and America as bases for its own expansion there. ICI because of its prewar cartel policy (dissolved so far as Europe was concerned by the war and in America by the anti-trust suit against Du Pont) has no worth-while manufacturing interests in the Common Market nor in America. [69]

ICI was embarking on a major investment program in Western Europe and taking over Courtaulds offered a ready solution to ICI's perceived need to expand its operations on the continent. ICI's sales in Europe had reached nearly £200 m. by 1971, a five-fold increase in a decade; it had invested over £100 m. in continental Europe over that decade and over 50 percent of its sales in the EC were now manufactured at its new plants in Germany and the Netherlands.

There are other examples in the 1960s of attempts by British companies to merge with other British companies in order to acquire access to the European market. This was a key component of the case that Guest, Keen & Nettlefolds Ltd (GKN), the metal working and engineering company, made to the Monopolies Commission in support of its merger with Birfield Ltd. GKN was looking for companies which, among other factors, "have established international operations, particularly in Common Market countries.... Birfield . . . through associated companies in France, Italy and Germany, has established bases in the Common Market which GKN lacked."[70] Domestic mergers were not solely driven by the desire to acquire monopoly status or simply a defensive response to increased international competition. They could also be part of an attempt to create an international position, either directly by acquiring a company that already had international interests or indirectly as a staging post towards international mergers.

Taking the evidence available in terms of the number of British firms engaging in FDI in Western Europe, especially the EC, from an early date plus the evidence that access to European markets could also play a role in domestic mergers, it does not appear that Stopford and Turner's criticism of an overly slow turn to Europe by British business is valid. The scale could have been greater but even here there were obstacles which acted as a deterrent to greater FDI. Given this, it seems reasonable to assume that British FDI to Western Europe and especially the EC would have been higher than it was had such investment been encouraged by the government. The reasons for this lack on encouragement can now be considered.

---

[69] "The Merger: ICI Power and Strategy," letter by Avison Wormald, *The Times*, 16 February 1962.

[70] The Monopolies Commission, *Guest, Keen & Nettlefolds Ltd and Birfield Ltd: A Report of the Merger* (London: HMSO, 1967) (Cmnd. 3186), 29.

BECOMING EUROPEAN AND THE
BRITISH GOVERNMENT

The purpose of exchange control was to help reduce overseas investment in order to alleviate Britain's recurring balance of payments problem. The British government was not keen to encourage FDI in Europe believing that FDI was an alternative to exports and that a failure to reach an accommodation with the Six would set off a bout of tariff wall-jumping FDI.[71] In contrast, business, in the form of the FBI and CBI, took a very different view, confident that FDI and exports were complementary. With a lack of evidence and given the complexity of the subject the two sides were to argue the case through the 1960s. The economic departments of the government were to change their position little from that set out in 1959:

> For domestic employment as well as balance of payments reasons, we presumably do not want too much capital to leave this country for the continent. But some increase in the interlocking of our industries with those of the Six might help to promote an outward-looking development of the Common Market.[72]

As a result, no positive encouragement was to be given to business to invest in Western Europe. In addition, it was argued that even if the commercial returns were the same, domestic investment had a higher net social return than overseas investment.[73] Related to this, Nicholas Kaldor, the Cambridge economist and Labour government economic adviser, believed that UK overseas investment was too high and treated too generously by government policy, hindering British economic growth.[74]

In contrast, business complained about the constraints on overseas investment arguing that exchange control was only needed in periods of crisis and that policy was being implemented "without any sure knowledge of what the effects will be" and that what was needed was "a thorough examination of the complex relations between investment and exports (visible and invisible)."[75] When the government refused to fund such a study, the FBI paid Brian Reddaway, an economist at Cambridge, to produce such a report. In the end, he produced an interim and a final report which, perhaps inevitably given the complexities of the subject, provided no clear answers to the issue and highlighted the diversity of experience.[76] In the eyes of the FBI's successor organization, the CBI, the reports provided substantial support to its criticisms of exchange control restrictions since 1961, but the

[71] TNA T318/918, "UK Investment in EEC Countries," by Hodges, 17 December 1959.
[72] Ibid.
[73] TNA T326/289, OI(WP)(64)24 (Final), June 1964, para. 155.
[74] See TNA T295/163.
[75] TNA T295/163, H.53.65, 21 May 1965.
[76] W. B. Reddaway, *Effects of UK Direct Investment Overseas: An Interim Report* (Cambridge: Cambridge University Press, 1967); W. B. Reddaway, *Effects of UK Direct Investment Overseas: Final Report* (Cambridge: Cambridge University Press, 1968).

Treasury reached the opposite conclusion.[77] Thus the issue remained highly contentious and unresolved with a significant gap between the Treasury and the representatives of business.

The CBI used the occasion of Reddaway's *Interim Report* to stress the importance of European integration as a context for British FDI: "The argument for entry into Europe which has gained the greatest acceptance in the last few years is that we must have a larger industrial base than the home economy can provide. Overseas investment is an important means of extending the range and scale of industrial operations and, whether we enter the European Economic Community or not, the need for it will grow."[78] This argument was rejected out of hand within the government on the basis that FDI and exports were alternatives.[79] Business organizations found such an argument outmoded in the emerging world of multinational enterprises and the internationalization of production in which exports and other forms of international activity, including FDI, were, in their eyes, complementary:

As Britain's external difficulties have increased, the outflow of investment has come under scrutiny and criticism, and it has been suggested that overseas investment is a luxury that we cannot afford. Critics sometimes imply that British companies should have sought to build up their overseas sales by means of direct exporting alone, and that investing overseas is an alternative, or addition to, exporting.

Such a view is based on a complete misunderstanding of the nature of international competition. Investments abroad are undertaken by manufacturing companies for many diverse reasons. Essentially, however, industry invests overseas because, in a particular commercial situation, foreign investment is the only appropriate competitive weapon.... All [reasons for overseas investment] are related to the requirements of establishing and maintaining an effective competitive position in world markets when failure to invest will strengthen foreign competitors. Hence, the consequences for the competitive stance of a particular company, and ultimately of the whole British economy, if overseas investment is discouraged can be extremely serious.[80]

By the late 1960s, Foreign and Commonwealth Office (FCO) commercial representatives were increasingly adopting a similar appreciation in their analysis of Britain's relations with the EC and becoming frustrated with the Bank of England, the Treasury and the Board of Trade. The commercial representative in the British embassy in Brussels gave examples of three other reasons for investment in Belgium beyond jumping tariff barriers: access to the distribution network of a local partner, expansion of sales from the home factories, and securing a better footing in preparation for eventual British

---

[77] TNA T295/165, meeting of the government's Overseas Investment Group, 3 March 1967.

[78] Ibid., "CBI Press Release on the Reddaway Interim Report," attached to Bracewell-Milnes (FBI) to Sir Denis Rickett, 17 March 1967.

[79] TNA T295/166, "NEDC Briefing on the Reddaway Report," Forsyth to Hodges, April 1967.

[80] TNA T295/639, Davies, "Overseas Investment: Two CBI Occasional Papers," September 1969, 15–6. See also MRC MSS200/F/3/E3/32/10, E.382.64.

entry into the EC.[81] He went on to voice his concerns about the essentially passive nature of government policy. A more positive and encouraging policy would make certain that more firms were aware of the opportunities in the EC and the potential benefits which could ensue. British embassy representatives across the EC endorsed these views. There was a political as well as an economic dimension to encouraging British direct investment in the EC at that time:

While we cannot make striking political moves forward, there is no doubt that our commerce is making its own way into the European area and there seems to be nothing (except perhaps government policy) to stop our industry moving into the same field. I myself am convinced that the shortest way into the European Community is to produce a "de facto" (to use a fashionable term) situation in which our industry is firmly placed within the borders of the Six.[82]

The British Ambassador in Brussels in particular urged that full weight should be given to the political arguments for greater British investment in Europe and this formed part of a request from the FCO to the Treasury to allow embassies to encourage industry to exploit the investment opportunities in the EC.[83] Nevertheless, embassy commercial officers also recognized the economic considerations. ICI was cited as an example of a company that had been asked if its investment program in the EC would have gone ahead even if the company had been certain of British entry. The response was "a very decided affirmative" and other examples of similar strategies were given.[84] It took six months of discussion within Whitehall for a cautiously more positive stance towards investment opportunities in both EFTA and the EC to be accepted. Even then the Board of Trade remained unyielding: If there was a likelihood of Britain entering the EC, it was argued, then this would provide a sufficient stimulus to investment of itself and that it was necessary to avoid this reducing domestic investment.[85] This position drew a scathing critique from the FCO, who could see no point in continuing "an acrimonious exchange with the Board of Trade on the philosophy of overseas investment." Put bluntly, "This attitude and the excessive preoccupation with visible exports is antediluvian in these days of international marketing and international firms."[86]

---

[81] TNA FCO70/1, "Local Investment and Trade," Hiller to Phillips, 13 February 1969.
[82] Ibid., Malcolm to Hancock, 24 January 1969.
[83] TNA FCO70/1, Hancock to Bell, 27 March 1969.
[84] Ibid., Rooke to Preston, 28 March 1969.
[85] Ibid., Hughes to Sir Thomas Brimelow, 20 June 1969.
[86] Ibid., "British Industrial Investment in Europe," by Jamieson, 30 June 1969.

A EUROPEAN CORPORATE STRATEGY

Emphasizing international marketing and the international nature of firms implied such firms had international corporate strategies. However, this did not mean that "Europe" or even the Six were regarded as a single homogenous entity by British business. While there was much talk of "going into Europe", it is clear that British industry (and its European counterparts) were very aware of differences between countries and that nationalistic sentiments in particular limited the extent of a single market within the EC, let alone within Western Europe. In this respect, there was often a contrast between American and European perspectives of the impact of European integration. Obviously, Servan-Schreiber's starting point, and that adopted by many since, has been to present the American approach as the better one. In many ways this must be qualified. The European Union is still a significant distance from being a single market and only "superficial analysis" would have seen the EC in the 1960s as a single market.[87] "The American advantage stemmed partly from a misconception – many Americans thought of Europe as one entity, and though this led to initial disasters when national differences were encountered in practice, the direction of planning, marketing and product development to the European market as a whole have produced some striking benefits," was how *The Times* expressed it.[88] But the argument can be taken further. Tolliday has shown that problems were created for Ford in Europe because its American management had an unrealistic view of European integration.[89] While the company's British and German managers emphasized the national differences that remained in Europe, management in Dearborn perceived a single market. More than this, the American managers worked on the assumption in the late 1950s and early 1960s that Britain and the rest of EFTA would soon join forces with the EC.[90] The veto of Britain's membership of the EC in January 1963 not only came as a shock to Ford's managers in the United States but also left their

---

[87] Mazzolini, *European Transnational Concentrations*, 97. See also A. Millington and B. Bayliss, "Non-Tariff Barriers and UK Investment in the European Community," *Journal of International Business Studies*, Vol. 22, No. 4 (1991), 695–710.

[88] R. Jones, "Europe: An Integrated Operation or Just Another Export Market?" *The Times*, 23 March 1970, 23.

[89] S. Tolliday, "The Origins of Ford of Europe: From Multidomestic to Transnational Corporation, 1903–1976," in H. Bonin, Y. Lang and S. Tolliday (eds.), *Ford, 1903–2003: The European History*, Vol. 1 (Paris: PLAGE, 2003), 177–241; S. Tolliday, "American Multinationals and the Impact of the Common Market: Cars and Integrated Markets, 1954–1967," in F. Amatori, A. Colli and N. Crepas, *Deindustrialization and Reindustrialization in 20th-Century Europe* (Milan: Franco Angeli, 2003), 383–93; and S. Tolliday, "Transplanting the American Model? US Automobile Companies and the Transfer of Technology and Management to Britain, France, and Germany, 1928–1962," in Zeitlin and Herrigel (eds.), *Americanization and Its Limits*, 93–119.

[90] Tolliday, "Origins," 177–8 and 182; and Tolliday, "American multinationals," 383–93.

European strategy in flux.[91] Even the creation of Ford Europe in 1967, often held up as a prime example of the foresight of American multinationals, was in part brought about because of hopes that Britain's second application at that time would be successful.[92]

Similarly, Bartlett and Ghoshal have used a comparison of the contrasting strategies of Procter & Gamble (American) and Unilever (Anglo-Dutch) in Europe at this time as a classic case study of business strategy.[93] Their point is to emphasize the importance of administrative heritage in business strategy but they also praise Procter and Gamble's internationalization strategy in Europe as "one of the best examples of how to manage such an organizational change."[94] In contrast, Unilever found it far harder to break the autonomy of its national subsidiaries and to adopt a pan-European strategy. This case has recently been reexamined by Jones and Miskell, using Unilever's archives, who conclude that while Procter and Gamble moved quickly to exploit European integration in the early 1960s, the differences between the two companies can be overdrawn.[95] Nevertheless, they argue, Unilever, despite being a strong advocate of European integration, faced major exogenous and endogenous barriers to restructuring on to a European basis compared with Procter and Gamble, and that these barriers inevitably meant that restructuring was slower.

Indeed, it would be wrong to assume that all US multinationals viewed the EC as a single market.[96] Equally, Europe was more of a single market for some industries than others. ICI was often held up as the exception to the failure of European companies to respond to European integration by adopting a pan-European strategy.[97] By the end of the 1950s, ICI had entered what one director called "the era of fallibility"; at that stage it was a national company with relatively small sales in Western Europe and the USA.[98] In 1960 Paul Chambers became chairman of the company and one of his first steps was to appoint a new European Council to examine the desirability of large-scale manufacture in the EC.[99] As a result, in February 1961, the

---

[91] Tolliday, "Origins," 184.　　　[92] Ibid., 190–1.

[93] C. Bartlett and S. Ghoshal, *Managing Across Borders: The Transnational Solution* (Boston: Harvard Business School Press, 2nd edn., 1998). See also Davis Dyer, Frederick Dalzell, and Rowena Olegario, *Rising Tide: Lessons from 165 Years of Brand Building at Procter & Gamble* (Boston: Harvard Business School Press, 2004).

[94] Bartlett and Ghoshal, *Managing Across Borders*, 166.

[95] G. Jones and P. Miskell, "European Integration and Corporate Restructuring: The Strategy of Unilever, c. 1957–c. 1990," *Economic History Review*, Vol. 58, No. 1 (2005), 125. In the text "cannot" is used but the authors have confirmed that it should be "can." See also G. Jones, *Renewing Unilever: Transformation and Tradition* (Oxford: Oxford University Press, 2005).

[96] Kindleberger, "European Integration and the International Corporation," 71–72.

[97] Servan-Schreiber, *American Challenge*, 5.

[98] Turner, *Business in Britain*, 143.

[99] *Imperial Chemical Industries: Compiled from a Survey by The Times* (London, 1962), 83.

company announced plans to invest £100 m. in the EC. The preference for investment over export related to four issues: the common external tariff, a concern that high levels of exports would lead to complaints of dumping from continental competitors, the belief that customers were more likely to accept a product manufactured in the Six compared to one from Britain, and, finally, the possibilities of economies of scale if producing for a large "home" market, instead of "living in a ghetto," as one ICI deputy chairman called Britain.[100] The attempt to takeover Courtaulds fitted into this strategy and when this failed further substantial direct investment in continental Europe was undertaken: By 1971, ICI's sales in Europe were more than five times what they had been in 1960 and over 50 percent of these sales came from the new plants in the Netherlands and Germany in 1970.[101] However, in many respects it was not ICI that was the exception but the chemical industry as a whole. There were clear economies of scale for operating on a pan-European level with plants serving the whole or large parts of continental Europe. The same could not be said of many other industries where the idea of creating a Eurochampion was often inappropriate and did little to improve the competitiveness of European industry, having nothing like the efficiency gains expected from large-scale manufacture.[102] Again, therefore, we should be careful not to be overly critical of European (including British) industry for not following the route advocated by Servan-Schreiber, or that followed by American multinationals operating in Western Europe. As Charles Kindleberger has written, "Many decisions in the field [of foreign direct investment] are so close that two firms in the same industry facing what appear to be similar circumstances will decide to act in different ways."[103]

CONCLUSION

It has been shown that with the growing internationalization of production it is not enough to deal only with trade: It is essential to incorporate foreign direct investment as well into any consideration of the economic realities of European integration in this period. British business adjusted their corporate strategies towards Europe earlier than has been commonly suggested. The

[100] J. Sudworth, "The Chemical Industry: A Case Study," in J. Dunning, *The Multinational Enterprise* (London: Allen & Unwin, 1971), 204–15; Turner, *Business in Britain*, 148–61; and F. V. Meyer, D. C. Corner and J. E. S. Parker, *Problems of a Mature Economy* (London: Macmillan, 1970), 329–30.

[101] Turner, *Business in Britain*, 152.

[102] P. Geroski and A. Jacquemin, "Industrial Change, Barriers to Mobility, and European Industrial Policy," *Economic Policy*, Vol. 1, No. 1 (1985), 169–218; and H. W. de Jong, "Concentration in the Common Market," *Common Market Law Review*, No. 4, (1966), 166–79.

[103] C. Kindleberger, "Summary: Reflections on the Papers and the Debate on Multinational Enterprise: International Finance, Markets and Governments in the Twentieth Century," in Teichova, Lévy-Leboyer and Nussbaum (eds.), *Historical Studies*, 236.

scale of direct investment in Europe may not have been great but a significant number of British firms participated in the process in the late 1950s and early 1960s. These economic developments had a close but complex relationship to political integration. The Foreign and Commonwealth Office took the side of business against the economic departments of government because its goal was political integration in the form of British membership of the EC and believed economic integration was the most promising route to achieving that political goal. This is a prime example of the interaction between political and economic integration. However, this relationship was not straightforward: Others viewed economic integration as reducing the urgency of political integration. ICI, so long an arch advocate of EC entry, was typical in this respect:

In 1962 they had very little base in Europe and were desperately anxious for our entry. . . . They now [1969] had substantial interests in several countries in the Six and were able to take a much more relaxed view than they could have done seven or eight years ago.

Dr Sisson's [of ICI] own view was that it was still right for us to join the EEC if we could do so on reasonable terms. He was emotionally a European, but at the same time he believed that economically, as well as politically, integration in Europe would pay. It was undeniable however that there would be a large adverse balance on agriculture if we went in on the basis of the current common agricultural policy. In these circumstances it would be foolish to be in a hurry to join the Community and certainly from ICI's point of view, there was no reason at all why we should hurry. If it were next year or in five year's time or even longer, it would not worry them provided that ultimately we joined.[104]

This and the previous chapter have drawn out some of the economic trends that were moving British business towards becoming European, the next section develops the political side by examining British business attitudes to political integration and the voice that it had in the long story of Britain joining the EC.

[104] TNA BT241/2156, Hughes to Preston, 4 August 1969.

PART II

THE DEVELOPMENT OF PERCEPTIONS OF EUROPEAN INTEGRATION

4

From 1945 to June 1955: The Marshall Plan and the European Coal and Steel Community

In 1995, Clemens Wurm noted that the role of industrial and economic interest groups in the early years of European integration had been little researched. Further, he believed, "The predominant academic view is that the attitude of European industry was in general one of scepticism or outright rejection."[1] Since then a number of studies have qualified this picture.[2] The conventional image of British industry at this time has been one of disinterest in European integration until at least the mid-1950s. Robert Lieber's key study of the role of the FBI, the Trade Unions Congress (TUC) and the National Farmers' Union (NFU) in the development of British policy on European integration starts in 1956.[3] Most other works take their lead from this. Indeed, prominent representatives of British industry themselves confirmed this position when looking back at the subject.[4] Sir Norman Kipping's memoirs only add further confirmation:

We thought of Europe as thickly populated with do-gooders putting forward idealistic plans for this, that and the other that had very little to do with us . . . . So with our continuing preoccupation with Commonwealth trade and the GATT [General Agreement on Trade and Tariffs] we light-heartedly christened this new European manifestation as "Schumania."[5]

Nevertheless, the period from the end of the war in 1945 to the opening of the talks in June 1955 at Messina in Sicily, which were to presage the next

---

[1] Clemens Wurm, "Introduction," in Clemens Wurm (ed.), *Western Europe and Germany: The Beginnings of European Integration 1945–1960* (Oxford: Berg, 1995), 5.

[2] Werner Bührer, "German Industry and European Integration in the 1950s," in Wurm (ed.), *Western Europe*, 87–114; Marine Moguen-Toursel, *L'Ouverture des Frontières Européennes dans les Années 50: Fruit d'une Concertation avec les Industriels?* (Brussels: P. I. E. Peter Lang, 2002); and Matthias Kipping, *La France et les Origines de l'Union Européenne: Integration Économique et Compétitivité Internationale* (Paris: Comité pour l'Histoire Économique et Financière de la France, 2002).

[3] Robert Lieber, *British Politics and European Unity: Parties, Elites and Pressure Groups* (Berkeley: University of California Press, 1970).

[4] Stephen Blank, *Industry and Government in Britain: The Federation of British Industries in Politics, 1945–65* (Farnborough: Saxon House, 1973), 143.

[5] Norman Kipping, *Summing Up* (London: Hutchinson, 1972).

stage of European integration, has been seen as a coherent and crucial stage in the development of Britain's attitude to European integration, first in relation to the Marshall Plan and then with regard to the European Coal and Steel Community (ECSC).[6] One of the main stipulations of American provision of Marshall Aid was for Western Europe to integrate economically.[7] To this end the Organization for Economic Co-operation and Coordination was created in 1947 by European national governments to divide the aid and to provide a framework for taking forward the economic integration of the sixteen recipients of Marshall Aid, initially in the form of a customs union whereby tariff duties between member states would be removed. In May 1950, Robert Schuman, the French Foreign Minister, announced the plan, drafted by Jean Monnet, for countries to pool their coal and steel industries under supranational control. From this the Treaty of Paris was signed in April 1951 and the six signatories (France, West Germany, Italy, the Netherlands, Belgium and Luxemburg) created the ECSC which was to prove to be the precursor to the European Community.

While discussion of the ECSC by business in Britain was dominated by the two sectors directly concerned, the wider business community did show interest in European integration as part of the Marshall Aid package and also came to recognize the wider implications of the ECSC toward the end of the period. More than this, it is a key period in the related debate on Britain's relative economic decline and the role of manufacturing in that process.[8] British business has generally not received a favorable press in this literature, and "the missed opportunity" to be at the forefront of the process of European integration has been seen as symptomatic of Britain's postwar defensiveness and lack of competitiveness.[9] This chapter begins by considering the proposals for European integration on a bilateral basis between Britain and France. It then turns to the multilateral efforts of the OEEC, finally turning to the Schuman Plan and the ECSC.

[6] John W. Young, "British Officials and European Integration, 1944–60," in Anne Deighton (ed.), *Building Postwar Europe: National Decision-Makers and European Institutions, 1948–63* (Basingstoke: Macmillan, 1995), 92.

[7] Alan Milward, *The Reconstruction of Western Europe, 1945–1951* (London: Methuen, 1984); and Michael Hogan, *The Marshall Plan: America, Britain, and the Reconstruction of Western Europe, 1947–1952* (Cambridge: Cambridge University Press, 1987).

[8] Alan Booth, "The Manufacturing Failure Hypothesis and the Performance of British Industry during the Long Boom," *Economic History Review* 56, No. 1 (2003), 1–33; and Stephen Broadberry and N. F. R. Crafts, "UK Productivity Performance from 1950 to 1979: A Restatement of the Broadberry–Crafts View" *Economic History Review* Vol. 56, No. 4 (2003), 718–35.

[9] Christopher Lord, *Absent at the Creation: Britain and the Formation of the European Community, 1950–2* (Aldershot: Dartmouth, 1996), 158–9; Stephen Broadberry, *The Productivity Race: British Manufacturing in International Perspective, 1850–1990* (Cambridge: Cambridge University Press, 1997), 153; and Alan S. Milward, *The European Rescue of the Nation-State* (London: Routledge, 2000), 366.

THE EARLY POSTWAR YEARS

As noted above, Norman Kipping, the director-general of the FBI, whimsically dismissed European integration as idealistic and little more than a joke. It is certainly hard to find any British industrialist who was an enthusiastic supporter of European integration in the early postwar years. None of the leaders of the FBI or the ABCC seem to have been active in the British Section of the European Movement, the main pressure group in favor of European integration at that time. Also, while there were efforts to recruit trade unionists to the European Movement there seems to have been little equivalent effort to enlist businessmen.[10] In April 1949, a related group of activists, the European League for Economic Cooperation (ELEC), organized a conference in London devoted to the consideration of European economic unification. This included an examination of basic industries, the possibilities for the coordination of production of different industries, and of the creation ultimately of a single currency.[11] Many continental industrialists attended the conference, and were active in ELEC, and the importance of the conference for French industry has recently been stressed.[12] Yet, despite a ministerial welcome and the participation of many British individuals, few British businessmen were interested and the FBI did not think that active participation in the European Movement was part of its remit.[13] This was an issue on which the FBI preferred to let individual members take their own positions.[14]

An apparent lack of enthusiasm for active involvement in European integration should not be interpreted as a complete lack of interest in the subject on the part of British business. Most significant in this respect was the FBI's involvement in the Council of Directors of European Industrial Federations (CDEIF), originally formed in the 1920s, and the Council of European Industrial Federations (CEIF, or CIFE as it was known on the continent), a new body.[15] In October 1946, the director-general of the Federation of British Industries (FBI) met with his French, Belgium and Dutch counterparts to revive the interwar meetings, and a year later, a meeting in The Hague formally marked the restart of the CDEIF annual meetings, although it took a

---

[10] Harvester microfiche series, "Britain and Europe since 1945," records of the British Section of the European Movement, fiche 161.

[11] "Economic Unity for Europe," *The Economist*, 30 April 1949, 796; and *The Times*, 21 April 1949, 4 and 22 April 1949, 2 and 26 April 1949, 2.

[12] Moguen-Toursel, *L'Ouverture*, 56–8. See also Bührer, "German Industry," 98.

[13] MRC MSS200/F/1/1/192, Kipping, Grand Council meeting, 14 October 1953.

[14] MRC MSS200/F/3/D3/3/15, notes of 7 April 1948 and 14 April 1948.

[15] Neil Rollings and Matthias Kipping, "Private Transnational Governance in the Heyday of the Nation-State: The Council of European Industrial Federations (CEIF)," *Economic History Review* Vol. 61 (2008), forthcoming.

number of years for its membership to widen.[16] Initially, discussions were limited to written reports and oral accounts of the economic conditions in each country; however, in 1949 at the Rome meeting the agenda was much wider including discussion of European integration.[17] This became the format of later meetings.

It would be easy to dismiss the CDEIF as little more than a social occasion given that there was always a full social program of cocktail parties and dinners, and from 1949, wives were invited too.[18] The Rome meeting even included an audience with the Pope. However, this would be to underestimate the importance of such informal networks, particularly given the uncertainty surrounding postwar Europe. Looking back, Kipping believed the meetings helped "in familiarising ourselves with this new world of international consultation and confrontation, to be able to discuss the problems informally among men of similar responsibilities. It helped even more to have made friends one could ring up or go and see in all these countries, both for 'grapevine' purposes, or as fellow members of sometimes invaluable 'old-boy networks'."[19] It was unclear how the postwar world would develop but there was also a need to know how business in other countries would react in the new postwar circumstances. With the world moving toward a multilateral framework, the CDEIF was one of the few multilateral forums available from which to learn about such issues and understand the range of opinions that existed. Moreover, given the hectic and reactive nature of much of the work of these directors, the meetings offered a rare opportunity to consider some of the long-range general issues of the time.[20] The CDEIF was, therefore, a key mechanism for building knowledge, understanding, and trust between the various directors of national industrial federations in Europe. Many of these individuals remained in post into the 1960s adding to the body's long-term significance.

Nevertheless, whatever their perceived value – and Kipping's Luxemburg counterpart felt that the meetings had a particular character "in which hearts and minds bloom" – single annual meetings could only achieve so much by themselves.[21] It was the combination of the informal CDEIF with the more formal, organized and regular CEIF that mattered. Indeed, for all Kipping's enjoyment and praise of the CDEIF, he was quite clear that it was the CEIF which he believed was the most useful of all the transnational organized business interests in which he was involved.[22] The CEIF was established in

---

[16] FBI, *Annual Report for 1946*, 15; and FBI, *Annual Report for 1947*, 19; MRC MSS200/F/3/E1/16/25 onwards cover each annual meeting.

[17] MRC MSS200/F/3/E1/16/27.   [18] Kipping, *Summing Up*, 72–5.   [19] Ibid., 72.

[20] MRC MSS200/C/3/S1/12/2, Kipping to Hayot, director-general of the Federation des Industriels Luxembourgois, 19 March 1954. This section is drawn from Rollings and Kipping, "Private Transnational Governance."

[21] MRC MSS200/C/3/S1/12/2, Hayot to Kipping, 27 July 1954.

[22] Kipping, *Summing Up*, 55–6.

1949 under French leadership following a request from the OEEC for the formation of a consultative industrial body.[23] The following February the OEEC formally ratified the CEIF as that body.[24] The CEIF's General Council of Federations consisted of representatives from the national industrial federations of OEEC member states plus representatives of the International Chamber of Commerce (ICC) and the International Employers Organization and met at least once a year. In addition, there was a Steering Committee, the first chair of which was Georges Villiers, President of the Conseil National du Patronat Français (CNPF), and a small secretariat, based in Paris and largely staffed by the CNPF, but which later included permanent representatives from the British, German, and Italian federations. Provision was also made for the establishment of Round Tables, which were to enable federations to cooperate in studying any subject that interested them.

The CEIF was represented on various OEEC consultative groups and tried to influence OEEC policy with varying degrees of success.[25] It also offered the opportunity for national federations to make their views known to US officials and industrialists.[26] This opportunity was at its greatest during a series of International Conferences of Manufacturers initiated as part of the productivity drive to inculcate European business leaders with American management methods.[27] The CEIF was also seen as a suitable forum for industrialists to discuss, among other topics, European integration.[28] Its meeting in July 1950 was followed by a meeting of the French, Italian, German, Dutch, and Belgium representatives to discuss the Schuman Plan, with the British there as observers.[29] Two years later the members of the CEIF agreed to the formation of the Union des Industries des Pays de la Communauté Europénne by the national industrial federations of the six member ECSC states and, later, it was to be a key forum for national industrial

[23] FBI, *Annual Report for 1949*, 7–8; MRC MSS200/F/3/E1/16/28, René Arnaud, secretary of the CNPF and of the CEIF, paper to the CDEIF, London, May 1950.

[24] OEEC, *The Organisation for European Economic Co-operation: History and Structure* (Paris: OEEC, 1953), 39.

[25] TNA LAB13/1231, unsigned to Slater, 31 October 1956; B. Boel, "The European Productivity Agency: A Faithful Prophet of the American Model?" in Matthias Kipping and Ove Bjarnar (eds.), *The Americanisation of European Business: the Marshall Plan and the Transfer of US Management Models*, (London: Routledge, 1998), 41–4.

[26] N. Tiratsoo, "What you need is a Harvard." The American Influence on British Management Education c. 1945–65," in T. R. Gourvish and N. Tiratsoo (eds.) *Missionaries and Managers: American Influences on European Management Education, 1945–60* (Manchester: Manchester University Press, 1998), 152.

[27] Kipping, *Summing Up*, 114–6; and Matthias Kipping, "Operation Impact: Converting European Employers to the American Creed," in Kipping and Bjarnar (eds.), *The Americanisation of European Business*, 55–73.

[28] Henry Ehrmann, *Organized Business in France* (Princeton: Princeton University Press, 1957), 401–2; FBI, *Annual Report for 1950*, 7–8.

[29] MRC MSS200/F/1/1/190, Grand Council meeting, 12 July 1950.

federations to discuss the establishment of the EC and the European Free Trade Association (EFTA).

After 1945 the leadership of the FBI, which quickly established a network of contacts across Western Europe, was more than aware of the proposals for European integration via this network, and was able to build up an understanding of the respective positions of its counterparts across Western Europe. The CEIF, and to a lesser extent the CDEIF, were to play key roles in the development of the FBI's policy on European integration until the 1970s. It was through these meetings in the early 1950s that the FBI's leadership came to appreciate the drive and determination to make the Schuman Plan a reality and that led to the appointment of Peter Tennant as the FBI's Overseas Director in 1952 "specifically to bring us [the FBI] knowledge of Europe and Europeans."[30] Tennant had no business experience, having been a linguist and in the Foreign Office from 1939 with postings in Stockholm and Paris; but he had a keen interest in European affairs and went on to play a central role in the development of the FBI's policy on European integration in the second half of the 1950s.[31]

The majority of British industry may have been disinterested in the subject of European integration but this cannot be said of the leadership of the FBI. The FBI's response to the measures introduced by the Labour government to deal with the 1947 economic crisis twice referred to the countries of Western Europe as a large part of Britain's traditional export markets and set out clearly how the FBI viewed the relationship between Britain, the Commonwealth, and Western Europe in the aftermath of the Second World War:

The economy of Britain, taken alone, is that of a small, highly industrialised country that has lost many of the advantages on which its industry was founded, and that cannot feed or support her population from her own resources.

If it were not for the closeness of our ties with the British Commonwealth, and for the great sacrifices that the Dominions have always made to help us, our position now would seem hopeless. We think of the Commonwealth first as our partners in present difficulties, but it is no detraction to believe also that we should recognise the inevitable closeness of our economic ties with Western Europe. A larger economic grouping of this kind represents, we believe, the essential foundation for the building of a system of expanding trade both in primary and manufactured goods. We urge the most strenuous efforts in response to the first moves made by Mr. Marshall, and the most earnest study of ways and means by which economic collaboration of this kind may be progressively developed . . . .

We, therefore, urge that all possible steps should be taken to indicate the desire of the United Kingdom to arrive at a basis of collaboration with the nations of Europe. Serious consideration should be given, even at the risk of some under-employment

---

[30] Kipping, *Summing Up*, 153–4; and MRC MSS200/F/1/1/192, Grand Council meeting, 22 July 1953.

[31] MRC MSS200/F/3/O2/2/8, Tennant to Macadam, 3 January 1955.

this winter, to making a good start with the export of coal to Europe, as an indication
of the genuineness of our wish to collaborate, and as a tangible means of assisting
the economic recovery of those countries that form a large part of our traditional
markets [emphasis in original].[32]

It would be hard to construe this statement as representing a lack of interest
in European integration even if the prospect of receiving Marshall Aid lay
behind it.[33]

A CUSTOMS UNION

This was the context in which the specific proposals for integration developed, and it is to these proposals that we now turn. Although discussions
on economic collaboration were soon to take a multilateral shape, initial
discussions were bilateral. Anglo-French discussions were the most prominent in this respect immediately after the war. In March 1947 the Anglo-
French Treaty of Dunkirk was signed. Mainly concerned with mutual security there was an economic element referring to "constant consultation" and
the promotion of prosperity.[34] Among the French proposals were discussions
between French and British industries to avoid clashes of policy, especially in
their investment programs. The French suggested that, "There was no reason
why the two countries should not exchange information as to their respective intentions and ultimately modify their own policy in whatever way was
desirable."[35] However, the relevant British government departments ensured
that in practice such economic links were minimal.[36] Taking their lead from
the government, the FBI responded to these advances in a similar fashion:
"their inevitable cartel flavour coupled with the timing vis-à-vis Marshall Aid
has made it seem undesirable to offer them any encouragement."[37] However, in April 1948, with the Foreign Office now encouraging such talks,
the FBI met the French representatives of the newly created Association
for Franco-British Economic Expansion (AFBEE). With close links to the
CNPF, including the same President, the AFBEE's object was "to develop
production and collaboration between French and British industrialists so

---

[32] TNA CAB124/1047, GEN179/28, Annex, 5 September 1947.

[33] Jeremy Moon, *European Integration in British Politics 1950–1963: A Study of Issue Change* (Aldershot: Gower, 1985), 98–9.

[34] Quoted in Roger Woodhouse, *British Policy Towards France, 1945–51* (Basingstoke: Macmillan, 1995), 19.

[35] TNA BT11/3327, 3rd meeting in the third series of the Anglo-French economic official committee, 20 January 1947.

[36] Alan S. Milward, *The United Kingdom and the European Community Vol. 1: The Rise and Fall of a National Strategy 1945–1963* (London: Frank Cass, 2002), 21–2.

[37] MRC MSS200/F/3/S1/21/47, D/6234, "Visit M. Gilbert, President of the Association for Franco-British Economic Expansion, 7 April 1948."

that they could work as a pivot round which the rest of European producers might be grouped."[38] Paul Gilbert, the head of the French delegation and the President of the National Association for Economic Expansion, suggested that there was also scope for organizing a degree of rationalization and mutual assistance, and for collaboration on the development of colonies. He also believed that the idea of a customs union would be impossible without a degree of integration or understanding among industries in the countries concerned, and that this seemed better done through consultation between industries than solely between governments. To this end, the FBI agreed to act as a conduit between French and British trade associations and the issue was given further consideration by an FBI committee, but little more followed. Generally, the FBI remained hesitant and cautious about such collaborations. A few years later when French industrialists made similar bilateral proposals to German industrialists, reaction in the FBI remained skeptical as there was "a significant undercurrent of talk about cartels."[39]

A major factor in the FBI's hesitancy toward such approaches was that they were overshadowed by Marshall Aid. The Americans were keen for European integration to take the form of a customs union. In Whitehall, the two main economic ministries, the Board of Trade and the Treasury, were implacably opposed to British involvement in such a venture because it would herald the end of Imperial Preference and weaken the British economy. In the opinion of the Board of Trade, "It would mean (as would *ex hypothesi* be its intention) the decline of industry here in favour of its competitors elsewhere, with all the discordant dislocation."[40] To what extent did business concur?

By February 1948 the FBI were pressing for a meeting between its Overseas Policy Committee and the Board of Trade at which it was intended to raise a number of issues worrying the FBI. These included progress on the European customs union and whether British industry should give it any detailed consideration.[41] It was considered at the Consultative Committee for Industry (CCI), a body comprising of representatives of peak-level business organizations and Board of Trade officials, but without the involvement of individual industries.[42] Following this meeting, the FBI's President, Sir Frederick Bain, told the FBI's Grand Council that since the war the FBI had concentrated on domestic issues but now was the time to give full cognizance

---

[38] Ibid.

[39] MRC MSS200/F/3/D3/6/50, "Short Report on Franco-German Industrial Talks in Dusseldorf on November 8 and 9, 1951," and Tennant to Kipping, 24 April 1952.

[40] TNA FO371/62552, "Customs Union for Western Europe," by the Board of Trade, 30 June 1947, quoted in Milward, *Rise and Fall*, 21.

[41] TNA BT11/3832, unknown to various, 12 February 1948.

[42] Ibid., Ramsden to Burns, 19 February 1948.

to international subjects.[43] Included among those topics mentioned by Bain were the custom union studies, the European Movement, and Franco-British interindustry collaboration, as well as Commonwealth issues, but the most important of all was Marshall Aid. To deal with these developments it was agreed that an ERP [European Recovery Program] Committee should be established. At its first meeting the key issue for Norman Kipping was "the question of consultation" as "it was imperative for British industry to secure a voice in matters connected with ERP and its operation."[44] He contrasted business–government relations in Britain with those he had experienced in France where "industry had secured an intimate form of consultation with its government," including the right to nominate members to OEEC technical committees. In addition, after "sustained representations" from the FBI, a subcommittee of the CCI was established to deal with ERP questions but discussion of the customs union issue remained limited.[45]

Moreover, when the FBI did express any opinion on the customs union it was cautious about the whole topic, concerned about the detrimental impact on Imperial Preference and the implications for UK trade.[46] The FBI's *Annual Report for 1949* reassured its membership that, "The government is in no way committed to participation in any form of customs union."[47] As the FBI became acquainted with the idea of a Western European customs union, it became increasingly concerned about the potential implications for Commonwealth trade. The ABCC was equally, if not more cautious, referring to the complexity of the subject and believing that expressing any hurried opinion would be unwise.[48] Nevertheless, the episode highlighted the FBI's dissatisfaction with the lack of consultation by the government in the development of its commercial policy and the need for new or revitalized mechanisms of consultation.

What is even more significant is that even in these early postwar years the CDEIF was already a valuable forum for learning about the views of other European national industrial federations and that the FBI was comparing how its counterparts were treated by their respective national governments. The FBI had a clear information network in Europe and was willing to envisage some degree of British involvement in European integration, as shown in its 1947 memorandum, but as soon as it became clear that such engagement would be at the expense of trading relations with the Commonwealth,

[43] Ibid., CCI 6th, 16 March 1948; and MRC MSS200/F/1/1/189, Grand Council meeting, 12 May 1948.

[44] MRC MSS200/F/1/1/146, ERP Committee 1st meeting, 23 June 1948.

[45] FBI, *Annual Report for 1948*, 5 and 9; and MRC MSS200/F/1/1/189, Grand Council meeting, 8 September 1948.

[46] TNA BT11/3832, CCI 7th meeting, 25 June 1948.

[47] FBI, *Annual Report for 1949*, 10.

[48] ABCC Overseas Committee, 7 April 1948, quoted in Moon, *European Integration*, 99.

support for the idea vanished. The Commonwealth relationship remained at the heart of British business' view of the world.

SECTORAL INTEGRATION

OEEC

For the rest of the period prior to the Messina talks, consideration of European integration focused on a sectoral approach, most famously the announcement of the Schuman Plan in May 1950 and the resulting creation of the European Coal and Steel Community. However, a sectoral approach to European economic integration also came to the fore within the OEEC. Only days after the Schuman Plan was announced, Dirk Stikker, the Dutch Foreign Minister, presented his "Plan of Action" to the OEEC, setting out an industry-by-industry approach to Western European integration.[49] The OEEC did embark on pilot studies but to little effect, with the British government in particular dismissive.[50] The pilot studies included paper and pulp, textiles, cement, nitrogenous fertilizers, plate glass, textile machinery, and motor cars.[51] Questionnaires were sent to each national government, which were then required to gather statistical information on the competitiveness of each of these industries and to consult with the industries themselves. Little more ensued within the OEEC, but in early 1953, the President of the Board of Trade recommended to his fellow government ministers that Britain should take the initiative in Europe by trying to secure a common market for a range of goods in order to avoid the Six going ahead further by themselves to Britain's detriment.[52] It was to the existing OEEC sectoral studies to which the Ministry of Supply turned in trying to build up a list of possible industries.[53] Although nothing further resulted in policy terms, these studies did represent a starting point for the British government's consideration of the implications of European economic integration for a range of sectors of the economy and included engagement with the respective sectors in that process.

The Schuman Plan and the European Coal and Steel Community

Far more significant, in both the short and long term, than the OEEC sectoral studies, was the Schuman Plan and the resulting European Coal and Steel

---

[49] See Milward, *Reconstruction of Western Europe*, 446–51; and Wendy A. Brusse, *Tariffs, Trade and European Integration, 1947–1957: From Study Group to Common Market* (Basingstoke: Macmillan, 1997), 100–4.

[50] Milward, *European Rescue*, 181.

[51] TNA SUPP14/340, "Integration Studies," by McLeod, 29 November 1950.

[52] TNA CAB129/59, "Commercial Policy in Europe," 19 February 1953.

[53] TNA SUPP14/391, Whitehouse to Ministry of Supply "E" divisions, 8 April 1953 and following correspondence.

Community. The story of Britain's decision not to enter the negotiations over the Schuman Plan and the later negotiations which led to association with the ECSC has been well documented from a variety of angles.[54] With Jean Monnet, the architect of the plan, Robert Schuman, the French Foreign Minister, announced the proposals on May 9, 1950 to establish a common market for the coal and iron and steel industries of all interested nations. The British government quickly responded that it could not participate, and following longer than expected negotiations the Treaty of Paris was signed in April 1951, and in July 1952 the European Coal and Steel Community came into existence. The six member states (France, West Germany, Italy, the Netherlands, Belgium, and Luxemburg) agreed to the creation of a range of institutions, of which the most significant was the supranational regulatory body, the High Authority.

For Britain, Ranieri has provided a detailed account of the iron and steel industry.[55] The wider business community was not particularly interested in either the Schuman Plan or the ECSC. Both the FBI and ABCC had limited roles in the development of policy. The ABCC remained cautious and noncommittal on the few occasions the subject arose and there was little consideration of the Schuman Plan in the FBI's various committees.[56] By way of explanation, Kipping later commented, "With some comfort, we could leave the study of it to the Iron and Steel Board, for we would have had little competence to offer comment ourselves."[57] While this modesty was somewhat disingenuous it did reflect the back-stage position of the FBI. Its officials ensured that they were well-informed observers but were not active beyond that. Thus the President of the Federation dined with Jean Monnet when the latter visited London to explain the Schuman proposals in May 1950.[58] In addition, the FBI remained informed of developments on the continent through the CDEIF and the CEIF.[59] When there was a private meeting on the Schuman Plan between the representatives from France, Italy,

---

[54] Milward, *Rise and Fall*; Lord, *Absent*; Edmund Dell, *The Schuman Plan and the British Abdication of Leadership in Europe* (Oxford: Oxford University Press, 1995); and John W. Young, "The Schuman Plan and British Association," in John W. Young (ed.), *The Foreign Policy of Churchill's Peacetime Administration 1951–1955* (Leicester: Leicester University Press, 1988), 109–34.

[55] Ruggero Ranieri, "Inside or Outside the Magic Circle? Italian and British Steel Industries Face to Face with the Schuman Plan and the European Coal Iron and Steel Community," in Alan S. Milward, Ruggero Ranieri, Frances M. B. Lynch and F. Romero, *The Frontier of National Sovereignty: History and Theory 1945–1992* (London: Routledge, 1993), 117–54; and Ruggero Ranieri, "Attempting an Unlikely Union: the British Steel Industry and the ECSC 1950–54," in Peter M. R. Stirk and David Willis (eds.), *Shaping Postwar Europe: European Unity and Disunity 1945–1957* (London: Pinter, 1991), 112–3.

[56] Moon, *European Integration*, 99–100; and GLA MS14487/6, Overseas Trade Committee meeting, 4 February 1953.

[57] Kipping, *Summing Up*, 152.   [58] Milward, *Rise and Fall*, 60.

[59] FBI, *Annual Report for 1951*, 28.

Germany, Belgium, and the Netherlands after a CEIF meeting, the FBI sat in as observers.[60] Beyond this, however, the FBI's direct policy role seems to have been non-existent. This contrasted markedly with the situation in France and Germany where the CNPF, the FBI's French counterpart, and, to a lesser extent, the BDI, its German counterpart, vociferously criticized the Schuman proposals.[61]

Government consultation with industry was, therefore, focused on the sectors affected directly by the Schuman Plan proposals. Even the steel-consuming industries, crucial in winning industrial support for the proposals in France, seem to have been hardly involved. Of the two industries consulted, the coal industry's position was straightforward. The industry was used to facing no competition in the home market and government support to keep domestic prices below export prices. In addition, it had recently been nationalized. The last things the newly created National Coal Board wanted was an opening up of the domestic market and having to hand over some control of the industry to the proposed supranational High Authority.[62] Its position was an unequivocal rejection of membership.[63]

The position of the iron and steel industry was more complex. The initial reaction was one of caution and uncertainty. There had already been efforts in 1949 to reestablish cartel agreements and the key issue was, therefore, whether the Schuman Plan represented an attempt to restore something like the interwar cartel or something else. Central here was the potential powers and purpose of the High Authority.[64] Most of the steel industry had not been party to the interwar cartel arrangements but had reached agreements with them.[65] Ideally, this was what the British steel industry wanted to see emerge once more, protecting its overseas markets in the Commonwealth and maintaining the heavily protected domestic market. The British Iron and Steel Federation, the industry's overarching trade association, was not, therefore, in favor of British membership on the basis of the Schuman Plan, as its members would lose their influence on price-setting and open up the domestic market. Equally, any continental agreement without the British steel industry could threaten its export position. However, to voice such negative views in public ran the risk of strengthening the argument of those

---

[60] MRC MSS200/F/1/1/190, Grand Council meeting, 12 July 1950.

[61] Matthias Kipping, "Inter-firm Relations and Industrial Policy: The French and German Steel Producers and Users in the Twentieth Century," *Business History* Vol. 38, No.1 (1996), 1–25; and Matthias Kipping, "Concurrence et Compétitivité, les Origines de la Législation Anti-trust Française après 1945," *Études et Documents* 6, (1994), 429–55.

[62] Milward, *Rise and Fall*, 56.

[63] TNA CAB134/294, FG (WP)(50)4th, 2 June 1950.

[64] Milward, *Rise and Fall*, 57–8; Ranieri, "Inside or Outside," 119–20.

[65] Clemens Wurm, *Business, Politics, and International Relations: Steel, Cotton, and International Cartels in British Politics, 1924–1939* (Cambridge: Cambridge University Press, 1993).

in favor of nationalization of the steel industry. Accordingly, a mildly positive and largely noncommittal position was adopted.

Two points emerge from the episode. First, the BISF, the industry's main trade association, and the Iron and Steel Board, the body that existed prior to nationalization of the industry and was reestablished from 1953 with the industry's privatization and which oversaw the development of the industry, were used to being involved in the formulation of policy. In 1947 the industry had representation (Sir John Duncanson) on the working party of government officials which had proposed what was considered the desirable level of German steel output.[66] Similarly, prior to the Schuman Plan, a Conservative Research Department paper on the Ruhr was sent to Sir Andrew Duncan, chairman of the BISF, for comment.[67] More generally, the ministry responsible for the steel industry, the Ministry of Supply, fixed steel prices after close collaboration and advice from both the BISF and the ISB.[68] It is unsurprising, therefore, to find industrial representation on the working party set up to consider alternative proposals once acceptance of the Schuman Plan had been rejected by the government. However, the majority of officials on the working party came to the conclusion that the steel industry was overprotected. The issue of protection was a cause of tension in what was otherwise "a very close entente between the industry's association and government departments."[69] Secondly, the episode illustrates the link between domestic and international policy. The BISF discussion of the Schuman Plan was dominated by the threat of nationalization by the Labour government. Even at this early stage in the history of British industry's attitude to European integration, this connection between domestic and external concerns is apparent and it was to reappear once the Conservative government, elected in 1952, privatized the iron and steel industry.

In the 1950 discussions of Britain's response to the Schuman Plan, the views of industry played a role in the decision to turn down negotiations, but far more important was the government's refusal to countenance a loss of national sovereignty.[70] The impact of industry's views was much more significant in the ensuing discussions about the possibility of British association with the ECSC. These discussions began soon after the Schuman Plan proposals were rejected, but did not make a significant advance until 1953. That July a new government committee of civil servants made the surprising recommendation that the British steel industry should be associated closely with the Six, and when the report was considered by the Economic Steering Committee, the most senior committee of officials dealing with economic

---

[66] Woodhouse, *British Policy*, 23.

[67] Sue Onslow, *Backbench Debate within the Conservative Party and its Influence on British Foreign Policy, 1948–57* (Basingstoke: Macmillan, 1997), 56–7.

[68] Ranieri, "Inside or Outside," 129–30.   [69] Ibid., 133.

[70] Milward, *Rise and Fall*, 74–6.

issues, the recommendations were extended not just to a freer market for steel but also for metal manufactures: The resulting greater competition, it was argued, would improve productivity, restrain restrictive practices, and would be for the long-term benefit of steel users.[71] Yet, the agreement on association between Britain and the Six was not reached until December 1954 and not ratified until the summer of 1955. The main provision of the Treaty of Association was a Council of Association. This "anodyne" agreement incorporated no interference in either the British coal or steel industries.[72]

The major historical studies of this topic agree that it was the reluctance of the government to override the objections of industry that explains the weakness of the final treaty compared to the 1953 recommendations. Indeed, Ranieri sees the government as "a hostage to the BISF's views" at this time.[73] How had the views of the steel industry become so influential? First, the NCB continued to see little benefit from association, wanting at most a short-term commercial contractual agreement: Its economic adviser, E. F. Schumacher, was vehemently critical, regarding the ECSC as "a flop."[74] Secondly, the steel industry's views hardened against any form of close link with the Six. In discussions with the UK delegation to the High Authority in February 1953, just prior to the opening of the common market for steel, the BISF representatives made no comment when the issue of UK association arose despite voicing other complaints.[75] However, soon after, the steel industry made its opposition clear, even before it was agreed that the industry should be consulted.[76]

Ranieri has focused on the discussions within the BISF. In its submission to the government the BISF opposed any form of association involving UK entry into a common market for steel but harked back to the interwar arrangements if there was to be some lesser form of association.[77] Ranieri explains its changed position from 1950 in terms of changed market conditions.[78] However, there were other factors involved as well. Most of the meetings with government were carried out by the Iron and Steel Board, which had concerns about its status following privatization. In July, Sir Archibald Forbes, the chairman of the ISB, met Sir Cecil Weir, "anxious to establish the Board with as high a standing as possible" in terms of representation in

---

[71] Ranieri, "Inside or Outside," 143–4.   [72] Milward, *European Rescue*, 346.

[73] Ranieri, "Inside or Outside," 153; and Milward, *Rise and Fall*, 161.

[74] TNA FO371/105954, "Note of a Meeting Held in the Foreign Office on Wednesday 25th February about UK Association with the ECSC on Coal Questions"; TNA FO371/111252, M601/54, "Consultations on the UK Association with the European Coal and Steel Community," by Crawford, 4 March 1954, and M601/73A, note by Christofas, 30 March 1954.

[75] TNA FO371/105954, M604/28, "Notes of a Meeting," 28 February 1953.

[76] TNA FO371/105956, note by Hope-Jones, 29 July 1953.

[77] TNA FO371/111252, M601/73A, Christofas, 30 March 1954.

[78] Ranieri, "Inside or Outside," 144–5.

Luxemburg to cement its position.[79] By October, Forbes and other representatives of the ISB were doing the rounds of Whitehall departments as part of the consultation process. At a meeting with representatives of the UK delegation, the Ministry of Supply and the Foreign Office, Forbes and Robert Shone, a member of the ISB, pointed to a range of perceived difficulties with the proposals for association and argued for a weaker form of association.[80] A few days later, the two had meetings with Foreign Office and Treasury officials. On both occasions, Forbes asked about the responsibilities of the Iron and Steel Board and its relationship with the High Authority in the formulation of policy.[81]

Following the meetings it was noted that Sir Edwin Plowden, chairman of the government working party drawing up the proposals for association, thought that Forbes "intensely dislikes the idea of a common market and will find any excuse for opposing it" and soon after, Sir Pierson Dixon in the Foreign Office observed that, "It was becoming clear that the Steel Board are not going to consider a treaty unless they are told that politically it is desirable."[82] The ISB's views were set out formally in a nine-page response to the Minister of Supply, Duncan Sandys, in February 1954.[83] The whole document was a critique of the suitability of a common market in steel between the Six and the UK. In particular, it focused on the problems of changing market conditions and of dealing with differences between these conditions on the continent and in the UK, as noted by Ranieri. However, the document also set out a raft of perceived practical difficulties and once more emphasized the position of the ISB, going so far as to argue that if association occurred then relations with the High Authority should be exclusively carried out by the ISB, as any involvement by government would compromise the Board. Even the Treaty of Association, so weak in its contents, was criticized by the ISB because of its failure to mention the Board, drawing forth a bitter rant from Forbes:

[The proposed agreement] completely fails to recognise the position of the Iron & Steel Board which is neither a contracting party nor even referred to in the agreement.

The only reason so far advanced for omitting any direct reference to the Board and the integral part which it plays in the supervision of the British steel industry is that M. Monnet does not like it. The ostensible ground of his dislike is that he is fearful that if the Board's position was referred to in the agreement he would be subjected to pressure from the European industry for representation. This may or may not be the real reason for his objection. It is at least open to question whether he

[79] TNA FO371/105961, M608/8, note by Crawford, 29 July 1953.
[80] TNA FO371/105957, "Note of a Meeting," 21 October 1953.
[81] Ibid., "Iron and Steel Board and the European Coal and Steel Community," undated; "Talk with Sir Archibald Forbes and Mr. Shone," 30 October 1953.
[82] TNA FO371/105957, M604/145, handwritten note by Sir Pierson Dixon, 28 October 1953; and TNA FO371/105956, written comment by Dixon, 9 November 1953.
[83] TNA FO371/111252, M601/51, Forbes to Sandys, 23 February 1954.

is not more concerned with establishing direct contact at all points with the British government. But even if his reason is as alleged it has no real merit because neither the European industry nor the Consultative Council to the High Authority have the statutory responsibilities of the Iron & Steel Board. There would seem to be an urgent need to explain the true position of the Board to European minds. The Board is just as concerned with its own position and its ability to perform its statutory functions in Great Britain as M. Monnet is with the position of the High Authority.[84]

Throughout this episode, the ISB, newly created after privatization of the steel industry, was extremely sensitive about its position, and vigorously opposed any action which might compromise or weaken its powers. In this light, any association with the High Authority was likely to be regarded with distaste, in addition to the perceived differences in market conditions between Europe and Britain. Just as nationalization impinged on the steel industry's consideration of the Schuman Plan, so the results of privatization impacted upon its response to the possibility of association.

Significantly, neither the BISF submission, nor that from the ISB to the Minister of Supply in the early months of 1954 hinted at anything other than a united position within the steel industry. However, Ranieri has shown that "the most powerful group within the industry was in favour of a more positive approach towards Europe."[85] Sir Ernest Lever, chairman of Richard Thomas & Baldwin, who was also on the board of the Steel Company of Wales, did not agree with the rigid negotiating position adopted by the majority of the BISF in March 1954. Nor was this a recent split. The previous October, as the consultation process began, Sir Cecil Weir had been invited to lunch with Lever and about fifty other directors and senior executives of the two companies at the Dorchester Hotel.[86] Weir was pleasantly encouraged by their interest in the issue of UK entry into a common market for steel. Harry Spencer, the managing director of Richard Thomas & Baldwin, informed Weir that personally he was in favor of joining the common market. The reason for these two companies support for UK entry was that, as tinplate producers and special steel producers, they had markets in Europe, unlike producers of other forms of steel.[87] Hidden by the apparent unanimity of the BISF and the ISB, there were major firms who took a contrary view. This well illustrates the wider lesson of overgeneralizing about attitudes to European integration in a sector from the pronouncements of the industry's representatives, and the need to understand the motives that fed into stated positions on European integration.

---

[84] TNA FO371/111254, M601/186, "Proposed Agreement with the European Coal and Steel Community: Effect on the Iron and Steel Board," by Forbes, October 1954.

[85] Ranieri, "Inside or Outside," 148.

[86] TNA FO371/105957, M604/140, Weir to Crawford, 16 October 1953.

[87] Milward, *Rise and Fall*, 159.

As the government was aware of the views of these two companies, why was the government so reluctant to override the opposition to British entry into a common market presented by the BISF and ISB? Two other factors help to explain this situation. For the first time steel consumers, in the form of the engineering industry, were consulted. As already mentioned, in France this group played a key role in supporting the Schuman Plan as a way of obtaining cheaper steel against the opposition of steel producers and showing that parts of industry were in favor of the proposals. The Foreign Office hoped that, similar to that in France, the engineering industry's interests might diverge from those of UK steel producers.[88] These hopes were pretty forlorn: Steel prices were artificially low in Britain, and while in the long term consumers would probably benefit, in the short term prices were likely to rise. As far as the Ministry of Supply was aware, although the implications were:

no less vital for our iron and steel consuming industries and notably the engineering industries . . . .

At present the engineering industries have taken very little interest in the Schuman Plan and have given little consideration to the possible impact of the Community on the UK; and so far as is known it has done no thinking at all about an association between the UK and the High Authority.[89]

Nevertheless, the ministry did not think it was difficult to guess what the reactions of the engineering industry were likely to be to the proposals. "The SMMT [Society of Motor Manufacturers and Traders] for one would go up in smoke if we were deliberately to increase the cost of their steel," was how a Board of Trade official saw the situation.[90] Unsurprisingly, therefore, the Foreign Office's hopes were dashed when the Engineering Advisory Council endorsed the views of the BISF.[91] In Britain there was no voice from industry to counter the steel producers' opposition, as there was in France.

In addition, there was no consensus of opinion within Whitehall in support of the idea of British entry into a common market for steel. In particular, the Ministry of Supply seems to have been happy for the consultation process to be dragged out and watered down. While the Foreign Office had no objection to the consultation process, it envisaged this as of a limited nature, whereas the Ministry of Supply wanted to make these consultations far broader even if this risked information being leaked about what was being proposed.[92] It had been hoped that the consultation process would be completed before Jean Monnet submitted his proposals on association to the British government but

[88] TNA FO371/111252, M601/54, "Consultations on the UK Association with the European Coal and Steel Community," by Crawford, 4 March 1954.
[89] TNA FO371/105956, note attached to Robinson to Dixon, 27 August 1953.
[90] TNA FO371/105957, Burns to Forward, 19 November 1953.
[91] TNA FO371/111252, M601/73A, note by Christofas, 30 March 1954.
[92] TNA FO371/105956, note by Christofas, 29 August 1953.

Sandys, the Minister of Supply, refused to press the ISB for a reply until after Monnet's proposals had been seen.[93] At the end of October, the Ministry of Supply hoped that a reply would be received during November.[94] In the end, the Cabinet agreed to further consultations with industry toward the end of January. In any case, the ISB's reply did not arrive until the end of February and the BISF submission came even later.

The Cabinet finally considered the issue in April, deciding to appoint a new ministerial committee to consider the issue.[95] Encouraged by the chairman's personal sympathy for a common market for steel, the Foreign Office hoped that "if the ministerial committee is in general agreement with this objective, they could try to overcome the objections of the Iron and Steel Board."[96] Again, this proved overly optimistic. From the outset this position was rejected given the steel industry's views.[97] Instead, a halfway house was proposed involving a reduction of the UK tariff on steel in return for a commitment from the ECSC not to dump steel on the British market in times of surplus. Sandys opposed even this, instead proposing that discussion of tariffs and a common market should be postponed, concentrating instead on setting up a Council of Association. His hope was that by this means the steel industry would be slowly persuaded of the merits of closer association, and it was this route that ministers endorsed. While, therefore, the views of the industry were a crucial obstacle to British entry into a common market for steel, they would not have had the same impact had the Minister of Supply and his officials not been so sympathetic. In this respect, association with the ECSC was not as vital to Britain as membership of the ECSC was to the Six, and public support for British association was also lacking.[98]

The ABCC and the FBI played virtually no role whatsoever in the decision. The ABCC's Overseas Committee appears not to have even discussed it. The subject of the ECSC did arise at the FBI's Overseas Trade Policy Committee in 1953, but only in the context of a meeting with Dutch industrialists, and was dealt with by Sir Archibald Forbes, who was a member of the committee. Forbes disingenuously told the Dutch that British industrialists had not studied the issue with the intensity of their European colleagues and therefore could not express any definitive views![99] On the FBI's Grand Council some firms supported association but when the subject was discussed in February 1954 it was the practical difficulties of the ECSC which were highlighted and it was concluded that the advantages to Britain were "by no means apparent" and the following October the Grand Council simply

---

[93] TNA FO371/105957, note by Crawford, 11 November 1953.

[94] Ibid., Robinson to Plowden, 28 October 1953.

[95] TNA CAB128/27, CC(54)27th, and TNA CAB129/67, C(54)126, 131, 132 and 133.

[96] TNA FO371/111253, M601/100, "UK Association with ECSC," by Crawford, 14 April 1954.

[97] Ibid., M601/130, "UK Association with the European Coal and Steel Community: Brief for Minister of State," by Crawford, 25 May 1954.

[98] Milward, *Rise and Fall*, 161–2.   [99] Moon, *European Integration*, 130–1.

endorsed the views of the steel industries.[100] Although representatives of the FBI did meet Jean Monnet, its Overseas Trade Policy Committee did not think this was an issue that needed their consideration.[101] Likewise, the FBI sent a delegation to a conference organized by the European Movement to discuss the European Coal and Steel Community, but only "to keep the British contribution on the rails as we saw it, by which we meant keep clear of involvement." [102]

Nevertheless, the first signs of a changing awareness of European integration were beginning to appear within the FBI's staff at least. A memorandum entitled "European integration and the Schuman Plan" was circulated in February 1953 urging the FBI to take the Schuman Plan seriously.[103] A few months later Norman Kipping reported to the Grand Council on the 1953 CDEIF meeting in Stockholm. Among the subjects discussed were European integration and the European Coal and Steel Community and Kipping was clearly influenced by what he heard:

The subject of European integration was almost a closed book to industry outside the steel industry: but the time was coming when it would have to be considered. The Coal and Steel Community was likely to have secondary effects some of which would be felt by British industry and would alter the structure and pattern of European industry.[104]

There were also some indications, if more belated, that the rest of British industry was slowly waking up to the significance of events on the continent and becoming more positive in its consideration. Very few articles on the ECSC had appeared in the *FBI Review* or the publications of the various regional Chambers of Commerce by 1955.[105] Then in June 1955, the same month as the Messina talks, the *Birmingham Chamber of Commerce Journal*, which was not noted to this point for the warmth of its feelings toward continental Europe, contained an editorial on "The changing economy of Europe." It referred to the ECSC in glowing terms, concluding:

So good has been the work done by the Community that there is little doubt but that further integration of industries will take place; and there is no doubt at all that the basis has been laid down for a functional Europe in which men of the various nationalities will sink their old differences and, working in harmony, forget the moods and prejudices that have bred war in the past. A strong Europe, intent on peaceful

---

[100] Keith Middlemas, *Power, Competition and the State, Vol. 1: Britain in Search of Balance 1940–61* (Basingstoke: Macmillan, 1986), 241.

[101] Moon, *European Integration*, 131.   [102] Kipping, *Summing Up*, 154.

[103] MRC MSS200/F/3/D3/6/50, "European Integration and the Schuman Plan," undated but February 1953.

[104] MRC MSS200/F/1/1/192, Grand Council meeting, 22 July 1953.

[105] For example, Sir Cecil Weir, "Progress with the Schuman Plan," *FBI Review* (February 1953), 25–9.

pursuits, free from trade barriers and inspired by a desire to promote the well-being of all concerned, cannot fail to provide the environment that will conduce to the increased prosperity and well-being of Great Britain.[106]

Further integration was indeed about to take a step forward and the precise nature of Britain's response to it was just about to become a key consideration for the government and for British business.

CONCLUSION

In the period from the end of the Second World War to 1955, British industry was not actively engaged in consideration of European integration. However, this should not be translated as complete disinterest. As Werner Bührer has found when looking at industry in Germany in this period, engagement with the subject changed over time.[107] In the early postwar years, there was some interest in European integration in the context of Marshall Aid and consideration of the sort of world that was going to be reconstructed. Interest then waned as the possibility of integration shifted from the macro-level to the sectoral level before reawakening toward the end of the period. Even then, the waning interest and a lack of desire for involvement did not mean that the subject was completely ignored; Europe was too important to British business for that. While the FBI and ABCC did not interfere in what were seen as sectoral issues for the coal and steel industries, the FBI at least kept a watching brief sufficient to inform Kipping that continental Europe was serious about European integration.

Secondly, it has been shown that one has to be careful not to read too much into the apparently unanimous positions voiced by the representatives of business. Often they can have their own agendas, as shown by the position adopted by the Iron and Steel Board, illustrating that such pronouncements cannot be seen as simply representative of the narrow economic interests of an industry on a particular topic. Thirdly, and related to this, the chapter has shown that it is necessary to place consideration of European integration into a wider policy context. The interaction between domestic and external policy considerations was most clearly illustrated not only in the steel industry's consideration of the Schuman Plan but also in relation to association. In the first case, nationalization of the industry was a paramount concern, and in the second, the ISB was desperate to establish itself following privatization.

Finally, while British industry tended to take its lead from the government in general in relation to European integration, this position was reversed in the case of association, where the objections of the steel industry in particular

---

[106] "The Changing Economy of Europe," *Birmingham Chamber of Commerce Journal* 54, (June 1955), 576.
[107] Bührer, "German Industry."

proved a fundamental constraint on government action. Significantly, the Ministry of Supply was often closer to the steel industry in its sympathies than to other departments in Whitehall, notably the Foreign Office, reflecting the fragmented nature of government and the strength of networks across the government–business boundary. Adding to the fragmentation and complexity, while the predominant relationship was between British industry and its national government, the CEIF/CDEIF network was an important source of knowledge and trust-building for the FBI in the uncertain postwar world, a network which was to remain valuable in the years to come when European integration shifted from a sectoral phenomenon to something altogether grander following the Messina talks in June 1955.

5

The Establishment of the Common Market and the Free Trade Area Proposals, 1955–1958

Few individuals at the time realized the significance of the talks at Messina in June 1955 at which the governments of the Six "recognised that the establishment of a European market, free from all duties and all quantitative restrictions, is the objective of their action in the field of economic policy."[1] What now with hindsight is often seen as a clear road of development from Messina to the signing of the Treaty of Rome in March 1957 and the establishment of the European Community itself in January 1958 was a most uncertain process. The possibility of Britain joining the EC was quickly ruled out by the British government as it would introduce discrimination against the Commonwealth countries and there was a "parting of the ways."[2] Just as some historians point to the Schuman Plan episode so others pinpoint Britain's reaction to the EC proposals as the crucial period when Britain "missed the boat."[3] Even if there was no boat to miss, as Moravcsik and others have argued, it was nevertheless clear from an early date that if the proposals were successful then there would be serious consequences for Britain as a non-member.[4] Politically, Britain would be marginalized as US attention would shift to the Six and, economically, exclusion from a common market containing Germany would not only hand over the markets of the member

---

[1] Quoted in Miriam Camps, *Britain and the European Community 1955–1963* (Princeton: Princeton University Press, 1964), 25–6.

[2] John W. Young, "'The Parting of the Ways'? Britain, the Messina Conference and the Spaak Committee, June–December 1955," in Michael Dockerill and John W. Young (eds.), *British Foreign Policy, 1945–56* (Basingstoke: Macmillan, 1989), 197–224.

[3] Simon Burgess and Geoffrey Edwards, "The Six Plus One: British Policy-making and the Question of European Economic Integration, 1955," *International Affairs*, Vol. 64, No. 3 (1988), 393–413; Miriam Camps, "Missing the Boat at Messina and Other Times?" in Brian Brivati and Harriet Jones (eds.), *From Reconstruction to Integration: Britain and Europe since 1945* (Leicester: Leicester University Press, 1993), 134–43; Wolfram Kaiser, *Using Europe, Abusing the Europeans: Britain and European Integration, 1945–63* (Basingstoke: Macmillan, 1996), 54–5; and James Ellison, *Threatening Europe: Britain and the Creation of the European Community, 1955–58* (Basingstoke: Macmillan, 2000).

[4] Andrew Moravcsik, *Choice for Europe: Social Purpose and State Power from Messina to Maastricht* (London: UCL Press, 1999), 123; Alan S. Milward, *The United Kingdom and the European Community, Vol. 1: The Rise and Fall of a National Strategy 1945–1963* (London: Frank Cass, 2002), 212.

states but also increase the competitive position of German exporters in third markets, including the Commonwealth. Unsurprisingly, given this, the British government set about finding a suitable counterproposal, first as an alternative and, once it became clear that the Six would go ahead with the EC in any case, as a way of including the Six in a wider and looser form of economic integration. After much discussion, the British government opted for what became known as Plan G in May 1956, a proposal to establish a free trade area (FTA) covering all OEEC member states for industrial products. Like the EC customs union the FTA would remove tariff barriers between member states on industrial products. The key differences from the EC were that agriculture was to be completely excluded and that as a free trade area there would be no common external tariff, allowing the maintenance of Imperial Preference on British manufactures sold in the Commonwealth and the retention of zero or very low tariffs on imports of raw materials from the Commonwealth.

Some suggest that Britain wanted the best of all worlds: "It was like taking a new wife without having to divorce, or even stop living with, the old one," was one description.[5] The Commonwealth preferential trading system would be maintained while British exporters would gain access to the markets of Western Europe; this was certainly the French view. As a result, progress toward agreement on a free trade area was slow: the Six, on French insistence, decided that the free trade area proposals would only be discussed once the discussions among the Six on the EC had been completed. Thereafter, discussions and eventually negotiations did occur but the proposals reached their demise at the end of 1958 when the French insisted on imposing trade liberalization within the Six, discriminating against other OEEC members for the first time. With the failure of the FTA, British policy had to be reassessed once more.

There is agreement in the existing literature over the growing influence of British business on government policy after the 1957 Suez crisis from which point the need for domestic consensus became a stronger influence on policy.[6] However, for the period before there is a clear division of opinion. Some, like Wolfram Kaiser, see British industry as cautious, disinterested, and lacking influence.[7] This position follows Robert Lieber's earlier study where he describes the FBI's response to emerging European integration as

---

[5] Michael Shanks and John Lambert, *Britain and the New Europe: The Future of the Common Market* (London: Chatto and Windus, 1962), 29; and "Are We Europeans?" *The Economist*, 12 October 1957, special supplement, 6.

[6] Milward, *Rise and Fall*, 265–6.

[7] Kaiser, *Using Europe*, 58–9. See also N. Tiratsoo and Jim Tomlinson, *The Conservatives and Industrial Efficiency, 1951–64: Thirteen Wasted Years?* (London: Routledge, 1998), 112–3; Moravcsik, *Choice for Europe*, 125; and Theodore Bromund, "From Empire to Europe: Material Interests, National Identities, and British Policies towards European Integration, 1956–1963," Ph.D. dissertation, Yale University, 1999.

not only slow but also "exceptionally cautious" and conditional, concluding that as far as the development of government policy was concerned, "the FBI operated more as a brake than a stimulus."[8] Others, however, have been more positive. John Young is typical here but again there is an earlier precedent in Miriam Camps' path-breaking study.[9] It will be argued here that these differences can partly be explained by incomplete use of the archives but also because of the complexity and diversity of British industry's views. These views will be considered first in general, then in relation to contemporary assessments of the impact of the free trade area proposals on different sectors of manufacturing industry, and finally with regard to the sensitive issue of safeguards, particularly the issue of origin.

THE VIEWS OF INDUSTRY

As shown in Chapter 2, it was in the context of growing concerns with British export competitiveness and economic performance that the proposal to establish a common market emerged. While there was a consensus that Britain could not join such a body, the potential economic implications were equally clear if such a body came into existence and Britain was not a member. Within weeks of the Messina conference a report by the Economic Section, a group of economists in the Treasury, noted that "we would certainly lose by the establishment of a common market without our participation."[10] Aware of this the committee of officials responsible for British policy on European integration, agreed to recommend to ministers in October 1955 that Britain could not join the common market but that "if it came into being with us outside it we should pay an increasing price commercially."[11] *The Economist* put the issue more explicitly in declaring its support for Britain to join the common market project "to the fullest possible extent": "if Germany is in the scheme, and Britain is outside it, the results could be disastrous for our trade."[12]

Industry had similar concerns. British business opposed Britain joining the EC as a full member because of the common external tariff's effect on Commonwealth trade and preferences.[13] Equally, it was appreciated that, if

---

[8] Robert J. Lieber, *British Politics and European Unity: Parties, Elites and Pressure Groups* (Berkeley: University of California Press, 1970) 57 and 66; and Stephen Blank, *Industry and Government in Britain: The Federation of British Industries in Politics, 1945–65* (Farnborough: Saxon House, 1973), 143.

[9] John W. Young, *Britain and European Unity 1945–1999* (Basingstoke: Macmillan, 2nd edn. 2000), 47.

[10] TNA CAB134/1029, MAC(55)136, 14 July 1955.

[11] TNA CAB134/1026, MAC(55)45th, 27 October 1955.

[12] "Opportunity in Europe," *The Economist*, 14 July 1956, 105.

[13] R. L. Wills, "The European Economic Community and the European Free Trade Area," *Monthly Record of the Manchester Chamber of Commerce* (May 1957), 143; and MRC

the EC came into existence, the status quo was doomed; taking no action would involve substantial risks for British industry.[14] Accordingly, the free trade area proposals tended to be presented as a compromise or "half-way house," rather than a situation where Britain got the best of both worlds.[15] Reflecting concerns about German competition, it was the views of Germany rather than the other five potential member countries that received the most coverage in business circles.[16] In general, support in industry for the free trade area proposals was driven by the fear of exclusion from continental markets and the resulting deterioration in British competitiveness in global markets.[17] Its views were, therefore, created in reaction to developments on the continent: the National Union of Manufacturers' *Annual Report for 1956–57* noted that the rapid emergence of the subject of Europe was "symptomatic of the suddenness with which they [the proposals] were presented to a country and industry largely unprepared for them."[18] Similarly, in November 1956, the then President of the FBI believed that it was only over the previous few months that there had been a growing awareness in industry of the situation.[19] One government official went further: In his view, no one outside of government had given serious consideration to the subject before September 1956.[20]

Industry, in general, was slow to pick up on the significance of moves towards European integration. Nor was industry prompted by government at this stage. Contrary to John Young's interpretation, industrialists were not sent a questionnaire by the Board of Trade shortly after the Messina conference. Instead, a questionnaire was sent to the relevant production departments of the government to report on the effects of a European customs union on certain UK industries, specifically iron and steel, chemicals, textiles, cars and other engineering goods, and agriculture and horticulture.[21] Indeed, the departments were specifically requested not to consult industry:

MSS200/F/1/1/193, Lincoln Steel, FBI Grand Council meeting, 10 October 1956. See R. L. Brech, "The Challenge of the Free Trade Area," *The European Common Market and Free Trade Area* (London: Institute of Bankers, 1958), 46.

[14] Wills, "The European Economic Community," 143; MRC MSS200/F/1/1/193, Lincoln Steel, FBI Grand Council meeting, 10 October 1956; and FBI, *European Free Trade Area: A Survey for Industrialists* (London, 1957), v.

[15] FBI, *European Free Trade Area*, v; and A. W. H. Scott, "Free Trade in Europe: Britain and the Customs Union Plan," *The Scottish Bankers Magazine*, No. xlviii, (1957), 209.

[16] Richard Bailey, "How Germany Sees the Common Market," *The Director* (October 1957), 93–4.

[17] Alan McKinlay, H. Mercer, and Neil Rollings, "Reluctant Europeans? The Federation of British Industries and European Integration, 1945–63," *Business History*, Vol. 42, No. 4, (2000), 101.

[18] NUM, *Annual Report for 1956–57*, 16.

[19] TNA CAB134/1240, ES(EI)(56)77, 6 November 1956.

[20] TNA BT258/229, Swindlehurst to various, 10 October 1956.

[21] TNA CAB134/1044, MAC(ECM)(55) 4.

"if industries were consulted . . . they might gain the impression that Her Majesty's government is in some way committed to the objectives of the Messina countries."[22]

However, as shown in the previous chapter, the subject of European integration did not go completely unnoticed in business circles before the summer of 1956. Within the FBI a small group of industrialists and FBI officials were considering the subject. In the late summer of 1955 the FBI's Economic Director wrote a paper on European integration which was then discussed by the Federation's Overseas Trade Policy (OTP) Committee.[23] Toward the end of the year the OTP Committee also established a working party "to study the functions of the various intergovernmental bodies concerned with economic questions on a European scale."[24] In October, European integration was discussed at the Consultative Committee for Industry, at which representatives of the FBI, ABCC and NUM, and other representatives met officials and ministers.[25] At the meeting, Lincoln Steel, the chairman of the OTP Committee, urged the government to adopt a more friendly attitude to the negotiations "to the interest and surprise" of Peter Thorneycroft, the most senior minister there.[26] By April 1956 when the report of the Spaak Committee, the body set up following the Messina conference to consider how best to carry forward European economic integration, was published, the OTP Committee's working party was known as the European Integration Panel. By that date it had already had meetings with representatives from the OEEC, the ECSC High Authority and with Russell Bretherton, Britain's representative at the Spaak Committee meetings.[27]

The subject of European integration was also dealt with at length at the International Chamber of Commerce (ICC) meeting in February 1956, at which British business had three representatives. Lincoln Steel, the chair of the FBI's OTP Committee, was one of these, as he was also the chair of the British National Committee of the ICC. He reported:

The British representatives held somewhat of a watching brief. They felt that the position was one of some delicacy and that what the "Six" did was primarily their own concern. At the same time, they felt they must show some sympathy with the idea of what was commonly called European integration, provided that any steps taken towards European integration did not adversely affect the position of this country. . . .

---

[22] Ibid.

[23] Bromund, "From Empire to Europe," 287–8n, referring to Matthias's unpublished history of the FBI.

[24] FBI, *Annual Report for 1955*, 15.

[25] TNA BT205/17, CCI 40th, 20 October 1955.

[26] Norman Kipping, *Summing Up* (London: Hutchison, 1972), 320.

[27] FBI, *Annual Report for 1956*, 11; and Michael Charlton, *The Price of Victory* (London: British Broadcasting Corporation, 1983), 193–4.

They tried – while showing sympathy with the idea of integration – to make it abundantly clear that if a Club was going to be formed, the rules must not be so exclusive as to prevent an associate from joining at some future date, if an associate member like the UK wished to do so. In any case, it was made clear that this country would not view with any enthusiasm the emergence of an economic bloc in Western Europe which would set up defensive walls against the rest of the world.[28]

Full membership of the proposed common market may not have appealed, but it is clear that some businessmen and FBI officials were not only well informed about events on the continent prior to the British government's proposal for a European free trade area, but were also very aware of their significance for British business.

More than this, even at this early stage this small group was willing to act on their concerns. In February 1956 Peter Tennant wrote a six-page internal memorandum on European economic integration based on recent trips to Brussels and The Hague. It also followed a meeting between Bretherton and the FBI's European Integration Panel.[29] Tennant emphasized that European integration could no longer be dismissed as "purely idealistic and impractical Europeanism."[30] He continued:

The issues are very serious ones for the economy of our country in the next two decades . . . . By adopting a more positive attitude now we might be able to steer the proposals towards a solution more of our own liking with which we could identify ourselves on our own terms instead of leaving events to proceed outside our control and then be faced some ten or fifteen years hence with a decision to join the club on its terms and at a high entrance fee. This would disrupt our economy far more severely than if we were founder members and were able to increase our competitiveness gradually to face the rigours of a free-trade area.[31]

Tennant then went on to set out what action he felt necessary for the FBI to take:

1. To persuade HMG of the necessity of adopting at least a friendly attitude from now onwards, however noncommittal we may feel it necessary to be in order not to let the opportunity go by default;
2. To arrange for the FBI to receive first-hand information and documentation on the discussions;
3. To define the issues;

---

[28] GLA MS16490, Executive Committee meeting, 19 April 1956.
[29] Charlton, *Price of Victory*, 194; Kipping, *Summing Up*, 320; and TNA BT11/5852, "The Development of Policy about the Common Market, and the Origin of the Negotiations for a European Free Trade Area, 1955/1957, with Special Reference to the Board of Trade," by Bretherton, June 1961, 19.
[30] Kipping, *Summing Up*, 316.   [31] Ibid., 318–9.

4. To discuss the issues not only with HMG but with industrial federations, government officials and economic organisations in Europe, the Commonwealth and the USA;
5. To present our findings to the FBI and take appropriate action with HMG in the light of industrial opinion.

In recognition of the importance and urgency of the first of these, Norman Kipping sent the memorandum to Frank Lee, the leading official in the Board of Trade.[32] His covering letter reiterated in more polite terms Tennant's call on the government "to abandon her dog-in-the-manger attitude and go back into the discussions."[33] Lee himself sympathized and agreed with much in Tennant's "interesting and timely" memorandum but he believed that it did not "really face up to the very difficult political and economic issues involved. Indeed, the FBI want us somehow to get full credit without commitment."[34] Even if their recommendations to government were deemed unrealistic, it would be harsh, therefore, to argue that the FBI's officials failed to be aware of the potential significance of the developments on the continent. As Kipping told Frank Lee, "the implications of Messina are far too important for this country to adopt a negative policy."[35] During the summer of 1956 the FBI continued to press the government to keep in the closest touch with the negotiations so that there was "no leap forward without us": the main issue was "how to associate with the Six and at the same time maintain a substantial share of our preferences."[36] However, at this stage this concern was driven by the fear that any such developments would damage the OEEC. Thus the government needed to get back into the discussions "in the hope that our influence might lead them in a more favorable direction for ourselves." This was not positive support for any initiative towards greater European integration per se.

Nor was there any evidence that the FBI's position was representative of the wider business community. To this end, the government asked the FBI for industry's views on the common market proposals to be submitted to it preferably by the middle of July and no later than by autumn.[37] The July deadline was deemed impossible and it was not considered by the Overseas Trade Policy Committee until the end of September but with little apparent consensus.[38] Prior to the ensuing Grand Council meeting the government had announced its intention to consider whether to negotiate an industrial free trade area in Western Europe.[39] Accordingly, in the middle of the Grand

---

[32] Ibid., 315.   [33] Ibid., 319.

[34] TNA BT11/5402, Lee, "European Economic Integration," 27 February 1956, and Lee to Glaves-Smith, 16 March 1956.

[35] Kipping, *Summing Up*, 315.

[36] TNA BT11/5402, "Note of Meeting," by Glaves-Smith, 13 July 1956.   [37] Ibid.

[38] MRC MSS200/F/1/1/193, Steel, Grand Council meeting, 10 October 1956.

[39] TNA BT258/146, Note from Dennehy, 10/10/56.

Council debate the FBI President announced that it had been decided "to take the unusual step of sounding the opinion of each of the FBI's individual members separately" and a special conference of the Grand Council would meet on October 31 to consider the responses prior to their submission to the government.

The results of this survey of its membership have always been the focus of attention when considering industry's views on the free trade area proposals. Indeed, analysis usually goes no further, although interpretation of the results remains divided. On the one hand, it was presented as signifying a wide measure of support for the government to open negotiations on a free trade area.[40] This was certainly the view adopted by the government and the FBI leadership: It was agreed that the results could be taken as a "green light to start negotiations."[41] Indeed, many have been surprised by the degree of support: *The Economist* found the FBI's response "broadly, and perhaps surprisingly, encouraging."[42] Norman Kipping notes with pride in his memoirs, "The publication of the results of this survey considerably surprised a lot of people. The press, having held the opinion that British industry was basically protectionist, was astonished. We were pretty surprised ourselves."[43] Some trade associations as well as government officials and ministers were equally surprised.[44] The basis for this surprise was the breakdown of the responses made by trade associations and member firms. Of the 128 trade associations that replied 67 could be said to be in favor of joining a European free trade area, that is, 52 percent, while 479, or 72 percent, of the 664 individual firms to reply felt the same.[45]

One needs to be cautious about taking these results at face value: "the strongest appeal to British industry was the negative one" that if German industry had access to a protected market in Western Europe, Britain could not afford to stay out.[46] This fear of exclusion was a powerful argument for involvement even if there seemed no positive reasons for joining.[47] Tariff barriers would limit access to fast-growing continental markets while the economies of scale gained by continental manufacturers would enhance their relative advantage in British and other third markets around the world.

---

[40] CPA CRD2/9/41, "European trade policy," by Dear (Conservative Research Department), 22 November 1956, 4.

[41] TNA CAB134/1240, ES(EI)(56)77, 6 November 1956.

[42] "Industry and Freer Trade," *The Economist*, 3 November 1956, 402.

[43] Kipping, *Summing Up*, 157.

[44] TNA BT258/146, Denman to various, 16 October 1956.

[45] E. Haas, *The Uniting of Europe: Political, Social, and Economic Forces 1950–1957* (Stanford, Stanford University Press, 1958), 212; and *Times Review of Industry*, March 1957.

[46] Miriam Camps, *The Free Trade Area Negotiations* (London: PEP, 1959), 32.

[47] Federation of Commonwealth and British Empire Chambers of Commerce, *Report of the Proceedings at the Nineteenth Congress* (London, 1957), 36; and UN, *Economic Survey of Europe in 1956* (Geneva, 1957), 24.

In addition, support for the proposal was highly conditional and dependent on a suitably long transition period (twelve to fifteen years) and satisfactory safeguards.[48] A more detailed breakdown of the responses from trade associations illustrates this conditionality. Of the 67 trade associations "in favour," fifty-two were in favor provided safeguards were worked out, with the further fifteen not opposing further negotiations, assuming that safeguards were worked out. In contrast, of the twenty-seven associations opposed to negotiations, eighteen were so unconditionally, the other nine unless certain safeguards were assured.[49] Obviously, the safeguards were a crucial element of industry's response and support for the free trade area was dependent to a large degree on them being obtained. Nearly two pages of the FBI's four-and-a-half page report to the government were spent setting out the eight principal safeguards.[50] Imperial Preference had to be maintained; tight rules over dumping and unfair trade practices would be required; non-tariff barriers, such as quotas, specification or registration regulations would need to be carefully scrutinized; safeguards against currency manipulation were essential as was provision of the greatest possible liberalization of payments and capital movements; British taxation needed to be reduced to allow competition on equal terms; labor costs, including rates of pay, hours of work, paid holidays, and the cost of social security and other welfare payments needed to be harmonized; there should be equal treatment of export agreements; and, finally, strategic industries would require special treatment.

These safeguards were wide ranging and those that focused on them emphasized the cautious and conditional nature of the response by business.[51] The other peak-level representative organizations of business at the time were equally if not more cautious once, like the FBI, one moves beyond the headline figures. The Deputy President of the ABCC noted, "there had been surprisingly little outright opposition to the proposals" with only six chambers of commerce, representing 5,000 members, opposed, against chambers representing 37,000 members in favor. Again, however, it should be noted this was in favor "of the principle of HMG entering into discussions with a view to examining the possibilities of association with the six common market countries by means of a partial free trade area," not of joining a free trade area.[52] Moreover, support was once more not without qualification. This time, six of the "most frequently cited safeguards" were set out, being

---

[48] MRC MSS200/F/1/2/84, "British Industry and European Free Trade Area," Hayman to Thorneycroft, 1 November 1956.

[49] CPA CRD2/9/41, "European trade policy," by Dear, 22 November 1956, 4.

[50] MRC MSS200/F/1/2/84, "British Industry and European Free Trade Area," Hayman to Thorneycroft, 1 November 1956.

[51] *FBI Review*, January 1958, 22, quoted in Lieber, *British Politics*, 66–7; and R. Lewis, *Challenge from Europe: Britain, the Commonwealth and the Free Trade Area* (London: Bow Group, 1957), 43.

[52] TNA CAB134/1240, ES(EI)(56)80, 12 November 1956.

broadly similar to those raised by the FBI. *The Times* reported the ABCC's response under the headline, "Qualified support of common market."[53]

With its history of support for Imperial Preference, the National Union of Manufacturers was even more cautious. It believed that "some kind of closer trade association with Europe may be in the long run inevitable," but that there was "a strong feeling that safeguards and exceptions in favor of certain industries are imperative if they are to survive."[54] This was because "considerable damage" was likely to result to individual firms and industries from the removal of protection.[55] The worries and proposed safeguards were even more extensive than those suggested by the FBI and ABCC. They included cushioning or protection of industries likely to suffer, fear of the effect on smaller manufacturing firms, and concerns about unequal transportation costs because of Britain's island position, as well as the usual demands for controls against dumping and subsidies, and the lowering of taxation in Britain.[56] "Fears for small firms under free trade plan" was how *The Times* summed up the NUM's position.[57]

This caution and conditionality were important elements of the view in business to the idea of a free trade area – British business did not think that it was getting the best of both worlds with a free trade area – but, it is argued here, that it is necessary to go even further to untangle the complexities of business opinion and to understand the key influences here. First, it is necessary to understand the reasoning behind the demand for safeguards. Demands for lower taxation can be seen as part of more general and common complaints about the excessive burden of public expenditure on industry (see Chapter 9). In addition, it was felt important politically for business to impress upon the government the importance of the safeguards.[58] Moreover, demands for clear guaranteed safeguards reflected a belief that continental countries were "less scrupulous than us in observing their undertakings."[59] Related to this, one of the main objections of those opposed to the proposed FTA was deep skepticism of the possibility of watertight safeguards to ensure competition on level terms.[60] This was a common and recurring theme in British industrialists' comments and relates to long-standing complaints about unfair competition and export subsidies.[61] Despite this, it was only the NUM that demanded protection beyond that for strategic industries. The FBI and the ABCC called for competition on equal terms. Obviously, the meaning of this was open to individual interpretation, but

---

[53] *The Times*, 10 November 1956, 4.
[54] TNA CAB 134/1240, ES(EI)(56)92, 4 December 1956.
[55] NUM, *Annual Report 1956–57*, 17.
[56] TNA CAB134/1240, ES(EI)(56)92, 4 December 1956.   [57] *The Times*, 4 April 1957, 6.
[58] MRC MSS200/F/1/1/193, Hayman, Grand Council meeting, 31 October 1956.
[59] TNA CAB134/1240, ES(EI)(56)80, 12 November 1956.
[60] MRC MSS200/F/1/2/84, "British Industry and European Free Trade Area," Hayman to Thorneycroft, 1 November 1956.
[61] See TNA T236/3486–8 and BT11/5090.

the difference has significance, reflecting a desire not to be exploited rather than something more defensive and protectionist.

This relates to the second point. The idea of joining a free trade area was seen by industrialists to be both of crucial importance and a major change of policy.[62] As the Overseas Trade Committee of the ABCC commented, this topic "was the most important with which the country had been faced since that of Tariff Reform, and a wrong decision at this time could jeopardize our entire future. Therefore, the most careful consideration must be given to every aspect of the matter, and the decision could not be rushed."[63] Significantly, the committee added that it could not take the issue any further at that time, "as the information at its disposal was not sufficient, nor had there been adequate time for due consideration of that which was available." Industry was being asked for its views on a free trade area when the form of that FTA remained no more than the broadest of concepts – the government itself had only set out its proposals in the broadest of terms at the start of October. Little information existed and some key issues had hardly been raised, let alone resolved.[64] For example, it was unknown whether the Six would even reach agreement and the contents of the Treaty of Rome did not become known until the spring of 1957. The membership of any free trade area was equally unclear as was the important issue of whether overseas territories would be included. These were only a few of the uncertainties. It would have been astounding if industry had been anything other than cautious at this stage in these circumstances.[65]

The views were also presented as preliminary, not industry's last word on the subject. Many trade associations had been unable to formulate their views in the time available (twenty-two of the trade associations replying to the FBI questionnaire).[66] This was a common theme in the various submissions to the government: The views expressed were not binding and that they expected the opportunity to make a further submission when the exact form of the free trade area became clear.[67] The example of J & P Coats Ltd, the thread manufacturer, provides a further complication. Coats already had extensive business interests in continental Europe. It was felt that the issue of Britain joining a FTA was "a matter of indifference" from the company

---

[62] MRC MSS200/F/1/1/193, Grand Council meeting, 10 October 1956.

[63] GLA MS14487/6, Overseas Trade Committee meeting, 3 October 1956.

[64] MRC MSS200/F/1/1/193, Grand Council meeting, 10 October 1956; and TNA BT258/20, CB588/56, "Proposed Free Trade Area in Western Europe: Problems for the Cotton Industry," by the Cotton Board, 28 December 1956.

[65] "Editorial comment," *Monthly Record of the Manchester Chamber of Commerce*, No. 68 (November 1957), 349.

[66] MRC MSS200/F/1/2/84, "British Industry and European Free Trade Area," Hayman to Thorneycroft, 1 November 1956.

[67] TNA CAB134/1240, ES(EI)(56)80, 12 November 1956 and ES(EI)(56)92, 4 December 1956.

point of view but the company was in favor of joining "from the point of view of the national interest."[68]

The views presented to government therefore were the product of a cocktail of considerations at the firm and trade association level. It was a balance of a range of opinions.[69] Much of the opinion took the middle ground, hedged by various qualifications. This was not simply because of the uncertainties involved but also the pasteurization of opinion. There were differences of opinion within sectors of an industry, for example, within the cotton industry, within trade associations, such as the Glass Manufacturers' Federation, and between leading personalities in a sector, for example, between Sir Ernest Goodale and Sir Kenneth Lee in the textile industry.[70] Few industries were able to report unanimity.[71] This created both a problem and an opportunity for the FBI's leadership. The problem was that the FBI had to distinguish between those in favor of opening negotiations and those who were opposed. Classifying several hundred replies in a short space of time was hard enough – the FBI borrowed tabulating machinery to help it – and, as Kipping wrote later, the officials despaired of making any sense of it all.[72] Ultimately, Kipping himself decided to divide the responses on the basis of tone rather than substance because so many referred to conditions or safeguards. He distinguished between those who were "in favour, provided" and those who were "opposed, unless" safeguards were assured. The FBI's submission to the government insisted that this distinction indicated "a real difference in attitude" but, as Kipping explained, this distinction had been devised "to get everyone to take up a position," that is, in favor or against.[73] Kipping later acknowledged: "The safeguards mentioned by each group were almost identical. In other words, those who said 'Yes, provided,' were really saying the same as those who said 'No,' unless, but from different points of view."[74] The line drawn by Kipping was, therefore, arbitrary, with the purpose of creating a dichotomy when one did not really exist, pigeonholing firms and trade associations into one camp or the other.

Adopting this approach provided the FBI leadership with the opportunity to create business opinion as presented to the government and the general public. We have seen that the FBI leadership, including Kipping, believed

---

[68] GUABRC UGD199/1/1/80, Executive Directors' Committee meeting, 1 November 1956.

[69] GLA MS16459/29, Council of the London Chamber of Commerce meeting, 13 November 1956, attached memorandum.

[70] See respectively, *The Times*, 9 October 1956, 10; MRC MSS200/F/3/D3/5/44, submission of the Glass Manufacturers' Association, October 1956; and MRC MSS200/F/1/1/193, Grand Council meeting, 10 October 1956, speech by Morton.

[71] MRC MSS200/F/3/D3/3/20, Kipping, "British Industry and the European Common Market," March 1957.

[72] Kipping, *Summing Up*, 156.

[73] MRC MSS200/F/1/2/84, Hayman to Thorneycroft, 1 November 1956.

[74] Kipping, *Summing Up*, 156.

that Britain could not ignore developments on the continent. Using the distinction he had devised allowed Kipping to set out the safeguards which business wanted but also to show that the weight of opinion was in favor of the proposals.[75] As he later commented, this was "a considerable act of leadership . . . . By accentuating the positive, even in those replies which were conditional negatives, a broad base of support for negotiations was located."[76] More than this, when there was division within a sector, like the cotton industry, he told the government:

All the firms whom one would admire were in favour of opening negotiations while it was the older type of firm which was opposed. From personal conversations it was also clear that where a trade association had come down in opposition to the proposals there were many individuals within the association who nevertheless supported them. He was confident that the better elements in most of our industries were clearly in favour of opening negotiations.[77]

The FBI's survey results were not, therefore, the outcome of considered deliberation and consensus within industries and trade associations but the creation of the FBI leadership in the context of the vast majority of responses being broadly similar, reflecting the ignorance, uncertainty, lack of consensus and rush involved in providing the responses. The importance of the survey was, therefore, not in its representation of business opinion but in the way the FBI leadership and the government were able to use the opportunity to endorse government policy to open negotiations on a FTA.

THE DEVELOPMENT OF THE VIEWS OF INDUSTRY

Following the October 1956 survey British business continued to give close attention to the free trade area proposals. Two developments were significant. First, direct discussions between sectoral trade associations and government grew. This was an inevitable response to the October 1956 survey by those trade associations who disagreed with the FBI's submission or felt that they had a special case or a particular issue relevant to themselves, which they wished to bring to the attention of government. Indeed, the first contact with government officials was often made by trade associations in October 1956 as part of the process of determining their response to the survey or in making an early attack on the proposals. Particularly noticeable in the latter respect were the efforts of the British Paper and Board Makers' Association (BPBMA). The BPBMA was to lead a stout and persistent attack on the free trade area proposals, as it would be "a mortal blow" to the paper industry by

---

[75] TNA CAB134/1240, "Note of a Meeting on Plan G with Representatives of the FBI."
[76] Kipping, quoted in Blank, *Industry and Government*, 163n.
[77] TNA CAB134/1240, "Note of a Meeting on Plan G with Representatives of the FBI."

exposing it to Scandinavian competition.[78] Many other trade associations contacted the government in the months that followed by whatever route became available.[79]

It would appear that in the first six months of 1957 British industry became less positive about the free trade area proposals, or those opposed became more vocal.[80] Certainly there was growing anxiety in business circles that the government was moving ahead in its commitment to negotiations "before industry was in any position to judge except in the very broadest terms the nature of the arrangements which might be made for establishing such a Free Trade Area" and representations to this effect were made to the government.[81] Having approved the opening of negotiations "at very short notice and with necessarily little reliable data" in October, it was now felt that the impression had been falsely created that industry "has given *carte blanche* to our negotiators," whereas, "Nothing could be further from the truth: industry as a whole has not given the green light to participation in the scheme; it has given a very cautious yellow to preliminary discussions."[82] These concerns among industrialists had not been allayed by May 1957 and continued to be relayed to the government.[83] As these anxieties became more explicit, the government became concerned at the lack of understanding of the main issues of the free trade area.[84] There are certainly many examples of ignorance in business circles about the FTA proposals.[85] Also business leaders stressed to their members that there was little point in complaining that the negotiations were taking place, rather attention should focus on studying the issues and potential problems of membership.[86]

Emerging from this was the importance attached to the dissemination of information on the free trade area proposals to the business community. The government played an important role in this process with ministers

---

[78] TNA BT258/91, Oliver to Thorneycroft, 25 October 1956 and McGregor to Robinson, 11 October 1956.

[79] TNA BT258/229.

[80] TNA BT11/5552, 8th weekly meeting on the free trade area in Europe, 8 February 1957.

[81] TNA BT258/10, Fraser, Secretary of the Wool Textile Delegation, to McGregor, 6 February 1957; and TNA BT11/5552, "Note of Meeting," by Swindlehurst, 7 February 1957.

[82] Presidential Address, *Monthly Record of the Manchester Chamber of Commerce* No. 68 (February 1957), 41.

[83] MRC MSS200/F/1/1/193, Grand Council meetings, 10 April 1957 and 8 May 1957; "Doubts on Free Trade Plan," *The Times*, 22 May 1957, 7; and "Fears for Small Firms under Free Trade Plan," *The Times*, 4 April 1957, 6.

[84] TNA BT258/135, Denman to Fisher, 18 March 1957; TNA BT258/28, 10th departmental meeting, 28 February 1957; and GLA MS17558, Wills, 1st meeting of the ABCC EFTA panel, 27 February 1957.

[85] TNA BT258/2, Stewart to Currall, 5 March 1957; and GLA MS16459/29, meeting of the Council of the London Chamber of Commerce, 11 June 1957.

[86] "We Must Join in Free Trade," *The Times*, 11 April 1957, 7; GLA MS17558, first meeting of the ABCC's EFTA panel, 27 February 1957; and NUM, *Annual Report for 1956–57*, 17.

visiting Glasgow, Birmingham, and Manchester to speak to industrialists.[87] However, the main role was played by the peak-level organizations, which the government told "to hammer home the essential facts on which the policy is based."[88] Indeed, the FBI's role has been described as "primarily educational" at this time.[89] Perhaps most crucial here was *European Free Trade Area: A Survey for Industrialists*, published in April 1957. Over ninety pages long, this FBI booklet aimed "to put before members as much as is known which may help them to form their own assessment of what is or may be involved."[90] It not only set out the free trade area proposals but also explained the Treaty of Rome and spent a chapter elaborating what action might be necessary in Britain as a result of joining the free trade area. The publication was rushed out as soon as the French text of the Treaty of Rome became available and was printed before the English version of the treaty. As a result, it was the first substantial review of the impact of the Treaty of Rome on Britain and, according to Norman Kipping, became a best seller.[91] Nor was the FBI alone in these efforts with studies also being carried out by the ABCC, the NUM, and individual companies and trade associations.[92]

Yet the divisions within business were to resurface during the second half of 1957. Following the October 1956 survey a working party had been set up by the FBI at the end of 1956 to act as a liaison group between the Board of Trade and representatives of business and chaired by Sir William Palmer, an ex-Board of Trade official.[93] This was to become a key conduit between business and government. From May 1957 it undertook a major study of the implications for British industry of joining a free trade area. Six study groups of the working party were established.[94] Respectively, these considered:

1. the consequences of the Treaty of Rome if the UK was not to be associated with the EC as a part of an industrial free trade area;
2. the degree of commitment to features of the EC in the Treaty of Rome required as a necessary safeguard against discrimination by the EC if the UK became a member of the free trade area;
3. the economic consequences for the UK, colonies, and Commonwealth of inclusion of overseas territories of member countries of the EC;
4. the effect of the customs union and free trade area on trade between the UK and the Commonwealth;

---

[87] TNA BT258/2, "President's Meeting with NUM at Glasgow," by Golt, 14 March 1957; and TNA BT258/28, note of 10th departmental meeting, 28 February 1957.

[88] TNA BT205/261, TN(FT)(57)14, "Board of Trade Progress Report No. 3," 8 March 1957.

[89] Blank, *Industry and Government*, 144.

[90] FBI, *European Free Trade Area: A Survey for Industrialists* (London, 1957), vii.

[91] Kipping, *Summing Up*, 158.

[92] ABCC Executive Council, *Annual Report for 1957–58*, 27; NUM, *Annual Report for 1956–57*, 18; and EIU, *Britain and Europe*, xi.

[93] MRC MSS200/F/3/E3/34/3, Please to all trade associations, 26 November 1956.

[94] MRC MSS200/3/E3/34/5, D/1274, Common Market Working Party meeting, 10 May 1957.

5. measures for hard-hit industries; and
6. problems arising from the abolition of export restrictions and dual pricing.

Controversy centered on the report of the first study group, which the main Palmer working group and others thought was too negative and one-sided in its emphasis on the problems associated with a FTA.[95] The outcome of the dispute was for two papers to be drafted, one setting out the pros of involvement in a FTA, the other the cons. They lacked balance and were the equivalent of manifestos for those for and against a FTA. Indeed, some sections of business, especially parts of the textile industries, were becoming sufficiently disgruntled to consider setting up a new political party to oppose the European free trade area proposals.[96] At its crux, the two sides disagreed on the consequences of standing aside and doing nothing while European integration developed.[97] For one group Britain had to be involved for its businesses to remain competitive, for the other Britain needed to stay out to ensure businesses were not wiped out by the competition.

The study group reports were put together into a single document. Part I was less contentious but Part II dealt with the work of study groups 3 and 6, and also included the two papers, which had emerged from study group 1 on the pros and cons of FTA membership. The decision on how to progress – what would be published, what was to be sent to the government and what would go to the members, as well as whether there would be a referendum on the issues raised – was to be made at an all-day meeting of the FBI's Grand Council on September 18, 1957. In preparation government officials briefed FBI staff prior to the meeting.[98] The FBI had been thinking of holding a referendum asking for approval of Part I of the report, with Part II included as background. It was made clear to the FBI officials that the government were very strongly opposed to this idea: A referendum could be "acutely embarrassing" to the FBI and the government if there was a large vote against the free trade area and it was hoped that Part II of the report would never be published. Those opposed to British involvement in a FTA also had a preparatory meeting, arranged by the BPBMA.[99] There, Lincoln Steel, the chairman of the FBI's Overseas Trade Policy Committee was criticized for being overly biased in favor of the FTA and a strategy for the forthcoming Grand Council meeting was agreed – both parts of the report were to go to the government, there should be a referendum and the government should take no further steps until the referendum results were known.

---

[95] MRC MSS200/3/E3/34/5, D/2117, Common Market Working Party meeting, 18 July 1957; and GLA MS17558, ABCC European Integration Panel meeting, 31 July 1957.
[96] *The Times*, 24 September 1957, 4.
[97] TNA CAB134/1862, ES(EI)(57)256, September 1957.
[98] MRC MSS200/F/3/S1/21/60, unsigned note, 12 September 1957.
[99] Ibid., Report of a meeting, 10 September 1957.

Although there were concerted efforts at the Grand Council meeting to get these points accepted, the government was more successful in achieving its goals: There was no referendum and Part II was never published but was sent to all members.[100] Part I of the report was published as a joint statement from the FBI, the ABCC, and the NUM and set out the proposed form of a European free trade area convention and had appendices on transport and hard-hit industries.[101] The focus was on the safeguards required but this was not simply a further manifestation of the defensiveness of British business. The purpose of the report was not to outline business opinion per se but to influence government policy as the negotiations on the free trade area were to resume in October 1957, following the lull in activity while the Treaty of Rome was being ratified by the Six.[102] In such circumstances it made sense "to outline the shape which we think an EFTA convention requires to take if it is to be acceptable to any but minority opinion in British industry and commerce."[103] Or, put another way, it would stipulate "the minimum terms that would be acceptable" to British industry.[104]

Confirmation of an increasingly positive mood about the FTA proposals came in November. Instead of a referendum, the FBI Grand Council meeting in September had agreed to hold a special conference to continue the debate on the proposals in which individual trade associations could set out their positions, on the basis of which FBI policy could be determined. This was a better indication of business opinion. Seventeen trade associations had submitted their views, while the rest presented them at the meeting. As shown in Table 5.1, the vast majority of those who spoke were in favor of a free trade area given the safeguards set out in the *Joint Report*. There were important industries, beyond the paper industry, which remained opposed, but despite the best efforts of representatives of these industries, the *Joint Report* was endorsed by a large majority at the meeting.

This marks a key stage in the development of British business thinking. Companies and trade associations were now far better informed about the implications of the FTA proposals than in October 1956 and most trade associations who had voiced an opinion then in support of the proposals were still positive and had been joined by the majority of associations which had not expressed a view back in 1956. The only significant industry that had clearly moved away from supporting the proposals was the cotton industry: In October 1956 opinion had been split, now it was "opposed, unless." By

[100] MRC MSS200/F/1/1/193, Grand Council meeting, 18 September 1957.
[101] ABCC, FBI, and NUM, *A Joint Report on the European Free Trade Area* (London: September 1957).
[102] MRC MSS200/F/1/1/193, Sir Hugh Beaver, Grand Council meeting, 18 September 1957.
[103] TNA CAB134/1862, ES(EI)(57)256.
[104] MRC MSS200/F/1/1/193, Beaver, Grand Council meeting, 13 November 1957.

Table 5.1. *Views Expressed at FBI Grand Council Meeting, November 13, 1957 on the Free Trade Area Proposals*

Speaker	Organization or Sector Represented	Views of Organization or Sector
J. O. Knowles	Electrical manufacturing industry	Split between "yes, provided" and "no, unless"
G. W. Clarke	N. Midland Regional Council of FBI	Recent swing of opinion to go in
J. Lindley	Cotton spinning and weaving industry associations	"No, unless"
Sir Ernest Goodale	Two trade associations including Furnishing Fabric Manufacturers' Federation	"Yes, provided"
Sir Graham Larmor	Irish linen industry	In favor
C. H. Mackenzie	Scottish Council of FBI	Government would push on for political reasons, i.e., make best of
J. Lilliman	Nottingham Lace Federation	Emphatically opposed
F. Johnstone	Lace manufacturer	In favor
J. W. F. Morton	Furnishing Fabric Federation	Split between sections year ago and still so
F. A. Martin	E & W Ridings Regional Council of FBI	"Yes, provided"
P. Thirkell Cox	Iron and steel wire industry	"Yes, provided"
E. H. Boas	Surgical Dressing Manufacturers' Association	Uncertain to vote in industry or national interest
E. Simons	British Jewellers Association including the Fancy Goods Association	"Yes, provided"
G. Brearley	Association of British Chemical Manufacturers	In favor
E. N. Hiley	Brass foundry industry	"Yes, provided"
T. C. Fraser	Wool Textile Delegation	"Yes, provided"

Name	Industry/organisation	Position
R. Viner	Sheffield Cutlery Manufacturers' Association and the silverware trade	Unequivocally opposed
K. Marshall	Iron industry	In favor
R. W. Todd	Building and civil engineering contractors working overseas	Little difference
N. J. Campbell	National Paint Federation	"Yes, provided"
C. E. Bridges	Society of British Paint Manufacturers	"Yes, provided"
E. S. Franklin	British Chemical Plant Manufacturers' Association	"Yes, provided"
E. H. T. Hoblyn	Food machinery industry	"Yes, provided"
H. Kennewell	Hosiery industry	Importance of safeguards
D. C. Bulloch	Not known	Opposed
H. M. Braid	Scottish whisky industry	"Yes, provided"
W. R. M. Watson	Paper and board industry	"No, unless"
J. S. G. Clark	Timber trade	"No, unless"
J. A. Talbot	Paper maker	"No, unless"
E. Edwards	Corsetry industry	Importance of definition of origin
H. E. Cookson	Not known	Could support the resolution

Source: MRC MSS200/F/1/1/193, FBI Grand Council meeting, 13 November 1957.

November 1957 Peter Tennant believed "those who opposed the free trade area within the FBI were weaker than they had been and now tended to be somewhat ashamed of their views."[105] The vote also marked a significant development in business' public position: The FBI was now committed to the idea of a free trade area "in a corporate sense."[106] This also had important implications for the government: It was no longer as necessary to frame policy in order to persuade domestic doubters.[107]

THE BASIS FOR BUSINESS VIEWS

On what basis had business reached this position? As mentioned previously, it is common to relate attitudes to trade liberalization to sectoral competitiveness and Moravcsik applies this model directly in his analysis of British business attitudes to European integration at this time.[108] Certainly economic interests were a key concern for business but it would only be after the negotiations were complete that such a judgment could be made definitively and the detail of the negotiations mattered. For example, one of the key safeguards raised by business related to the origin of goods.[109] It was necessary to know where each shipment of goods had come from in order to determine which goods should genuinely qualify as having been produced in the free trade area and thus be free of duty. There were two possible criteria for determining this: a percentage criterion, where a specified percentage of the price or cost of the good had to originate within the free trade area; or a process criterion, where certain manufacturing processes had to occur within the free trade area for the goods to be deemed to have originated there.

British industry was used to operating such a rules of origin scheme as part of Imperial Preference. Nevertheless, it was quickly realized that this was "one of the most important technical problems to be solved" in any European free trade area.[110] A 25 percent origin criterion was originally proposed but this was quickly raised to 50 percent, yet this was still criticized by some as being too low while others complained about its impact on raw material imports from the Commonwealth.[111] In addition, most textile

---

[105] TNA BT258/28, report by Percival, 10th departmental meeting, 14 November 1957; and BT205/262, TN(FT)(57)60, "Board of Trade Progress Report No. 8," 18 November 1957.
[106] MRC MSS200/F/3/D3/3/23, Kipping, note of a telephone conversation, 18 April 1958.
[107] TNA BT205/262, TN(FT)(57)60, "Board of Trade Progress Report No. 8," 18 November 1957.
[108] Moravcsik, *Choice for Europe*, 38 and 125.
[109] Miriam Camps, "Problems of Freer Trade in Europe," *Planning*, Vol. 24, (1958), 118.
[110] TNA BT258/2, letter to trade associations, 3 January 1957 and TNA BT205/261, TN(FT)(57)1, 1 January 1957.
[111] TNA BT258/135, Lacey to various Board of Trade officials, 27 February 1957, and TNA BT11/5552, Munro to Nowell, 2 January 1957.

industries rejected out of hand any use of the percentage criterion, preferring to rely solely on a process definition.[112] Perhaps the most vehement critic was the Wool Textile Delegation, which was in favor of the free trade area proposals in general but was clear that it saw this issue as "very important" and that it was "very emphatic" in rejecting a percentage criterion.[113] Until this technical issue was resolved its views on the wider proposals were preliminary and fragile.

Secondly, calculating the economic interests of a business sector was not a straightforward exercise. During 1956 and 1957 various studies of the likely impact of the free trade area proposals on British industry were made. Some focused on particular sectors, while others looked at the overall impact. Table 5.2 sets out the findings of five such studies by the government, A. R. Smith, head of ICI's intelligence department, the Economist Intelligence Unit, *The Economist*, and the economist Hans Liesner. All of these studies admitted they were fairly rudimentary and were based on different assumptions and timescales. In looking at Table 5.2 it can be seen that while there was some agreement on certain sectors which were expected to gain, such as most woolen goods, and others which would lose, such as clocks and watches, there was considerable disagreement about many sectors. For example, three of the studies had the paper industry as a sector likely to lose out but Liesner believed it might gain. The leather industry and the iron and steel industry were similarly presented with conflicting accounts of the impact of a free trade area.

Perhaps most interesting is the case of the car industry. According to the Economist Intelligence Unit in *Britain and Europe*, a free trade area "will provide a magnificent opening" for the British motor vehicle industry: it would increase its share of the FTA import market from 16.1 percent in 1955 to 20 percent in 1970 and sales to Europe would rise from 7 percent of sales to 21 percent over the same period.[114] The study found the motor vehicle industry would gain the most from a free trade area, in a context where most sectors benefited. The other two studies to specify the motor vehicle industry were much more circumspect, being uncertain of the outcome, while a survey for the Standard Motor Company contrasted markedly:

Competition when the free trade area is finally established will be very severe. The only sector of the market where the UK position seems reasonable assured is that of heavy commercial vehicles. With regard to cars the competition both design and price wise will be extremely severe....

[112] TNA BT258/229, "Process Definition and IM3 Industries," February 1957, and "Trade War on Two Fronts," *The Times*, 22 October 1956, 3.
[113] TNA BT258/10, "Notes of a Meeting with Representatives of the Wool Textile Industry to Discuss the Proposed European Free Trade Area . . . on 21 February 1957."
[114] EIU, *Britain and Europe*, 147–8.

Not only will the free trade area result in more fierce competition on the continent, but also within the UK . . . the home market will be eliminated.[115]

Expectations within the car industry were apparently divided, just like the economic assessments.[116] Nevertheless, despite the mixed picture which emerged from these studies and the dangers set out in the study by Standard, the Society of Motor Manufacturers and Traders (SMMT) supported the opening of negotiations on a free trade area in the FBI's October 1956 referendum. This position of favoring the FTA was later endorsed again by the SMMT provided certain safeguards were met.[117] Similarly, the studies showed a mixed position for the iron and steel industry, yet the British Iron and Steel Federation (BISF) was even more positive than the SMMT about the free trade area in October 1956 and maintained this position in November 1957.

How can this apparent discrepancy be explained? The problem is the focus in the economic assessments on the trade effects of a free trade area, that is the gains from free access to the markets of other member states compared to the losses from opening up the British domestic market to continental competition. European integration was being viewed in terms of market integration. Businessmen viewed the topic differently. At a British Institute of Management conference to consider *Britain and Europe*, K. D. Bull, the head of marketing analysis at Ford Motor Company Ltd, rejected the assessment of the impact of a free trade area on the motor industry. "Disappointing as it might seem," he remarked, "he thought it futile to try to estimate the gains and losses. In highly competitive markets national distinctions would cease to exist and the British industry's volume would be determined by the individual successes of its constituent companies."[118] He added, "The initial importance of the changes would not be in the gains and losses but in the impetus they would give to development of the best techniques of design, development and marketing." Firms, not sectors, were the relevant unit of analysis when considering the impact of integration. More than this, Bull was also implying that the response of individual firms mattered and that this response was inappropriately measured in terms of short-term trade changes. As a number of commentators pointed out at the time, the free trade area would be a challenge for management. To sum up, the impact

---

[115] MRC MSS226/ST/3/O/EU/6, "Survey of the European Motor Industry with Special Reference to the European Common Market and Free Trade Area," by the Market and Economic Analysis Department, undated but around 1958. See Timothy Whisler, "The Outstanding Potential Market: The British Motor Industry and Europe, 1945–75," *Journal of Transport History*, Vol. 15, No. 1 (1994), 1–19.

[116] TNA SUPP14/391, Cullen to Moore, 5 November 1956.

[117] MRC MSS226/ST/3/O/EU/2, "European Integration: Customs Union or FTA," by the British Manufacturers Committee (probably of the SMMT), undated.

[118] "Impact of Free Trade," *Birmingham Chamber of Commerce Journal* (April 1958), 453.

Table 5.2. *Assessments of Sectors Likely to Win or Lose in a Free Trade Area*

(1)	(2)	(3)	(4)	(5)
		Sectors likely to gain		
Most engineering	Aluminum	Motor vehicles	Wool	Aircraft
Most capital goods	Chemicals	Chemicals	Chemicals	Tractors
High quality woolen goods	Aircraft	Wool	Some engineering – diesel engines	Power-generating machinery
Man-made fibers except rayon	Furniture	Electrical engineering	Some electrical equipment	Cosmetics, soaps and polishes
Iron and steel	Shipbuilding	General engineering		Rubber tyres and tubes
	Plastics	Rubber manufactures		Paints and varnishes
	Electrical engineering	Steel		Nickel
	Radio and electronic components	Hosiery		Mineral tar and related crude chemicals
	Rubber	Clothing		Textile machinery
	Wool	Nonferrous metals		Woolen and worsted fabrics
	Some iron and steel	Metal manufactures		Plastics
	Leather	Aircraft		Bicycles
	Some heavy engineering	Shipbuilding		Leather
	Atomic energy	Oil refining		Shipbuilding
		Building materials		Pulp and paper products
		Glass		
		Scientific instruments		
		Sports goods		

Sectors likely to lose

Cotton	Cotton	Optical goods and instruments	Zinc
Optical and scientific instruments	Surgical instruments	Clocks and watches	Watches and clocks
Some fine chemicals	Paper	Some scientific instruments	Wood and cork manufacture
Clocks and watches	Pottery	Paper	Lead
Silk	Cameras	Rayon	Travel goods
Rayon	Glassware	Cotton	Cement
Some electrical equipment	Optical goods		Iron and steel
Dyestuffs	Timber		Tin
Pharmaceuticals	Iron founding		Pottery
Cheap woolens	Clocks and watches		Synthetic fiber fabrics
	Cutlery		Essential oils
			Glass and glassware
			Jute manufactures
			Prefabricated buildings
			Furniture
Uncertain/neutral impact	*Uncertain*	*Uncertain*	
Motor vehicles	China	Machine tools	
	Footwear	Electrical engineering	
	Toys	Motor vehicles	
	Neutral	*Neutral*	
	Railway engineering	Shipbuilding	
	Jute manufactures	Coal	
	Furniture	Steel	
		Some engineering components	

The studies are not strictly comparable as they are not consistent, and not always clear, in the timescales of their studies. Nor are the lists comprehensive. (1) TNA CAB134/1239, ES(EI)(56) 2, Appendix D, 23 July 1956. (2) A. R. Smith, head of ICI Intelligence Department, Liberal Summer School, *The Times*, 6 August 1957, 3. (3) EIU, *Britain and Europe* (EIU, London, December 1957). (4) *The Economist*, 12 October 1957, Supplement. (5) H. H. Liesner, "The European Common Market and British Industry," *Economic Journal* (June 1958), 302–16.

depended on firms' responses to the challenge and the dynamic effects that would ensue.

In this respect, business perceptions, rather than just the economic realities, were what counted. These perceptions of the free trade area were influenced by a wide range of factors, including their perceptions of the comparative advantages and disadvantages in their working and institutional environment or landscape. The trade effects were only one part of this story. Significantly, the SMMT's study concluded that the British motor vehicle industry ought to be able to meet the challenge of the free trade area as long as government created and maintained the right economic conditions.[119] More specifically, this meant the level of purchase tax on motor vehicles ought to be reduced closer to European tax levels and that the SMMT's preference was for a general flat rate tax levied on end-products (see Chapter 10).[120] Such domestic issues mattered: In considering the state of the car industry across Western Europe, it was usual not simply to consider the relative position in terms of production, design, and marketing but also the relative tax position applied to cars.[121] Thus the commercial consequences for the sector was still the dominant consideration but these went beyond just the net trade effects and reflected an awareness that European integration raised issues of political as well as economic integration even in a free trade area. Recognition of this helps to explain the apparent paradox of sectors' opinions on the FTA proposals not always matching up to the expected trade effects. The nature and importance of these wider considerations differed between sectors and even between firms but, as shown in Part III of this book, they played an important, but to date largely neglected, role in the attitudes of British industry to European integration.

CONCLUSION

The free trade area was a key episode in the history of Britain and European integration. The existing historiography is divided over the attitude and role of British industry in this episode. One school depicts industry as surprisingly positive and relatively influential in policy. The other paints a much more critical picture of industry being defensive and on the periphery of policy-making. Here, it is argued, both sides overstate their cases. More than this, like the FBI at the time, their focus on the either/or nature of business opinion clouds the issue more than it illuminates it. There was much similarity in the overall view of business – it was the emphasis on safeguards that mattered, rather than the position of being in favor or opposed – but ultimately this

---

[119] MRC MSS226/ST/3/O/EU/2, "European Integration: Customs Union or FTA," by the British Manufacturers Committee (probably of the SMMT), undated.

[120] TNA BT258/176, "European Free Trade Area," 21 March 1957.

[121] MRC MSS226/ST/3/O/EU/6, "Survey of the European Motor Industry."

was a balance of opinion. Agreement on the importance of safeguards did not mean consensus on the form of those safeguards, as has been shown here with regard to rules of origin. It is only when one acknowledges the importance of these details, the wide range of factors, not just trade effects, which fed into the creation of business opinion, and the resulting diversity of that opinion, that one comes to appreciate the complexity of the subject. From an early date, business viewed European integration as more than negative integration but as something that could alter the whole landscape in which firms operated.

Secondly, if one turns to business' influence on policy at this time, it is clear that the peak-level business organizations played a crucial role as intermediaries between government and the wider business community. On the general issue of the free trade area, it was to these bodies that government turned for advice and on which the government relied to create the desired public position of business on Europe, and in this these organizations were broadly successful at this time. As Norman Kipping suggested, these were acts of leadership. However, even the case of a free trade area, deliberately intergovernmental and limited in scope, raised detailed and technical issues. In these circumstances, the peak-level representative bodies had a limited role and the government turned to the meso-level of trade associations for business opinion and advice. In this sense the peak-level organizations were neither representative nor able to represent the wider business community on key aspects of European integration.

Finally, despite these issues and uncertainties, the response in November 1957 was strongly in favor of a free trade area. One needs to remember this when faced with the common image of British industry at this time as overly defensive and protectionist. The chemical industry was heavily protected but it was one of the strongest supporters of the free trade area proposals. There was no desire to turn Britain's back on the Commonwealth but there was a realization of the need to be engaged with European integration: Britain could not just stand by and do nothing. However, British business was soon to find out that the rest of the world was not standing still either and that an unpalatable choice would have to be made between Europe and the Commonwealth.

6

Creating EFTA, Applying to the EC and de Gaulle's Veto, 1958–1963

The free trade area was seen as a way for Britain to accommodate the common market and the Commonwealth. Its failure to win support in the common market countries, notably France, left the British government and British industry with a problem: how to respond? It could turn its back on the Six, it could try to find some accommodation, supported by the other non-European Community members of the OEEC, or it could apply to join the EC itself. Although the first of these seemed appealing to some in the immediate aftermath of the collapse of the FTA negotiations, the real choice was between the second and third options. The preference remained the second option, to continue to try to create an open trading bloc across Western Europe. It was to this end that Britain helped to establish the European Free Trade Association (EFTA) with other countries that were unable or unwilling to join the EC.[1] Over time, it became clear that an accommodation between the two groups was unlikely to occur and so opinion began to move to the third option, joining the EC. Finally, on July 31, 1961 the British government announced its attention to open negotiations with the Six on the possibility of Britain becoming a member of the EC. However, after a lengthy period of negotiations, President de Gaulle effectively vetoed the British application in January 1963 and the negotiations ended later that month.

   For most historians the decision to apply for membership represented an historic turning point in British policy.[2] However, for some, the change, while still significant, was less dramatic: "The British bid was not a bold leap into a new European future, as it is sometimes portrayed, but a defensive, rearguard action of a government that was quickly running out of ideas."[3] In the official history of the negotiations, Alan Milward highlights the

---

[1] The initial members of EFTA were Britain, Sweden, Norway, Denmark, Switzerland, Austria, and Portugal.

[2] Oliver Daddow, *Britain and Europe since 1945: Historiographical Perspectives on Integration* (Manchester: Manchester University Press, 2004).

[3] R. T. Griffiths and Stuart Ward, "The End of a Thousand Years of History": The Origins of Britain's Decision to Join the European Community, 1955–61," in R. T. Griffiths and Stuart Ward (eds.), *Courting the Common Market: The First Attempt to Enlarge the European Community 1961–1963* (London: Lothian Foundation Press, 1996), 7–37.

significance of 1962 rather than 1961, for it was only then that the British government acknowledged that the Commonwealth's central position in Britain's national strategy could no longer be maintained.[4]

Again, there is a split both over the extent to which business moved in favor of entry into the EC and its influence on policy. Those that see British business as on the whole positive in its response to the FTA, similarly bring out the change of opinion in industry in the course of 1960 away from EFTA towards EC membership.[5] Equally, those who present business attitudes as more constrained and conditional in the earlier period, continue to highlight these elements, for example, the cautious tone of the FBI's policy statement *British Industry and Europe*, which was released two weeks before the government announced its intention to apply for membership in July 1961, and to play down the influence of business on policy-making.[6] Thus, Lieber notes, "the major interest groups played a rather limited role in the common market decision," but significantly adds, "Had the business sector been opposed, it is scarcely conceivable that Britain could have sought entry."[7]

Building on the arguments in the previous chapters, it will be suggested here that, once more, it is too simplistic to depict business opinion as a homogeneous entity pro- or anti-EC membership and that influence on policy took a variety of forms from a variety of different locations. Business organizations were more directly influential over membership of EFTA than over the application to join the EC, but as shown in Chapter 3, the changing investment strategies of individual firms had an indirect influence. Even in the case of EFTA, business influence came from interaction with its counterpart organizations in Western Europe, not through direct influence over government policy. Concentrating on the direct political influence of business on the development of national government policy ignores these wider influences. The chapter is divided into three main sections, dealing with the creation of EFTA, the shift towards EC membership, and the period from July 1961 to de Gaulle's veto.

---

[4] Alan S. Milward, *The United Kingdom and the European Community, Vol. 1: The Rise and Fall of a National Strategy 1945–1963* (London: Frank Cass, 2002), 1–9.

[5] Robert L. Pfaltzgraff, *Britain Faces Europe* (Philadelphia: University of Pennsylvania Press, 1969), 48–51; Nora Beloff, *The General Says No* (Harmondsworth: Penguin, 1963); John W. Young, "Britain and the EEC, 1956–73: An Overview," in Brian Brivati and Harriet Jones (eds.), *From Reconstruction to Integration: Britain and Europe since 1945* (Leicester: Leicester University Press, 1993), 105; and Milward, *Rise and Fall*, 359.

[6] Robert Lieber, *British Politics and European Unity: Parties, Elites and Pressure Groups* (Berkeley: University of California Press, 1970), 96–7; Jacqueline Tratt, *The Macmillan Government and Europe: A Study in the Process of Policy Development* (Basingstoke: Macmillan, 1996), 103–4; and Wolfram Kaiser, *Using Europe, Abusing the Europeans: Britain and European Integration, 1945–63* (Basingstoke: Macmillan, 1996), 171.

[7] Lieber, *British Politics*, 132–3.

THE CREATION OF EFTA

Just as British industry was coming to terms with a free trade area towards the end of 1957, business in the Six seemed to be moving against it. In particular, French industry, like the French government, was hostile with its peak-level association, the Conseil National du Patronat Francais (CNPF), leading the opposition.[8] With progress towards the free trade area stalling during 1958 in the face of this hostility as well as political instability in France, attention in Britain turned to how to increase the pressure on the Six to agree to the FTA before January 1, 1959 when tariff discrimination between the Six and the rest of the OEEC would occur for the first time if there was no agreement. The government told business representatives that "contacts on an industrial level could be of great importance at this stage, as it was possible that the industrialists and unionists of Europe might be more receptive to argument than their politicians."[9] They were encouraged to highlight the potential opportunities in the FTA and the potential "unpleasant alternatives" if there was no settlement.

Accordingly, the peak-level business organizations renewed their efforts to sell the FTA to their counterparts in Europe and to put pressure on the CNPF, which in turn might persuade the French government. At least four channels were used. First, there were bilateral meetings with their national equivalents.[10] Secondly, there was the International Chamber of Commerce (ICC). In May 1958, the ICC Council adopted a statement supporting the creation of a free trade area, linked to the EC. It concluded that the ICC would "deeply deplore failure to establish the FTA in 1958 . . . . Failure of the negotiations might in fact lead to the economic and political division of western Europe, carrying with it the danger of a return to methods of trade discrimination."[11] Significantly, the statement had been drafted by Lincoln Steel, who was not only chairman of the FBI Overseas Trade Policy Committee but also a Vice-President of the ICC.[12] The statement's unanimous adoption was seen as evidence that the British strategy of working via business federations was having an impact: It was believed that the CNPF was now split on the issue of a FTA and that those in favor were a substantial minority, if not a majority.[13]

---

[8] MRC MSS200/F/3/S1/21, Tennant to various, 3 October 1957; MRC MSS200/F/3/O5/2/2, Pilkington to Tennant, 26 March 1958; and TNA BT11/5616, CCI 54th meeting, 12 December 1958.

[9] TNA BT11/5616, CCI 52nd meeting, 26 March 1958.

[10] Ibid., Wills, CCI 52nd meeting, 26 March 1958; and FBI, *Annual Report for 1958*, 22.

[11] TNA FO371/134501, ICC Council, "The Linking of a Free Trade Area with the European Economic Community," 6–7 May 1958.

[12] Ibid., "Note for the record," by Warner, 9 May 1958.

[13] Ibid., "Note for the record," Bretherton, 10 May 1958 and related correspondence.

The third channel used by British industry was the Council of European Industrial Federations (CEIF) and the closely related Council of the Directors of European Industrial Federations (CDEIF). The latter body met annually, partly as a social gathering but also as a forum to allow the directors of the main national industrial federations to discuss issues in depth. The CEIF was more formal and met more regularly, with a secretariat based in Paris.[14] Both forums had discussed European integration previously and the FBI made strenuous efforts at the 1958 meetings to explore the possibilities of agreement between the Six and the "Outer Six."[15] To this end, the CEIF established a working party under Axel Iveröth (of the Industriförbundet, the Swedish national industrial federation) with the aim of producing a statement acceptable to all the member federations, including the CNPF, on the issue.[16]

Finally, there were the close relations among the "Outer Six" which helped in the creation of EFTA. Towards the end of February 1958 a three-day "European industrial conference" took place in London organized by the UK Council of the European Movement. The conference was attended by industrialists and trade unionists from across Western Europe.[17] Unlike previous such conferences the British contingent, the largest of any nation, contained "a strong FBI delegation." Although *The Director* felt that the conference "fell rather flat," it proved to be a significant turning point in relations between the national industrial federations.[18] First, the extent to which French business was still opposed to the FTA proposals became apparent. Secondly, by contrast, it highlighted the degree of unity of opinion among the non-Six delegates. [19] As a result, the Swedish federation proposed a meeting of representatives of the industrial federations of Austria, Denmark, Norway, Sweden, Switzerland, and the UK. From this and subsequent meetings an approved joint statement, *Free Trade in Western Europe*, emerged in April 1958.[20] Proposing the title "Euromarket" for the free trade area, it set out agreed positions on a wide range of issues. In British eyes the purpose of the statement was, first, as a show of unity but also as an appeal to Germany and the Benelux countries while maintaining pressure on the French.[21] However, it failed to make the hoped for breakthrough in the OEEC negotiations

[14] Neil Rollings and Matthias Kipping, "Private Transnational Governance in the Heyday of the Nation-State: the Council of European Industrial Federations (CEIF)," *Economic History Review*, Vol. 61 (2008), forthcoming.

[15] FBI, *Annual Report for 1958*, 11.

[16] TNA FO371/134501, Tennant to Gore–Booth, 13 May 1958.

[17] UK Council of the European Movement, *European Industrial Conference* (London, February 1958).

[18] *The Director*, April 1958, 62.

[19] MRC MSS200/F/3/O5/2/2, Note for Grand Council, 14 March 1958.

[20] *Free Trade in Western Europe: A Joint Statement by the Industrial Federations and Employers' Organisations of Austria, Denmark, Norway, Sweden, Switzerland and the United Kingdom* (Paris, 1958).

[21] MRC MSS200/F/3/O5/2/2, Tennant to Palmer, 31 March 1958.

on the FTA. A further meeting and communiqué by the national industrial federations of the "Outer Six" in November was equally unsuccessful; the FTA negotiations collapsed and tariff discrimination within the OEEC occurred.[22]

Gloom, despondency and some bitterness quickly evaporated as the need for action was realized.[23] Although the marginal discrimination British industry would experience would not be that harmful, Lincoln Steel told the government that "the psychological effect of uncertainties about the long-term prospect could be serious."[24] He added that business could see no satisfactory alternative to a free trade area. Given this, there seemed to be a consensus that it was crucial for the non-Six to continue to work closely together. To this end, the FBI representatives went to Stockholm a few days later to meet their Swedish counterparts. There it was agreed to study the feasibility of a free trade area of the UK, Scandinavia and possibly Austria and Switzerland as well.[25] Other meetings followed and these discussions were still ongoing when the governments of the Outer Six, now joined by Portugal, began active consideration of joining in some form of association.[26] Agreement was reached remarkably quickly, with the Seven signing the Stockholm Convention in November 1959 to create EFTA. The role of organized business does stand out at the outset of the EFTA initiative. To Lieber, the FBI played a "prominent" role in the establishment of EFTA: "Not only did the Federation lead the government on the issue, but it provided an important impetus for the whole arrangement" with Norman Kipping, the FBI director-general "sometimes dangerously in the lead."[27] The way in which the national federations worked together ahead of their governments was an important factor in starting the EFTA initiative. In this respect, Tratt may be right in suggesting that the role of these federations "should not be over-emphasized as a source of government policy."[28] However, such an argument adopts a very narrow perspective for considering the influence of business and a very traditional view of government–business relations: organized business cannot draft and enact an international treaty. A more encompassing approach is to consider what role the FBI played in the creation of EFTA. The importance of the FBI came from the information which it gained and its contacts in Western Europe, and that its officials had equally close relations with government officials. These contacts provided

[22] MRC MSS200/F/3/S2/2/10, Grand Council meeting, 12 November 1958.

[23] MRC MSS200/F/3/E3/34/8, Pilkington to Tennant, 8 November 1958; and TNA BT205/264, TN(FT)(58)25, "Board of Trade Progress Report No. 15," 14 November 1958.

[24] TNA BT11/5616, CCI meeting, 12 December 1958; and MRC MSS200/F/3/S2/2/10, Grand Council meeting, 10 December 1958.

[25] MRC MSS200/F/3/S2/2/10, Grand Council meeting, 14 January 1958; and TNA BT205/265, TN(FT)(59) 1, "Board of Trade Progress Report No. 17," 7 January 1959.

[26] MRC MSS200/F/3/S2/2/10, Grand Council meeting, 14 January 1958.

[27] Lieber, *British Politics*, 74 and 82.   [28] Tratt, *Macmillan Government*, 43 and 52.

the FBI with information unavailable to the government.[29] Equally, the FBI did not embark on the EFTA initiative without the blessing of ministers. Indeed the government found it helpful.[30]

The role of individuals and informal contact was important in this respect. Peter Tennant, the FBI's Overseas Director, played a crucial role here with his many contacts on the continent and in government.[31] Norman Kipping was also a key player, given his good friendship with Frank Lee, the most important government official in the development of policy on European integration in this period. Similarly, the winding down of the FBI's explicit efforts to move the EFTA discussions forward coincided with a change in the FBI president: Sir Hugh Beaver had come to the end of his term of office and was replaced by the relatively less activist Sir William McFadzean.[32]

The way in which the FBI found out that the British government had started its own discussions with other non-Six governments is illustrative of the complex set of relationships involved and how international links between national federations were sometimes more informative than relations between the FBI and the government, rather than of how the national government had "overtaken" the FBI.[33] The FBI "learned almost by accident" that the discussions were taking place: an FBI official was in Stockholm for a CEIF committee meeting and found out at a dinner with a Swedish official. Surprised to discover this, a FBI representative met with the minister responsible for the EFTA negotiations and extracted a promise from the government to consult fully with the FBI before entering into any commitments.[34] That the FBI did not know about the government talks despite the government blessing talks between the industrial federations shows that the relationship between the FBI and the government was not straightforward and open. However, that the FBI was able to obtain a promise to be consulted does not suggest that after March the government ignored industrial opinion.

Similarly, it has been suggested that British business began to lose its enthusiasm for EFTA over the course of 1959, in part as an explanation for the FBI withdrawing from its leading role.[35] However, the NUM, the ABCC and the FBI were all agreed in their support for EFTA.[36] More than this, the

[29] TNA FO371/134501, Golt to Wilson 9 May 1958, and Gore–Booth note, 16 May 1958.

[30] Norman Kipping, *Summing Up* (Hutchinson, London, 1972), 163; and TNA BT205/264, "Board of Trade Progress Report No. 15," 14 November 1958.

[31] MRC MSS200/F/3/O2/2/16, note of meeting of enlarged steering committee, 17–19 January 1959 and Tennant to Maudling, 22 January 1959.

[32] Lieber, *British Politics*, 79.   [33] Kipping, *Summing Up*, 164.

[34] MRC MSS200/F/3/S2/2/10, McFadzean to Grand Council members, 16 April 1959.

[35] Miriam Camps, *Britain and the European Community 1955–1963* (Princeton: Princeton University Press, 1964), 215–6; and Lieber, *British Politics*, 79.

[36] NUM, *Annual Report for 1959–60*, 11.

FBI's position was informed by a survey of its membership. On summarizing the replies of 114 trade associations and twenty individual members of the Grand Council, it was noted that about 60 percent of the replies thought the formation of the proposed association was desirable "as offering benefits on its own." Expanding on this, it suggested,

Taking into account considerations of wider policy, as well as of direct benefit, about 70% of those replying favoured the negotiation of the proposed association; more than half the rest were prepared to acquiesce in it. Thus almost 90% were prepared to support the proposed association with varying degrees of enthusiasm.[37]

It was estimated that the net industrial output of the industries definitely opposed amounted to not more than 5 percent of total industrial output.[38]

One of the main motivations here was the desire to ensure that Britain did not become isolated in Europe but also it remained a hope that unity among the Seven would persuade the Six to accept the wider free trade area proposals; EFTA was seen as a bridge-building exercise.[39] There was virtual unanimity in the responses to the FBI questionnaire that the form of EFTA should help association. However, important as this was, the intrinsic benefits to British business of membership of EFTA were played up as just as important. As the ABCC's free trade area panel concluded, "Any proposals for a partial free trade area of the Outer Seven must stand by themselves and the UK must be prepared for such a free trade area to go forward alongside the EEC if it proved impossible to reach agreement with it."[40] Accordingly, efforts were made to assuage the concerns of the "sensitive" industries such as the paper and watch industries that were likely to be hit hardest by EFTA competition and to play up the potential compensations from vulnerable German trade to EFTA.[41] There is little sign here then of any waning of business support for EFTA as expressed publicly by the peak national federations.

The results of the 1959 FBI questionnaire on EFTA did offer some hint of discontent, however.[42] In addition, to those sectors who opposed EFTA outright, there was a second group who tended to acquiesce to EFTA, or even favored it, but who often saw no direct benefit for themselves. Significant here are the trade associations and company representatives concerned. Those that saw no direct benefit included the British Non-Ferrous Metals Federation, the Joint Iron Council, the Aluminium Industry Council, BEAMA, the British Man-Made Fibres Federation, the Association of

[37] TNA CAB134/1870, ES(EI)(59)32.
[38] TNA BT11/5729, "Consultative Committee for Industry: Brief for Meeting at 2 pm on 29th July 1959," no date.
[39] GLA MS17558, ABCC Free trade area meeting, 21 May 1959.   [40] Ibid.
[41] MRC MSS200/F/3/O5/2/1, Whitehorn to trade associations, 22 June 1959.
[42] Miriam Camps, *The European Free Trade Association: A Preliminary Appraisal* (London: PEP, 1959), 10–1.

British Chemical Manufacturers, and the British Iron and Steel Federation, all major trade associations and representing a significant proportion of total industrial output. Many of them had supported the free trade area proposals in 1956 and 1957.

More than this, individual businessmen who were actively involved in FBI work in this area were associated with these trade associations. The President of the Aluminium Industry Council was Fred Catherwood, soon to become director-general of the National Economic Development Office; Sir Archibald Forbes, an ex-president of the FBI (1951–53) and frequent chairman of FBI committees, was the chairman of the Iron and Steel Board 1946–49, 1953–59, and Sir William Palmer, who chaired the working group which consulted with government on European integration, was a leading member of the British Man-Made Fibres Federation.

Most noteworthy in this respect was Lincoln Steel, ICI director, and chairman of the FBI's Overseas Trade Policy Committee since 1950 and also of its European Integration Panel since its creation. He was also an FBI representative on the government's Consultative Committee for Industry, chairman of the British National Committee of the ICC and a vice-president of the ICC. Steel had been criticized for his bias towards the FTA proposals (see Chapter 5) but now he set out his "misgivings" about EFTA and the importance of keeping parity with EC trade liberalization.[43] Speaking in a personal capacity, Steel reiterated his concerns about EFTA to ministers: "As a commercial proposition from the chemical industry's point of view the proposal had little or no merit."[44] Indeed, Steel used his position to criticize the FBI's draft EFTA questionnaire and to get it changed. The most important change related to the second question. Here it was added that although government officials saw intrinsic merit in EFTA and that it might improve the prospects of an accommodation with the Six, there could be "no guarantees" that this was the case and that EFTA might "soften or harden the diplomatic outlook" in the Six.[45] Although the FBI leadership was committed to EFTA and to presenting it in a positive light, not all of its leaders held this position. What is significant is the way in which the balance over EFTA was very different from that over the free trade area, and, as we shall see later, over EC membership: Opinion shifted in relation to the particular features of the proposals.

Once the peak level associations had declared their support for the EFTA proposals and the government had announced its intention to negotiate an agreement, the role of these peak-level bodies was limited. Given the speed

---

43 Theordore Bromund, "From Empire to Europe: Material Interests, National Identities, and British Policies towards European Integration, 1956–1963," Ph.D. dissertation, Yale University, 1999, 389–91.

44 TNA BT11/5616, CCI meeting, 27 May 1959.

45 Bromund, "From Empire to Europe," 395–7.

of the negotiations, there was little time for education or publicity about the potential opportunities in EFTA for British industry. Technical issues came to the fore of which one is particularly noteworthy, that is the issue of origin and dumping. As shown in Chapter 5, the issue of the criterion of origin of goods had been a highly contentious issue for some parts of British industry, notably textiles, in their consideration of the free trade area proposals. In the EFTA negotiations, the issue remained a complex and contentious issue but officials were determined to reach agreement, in part to make sure that it did not become a stumbling block the way it had in the FTA talks and in part to show the Six, and especially France, that such a system was feasible.[46] For most goods, importers could choose either a 50 percent criterion or a process criterion, that is, no more than half of the value of the goods to consist of non-EFTA materials or that one of a specified list of processes had occurred within EFTA in the goods' production. However, for certain specified products – mainly textiles and clothing – only the process criterion applied, a victory for the British textiles industries.[47]

However, it was the concerns expressed by other industries about the rules of origin which were more significant in many ways. This is because it helps to explain the anxieties over EFTA that we have seen from Lincoln Steel with regard to the chemical industry and from other industrialists. It was not simply that EFTA offered few market opportunities to these industries compared to an association which included the Six. In addition, industrialists from these sectors feared dumping, a contentious issue throughout the 1950s. It was a particularly sensitive issue at this time because the government had enacted a new piece of legislation, the UK Customs Duties (Dumping and Subsidies) Act, 1957, which had brought forward many complaints from industry because the onus of proof of dumping rested with the complaining industry rather than government. Within the EFTA negotiations, the Scandinavians and the Swiss favored even more liberal rules of origin than in the FTA negotiations because of their reliance on imports of semi-manufactures from the Six. In contrast, parts of British industry viewed this as opening the doors for a flood of goods being indirectly dumped in Britain.[48] In January 1960, Courtaulds and British Nylon Spinners Ltd. submitted a memorandum to the FBI's OTP committee setting out these concerns, beginning by listing the fifteen trade associations who had raised anti-dumping provisions as one of their issues of concern in the FBI's June 1959 questionnaire.[49] At

[46] TNA BT205/265, TN(FT)(59)5, 22 June 1959.
[47] MRC MSS200/F/3/S2/2/10, D/1113, White, Grand Council meeting, 9 September 1959.
[48] TNA BT205/265, TN(FT)(59)5, "The Stockholm Group: Definition of Origin," 22 June 1959.
[49] MRC MSS200/F/3/O2/4/6, D/1625, "Dumping and the EFTA," Courtaulds Ltd and British Nylon Spinners Ltd, January 1960.

the meeting that discussed the paper, the concerns of British producers of semi-manufactures were expounded:

Many sections of the chemical, textile and steel industries were largely suppliers to other producers. It had been clear in the Stockholm negotiations that there was a conflict of interest between the United Kingdom, whose industries in general embraced all stages of manufacture, and the other members of the EFTA, whose industries were largely finishing industries. His [Sharman's] fears were largely of indirect dumping through EFTA countries from outside the Area, since it was very probable that the finishing industries of the other EFTA countries, so far from resisting the dumping of semi-finished manufactures, would indeed welcome them.[50]

This view received considerable support at the meeting, but little ensued as it was impossible to adjust the Stockholm Convention. Nevertheless, the episode illustrates that important sectors of British industry and major British companies were unhappy with the provisions in the Stockholm Convention and did not feel committed to EFTA. They were willing to acquiesce to EFTA in the hope that it would act as a bridge between the Six and the Seven. When this did not seem to be working, these concerns were voiced more openly, but the underlying concerns had been there from the outset of EFTA.

BETWEEN EFTA AND THE EC

Having signed the Stockholm Convention in November 1959, British government policy was to change rapidly. Less than two years after the signing of the Stockholm Convention and little more than a year after EFTA formally came into existence, Harold Macmillan, the Prime Minister, announced Britain's intention to open negotiations over possible EC membership in July 1961. Some emphasize the importance of political considerations, often US opinion, and the role of Harold Macmillan in changing the direction of government policy.[51] Others, however, make more of the role of business, highlighting how opinion in industry was shifting towards membership from 1960 but that the FBI, even in its statement *British Industry and Europe*, released only weeks before the government announced its intention to apply for EC membership, remained cautious.[52]

What is significant is that those, like Jacqueline Tratt, who downplay the role of business, focus on the FBI and the lack of concerted action to pressure the government to join the EC.[53] Again, it is suggested here that this is looking for too simple and too direct a form of influence. The FBI

---

[50] Ibid., Sharman, FBI Overseas Trade Policy Committee meeting, 20 January 1960.

[51] Richard Mayne, *The Community of Europe* (London: Victor Gollancz, 1962), 148.

[52] Beloff, *General Says No*, 91; and Griffiths and Ward, "End of a Thousand Years of History," 20. See FBI, *British Industry and Europe* (London, July 1961).

[53] Tratt, *Macmillan Government*, 190.

was restrained in its support for EC membership but this does not mean that business had no influence on the decision. It was in this period that British companies embarked on a major investment drive in the Six (see Chapter 3). As Miriam Camps has noted, "without the industrial interest in expanding trade with Europe . . . the first application to join the Community would not have been made as early as 1961."[54] What is clear is that business influence did not flow directly from the peak-level associations but here relied on the actions and the demands of individual firms for EC membership.

We have seen how some industrialists, like Lincoln Steel, had their doubts about EFTA from the outset. Although *The Economist* published an article in December 1958 asking "Join the Common Market?," it detailed significant reservations about joining the EC at that stage.[55] Few industrialists or trade associations made the leap from dislike of EFTA to support for EC membership.[56] Most, like *The Director*, simply dismissed the notion of EC membership out of hand: "There are now few people who see Britain's future as a partner in an exclusive common market group."[57] EFTA was still seen as the best way of bringing about some form of reconciliation between the Six and the Outer Seven and so once it was created business held on to this hope.[58] The situation was then reported and updated regularly in the business press.[59] The prospects of a bridge between the Six and the Seven was still industry's main concern well into the spring of 1961, only weeks before the government was to apply to the EC for membership.[60]

Both for intrinsic reasons and to support this bridge-building aim, it was important for EFTA to flourish. Peak-level business organizations invested their time and money in this. One way was by supporting and publicizing the work of the Export Council for Europe (ECE) to their members. The ECE was set up in November 1960 by the government but also funded by the FBI,

[54] Miriam Camps, "Missing the Boat at Messina and Other Times?" in Brivati and Jones (eds.), *From Reconstruction to Integration*, 141.

[55] "Join the Common Market?" *The Economist* (27 December 1958), 1138–9.

[56] "The Outer Seven," *The Chamber of Commerce Journal* No. 90, (June 1959), 5.

[57] "No Little Europe," *The Director*, Vol. 11, No. 11 (May 1959), 233; and "The Common Market and After," *The Director*, Vol. 11, No. 10 (April 1959), 28–9.

[58] TNA BT258/92, EFTA(WP)(60)13, "Attitude of Industry. Board of Trade Regional Controllers' Reports," Note by the Board of Trade, 5 February 1960; TNA CAB134/1815, EPB(60)4th, 2 May 1960, EPB(60)5th, 30 May 1960, EPB (60) 6th, 4 July 1960; and TNA BT11/5559, Consultative Committee for Industry meeting, CCI 58th, 8 April 1960, and "Palmer Group," note of a meeting 22 March 1961.

[59] "The Next Step," *The Chamber of Commerce Journal* No. 91. (July 1960), 9; "One Europe," *The Chamber of Commerce Journal* No. 91, (September 1960), 9; and "European Outlook," *The Chamber of Commerce Journal* No. 91, (December 1960), 9 are typical.

[60] TNA BT11/5559, EFTA(WP)(61)15, Attitude of industry. Board of Trade Regional Controllers' reports, 20 March 1961; and report on Sir Edward Beharrell's speech as chairman at the Dunlop Rubber Co. Ltd AGM on 29 May 1961, *Rubber and Plastics Weekly*, June 10 1961, 882.

ABCC, NUM, TUC, and City of London and was chaired by Sir William McFadzean, at that point still president of the FBI. It began its work by organizing fact-finding missions to European countries as well as promoting exports to Europe.[61] The general aim was to increase exports to European markets without distinction but at the ECE's first meeting it was agreed that the Council should first prioritize EFTA markets above those in the EC.[62] This was driven by the desire to exploit any tariff advantages, for example, over German goods, and any goodwill towards Britain that might exist as a result of the creation of EFTA.[63] Business organizations also highlighted export opportunities in EFTA themselves. The ABCC and FBI were active in providing information on selling in EFTA markets: The former followed up its pamphlet *The Seven* with another, *EFTA Markets*, 10,000 copies of which were distributed and a further 6,000 sold, while the FBI organized conferences in London, Birmingham and Glasgow, the proceedings of which were then published.[64]

These organizations also maintained bilateral and multilateral links with their continental counterparts.[65] In this context, they helped to build up EFTA by creating networks and arenas for discussion within EFTA. The ABCC was active in bringing together the national chambers of commerce of the Seven to discuss policy on issuing certificates of origin.[66] Arising from these efforts in May 1961 the EFTA Association of Commerce was formed with a secretariat based in London.[67] Similarly, the FBI was active in the creation of the Council of the Industrial Federations of the Outer Seven (CIFEFTA), with its first meeting held in Vienna in January 1960.[68] The

[61] For example "Opportunities in Europe," *Monthly Record of the Manchester Chamber of Commerce*, (30 June 1961), 182–3.

[62] GLA MS14487/6, ABCC European Panel meeting, 7 December 1960.

[63] TNA BT11/5559, EFTA(WP)(60)61; TNA BT258/521, ESC/MTAC(60)(1960)31st meeting, 15 November 1960; and MRC MSS200/F/3/E3/34/7, note of meeting of trade association representatives at the FBI, 11 May 1960.

[64] Lewis Payne, *The Seven: Stockholm Plan for a European Free Trade Association* (London: Chamber of Commerce Publications, 1959); "EFTA markets," *The Bradford Chamber of Commerce Journal*, (November 1960), 27; and FBI, *United Kingdom Trade with Scandanavia and Finland* (London, November 1959).

[65] GLA MS14487/6, report by Sir James Hutchinson on German efforts at bridge-building, 6 April 1960; TNA BT11/5559, Nixon to Ackroyd, 23 June 1960; GLA MS17371, report on request by the French Chamber of Commerce for talks, 7 June 1961; and MRC MSS200/F/3/O2/2/19, letter from McFadzean to leaders of the industrial federations of EFTA, 4 September 1959, reporting on discussions with Berg (President of the BDI) and Bekaert (President of the Belgian federation).

[66] GLA MS17558, European Panel meeting, 26 January 1961.

[67] "EFTA Association of Commerce," *The Times*, 19 May 1961, 23.

[68] Neil Rollings and Matthias Kipping, "Private Transnational Governance in the Heyday of the Nation-State: The Council of European Industrial Federations (CEIF)," *Economic History Review*, Vol. 61 (2008), forthcoming.

FBI also offered to provide the central administration for the operation of CIFEFTA.[69]

This commitment to making a success of EFTA was central to the FBI and ABCC's thinking. Peter Tennant, the FBI's overseas director, set out the issues clearly in the spring of 1960:

We must at the moment give priority to making EFTA as practical a proposition as we can and rally round the weaker brethren in some of the member countries who show little faith in its potential from the point of view of what they can get out of it. But if our bluff is called by the Hallstein proposals [to accelerate the EEC's tariff program] being postponed, we must be ready to negotiate on something more fundamental than just putting off the evil day as far as discrimination is concerned. We must make our minds up as to whether we can live with EFTA and EEC as separate units for an appreciable time or whether we should in fact take some new initiative for a more permanent solution of the European problem. This would involve undoubtedly immediate and appreciable sacrifices in the present in the realm of tariff protection and Imperial Preference in return for ultimate benefits from a wider market. The forthcoming GATT negotiations may offer opportunities for some manouvre in this field in negotiating with EEC but the price of a European solution acceptable to the EEC and to the USA would be a high one to pay and it would mean eating many of the words we have uttered in the past about the sacredness of certain cows.[70]

Here was the corner in which Britain found itself in: accept EFTA and work within it, or make what were perceived to be major sacrifices in order to gain easier access to the markets of the Six. Faced with this increasingly clear choice, it would seem that the FBI leadership still baulked at the idea of EC membership. In September 1960, Sir William McFadzean, the FBI president, told an audience in Copenhagen that there was no possibility of Britain making some bilateral agreement with the Six.[71] Two months later Kipping went further over dinner with Frank Lee and another leading government official.[72] Kipping suggested that opinion in industry had shifted over the previous nine months. A bridge between the Six and the Seven had been seen as essential but this was now felt to be impossible, that Britain could survive without it and that "it would be much better during the next two or three years to put this problem aside as an immediate preoccupation."[73] Instead, EFTA should be built up. In passing this view on to Edward Heath, the minister now responsible for policy on Europe, Lee, who knew Kipping well, added that Kipping reflected "pretty well what the average intelligent industrialist/trader is thinking." With the FBI firmly committed to making a go of EFTA it is not surprising that the FBI played no leading role at this

---

[69] TNA BT11/5559, meeting of the Presidents of the Industrial Federations of EFTA countries, Vienna, 15–16 January 1960.
[70] MRC MSS200/F/3/D3/6/50, "BDI–FBI Talks, 31 March–2 April 1960," by Tennant.
[71] "EFTA 'Step in Right Direction'," *The Times*, 21 September 1960, 8.
[72] Tratt, *Macmillan Government*, 157–8.   [73] Quoted in Ibid., 157–8.

stage in the run up to Britain's application to join the EC during the first half of 1961.[74] The organization's leadership was unwilling or unable to provide a lead on Europe on this occasion. Kipping's memoirs are strikingly brief in their discussion of this period in comparison to the detail before.

Similarly, the FBI's Overseas Trade Policy Panel did not meet from September 1960 until June 1961 when it first considered the draft statement, issued the following month as *British Industry and Europe*, and described as the FBI's "lukewarm" endorsement of British membership of the EC.[75] The five-page statement noted the ongoing discussion about the possibility of Britain applying for EC membership. In this context there were perceived to be three key issues: the negotiation of exceptions to EC policies for Britain, Commonwealth trading relations, and relations with EFTA members.[76] On the last two issues the FBI statement was forthright and illustrated little change of opinion towards EC membership:

First, we would not support any solution which in effect meant that the Commonwealth was to pay a substantial part of the price for British association with the Common Market. Second, it is imperative that Britain's obligations to EFTA, to which this country is not only contractually but morally committed, must be honoured in full. [77]

In conclusion, the statement reiterated the FBI's support for a Europe-wide multilateral trading system and that an end to the Six/Seven divide would be welcomed but that "a large majority of us are of the opinion that it is right not to become committed to formal negotiations with the Six until existing differences over the problems outlined above have been so far narrowed as to offer the prospect of a satisfactory outcome."[78] It was indeed lukewarm about EC membership.

A number of points need to be made about the statement. First, there was some criticism at the FBI Grand Council that the document was too vague and provided no lead for industry.[79] However, whatever his personal views, Lincoln Steel emphasized the need for caution and the conditional nature of any approach towards the Six.[80] This reflected the mood in business: No other key document on European integration was received at the Grand Council or later at the CBI Council with so little apparent contention. In this respect, it was representative of wider business opinion rather than leading it. Yet even this was no mean achievement because it was also clear at Grand Council that business opinion in the country was divided over the whole

---

[74] "Calling on the FBI: 2–the Problem of Europe," *FBI Review* (February 1961), 31–3.

[75] MRC MSS200/F/1/1/217, O.152.61, FBI OTP Panel 4th meeting, 8 June 1961; and "FBI's Provisional Support," *The Times*, 15 July 1961, 8.

[76] FBI, *British Industry and Europe*, 1.   [77] Ibid., 2.   [78] Ibid., 5.

[79] MRC MSS200/F/3/S2/2/11, Grand Council meeting, 12 July 1961, comments by Hirst and Le Mare.

[80] MRC MSS200/F/3/S2/2/11, Grand Council meeting, 12 July 1961.

topic. Much also remained uncertain about the nature of any negotiations. In the article of the Treaty of Rome dealing with applications to join the Community (Article 237) the English language version referred to "amendments" to the Community, while the French version used "adaptations": the former implied the possibility of derogations from the Treaty for new members while the latter did not.[81]

Secondly, there seems to have been little discussion with the government in advance of the statement's publication. Rather, the Foreign Office, if not the government as a whole, were "proceeding on the assumption that we have the backing of industry for an approach to the Six, without having a special review of their reactions," disingenuously arguing that the September 1957 joint statement by the FBI, NUM, and ABCC made it clear that "the general opinion of industry is in favor of an association with the Six, but not at any price" and that the FBI's 1959 questionnaire on EFTA had not invalidated that position.[82] The Foreign Office was accordingly surprised by the ambivalence of the statement and criticized the FBI for its perceived disloyalty.[83] There was, therefore, a distance between the views of the main supporters of EC entry in government (Foreign Office officials) and the leadership of the FBI at this point. In part, this was because of constraints imposed by smaller firms who were less committed to EC membership and who were overrepresented on the FBI's Grand Council, as Lieber has argued.[84] However, it also reflected uncertainty about what membership would entail. Finally, there were moral obligations. As Lincoln Steel put it in relation to EFTA, "it would be disastrous for the good name of the country and indeed of the FBI if the UK appeared to run out on its obligations."[85]

Like the FBI, the ABCC was not particularly active in discussion of EC membership. The last meeting of its FTA panel was in May 1959 but it was not wound up until June 1960 when it was replaced by a new European Panel.[86] At its meeting, the panel agreed on a stance on the same lines as the FBI – on no account taking action adversely affecting Commonwealth exports or breaking obligations to other EFTA countries.[87] In January 1961 the panel continued to stress the priority of making EFTA work above bridge-building with the Six as long as France seemed likely to maintain its opposition to any form of association.[88] Nevertheless, by April the ABCC's Overseas Committee was concerned that the government was

---

[81] Ibid.
[82] TNA BT11/5559, draft letter to Sir Roderick Barclay, unsigned and undated but July 1961.
[83] Kaiser, *Using Europe*, 171.   [84] Lieber, *British Politics*, 97.
[85] MRC MSS200/F/3/S2/2/11, Grand Council meeting, 12 July 1961.
[86] GLA MS14476/17, ABCC Executive Council meeting, 1 June 1960.
[87] GLA MS17558, European Panel meeting, 29 September 1960.
[88] Ibid., European Panel meeting, 26 January 1961.

seriously considering much closer relations with the Six.[89] As the government had not sought the opinion of the regional chambers of commerce it was felt necessary for the ABCC to do this.

Asked if they thought the UK should join the EC, thirty-six chambers had replied by June. Only two chambers were against, a further four too divided and the remaining thirty in favor, though with a range of conditions attached (only one was unconditional).[90] Although many chambers had not replied, the thirty-that had represented 36,000 members and so it was felt safe to conclude that "in broad terms UK chambers of commerce are in favor of the UK joining the common market, that this should be as soon as possible, and if necessary with some problems unresolved and subject to future negotiation." This view was then endorsed at the ABCC's annual conference.[91]

The survey illustrated to the ABCC leadership that the business community was more positive towards the common market than had been expected and ahead of the leadership of these representative organizations. As business became increasingly concerned about the continuing delay in an agreement being reached between the Six and the Seven, it also wanted an end to the resulting uncertainty that was hampering forward planning in some industries.[92] While the FBI and ABCC viewed this in terms of making the most of EFTA, some individuals and trade associations, were becoming increasingly disillusioned by EFTA and began to favor EC entry. The Whitehall report most often noted as marking a change in the government's position by calling for a "near identification" with the EC, and written by a committee chaired by Frank Lee in May 1960, noted the "great uneasiness, amounting to almost dismay, among leading industrialists" at the prospect of exclusion from the markets of the Six.[93] If EFTA could not deliver a bridge to a wider European economic grouping then EC membership was increasingly preferable to these individuals. The business press was also moving in favor of joining the EC: *The Economist* and the *Financial Times* both announced their support for British entry during 1960 and *The Director*, the journal of the Institute of Directors, in April 1961.[94]

During 1960 most companies still wanted an economic grouping covering the whole of Western Europe but it is clear that they were increasingly developing a strategy to deal with a Six–Seven split. Company annual reports

---

[89] GLA MS14487/6, Overseas Committee meeting, 12 April 1961.

[90] Ibid., Overseas Committee meeting, summary attached to minutes 7 June 1961.

[91] "Association of British Chambers of Commerce 101st Annual Conference," *Monthly Record of the Manchester Chamber of Commerce*, No. 72, (31 July 1961), 209–13.

[92] Timothy Whisler, "The Outstanding Potential Market: The British Motor Industry and Europe, 1945–75," *Journal of Transport History*, Vol. 15, No. 1 (1994), 10; and TNA CAB134/1816, EPB(60)20, "The Prospects of the Motor Industry," 24 June 1960.

[93] TNA CAB134/1819, EQ(60)27, 27 May 1960.

[94] Lieber, *British Politics*, 219; and Robert L. Pfaltzgraff, *Britain Faces Europe* (Philadelphia: University of Pennsylvania, 1969), 51.

showed a marked increase in direct investment in the Six (see Chapter 3) and some company chairmen began to call openly for UK membership of the EC.[95] An increasing number of groups of prominent individuals announced their support for British entry too, and these often included industrialists.[96] In July 1960, forty-two signatories called for Britain to join the EC and this included some industrialists.[97] By September the ABCC's European panel commented on the growing body of opinion wanting EC membership.[98] This support continued to grow such that by the time that Britain did apply in July 1961 a wide range of individual businessmen and companies had come to prefer EC membership above continued membership of a limited EFTA. These included the linen industry, the worsted industry, fine spinners and doublers, Courtaulds and J & P Coats.[99] In May 1961, another letter appeared in the press in favor of EC membership, this time signed by 140 individuals of whom at least twenty-seven were industrialists or bankers.[100] This letter was also supported privately by Sir William McFadzean, who had only recently stood down as president of the FBI.[101] He now believed business leaders in Britain were "very much in favor of the United Kingdom joining the EEC."[102] A *Sunday Times* survey of 130 top firms in July 1961 confirmed a growing consensus among Britain's largest firms in favor of EC entry.[103]

This growing support emerged for a variety of reasons. Obviously, industries such as the paper industry continued to support EC entry.[104] Similarly, the chemical industry continued to see little intrinsic value in EFTA, and so full EC membership seemed the only solution.[105] There was also concern that the more EFTA was built up, rather than increasing the chances of accommodation between the two groups as the FBI hoped, the more this accentuated the split between the Six and the Seven and the harder any reconciliation would become.[106] Some British industries were also finding the

---

[95] Pfaltzgraff, *Britain Faces Europe*, 49. For examples of calls to join the EC see "Bowaters," *The Times*, 3 June 1960, 23; and "Beecham Group," *The Times*, 28 July 1960, 17.

[96] Pfaltzgraff, *Britain Faces Europe*, 39.

[97] "Britain Urged to Join Six," *The Times*, 25 July 1960, 7.

[98] GLA MS17558, European Panel meeting 29 September 1960.

[99] TNA BT11/5559, POM 356, "President's Visit to Northern Ireland," 27–28 March 1961; "Worsted Industry Facing a Growing Challenge," *The Times*, 5 July 1961, 23; "Fine Spinners and Doublers Limited," *The Times*, 6 July 1961, 22; and GUABRC UGD199/1/181, Coats Executive Committee meeting, 26 June 1961.

[100] "Government Declaration for Common Market Sought," *The Times*, 26 May 1961, 8.

[101] Bromund, "From Empire to Europe," 448–9.   [102] Pfaltzgraff, *Britain Faces Europe*, 51.

[103] Lieber, *British Politics*, 97.

[104] TNA BT11/5569, Langley to Charlish, 22 August 1961.

[105] George Brealey, "The British Chemical Industry – from KID to Outer Seven," *Chemistry and Industry* (8 July 1961), 1006–8; and MRC MSS200/F/3/S2/2/11, D/2288, Lincoln Steel, Grand Council meeting, 11 May 1960.

[106] MRC MSS200 F/3/E3/34/7, D/2283A, note of a meeting of trade association representatives at the FBI, 11 May 1960.

rewards from EFTA membership disappointing. This was particularly true of the car industry, originally expected to be one of the main beneficiaries from the creation of EFTA. First, it was increasingly predicted that the larger growth rate in sales would be in the EC rather than EFTA. However, the common external tariff and decreasing internal tariffs would hamper British efforts to increase exports there so firms began to invest in assembly plants to jump the tariff wall.[107] At the same time there proved to be relatively little price advantage in EFTA markets.[108] In addition, the Norwegians had refused to include their revenue duties on motor vehicles within the EFTA tariff reduction framework. Thus, British sales in one EFTA national market remained restricted, much to the annoyance of the British car industry.[109]

Accordingly, in the lead up to Harold Macmillan's announcement that Britain intended applying for membership of the EC in July 1961, individual businessmen moved to the fore in calls for EC membership, filling the vacuum left by the FBI and ABCC's relative silence on the issue. These demands came from the bottom up in this respect with the peak-level organizations offering no steer and making no effort to create business opinion as they had over the FTA proposals. Also, it was to individual industrial leaders rather than formal meetings with business representatives from the FBI that the government turned in considering its policy on European integration at this time.[110] Harold Macmillan had been holding such meetings since the October 1959 general election. At these meetings the industrial leaders came to urge more rapid progress towards European integration. It was these appeals and the more general evidence of British business turning its attention towards the Six (see Chapters 2 and 3) to which the government responded rather than any direct pressure from the FBI, the ABCC or the NUM as the main peak-level representative bodies of industrial opinion.

THE PERIOD OF NEGOTIATIONS, 1961–1963

Plenty has been written on Britain's negotiations with the Six in the early 1960s even before Milward's official history was published.[111] All such

---

[107] For example, MRC MSS226/ST/1/9/3, Standard Motor Company, minute 28, 6 November 1959.

[108] Whisler, "The Outstanding Potential Market," 10.

[109] TNA BT11/5812, draft letter by Savage to Rootes (SMMT), 8 May 1961 and draft note for President of the Board of Trade, c. March 1963.

[110] Lieber, *British Politics*, 98; and Kaiser, *Using Europe*, 172.

[111] N. Piers Ludlow, *Dealing with Britain: The Six and the First UK Application to the EEC* (Cambridge: Cambridge University Press, 1997); Kristian Steinnes, "The European Challenge: Britain's EEC Application in 1961," *Contemporary European History*, Vol. 7, No. 1 (1998), 61–79; Anne Deighton and Alan S. Milward (eds.), *Widening, Deepening and Acceleration: The European Economic Community 1957–1963* (Baden-Baden: Nomos Verlag, 1999); and Milward, *Rise and Fall*.

accounts focus on the three key areas of difficulties in the negotiations: the Commonwealth, domestic agriculture, and EFTA. Domestic business was not a major issue of contention – even less than was expected – and hence has received little attention in accounts of the negotiations.[112] This does not mean, however, that there were no business-related issues nor that industry was not politically engaged with the negotiations but it was the case that the role of the peak-level organizations was limited. These organizations were involved at the outset but thereafter were awaiting the outcome of the negotiations in order to decide if the terms of entry were suitable. In the meantime, their main activities revolved around educating members about the EC while technical issues were dealt with by trade associations and individual firms.[113] The Palmer working group did operate as a key channel between business and government but again tended to focus on technical issues. The one exception to this was the development of competition policy in the EC (see Chapter 9).

The initial urgency was to ensure that government took on board business opinion prior to the negotiations opening.[114] One issue that both the ABCC and the FBI did take up at this stage was that of "sensitive" or "hard-hit" industries, those that were likely to suffer from EC entry. The FBI sent a questionnaire to all its trade association members asking whether they believed their industries would suffer hardship as a result of the application of the EC's common external tariff (including on imports from the Commonwealth), from reduced protection on finished goods from outside the EC and from increased competition from within the EC. While many trade associations did believe that one or more of these aspects would cause hardship for their industry, the FBI concluded that "not many industries are likely to find themselves so adversely affected as to be 'hard-hit' within any reasonable definition of the term."[115] However, for many this was dependent on the outcome of negotiations on the application of the common external tariff to raw material imports and that British firms were not disadvantaged by UK taxation, notably purchase tax (see Chapter 10).[116] There remained two groups of firms, believed to be few in number, where their particular circumstances could warrant special treatment. One group was industries such as precision optical instruments, which had previously received substantial

[112] George Wilkes, "The First Failure to Steer Britain into the European Communities: An Introduction," in Wilkes (ed.), *Britain's Failure to Enter the European Community 1961–63: The Enlargement Negotiations and Crises in European, Atlantic and Commonwealth Relations* (London: Frank Cass, 1997), 11.

[113] Anne Deighton, "The United Kingdom Application for EEC membership 1961–63," in Griffiths and Ward (eds.), *Courting the Common Market*, 41.

[114] MRC MSS200/F/3/S2/2/11, GC.58.61, Grand Council meeting, 13 September 1961.

[115] MRC MSS200/F/3/O5/2/11, O.297.61, "Hard Hit industries and the Common Market," October 1961 and attached summary.

[116] MRC MSS200/F/3/S2/2/13, Grand Council meeting, 13 December 1961.

protection, often for strategic reasons. The other broader group was those industries already under severe competitive pressure from the free entry of Commonwealth manufactures, which would face even greater competition with EC entry. By and large, this meant sections of the textile industries. Nevertheless, having examined the issue, both the ABCC and the FBI "could not take up the cudgels or make a case for any individual industry or firm."[117] This was for the firms themselves and their trade associations.

The peak-level business organizations also continued to interact with their counterparts elsewhere in Europe and, most significantly of all, they also embarked on a major education exercise for their members. In addition to bilateral links with sister national business organizations, the FBI maintained its links with other national business federations via the CEIF, covering the whole of Western Europe, CIFEFTA and with meetings with the Union des Industries de la Communauté Européenne (UNICE) covering the Six.[118] Similarly, the ABCC held bilateral meetings with its national counterparts to discuss British entry into the EC, learning soon after the British application that French business now welcomed an "economic agreement" with Britain.[119] The ABCC was also invited to observe the meetings of the Permanent Conference of the Chambers of Commerce of the Six.[120] While the ABCC representatives were not allowed to contribute in the sessions, points were made "in the corridors" and that "it should be possible to learn a great deal of the way official thinking amongst the Six was going and at the same time we could convey some ideas of thinking in this country."[121]

However, the main role of these organizations related to education and publicity: during the negotiations business was "one of the most important sectors of the British political community actively promoting the European cause."[122] The government itself felt constrained in undertaking such an exercise to sell its own policy until late in 1962 and so the activities of business were all the more important.[123] Activities by the peak-level organizations of business took a variety of forms. They produced pamphlets, published articles in their journals and organized conferences. These were sometimes general, like the NUM's *If Britain Joins* and the FBI's *The Rome Treaty*,

---

[117] GLA MS14487/6, ABCC European Panel meeting, 4 October 1961; and MRC MSS200/F/1/1/217, O.263.61, Overseas Trade Policy Panel meeting, 3 November 1961.

[118] Neil Rollings and Matthias Kipping, "Private Transnational Governance."

[119] GLA MS14476/17, report of visit of representatives of French chambers of commerce, July 1961.

[120] GLA MS17558, ABCC European Panel meeting 23 November 1961.

[121] GLA MS14476/17, ABCC Executive Committee meeting, 5 December 1962 and GLA MS17558, ABCC European Panel meeting 23 November 1961.

[122] Lieber, *British Politics*, 104.

[123] N. Piers Ludlow, "A Mismanaged Application: Britain and the EEC, 1961–1963," in Deighton and Milward (eds.), *Widening, Deepening*, 279.

and at other times more focused on particular aspects of the EC.[124] They also stressed the need for improved foreign language skills and provided material on the market situation for exporters in the Six.[125] Individual trade associations, other business organizations, and banks also published material and ran conferences on the same lines.[126] There was a plethora of such activities:

If any British businessman has not yet attended a Common Market conference, it can hardly have been for lack of an invitation. Scarcely a day passes without news of some fresh gathering to discuss the effects of "going into Europe", whether it is a mass jamboree by the seaside or a select houseparty of two dozen industrialists in a provincial town.[127]

Even when the government did begin to organize a publicity campaign about the EC late in 1962, it still felt unable to front it, instead using existing bodies which included the FBI, the British Employers' Confederation, the ABCC, the National Association of British Manufacturers (the renamed NUM), and the Institute of Directors.[128] Indirectly, business also had a role in these campaigns: It was common to state how beneficial entry would be for British business or to quote British business leaders positive views on EC entry.[129]

Accordingly, while business' direct role in the negotiations was limited to largely technical matters, its role in the publicity and educational campaigns associated with membership of the EC, both directly and indirectly, should not be overlooked. Even if the campaign was to prove fruitless in the end with de Gaulle's veto of the British application in January 1963, the British business community was much better informed and knowledgeable about the EC by the time of the veto than it had been in 1961. Also, by 1963 many businessmen coming from a full range of business activities had professed

---

[124] EIU (for the NUM), *If Britain Joins: A Guide to the Economic Effects of Membership of the Common Market* (London, 1961), and FBI, *The Rome Treaty* (London, 1962).

[125] FBI, *Foreign Languages in Industry: Report of a Working Party* (London, June 1962); "The Challenge of Western Europe: Increased Exports but More Home Competition," *Monthly Record of the Manchester Chamber of Commerce* (31 January 1962), 8–10; and "The Challenge of Europe: Review of ECE Conferences," *Monthly Record of the Manchester Chamber of Commerce* (31 December 1962), 356.

[126] Midland Bank Ltd., *Bridging the Channel: The Businessman and Europe* (London, 1962); Lloyds Bank (Foreign) Ltd., *Europe and You: A Word to British Manufacturers Interested in Europe* (London, 1961); and British Institute of Management, *Management and the European Common Market: Convention 1962 – Papers and Discussion* (London, 1962).

[127] *The Observer*, 6 May 1962, quoted in Robert Pfaltzgraff, "The Common Market Debate in Britain," *Orbis*, Vol. 7, No. 2 (Summer 1963), 280.

[128] TNA PREM11/4415, Oliver Poole to Macmillan, 30 November 1962.

[129] Federal Trust, *Industry and the Common Market* (London, 1962); and William Rees-Mogg, "Industry and the Common Market," *The New Europe: Oxford Lectures 1962* (Conservative Political Centre, August 1962).

their support for British entry.[130] An ABCC survey of its individual members in 1962 found that 75 percent of those responding supported EC entry.[131]

The FBI did not carry out a similar survey but was planning one from the autumn of 1962 in readiness for the expected completion of the negotiations.[132] Ironically, only days before de Gaulle's veto, the FBI were preparing to send their members a summary of the terms of the negotiations and asking whether the FBI should "say yes or no to Britain's entry."[133] There the issue rested. It was not to be until 1967 that the membership of the largest representative organization of business in Britain, now the Confederation of British Industry, which was formed in 1965 out of the merger of the FBI, the BEC, and the NABM, was given the opportunity to voice its opinions on British entry to the EC in any systematic way.

CONCLUSION

Much changed over the period 1958–1963. It was a crucial period in the development of British policy on European integration. At the start of the period all hopes lay with the idea of a wider free trade area. When that was dashed, EFTA was quickly put in place both as an alternative and as a potential bridge to some association with the EC. When that bridge failed to emerge some sectors of business, unhappy with EFTA, began to support EC membership. At times, notably in the creation of EFTA, the peak-level business organizations played a crucial role in these developments, while at other times such leadership was lacking. Crucially, the ABCC and the FBI (even more so) felt tied to EFTA. The FBI had played such a central role in the creation of the body that it felt morally obliged not to renege on this commitment by turning to the EC. In these circumstances, pressure for EC membership came from below, from individual companies and businessmen. This took the form, first, of economic integration in the form of increased investment in the EC (see Chapter 3) and, second, as demands for political action. With the government's announcement of the intention to open negotiations in July 1961, the position changed once more. There was now an increased role for the peak-level organizations but this now related to their contacts with other national federations and to their efforts to educate their memberships and to influence public opinion.

These developments illustrate the limits of viewing business representation as a hierarchy where views flow up to the peak-level organizations that then

---

[130] Conservative Party Central Office, *Leaders of Industry and the Common Market* (London, 1962); and TNA PREM11/4529, Dunphie to Macmillan, covering a letter from twenty leading companies on EC entry, 1 January 1963.

[131] Lieber, *British Politics*, 101, and Moon, *European Integration*, 181.

[132] MRC MSS200/F/3/S2/2/13, GC.42A.62, "Britain and the EEC: The Brussels Negotiations," August 1962; and GC.48.62, Grand Council meeting, 12 September 1962.

[133] MRC MSS200/F/3/S2/21/3, Felgate to Tennant, 10 January 1963.

transmit these views to national governments. Similarly, they highlight the dangers of an overly narrow focus on direct influence on government policy. The FBI was at its most influential in the creation of EFTA not through its direct impact on government policy but via the actions that it took with the other national business federations of the Seven. Equally, it was contact between individual businessmen and government which was the route by which business encouraged the government to apply for EC membership. These relationships were complex, diverse, and shifting over time. As will be shown in the next chapter, with de Gaulle's veto these relationships shifted once more.

7

After de Gaulle's First Veto, the Second Application and the Second Veto, 1963–1968

De Gaulle's veto in January 1963 marked the end of negotiations over British entry at that time. It was a further ten years before the UK finally joined the European Community. A Labour government was elected in 1964 with little overt interest in European integration. However, led by Harold Wilson, the government shifted its position, launching a second bid for entry in 1967, but again de Gaulle vetoed the application. This left little prospect of EC enlargement in the foreseeable future but also created a crisis in the EC. The attitude of British business to European integration also developed considerably after the first veto. The first reaction to the 1963 veto was a mixture of relief that at least business knew where it stood and an ensuing sense of reflection and reassessment, which, in turn, led to a diverse range of responses. Slowly this was replaced by renewed enthusiasm for entry, stimulated by the creation in 1965 of the Confederation of British Industry (CBI) out of the merger of the Federation of British Industries (FBI), the British Employers' Confederation (BEC) and the National Association of British Manufacturers (NABM) (until 1963 the National Union of Manufacturers). This created a single voice for British industry, with the Association of British Chambers of Commerce (ABCC) taking much more of a backseat role. With Norman Kipping's retirement from the post of director-general of the FBI there was also a new head of the new organization's staff, John Davies, who described himself as "a passionate European."[1] British business was more positive about British entry to the European Community (EC) at the time of the second application in 1967 than at any other time before Britain joined the EC in 1973. This positive approach was in part aimed at drawing a commitment to EC entry from the government, in which it was successful, but also reflected the particular circumstances of the time which made UK entry seem at its most appealing for British business. In this sense, the veto from de Gaulle in 1967 was even more of a body blow than the first one in 1963.

The perceptions held by British business about European integration are also significant. For the early part of the period under consideration in this chapter there were grave concerns about trade discrimination as the common external tariff came into play. However, the trade liberalization achieved by

---

[1] MRC MSS200/C/1/1, CC.16.65, September 1965.

the Kennedy Round removed this as a fundamental concern for most sectors of business. Separately, other aspects of European integration were coming to the fore as British firms expanded their investment on the continent and concerns about Americanization rose (see Chapters 3 and 11). It was to gain the advantage of a large domestic market, allowing rationalization and the achievement of economies of scale that increasingly mattered. This was true not only of British business but also of the Labour government which found arguments about economies of scale and rationalization more appealing than arguments about trade liberalization. For business, a larger domestic market also had clear implications for harmonizing economic policy.

For historians, the records of this period have only recently become available. Analyses of the 1960s have led to a reassessment of the importance of Britain's second application to join the Community in 1967. It was common to depict this application as bound to fail until French attitudes changed and hence a waste of time.[2] However, recent work has refuted this by showing how the second application, in drawing a second veto from de Gaulle, had a profound impact on European integration, with the Dutch refusing to countenance any further moves towards deeper integration until the issue of British membership had been dealt with. Britain may have lost that battle but the long-term war over UK entry had been won.[3]

However, there is as yet no consensus in the historical literature on the forces that underpinned the second application. Among contemporary works Camps and Frey argued that business opinion was ahead of the government on the issue of a second application, whereas Kitzinger suggests the primacy of political considerations.[4] Similarly, today there is one group of historians who tend to emphasize the importance of economic considerations and the role of business interests in pushing for the second application, while on the other, a second group views the issue in political and strategic terms and downplays the role of business on policy formation. Typical of the first group would be John Young, who has singled out business interests as the fundamental reason for the application, although in his most recent work this is presented as one of a number of economic and political considerations.[5] Helen Parr would be representative of the second group, arguing that the

[2] Uwe Kitzinger, *The Second Try* (Oxford: Pergamon, 1968), 14.

[3] N. Piers Ludlow, *The European Community and the Crises of the 1960s: Negotiating the Gaullist Challenge* (Abingdon: Routledge, 2006), 146–73; and Helen Parr, *Britain's Policy towards the European Community: Harold Wilson and Britain's World Role, 1964–1967* (Abingdon: Routledge, 2006), 152–3.

[4] Miriam Camps, *European Unification in the Sixties* (London: OUP, 1967), 158 and 182; and C. W. Frey, "Meaning Business: The British Application to Join the Common Market, November 1966–October 1967," *Journal of Common Market Studies*, Vol. 6, No. 3 (1967–68), 217–9.

[5] John W. Young, "Britain and the EEC, 1956–73: An Overview," in Brian Brivati and Harriet Jones (eds.), *From Reconstruction to Integration: Britain and Europe since 1945* (Leicester: Leicester University Press, 1993), 109. More recently, John W. Young, *The Labour*

government's decision to apply was primarily driven by political and strategic concerns: "the significance of Wilson's application is that it clearly was about Britain's international role on the world stage."[6] Yet even more than previous chapters there is a distinct lack of knowledge about business attitudes to European integration in general in this period.[7] The chapter begins with a consideration of reactions and responses to the veto, followed by a section on the growth in business interest in EC membership after 1965, leading to the publication of the first volume of the CBI's study on European integration, *Britain and Europe*. The third section analyses the reaction in the business community to this report and illustrates the way in which the study used European integration to provide a critique of the economic policy of the Labour government.

RESPONSE TO THE VETO

De Gaulle's veto on January 14, 1963 not only ended Britain's immediate hopes of entry into the EC but also left government policy in limbo.[8] The Prime Minister believed, "all our policies at home and abroad are in ruins."[9] It is also clear that the veto in January 1963 was not expected by British business. Such was the sense of astonishment that it was even suggested by one commentator that the shock of non-entry was at least as great as entry.[10] However, there was also a sense of relief. From the summer of 1962 business had been becoming increasingly perturbed that the negotiations were taking so long and that this was impacting detrimentally on business investment plans.[11] These concerns were also voiced to government via the Palmer

Governments 1964–70, Vol. 2: International Policy (Manchester: Manchester University Press, 2003).

[6] Helen Parr, "A Question of Leadership: July 1966 and Harold Wilson's European Decision," *Contemporary British History*, Vol. 19, No. 4 (2005), 452; and Helen Parr, "Britain, America, East of Suez and the EEC: Finding a Role in British Foreign Policy, 1964–67," *Contemporary British History*, Vol. 20, No. 3 (2006), 403–21.

[7] Neil Rollings, "The Confederation of British Industry and European Integration in the 1960s," in Oliver Daddow (ed.), *Harold Wilson and European Integration: Britain's Second Application to Join the European Economic Community* (London: Frank Cass, 2003), 115–134.

[8] Richard Davis, "The 'Problem of de Gaulle': British Reactions to General de Gaulle's Veto of the UK Application to Join the Common Market," *Journal of Contemporary History*, Vol. 32, No. 4 (1997), 453–64.

[9] Alastair Horne, *Macmillan, 1957–1986, Vol. 2* (London: Macmillan, 1989), 447.

[10] Andrew Shonfield, "The Economic Implications of the Brussels Breakdown," in Kenneth Younger, Andrew Shonfield, L. Beaton and D. Pickles, *Implications of the Brussels Breakdown* (London: RIIA, 1963), 19.

[11] W. I. French (Sir William Arrol & Co. Ltd.), "What FBI Members are Saying," *FBI Review* (June 1962), 69; "Britain and the EEC," *Journal of the Birmingham Chamber of Commerce* (November 1962), 953; and GLA MS17558, European Panel meetings, 27 June 1962 and 4 December 1962.

committee, and within the government, there seemed to be an acceptance that the uncertainty over the negotiations was the main cause of business pessimism at that time and that this was adversely affecting levels of investment.[12] In this respect, if no other, the ending of the negotiations, even in failure, was a relief to British business. It is only in this context that sense can be made of the FBI's statement "Forward from Brussels" which it released on 15 February, 1963 and which was to cause a furor.[13] The final sentence was the problem: it said, "The break is clear and, in our opinion, final."

Some industrialists supported the apparent finality of the statement but others, like Sir William McFadzean, the previous FBI President and chairman of the Export Council for Europe, were furious.[14] McFadzean's criticisms were part of a wider outburst of discontent among the FBI's members. The reaction to the statement outside the membership was even more significant. The statement was picked up widely by the press not just for its tone but also because Ted Heath had addressed the FBI's Grand Council shortly before the statement was issued. Heath was incensed that the final sentence would be construed as reflecting his own sentiments and it was only as a result of his vehement criticism of the original draft that the words "in our opinion" were added to the sentence.[15] Although Kipping later believed the statement was "an error of judgment" at the time, he defended its firmness, picking up on the detrimental impact on business decision-making of continued uncertainty: Until the French government changed its views, there was little prospect of British entry into the EC and it would have been wrong of the FBI to encourage any such hopes.[16]

What business should do was less straightforward. There was the inevitable period of reflection and reassessment: as one leading businessman put it, "We must behave like any rejected lover, and take a long walk in the country."[17] Like rejected lovers, some wanted to turn their back on Europe. John Holt, the chairman of John Holt & Co. (Liverpool) Ltd., a trading company with widespread interests, called for a return to a focus on Commonwealth markets.[18] Unsurprisingly, the Federation of

---

[12] TNA BT11/6045/1068/1963, Brown to Edwards, reporting comments of Gray (NABM) at the Palmer committee meeting, October 1962, and subsequent documents.

[13] *The Times*, 15 February 1963, 14.

[14] MRC MSS200/F/3/O5/2/8, Sherborne to Kipping, 27 February 1963, and McFadzean to Kipping, 1 March 1963.

[15] MRC MSS200/F/3/S2/21/3, Grand Council meeting, 13 February 1963; Sir Cyril Harrison, FBI President, to Heath, 14 Feb. 1963; and Norman Kipping, *Summing Up* (London: Hutchinson, 1972), 177; *The Times*, 15 February 1963, 4.

[16] MRC MSS200/F/3/S2/21/3, Kipping to Marshall, director of the Joint Iron Council, 19 February 1963; and Kipping, *Summing Up*, 176.

[17] Nora Beloff, "What Happened in Britain after the General Said No," in Pierre Uri (ed.), *From Commonwealth to Europe* (Harmondsworth: Penguin, 1968), 53.

[18] "After Brussels," *Commerce* No. 15, (March 1963), 7; and MRC MSS200/F/3/O5/2/8, "Bill" (John Holt & Co.) to Kipping, 15 February 1963.

Commonwealth and British Chambers of Commerce and the Commonwealth Industries Association supported this, and there were also calls for measures to stimulate private direct investment there.[19] A similar reaction was to emphasize the still-unexploited potential in EFTA markets.[20] Acceleration of the tariff reduction program within EFTA in order to ensure parity with the EC and to bind the member states together was one possibility, though this only raised the hackles of the paper industry once more.[21] This approach also looked rather hollow once the newly elected Labour government introduced a 15 percent import surcharge on gaining power, directly flouting EFTA regulations and infuriating other EFTA member governments. Others pointed to export opportunities elsewhere in the world, including the Soviet bloc, as a third option.[22]

The response of the peak-level business associations was to restate their commitment to multilateral trading but with greater emphasis on the importance of achieving significant trade liberalization so that the EC's common external tariff did not prove insurmountable.[23] This line was apparent in the FBI's policy statement, *Overseas Trade Policy*, published in September 1963, with its emphasis on the role of GATT.[24] Given that membership of the EC was discounted for the foreseeable future, global trade liberalization offered, among other things, the best alternative route to gaining freer access to the markets of the Six. As the statement itself put it, "The lowering of Community tariffs must clearly be a main object of policy."[25] Fear of exclusion from these markets remained a potent concern and made the successful conclusion of the Kennedy Round of negotiations all the more imperative.[26]

The alternative for business was to jump the tariff wall by investing in, or acquiring, firms based in the Six. Some firms did embark on this strategy (see Chapter 3), yet for others who had already established a foothold within the Six the impact of the common external tariff and the breakdown of the negotiations were of less concern. A number of firms argued that it made no difference to their strategy of continuing to develop links with

[19] MRC MSS200/F/1/1/217, O.65A.63, meeting of the FBI's Overseas Committee, 5 March 1963; TNA BT11/6148, Reid to Huijsman, 24 January 1964, note of a meeting between the Prime Minister and the Commonwealth Industries Association Parliamentary Committee; and TNA BT11/6289, DuCann to the Prime Minister, 15 May 1964.

[20] "The Future of EFTA," *Commerce* No. 24 (December 1963), 7; and FBI, *Annual Report for 1963*, 10.

[21] TNA BT258/93, various correspondences.

[22] TNA BT11/6045/1068/1963, Terry, note of a meeting by the President of the Board of Trade with Redditch industrialists, 30 January 1963; and "After Brussels – by the Editor," *Tees-Side Journal of Commerce*, Vol. 28, No. 2 (February 1963), 19.

[23] MRC MSS200/F/1/1/217, O.65A.63, meeting of the FBI's Overseas Committee, 5 March 1963. For the ABBC see GLA MS17558, European Panel meeting, 19 February 1963.

[24] FBI, *Overseas Trade Policy* (London, 1963).   [25] Ibid., 10.

[26] TNA BT278/27, Noble to Sir Patrick Reilly, 28 March 1963; and TNA BT11/6168, "British Trade Policy: Notes on European aspects," unsigned and undated but about July 1964.

European firms or to make further acquisitions.[27] Sir Malcolm McDougall, the chairman of Coats, Patons & Baldwins Ltd, the thread manufacturer and early multinational, was perhaps the most explicit in this respect: "The main event in Europe was, of course, the breakdown of the European Common Market negotiations. I mentioned in my statement last year that Coats was producing in most of the ECM [European Common Market] markets. For us, therefore, entry or non-entry did not present any major problems."[28] Similarly, banks continued to develop their links on the Continent after the veto.[29] For these firms with subsidiaries in the Six a process of being "automatically Europeanized" was occurring.[30] For others, the response to the veto varied, though trade liberalization was generally supported, but few turned their back on the EC even if there was little prospect of entry in the short-to-medium term.

RENEWED INTEREST IN EC MEMBERSHIP, 1965–1967

Once it became clear that the Kennedy Round offered no quick and easy solution to EC tariff discrimination and the growth in exports to the Six began to slow in 1964, it was always likely that the issue of European integration would re-emerge.[31] As early as June 1964 the Birmingham Chamber of Commerce issued a statement saying that it was in favor of EC entry and others followed suit.[32] Of more lasting significance was the airing that the issue received in January 1965. As a forerunner to a possible merger, the FBI, BEC, and NABM organized a joint conference to consider "Britain's Economic Problems and Policies: The Next Five Years." One hundred and fifty leading businessmen met at the Grand Hotel, Eastbourne to spend three days discussing these issues. The first speech by Lord Plowden, the ex-economic adviser to the government and ex-chair of the UK Atomic Energy Authority, called, among other things, for British businessmen to consider the UK's relationship with the EC as "soon we shall be the only great manufacturing nation who will not have a market of between 100 million and 200 million people, with all the opportunity that gives for mass production and

---

[27] "Future of Metal Box, In or Out of EEC," *The Times* (31 January 1963), 19; and MRC MSS200/F/3/O5/2/8, Sherborne (Yorkshire Imperial Metals Ltd) to Kipping, 27 February 1963.

[28] *The Times*, 30 May 1963, 21.

[29] "Eurosyndicat: Developing Trade with the Common Market," *Monthly Record of the Manchester Chamber of Commerce* (31 May 1963), 137; and Duncan Ross, "Clubs and Consortia: European Banking Groups as Strategic Alliances," in Stefano Battilossi and Yousef Cassis (eds.), *European Banks and the American Challenge: Competition and Cooperation in International Banking under Bretton Woods* (Oxford: Oxford University Press, 2002), 135–60.

[30] Beloff, "What Happened," 54.   [31] Camps, *European Unification*, 157–8.

[32] TNA BT11/6168, Farrow, note of a meeting, 31 December 1964.

specialisation."[33] The following day the conference divided into five groups to agree policy recommendations relating to different aspects of the economy. Group V considered Britain in the world economy, concluding in relation to European integration:

British industry has for many years actively wished to see an economically integrated Europe. We greatly regret the continued division. While we see no early prospect of an end to the division we think its implications for industry must continually be subjected to critical scrutiny. Equally the objective of healing the breach must remain in the forefront of policy, and where in managing our own affairs there is an element of choice, this should be exercised so as to help not hinder this aim.[34]

Clearly then, European integration remained a concern for leading British businessmen even if there was little prospect of advance. Although it was not to appear in the final report of Group V and was not supported by FBI staff, Group V had proposed a study of the consequences for industry of (a) remaining outside the EC and (b) joining the EC under various hypotheses.[35]

BRITAIN AND EUROPE

In the short term nothing happened about the proposal for such a study. Business leaders were tied up with the creation of the new CBI and all that entailed in terms of new machinery and new staff – Norman Kipping, for so long the director-general of the FBI, for example, retired. In addition, the Six were having to deal with the empty chair crisis when de Gaulle removed French representation from the Council of Ministers, making progress on any major decisions almost impossible during the second half of 1965, and raising the prospect of the EC breaking up.[36] The idea of examining Britain's relations with Europe quickly reappeared, however, in the autumn of 1965 once the CBI was up and running. John Davies, the new director-general and a self-professed "passionate European," announced to the press in September that one of the new body's six "points of attack" would be that, "Britain should seek every opportunity of moving closer to Europe with the objective of Common Market membership."[37] To this end, he told the CBI Council's first meeting that the time was ripe to test the desire of British industry to

---

33 Quoted in "The Management of Change," *The Economist*, 30 January 1965, 414.
34 MRC MSS200/F/3/O3/8/2, "Britain's Economic Problems and Policies: The Next Five Years. Conclusions of Group V," undated.
35 Ibid., Whitehorn, "Eastbourne Conference Group V," 4 February 1965.
36 Jean-Marie Palayret, Helen Wallace and Pascaline Winand (eds.), *Visions, Votes and Vetoes: The Empty Chair Crisis and the Luxembourg Compromise Forty Years On* (Brussels: P. I. E. Peter Lang, 2006); and Ludlow, *European Community*, 71–93.
37 *The Times*, 15 September 1965, 15.

Table 7.1. *Membership of the CBI Europe Steering Committee*

Name	Company or Institutional Affiliation
A. G. Norman	De La Rue Co.
G. A. H. Cadbury	Cadbury Brothers Ltd.
E. J. Callard	ICI Ltd.
Alun Davies	Rio Tinto-Zinc Corporation Ltd.
Stuart Douglas	British Man-Made Fibres Federation
M. F. Dowding	Davy-Ashmore International Ltd.
Derek Ezra	National Coal Board
L. Franck	Samuel Montagu & Co. Ltd.
A. H. C. Greenwood	British Aircraft Corporation (Operating) Ltd.
G. Ingram	Samaritan Equipment Ltd
Martin Jukes QC	Engineering Employers' Federation
Lord Layton	The Steel Company of Wales Ltd.
H. R. Mathys	Courtaulds
Keith Newlands	Elliott-Automation (Overseas) Ltd.
T. Normanton	Normanton Engineers
F. U. J. O'Brien	Shell International Petroleum Co. Ltd.
P. Parker	Bookers Engineering and Industrial Holdings Ltd.
Hon Maxwell Stamp	Maxwell Stamp Associates Ltd.
S. F. Steward	British Electrical & Allied Manufacturers' Association
H. M. Threlfall	Unilever Ltd.
R. L. Wills	George Wills & Sons (Holdings) Ltd.
Kenneth Younger	Royal Institute of International Affairs

Source: CBI, *Britain and Europe* –vol. 1, p. iii.

forge closer links with Europe and at its next meeting the Council approved the proposal for a CBI study of the European communities.[38]

To oversee the study a new committee, the Europe Steering Committee, was set up.[39] It was chaired by A. G. (Gerry) Norman, the chairman of De La Rue Co. and chairman of the CBI's Overseas Committee. The full membership is shown in Table 7.1. Its first meeting was in December 1965. Work was devolved to the various directorates of the CBI staff with special reports to be done on coal, steel, and agriculture.[40] In addition, a working party of the Overseas Committee was set up under Derek Ezra, the Chairman of the National Coal Board, to consider the implications of tariff changes if Britain

[38] MRC MSS200/C/1/1, CC 16.65, October 1965; MRC MSS200/C/1/1, CC.21.65, CBI Council meeting, 20 October 1965.
[39] MRC MSS200/C/1/2/O, CO.55.65, CBI Europe Steering Committee first meeting, 2 December 1965.
[40] Ibid., O.26.66, "CBI Study on Europe: A Progress Report," February 1966.

joined the EC.[41] Finally, another separate smaller Europe Panel was also created to advise the CBI staff, to coordinate the various specialist papers and to iron out any inconsistencies. It consisted of Arthur Knight (Courtaulds), S. A. Clark (Imperial Tobacco Co.), Steward (BEAMA), J. Wood (AEI) and M. Zinkin (Unilever).[42] Fiscal aspects were left to the CBI's Taxation Committee, and prices and incomes issues were excluded from the study.

A number of points need to be made at this point. First, the membership of the steering committee consisted mainly of representatives of large international companies or export-orientated sectors. This was especially the case with the Europe Panel. Secondly, as the papers were to be drafted by CBI staff members, the views of this new staff, led by the "passionate European" John Davies, would be influential. Thirdly, the steering committee's report was to form the basis of consultation with the membership.

The terms of reference of the steering committee were also important. Not only was there value, it was believed, in identifying where changes in British policy would be needed but that some of these changes might be desirable in their own right, in which case the CBI "would begin positively advocating them to the government without delay."[43] This is significant because the CBI was highly critical of elements of the Labour government's domestic policy and contrary practice in the Six could be used as a stick with which to beat the government. Finally, one further key decision was that the "closer relationships" between Britain and the EC referred to in the terms of reference were to be interpreted as meaning full membership of the EC and that this would apply to most EFTA countries as well as Britain.[44] This single assumption removed one of the major potential obstacles to support for Britain's EC entry before the study had even started, that is, the desire shown in the previous chapter by British business not to sell out EFTA and for as large a grouping of countries as possible to participate.[45] This assumption plus the other aspects set out above set a clear path towards recommending EC entry if the steering committee so wished. While the CBI's Overseas Director told CBI members that the study was not prejudging the issue of EC entry and might even conclude that EC membership was not appropriate, in practice this was not likely to be the case.[46]

Initially, work concentrated on Ezra's working party and the tariff aspects of British entry. From this work it was concluded that, "From British

[41] Ibid., O.15.66, CBI Overseas Committee working party on Europe, "What are the Main Structural Differences in the UK and EEC tariffs?" January 1966.

[42] MRC MSS200/C/1/1/2, CBI Europe Panel meeting, 2 March 1966.

[43] MRC MSS200/C/1/2/O, O.26.66, "CBI Study on Europe: A Progress Report," February 1966.

[44] CBI, *Britain and Europe, Vol. 1: An Industrial Appraisal* (London, 1966), 1.

[45] MRC MSS200/C/S1/3/12/8, Davies to Whitehorn, 3 June 1966.

[46] MRC MSS200/C/1/2/O, CO.45.65, "Overseas Director's Newsletter No. 19," 11 November 1965.

industry's point of view, the success of the negotiations will be determined principally by the extent to which (a) any increase in British domestic costs (b) any detrimental effects on British trade with (and investment in) non-EEC countries, especially the Commonwealth, are kept to a minimum."[47] As Peter Tennant, the previous Overseas Director in the FBI, put it, "So much of this is fearfully hypothetical since we know little of the conditions of entry and whether there would be any phasing of tariffs on the industrial front."[48] Yet, such qualifications in the draft report were criticized and all the proposed changes either played down the negative outcomes of UK entry or played up the positive outcomes, as well as launching an attack on UK exchange control policy as a barrier to the free movement of capital and the achievement of economies of scale by British companies in the EC.[49] The other detailed studies were extensive and wide ranging, and like the final version of Ezra's working party report, most were published as supporting papers to the Europe Steering Committee's report.[50] In addition to commercial policy, those published covered agriculture, the free movement of workers, vocational training and the European Social Fund, equal pay, harmonization of social security, energy, coal, iron and steel, transport, liberalization of capital movements, taxation, restrictive practices and monopolies, and monetary implications of EC membership.

While this work was progressing, CBI representatives used the various bilateral and multilateral links at their disposal to discern opinion on the continent. In April they met the BDI.[51] In the next month there were two trips, one to Brussels to meet the Belgian government and European Commission officials, the other to Rome.[52] These were followed by a visit to the Netherlands in July, to Sweden in September and in October to Denmark, before rounding off these consultations with a trip to Paris to see the CNPF.[53] In addition, the CBI held a special lunch party with two key government ministers, George Brown and George Thomson.[54]

[47] Ibid., O.89.66, "Draft Report of Overseas Committee Working Party," April 1966.

[48] MRC MSS200/C/3/S12/8, Tennant to Thurn, 7 June 1966.

[49] MRC MSS200/C/1/2/O, O.103.66, CBI Overseas Committee meeting, 21 June 1966.

[50] CBI, *Britain and Europe, Vol. 2. Supporting Papers* (London, 1967).

[51] MRC MSS200/C/1/2/O, O.82.66, "Note of a Visit to Germany by A. G. Norman and John Whitehorn," April 1966.

[52] Ibid., O.83.66, "Visit to Brussels, 28–29 May 1966", and O.92.66, "Visit to Rome, 19 May 1966."

[53] Ibid., O.122.66, "Note of a Visit to Holland, 11–12 July 1966", O.152.66, "Note of a Visit to Sweden, 12–13 September 1966", O.179.66, "Note of a Visit to Denmark 31 October–1 November 1966", and O.180.66, "Notes of Discussion between Representatives of the CBI and CNPF in Paris, 27–28 October 1966." See also MRC MSS200/C/3/S1/12/8, Whitehorn to Carstens (industriraadet denmark), 16 September 1966.

[54] Ibid., O.102.66A, "Note of a Discussion at the CBI Lunch Party for George Brown and George Thomson, 20 June 1966," 27 June 1966.

The work of the steering committee was then to digest the various result-ing reports and to produce a much briefer overarching report. The detailed studies were all, with the exception of the National Farmers Union's (NFU) on agriculture, broadly positive in their conclusions about closer association with the EC. Yet the steering committee's report was, if anything, even more positive, fudging or ignoring a number of difficulties and sensitive issues. As one member of the steering committee suggested, presentation was the key issue: "we have to bear in mind that we want a positive, useful contribution as the paper will be read by all concerned; those anxious to get in; those who are hesitant; and also those on the continent who will be engaged in the negotiations when they arise."[55] A number of other substantive alterations were made all of which created a more positive picture of the balance of advantages and disadvantages of British entry into the EC. For example, a sentence was deleted from the section on general economic policy which advocated urgent consultation on the problems of redundancy and redeploy-ment, following the rationalization of British industry which was expected to result from membership.[56] Most significant, however, was the way the steer-ing committee dealt with the fundamental issue of the cost of the Common Agricultural Policy (CAP) to Britain's cost of living and balance of payments. The NFU had supplied the supporting paper on agriculture in which the var-ious concerns of British farmers were set out. In addition, they supplied a paper estimating the costs to Britain of implementing CAP – £685 m. to the cost of living, and £350–400 m. to the balance of payments. However, at the final meeting of the committee prior to the publication of the report, its members considered a paper on the costs of CAP prepared by Unilever. This put the respective costs at £500 m. and £165 m., significantly lower than the NFU estimates. The steering committee, acknowledging its lack of expertise, agreed to publish both papers as appendices to the report but still felt able to state in the report itself, "It seems a reasonable assumption for industry to make that the true outcome may lie somewhere between the two, with the long term trend probably in the direction of the lower estimate," that is, Unilever's.[57]

Accordingly, the steering committee's report, published in December 1966, as *Britain and Europe, Vol. 1* was forthright and positive in tone through-out. For example, the ability of British industry to compete was not seen as a problem and it was believed that tariff changes should not result in any "intolerably adverse effects."[58] As *The Times* put it, "British industry has

[55] MRC MSS200/C/3/S1/12/8, Mathys (Courtaulds) to Felgate, 5 September 1966.
[56] MRC MSS200/C/1/2/O, O.170.66, CBI Europe Steering Committee 9th meeting, 12 October 1966.
[57] Ibid., CBI Europe Steering Committee 11th meeting, 8 November 1966; and CBI, *Britain and Europe, Vol. 1*, 15.
[58] CBI, *Britain and Europe, Vol. 1*, 2 and 24, and 3 and 11, respectively.

given an emphatic yes to joining the Common Market."[59] Its main conclusions were set out boldly in the report's first paragraph, which, ever since, has been the focus of attention:

This Committee is firmly convinced that, from an industrial point of view

  i)   there would be a clear and progressive balance of advantage to British industry from membership of an enlarged European Economic Community;
 ii)   the Treaty of Rome and the Community's method of operation are acceptable given reasonable transitional arrangements; and
iii)   entry should be negotiated as soon as possible.[60]

Gone was the preceding qualification of the draft report:

This is essentially an exercise in judgment. There is much in it that must be subjective. The areas of uncertainty are many. Different industries, different companies, will view the question from different viewpoints and in different lights.[61]

Clearly the CBI leadership was taking every opportunity to present as positive and unified a view as possible.

FOLLOWING UP ON *BRITAIN AND EUROPE*

The line adopted by the CBI leadership had multiple purposes. One was to "educate" the CBI's members about the advantages of EC entry. The report and the background papers, the latter published as *Britain and Europe, Vol. 2*, were followed up by a consultation exercise with the membership.[62] This took four forms: a survey questionnaire to 1700 firms, through the meetings of the CBI's twelve regional councils and its Small Firms Steering Group, through submissions by member trade associations and employers' organizations, and through enquiries among other bodies related in their activities to manufacturing industry.[63]

The four-page survey questionnaire was the first to be completed with a response rate of over 50 percent, 865 replies from individual firms in all.[64] Somewhat surprisingly, it was the first time that the membership had been asked directly about entry into the EC – previous questionnaires had related to the free trade area proposals or, as in 1963, had been planned

---

[59] *The Times*, 22 December 1966, 17.   [60] CBI, *Britain and Europe, Vol. 1*, 2.
[61] MRC MSS200/C/1/2/O, O.173.66, CBI Europe Steering Committee 10th meeting, 20 October 1966.
[62] CBI, *Britain and Europe, Vol. 2*.
[63] CBI, *Britain and Europe, Vol. 3: A Programme for Action Together with a Report on Consultations with Industry* (London, 1967), 3.
[64] MRC MSS200/C/1/2/O, O.3.67, Norman to the individual companies, 17 January 1967 and Norman to members, 7 March 1967.

Table 7.2. *Representativeness of the 1967 CBI Sample Survey*

Industry	National Industrial Output (%)	CBI Response (%)
Mechanical engineering	14.14	24
Electrical engineering	9.04	11
Metals and metal manufacture	13.33	12
Vehicles	13.03	6
Textiles, clothing, footwear and leather	11.59	13
Food, drink and tobacco	11.22	7
Chemicals	10.78	8
Building materials, pottery and glass, timber and wooden furniture	6.63	6
Paper and printing	7.76	5
Other industries	2.49	10
Size of company (by no. of employees)		
0–199	17.8	29
200–499	13.8	19
500–4999	30.2	39
>5000	38.1	13

Source: MRC MSS200/C/1/2/O, Norman to members, 7 March 1967, appendix to press release.

but never introduced because of de Gaulle's veto.[65] Although the original sample was meant to be representative of industry, inevitably the actual pattern of response did not replicate this. The sector most underrepresented was vehicles while mechanical engineering was most overrepresented, and it was decided not to publish the sectoral breakdown of results.[66] In terms of firm size, small companies were overrepresented and large companies significantly underrepresented, as is shown in Table 7.2. This is relevant given the widely held belief that small firms tended to be less in favor of EC entry than larger ones.

The responses to the three main conclusions in the steering committee's report have always been the center of attention. Individual companies were, in general, positive about the effect of membership for them, or saw little effect, and few expected a detrimental effect. There was an astonishing degree of support for the conclusions of the steering committee: 91 percent believed there would be a clear and progressive balance of advantage to British industry as a whole from membership, 90 percent thought the Treaty of Rome and the Community's method of operation acceptable given rea-

[65] MRC MSS200/C/3/S1/12/8, Felgate to Shanks, 24 June 1966.
[66] MRC MSS200/C/1/2/O, O.26A.67, CBI Europe Steering Committee 12th meeting, 2 March 1967.

sonable transitional arrangements, and 89 percent agreed that entry should be negotiated as soon as possible.[67] CBI officials believed these results were "too good to be true" and agreed that their presentation to the press should be "dead-pan" as "there was a danger of appearing too euphoric about the degree of support by industry for entry."[68] Nevertheless, the press release has been seen as the "most important single CBI announcement" on Europe in this period.[69]

The survey offers much more than this: It was the most detailed of any of the surveys undertaken of business opinion on Europe and so the responses do allow a quite detailed picture of business opinion to be constructed. It asked for consideration of the effects of British membership of an enlarged EC on various aspects of the individual company's operations, on its markets, on its need to adapt, and on the balance of advantage with regard to costs, profitability and growth, in addition to the firm's attitude to the conclusions of the steering committee. In all there were thirty-four questions.

Table 7.3 sets out the results in relation to the perceived impact on the individual respondent firm. This throws up a number of important issues. Most significant is the difference between the perceived overall balance of advantage of entry for British industry as a whole (91 percent) highlighted at the time and ever since, and the perceived balance of advantage to the individual firm (68 percent), as shown in the final column of Table 7.3. How was it that over a fifth of respondents thought that there was a clear and progressive balance of advantage for industry as a whole but not for their own company? In this respect, the CBI's efforts to "educate" the wider membership had proved extremely successful with the report clearly persuasive and convincing. However, there must have been other reasons. One possibility is that political considerations explain the difference. Certainly, when the second application was made it was often stated by businessmen that the motive for the application was political rather than economic but this is not relevant in this case because firms were asked for their views on the balance of advantage to industry as a whole, not the country as a whole.[70]

Another possible factor was that sectoral or scale differences explained the situation. Companies might have thought that other sectors of the economy or companies of a different size would benefit more than their own. Two sources allow this proposition to be examined more closely: The CBI drew up its own unpublished breakdown of the overall results by sector and by size of company and it followed this up with a survey of member trade associations.

[67] *The Times*, 8 March 1967; and Kitzinger, *Second Try*, 168–70, for the results of the survey.

[68] MRC MSS200/C/3/IA/1/14, Melville to Davies, 2 March 1967; and MSS200/C/1/2/O, O.26A.67, Europe Steering Committee 12th meeting, 2 March 1967.

[69] Frey, "Meaning Business," 218.

[70] MRC MSS200/C/3/S1/12/4, Binder, Hamlyn and Co., secretaries to the Federation of Manufacturers of Construction Equipment, to the CBI, 13 March 1967.

Table 7.3. *Results of the 1967 CBI Questionnaire on the Effects of Entry into an Enlarged EC on the Individual Company on the Basis of* Britain and Europe, *Vol. 1 (%): Balance of Advantage for Company*

	Up	Same	Down	Don't Know	Yes	No
(i) *Costs*: In the light of the analysis contained in the report, how would you expect your company's costs on balance to be affected by British membership of an enlarged EC?	19	53	22	6		
(ii) *Profitability*: In the light of all of the above, how would you expect your company's profitability to be affected by British membership of an enlarged EC?	41	35	17	8		
(iii) *Growth*: In the light of all of the above, do you think there would be a clear and progressive balance of advantage to your company from membership of an enlarged EC?					68	30

Source: MRC MSS200/C/1/2/O, attached to letter from Norman to members, 7 March 1967.

In relation to the size of operation the results broadly replicated the overall picture with smaller firms less positive in each case. The sectoral analysis is more interesting. Support for the first conclusion of the steering committee's report was remarkably consistent across the sectors, never falling below 87 percent. The response to the final question was much more mixed, ranging from 74 percent endorsement from mechanical engineering down to only 45 percent of those surveyed in food, drink and tobacco believing that their companies would gain a clear and progressive advantage. From the answers to the other questions it is clear that the food, drink, and tobacco sector did not envisage entry into the EC as offering many gains or, indeed, having anything like the impact perceived in other parts of the economy.

The questionnaire to individual firms was followed up by a survey of trade associations where it was hoped that the detailed differences between industries would emerge, something in which the CBI and the government were "very interested."[71] The questionnaire for member trade associations was much shorter, asking just four questions about whether the association agreed with the conclusions of *Britain and Europe, Vol. 1*, whether the impact would be advantageous or not, the main reasons for this and if there were any particular issues in relation to future negotiations over EC entry. A short eight-page summary of the responses was published as part of *Britain and Europe, Vol. 3* but there was also a seventy-seven-page internal document which summarized each of the over ninety responses.[72] From this longer document some firmer conclusions about sectoral differences and their impact on perceptions of European integration emerge. A number of sectors, for example, mechanical engineering, were in favor of UK entry into an enlarged EC for the standard reasons, with trade associations from the sector mentioning the removal of tariff barriers (the British Chemical Plant Manufacturers' Association and the Roll Makers' Association), the larger "home" market (British Chemical Plant Manufacturers' Association and the Steel Works Plant Association) and the opportunities for economies of scale (British Mechanical Engineering Federation and the Business Equipment Trade Association).[73]

However, removal of tariffs was only part of the story. As the steering committee report noted: "At least as important [as tariffs] would be the gradual assimilation of the economies of the Member States. . . . Tariffs are merely one group among the complex factors, tangible and intangible, that would influence the scope and direction of British industrial thought and action."[74] This was borne out in the responses from both individual companies and trade associations. Many referred to the issue of tax harmonization and of shifting the tax burden towards indirect taxation in the context of introducing a value added tax like the Six (see Chapter 10). Other aspects of harmonization, such as of patents and standards, were also particularly important to some, like the engineering firms. Technological collaboration was cited by some respondents. Factors were often sector specific: For producers of bulky goods, transport facilities and freight rates were important factors (the British Mechanical Engineering Federation, the Chemical Industries Association, the Council of Ironfoundry Associations and the British Non-Ferrous Metals Federation).[75] For some the removal of exchange

---

[71] MRC MSS200/C/3/S1/12/12, Felgate to Douglas, 9 January 1967.

[72] CBI, *Britain and Europe, Vol. 3*; and MRC MSS200/C/1/2/O, O.36.67, "Britain and Europe: Consultations with Industry: Views of Trade Associations and Employers' Organisations," July 1967.

[73] MRC MSS200/C/1/2/O, O.36.67, 1–12.   [74] CBI, *Britain and Europe, Vol. 1*, 8.

[75] MRC MSS200/C/1/2/O, O.36.67, 2, 19, 21 and 52.

control on capital movements was important (the Electronic Engineering Association, the Chemical Industries Association and the Tyre Manufacturers' Conference Ltd.) and, along with others (the Society of British Aerospace Companies Ltd.), these also emphasized the importance of the removal of barriers to mergers and joint ventures.[76] Here, then, is part of the explanation for the disparity in perceptions of impact on the individual company and industry as a whole. The benefits of British entry did not relate simply to sales but also to possible changes in the wider business environment. The importance of these potential changes varied from sector to sector, although taxation was a common theme for many.

Yet this is not the whole story. A number of trade associations made reference to the benefits in efficiency that would be gained by British business as a whole from the greater competition that would follow from UK entry. As the Machine Tools Trade Association put it, "An additional spur would be given to our manufacturing industries by the increased competition which we anticipate would result from entry."[77] Similarly, the British Ball Clay Producers' Federation Ltd. noted that its exporters already had duty free entry into the EC but were still in favor of entry because "it should increase the overall volume of trade and the interchange of capital investments and generally strengthen the markets we have already developed."[78] It was these general economic benefits and the potential changes in the domestic business environment which together explained why British business was so much more positive about the impact on British industry as a whole than it was about its own prospects. Nevertheless, it should not be forgotten that almost 70 percent, a very sizeable majority, saw a balance of advantage to their industry from EC entry.

As already mentioned, many factors were sector-specific or even firm-specific, and there had been a concern that this situation would only result in "an avalanche of paper" from trade associations setting out their particular issues and diluting the initial impact of the report.[79] As the director of the Glass Manufacturers' Federation put it:

There must certainly be many industries in this country which are very much like the glass industry and which are composed of very different industries, although working in the same basic material. In those cases, each section of the industry will see the advantages and disadvantages of Britain becoming closely associated with Europe in a different light. . . . I think there will be quite distinct differences of opinion within industries and it will be very difficult to reconcile them and really make some assessment for the balance of long-run advantage.[80]

[76] Ibid., 15, 27–28, 51 and 75.   [77] Ibid., 6.   [78] Ibid., O.36.67, 74.
[79] MRC MSS200/C/3/S1/12/12, Douglas, British Man-Made Fibres Federation, to Felgate, 6 January 1967.
[80] Ibid., Rider to Felgate, 3 January 1967.

Exactly the same point was made in relation to the textile industry.[81] There was the expected avalanche of responses and many did make reference to short-term difficulties, but what is so significant is that so many ended up at the same conclusion, endorsing UK entry, even if they reached it by different routes. The CBI leadership may have led opinion by casting *Britain and Europe* in such a positive light but it cannot be accused of taking British business down a path it did not want to go on this occasion. The other forms of consultation merely confirmed this, for example with overwhelming support for the report in the CBI Regional Councils.[82] Thus the CBI had as good as completed its consultation process on *Britain and Europe* prior to the Labour government's formal announcement of a second application. *Britain and Europe, Vol. 3* was not misleading then in stating that there was "virtually unanimous support" (with the notable exception of the NFU) for the conclusions of the steering committee report, despite a belief in Whitehall that the report was full of unconvincing assertions and was "unlikely to persuade the sceptics."[83] A similarly overwhelming level of support for entry into the EC was also found in the ABCC's referendum on the subject carried out at the same time.[84]

A clear voice was important for the second aspect of the whole *Britain and Europe* exercise, which was to put pressure on the government. Growing interest from business in 1965–66 in greater engagement with the EC was only part of a wider trend in Britain by which Europe had become "fashionable."[85] The underlying philosophy of the CBI leadership was as follows:

Commitment of this kind will both strengthen the government's determination to succeed and make an importantly favourable impression upon the Six. Faint John Bull never won fair Europe. . . .

Since a Labour government will be more vulnerable (or even sympathetic) to opposition within Britain, industry must stick in its toes and refuse to mortgage its future by undue tenderness towards special interests.[86]

Making this clear to government ministers was not so straightforward, however. Lieber has argued that CBI was in a position of "unprecedented weakness" when it came to influencing the government's European policy because the CBI's fervor for EC entry meant that the government "had

---

[81] Ibid., Douglas to Felgate, 6 January 1967.

[82] MRC MSS200/C/1/2/O, O.26A.67, Europe Steering Committee 12th meeting, 2 March 1967.

[83] CBI, *Britain and Europe, Vol. 3*, 15; and TNA EW5/21, Stevens to Charles, 6 January 1967.

[84] TNA EW5/22, Maclean, President of the ABCC, to Stewart, 20 April 1967.

[85] "After the Election," *Commerce* (April 1966), 9; MRC MSS200/C/3/S1/12/5, Melville to Boyd, covering PEP, "Were Britain to Try Again," 14 June 1966; and "ICI Chief says Britons Want to Join Europe," *The Times*, 20 January 1967, 8.

[86] MRC MSS200/C/3/S1/12/5, Melville to Boyd, covering a paper by PEP, "Were Britain to Try Again," 14 June 1966.

little compulsion for seeking to bargain in detail."[87] He then illustrates this weakness by showing how meaningless and unimportant the Industrial Consultative Committee on the Approach to Europe was. The committee was inconsequential. Harold Wilson, the Prime Minister, announced its creation in his 1966 Mansion House speech.[88] Despite its title it was never intended to be consultative. As government officials bluntly put it, the committee "would in practice be used as little more than a recipient of reports from the government on developments" but it would, "at least, have a useful PR role."[89] When in March 1967 Wilson announced on television that the work of the consultative committee was to be intensified, officials were rather bemused.[90] In fact, all Wilson had in mind was a meeting to be called so that it could be manifestly shown that there had been consultation with industry before the government reached its decision on whether to apply to enter the EC.[91] In all, the committee was to meet only four times between December 1966 and May 1967. Its chair, Michael Stewart, the Secretary of State for Economic Affairs, was happy to allow the committee to die quietly in July 1967, mourned by none of its members, including those from industry.[92]

However, Lieber is mistaken in two respects. First, business was deliberately forthright in its views because it was trying to get a commitment from the Labour government to make the second application. This was the key goal. Secondly, to suggest that the consultative committee typified relations between business representatives and the government is too sweeping. The CBI acknowledged that there were problems with business–government relations as, "There is no mechanism whereby on a continuing basis ministers and officials of the Board of Trade can be brought face to face with the thinking of leaders of industry on matters of long-term commercial strategy. Inevitably this tends to result in the government taking the initiative very often and industries being consulted afterwards."[93] Yet the position was more complex and varied. There was ongoing consultation between business and government officials prior to the government deciding to apply for membership. Once the government had announced its intention to mount a

---

[87] Robert Lieber, *British Politics and European Unity* (Berkeley: University of California Press, 1970), 265 and 269.

[88] TNA PREM13/1474, Wilson to Stewart, 11 November 1966; and TNA EW5/21, Burgh to Mitchell, 14 November 1966.

[89] TNA EW5/21, Hodges to Thornton, 15 November 1966 and meeting of officials, 15 November 1966.

[90] TNA EW5/22, Charles to Stock and Mitchell, 29 March 1967.

[91] TNA EW28/20, Halls (PM's Office) to Burgh (DEA), 14 March 1967.

[92] TNA PREM13/1474, Burgh to Stock, 20 July 1967; and TNA EW5/22, Burgh to Stock, 6 July 1967.

[93] MRC MSS200/C/1/2/O, CO.10.66, "Methods of Consultation between Government and Industry on Overseas Trade Policy," undated but about January 1966.

second application in May 1967, it was agreed that the Foreign Office would create a small committee to consult business on strategic issues and to act as a clearing house for intelligence, including that gathered by the CBI through its contacts with its counterparts on the continent, while more detailed aspects would be handled by small informal meetings with the Board of Trade.[94]

The presentation of *Britain and Europe, Vol. 3* to the government is illustrative of the complex relationship. The volume set out a "programme of action," a set of recommendations on the steps that were needed to ease any transitional difficulties and to make the most of entry once it occurred.[95] It was handed over to the Prime Minister and other ministers at a specially arranged meeting at No. 10 Downing Street. While Harold Wilson commended the CBI on their work there was no sense of a warm and open dialogue and, although he did not reject the CBI's proposals for liaison during the negotiations, Wilson suggested that there was unlikely to be detailed discussion of business-related issues in any negotiations.[96]

On the other hand, the purpose of the meeting was to hand over the report "in the glare of the fullest possible publicity" as a way of maintaining the momentum of the approach to the EC, a goal also supported in Whitehall.[97] As was reported to the CBI Council, it was agreed that "the CBI and government should work together to maintain the momentum, both at home and abroad, in the approach to Europe."[98] In other words, the need was for the public appearance of unity. Moreover, Wilson went on to note that contact with the CBI would be necessary "on the question of assimilating our laws and practices with those in the Community," mentioning "such matters as company law and fiscal practices."[99] This was a significant concession because the program of action listed many steps which government would need to take in the eyes of the CBI.[100] As the brief that officials supplied for Wilson told him:

At many points [the report] involves government action, sometimes in line with government policy, sometimes not necessarily so, or involves action expressed in terms that imply a much firmer commitment than the government would wish to take on without a great deal more thought. This is very evident for instance in the section "The management of the economy." There is a call for greater incentives

---

[94] Ibid., O.51A.67, CBI Europe Steering Committee 14th meeting, 21 May 1967; and TNA EW5/22, Mitchell to Charles, 12 May 1967.

[95] CBI, *Britain and Europe, Vol. 3*, 5–13.

[96] TNA PREM13/1474, "Note of a Meeting between the Prime Minister and Representatives of the Confederation of British Industry at No. 10 Downing Street on July 4, 1967."

[97] TNA PREM13/1474, Charles to Burgh, 3 July 1967, and unknown to Nield, 3 July 1967.

[98] MRC MSS200/C/1/1, C.61.67, director-general's report to Council, July 1967.

[99] TNA PREM13/1474, "Note of a Meeting between the Prime Minister and Representatives of the Confederation of British Industry at No. 10 Downing Street on July 4, 1967."

[100] CBI, *Britain and Europe, Vol. 3*, 7–13.

and for a radical review of many areas of policy – particularly in the fiscal sphere. Again in the section on taxation there is a call for the transfer of part of the tax burden from direct to indirect taxation with a reduction in the load on profits and on incomes, and the report recommends a reduced rate of withholding tax payable on dividends.

These are illustrations of the impossibility of welcoming this report wholeheartedly, and without qualification.[101]

The quote helps to explain Wilson's cool welcome of the document but also why British business was so positive about British entry into the EC at this particular time. At the start of the Labour administration in 1964, relations between the CBI and the government were good but this relationship began to deteriorate markedly as policy differences emerged. British business believed that the policy framework in Britain unfairly disadvantaged them. Membership of the EC would offer a way out of these difficulties: EC member states' growth rates were higher, their industries were becoming increasingly competitive and, in business' view, this was not just because of the larger market but also because of different economic policies. Becoming a member of the EC would force the British government to adjust its policies and also through expected policy harmonization also provide a similar business environment. *Britain and Europe, Vol. 1* had recognized this: "if entry into the EEC is made a conscious objective, then it follows that future policy ought to be judged not only on the criteria of whether it is sound in itself but whether it may be expected to facilitate Britain's joining the Community."[102] This approach offered the opportunity to recommend a raft of policy reforms, including a conscious effort to bring British law closer to Community practice, a re-examination of the structure and balance of the fiscal system, and in particular a reconsideration of Selective Employment Tax and Investment Grants, a reduction of direct taxation and the introduction of VAT (see Chapter 10), government encouragement of profitable investment, including freer movement of capital overseas, the easing of merger legislation, government support for the rationalization of industry to achieve economies of scale, and the improvement of transport facilities to the continent. The EC was being used as a lever to push for adjustments in domestic economic policy to make it more business friendly.

De Gaulle's second veto towards the end of 1967 therefore not only killed off hopes of Britain's early entry into the EC but also removed the force of this stick with which to prod the Labour government. It is significant that the one area of continued collaboration between business and the government related to European technological collaboration and this was to take an increasingly prominent position in the consideration of European integration. More generally, the Labour government did leave the application on

---

[101] TNA PREM13/1474, Charles to Burgh, 3 July 1967, attached brief.
[102] CBI, *Britain and Europe, Vol. 1*, 3.

the table by not formally withdrawing it. The CBI's leadership also remained committed to the goal of EC entry. Having taken stock of the situation following the second veto the CBI Council issued a new policy statement on Europe. It reaffirmed the position of the 1966 report, argued that, while the successful completion of the Kennedy Round of GATT negotiations and the resulting program of trade liberalization when added to the effect of the November 1967 devaluation of sterling had mitigated the worst trading effects of exclusion from the EC, there were other "compelling reasons" for entry.[103] It suggested, therefore, that Britain should continue to pursue its application and that the differences between Britain and the EC needed to be narrowed.

In sharp contrast to 1963 the CBI statement received virtually no wider acknowledgement. Within the business community the appeal of EC entry began to wane after the second veto for a variety of reasons. First, even if it was believed UK entry into the EC was no less desirable than before, it was recognized that "it is not attainable in the foreseeable future."[104] A further reason for the popularity in business circles of the 1967 application was the perceived need to get into the EC as soon as possible. As the response to the third conclusion of *Britain and Europe, Vol. 1* made clear, British business wanted a speedy entry into the EC. "Because so much of Community policy is still in embryo, the quicker Britain can share in the decision-making process the better," lay behind this feeling.[105] In the eyes of business, the mid-1960s offered a window of opportunity: EC institutional structures were appearing, some of which seemed preferable to those in Britain, but the longer before Britain entered the further the EC would continue to develop without an input from Britain (and British business) and be formulated without Britain in mind.[106] This was particularly true of the Common Agricultural Policy, the implementation of which would increase the cost of living significantly as well as imposing a sizeable financial burden on Britain through contributing to its operation. As the CAP was gradually settled so the cost to Britain became more apparent and of greater concern to business. In addition, at home, industrial relations were deteriorating and there were growing concerns that Britain was no longer competitive – a period of preparation might be necessary for business to ready itself for facing competition from the continent.

Just as the costs of EC membership seemed to be rising so the benefits appeared to be diminishing. The completion of the Kennedy Round in 1967 ensured that there would be significant reductions in the EC's common

---

[103] MRC MSS200/1/1, C.21.68, "Britain and Europe: The Way Ahead," C.21A.68, "CBI Statement on Policy on Europe," both undated but March 1968, and C.28.68, CBI Council meeting, 20 March 1968.
[104] TNA FCO30/481, CBI Europe Steering Committee paper, 16 October 1968.
[105] CBI, *Britain and Europe, Vol. 1*, 3.   [106] Ibid., 6.

external tariff by 1972 making UK access to the markets of the Six easier from outside the EC than would otherwise have been the case, while devaluation meant that in the short term at least UK exports were more price competitive. In addition, many large companies had been investing heavily in the EC and this reduced the urgency of membership for them (see Chapter 3). With the prospect of imminent EC entry receding and reduced incentives to push the idea of EC membership, so the appeal of EC entry waned among business circles. There was almost a sense of resignation that EC entry would not happen in the foreseeable future and that companies just had to get on with life as best they could – there were far too many other problems to worry about. As a result, the popularity of EC entry was never to reach the same heights as at the time of second application.

CONCLUSION

In many respects there was little change between 1963 and 1968. Britain was not a member of the EC because of de Gaulle's veto in 1963 and that was still the case in 1968. However, in other respects there had been enormous shifts. In 1963 the veto was a shock but there was also a sense of relief that uncertainty had been removed, whereas in 1967 it was disappointing but not unexpected. Yet, for business, the 1967 veto had a more negative impact than in 1963. In 1963 companies had responded by increasing their overseas investment in Europe and by looking for export opportunities around the world, including in the Six. After the second veto, business was much more pessimistic and at a loss what to do. To a considerable extent this was the consequence of the degree of support for EC entry that existed in British business at this time. As EC entry was so strongly wanted the reaction to the veto was an even greater sense of disappointment. Ludlow has recently argued that the second application lost the battle but won the war over enlargement.[107] This was not how it felt to British business at the time. The appeal of European integration to business was multi-faceted and complex. To some it remained an issue of tariffs even after the Kennedy Round but other factors increasingly came to the fore and reflected a wide and dynamic definition of what constituted European integration in which economic and political integration interacted. Its appeal was also relative and there was an issue of timing too: It was important to get into the EC before policies developed too extensively without a British input.

In all of this the role of business leaders remained central. Their influence on business opinion remained crucial. However, the leaders of the new CBI were not swimming against the tide in this period. The business community

[107] Ludlow, *European Community*, 146–73.

may have been led toward Europe but it was not reluctant to move in that direction. Similarly, Lieber is mistaken to criticize the CBI's lack of influence on government policy. The CBI wanted a second application and it got it. It not only maintained consultation and influence through a variety of forums with government departments but also with its counterpart organizations in the Six.

8

The End Game: From the Hague Summit to British Accession, 1969–1973

The dismay and disillusionment that followed de Gaulle's second veto was not limited to Great Britain. There was a wider sense of frustration, with certain member states, especially the Dutch, refusing to countenance any measures to deepen integration, particularly those proposed by the French, until the issue of British membership had been addressed. The result was a stalemate and stasis in the European Community.[1] The standoff began to thaw after April 1969 with de Gaulle's resignation as the French President and his replacement by Georges Pompidou. As Ludlow puts it, with this event the end game in the story of British entry into the EC had begun, although the topic remained complex and British entry was no foregone conclusion. The Hague summit of December 1969 marked the crucial breakthrough with the resulting commitment to deeper integration in the community, notably via economic and monetary union, and also to enlargement. Negotiations between Britain, the Six, and the Commission opened in 1970 and the outcome was ratified by Parliament the following year: On January 1, 1973, the UK, Ireland, and Denmark became members of the EC and the Six became the Nine. Historians are only now beginning to get access to the relevant documents on these events. Recent publications have dealt with the Hague summit but there is yet to be an archive-based account of the negotiations.[2] Indeed, the literature on the negotiations is relatively sparse, though reference should be made to Con O'Neill's official account of the negotiations, written at the time but only published in 2000.[3]

---

[1] N. Piers Ludlow, *The European Community and the Crisis of the 1960s: Negotiating the Gaullist Challenge* (London: Routledge, 2006), 146–73.

[2] Ludlow, *European Community*, and the special issue of the *Journal of European Integration History*, Vol. 9, No. 2 (2003).

[3] Uwe Kitzinger, *Diplomacy and Persuasion: How Britain Joined the Common Market* (London: Thames and Hudson, 1973); Simon Young, *Terms of Entry: Britain's Negotiations with the European Community 1970–1972* (London: Heinemann, 1973); Christopher Lord, *British Entry to the European Community under the Heath Government of 1970–4* (Aldershot: Dartmouth, 1993); and Sir David Hannay (ed.), *Britain's Entry into the European Community: Report by Sir Con O'Neill on the Negotiations of 1970–1972* (London: Whitehall in association with Frank Cass, 2000).

The topic of British business and European integration in this period has received even less consideration.[4] This chapter, therefore, not only extends the story told so far but also is one of the first archive-based accounts covering the period of the negotiations. At the end of the previous chapter, it was shown how business opinion in Britain on European integration had begun to diversify given no early prospect of British membership of the EC. Three responses can be recognized: those still committed to British membership, those who began investigating alternative proposals, and those who had, like ICI, integrated themselves economically in Europe and for whom political integration was no longer an urgent issue: As the *Financial Times* put it, this last group had already joined the EC, even if Britain did not.[5]

De Gaulle's resignation in the spring of 1969 impacted upon all of these positions and within the business community, whichever position was held, there was a case for taking this opportunity to reappraise Britain's relations with Europe. The chapter begins with this decision and the study that followed. The second section then tries to explain the changes in business opinion shown by the response to the study. Next, the build up to the negotiations and the negotiations themselves are considered before ending with the preparations in business for entry.

THE SECOND APPRAISAL

After the 1967 veto the CBI issued a new statement reiterating its belief that British membership of the EC remained the desired policy. To this point relations between the Foreign Office and the CBI had been broadly harmonious – the Foreign and Commonwealth Office (FCO), as the Foreign Office had now become, regarded the CBI as a pro-European ally, while the CBI found discussions with FCO officials more open and rewarding than those with either the Board of Trade or the Ministry of Technology. However, during 1969 this position changed with FCO officials hearing reports of CBI representatives and staff making what the FCO regarded as inappropriate comments in relation to European integration, be it on floating exchange rates, the nature and cost of the Common Agricultural Policy and the possibility of something less than full EC membership for Britain.[6] Kit Cope, the CBI's Assistant Overseas Director, explained the situation as he saw it:

When the CBI approval had been given for the British application in 1966–67, the question had been rushed through and the cost to Britain of joining had been rather

---

[4] Robert Lieber, *British Politics and European Unity: Parties, Elites and Pressure Groups* (Berkeley: University of California Press, 1970).

[5] *Financial Times*, 1 February 1970, quoted in Lord, *British Entry*, 20.

[6] TNA FCO30/481, Hannay to Petrie, "CBI/UNICE meeting," 2 April 1969 and attached CBI paper, "International monetary policy," 17 March 1969, and Killick to Sir Thomas Brimelow, "The CBI and Europe," 15 May 1969.

glossed over. He did not think that the CBI had departed from the basic belief that British membership was the right answer *ultimately*, but during the intervening period various factors had influenced their thinking about what our immediate policy should be. First, they had done their sums about the balance of payments costs – particularly in the agricultural field. Second, the prospects within the Community itself had become much more gloomy and in general the likelihood of access to the Community offering the United Kingdom greatly improved trade prospects in the industrial field seemed a good deal less. (Presumably the Kennedy Round is also relevant here). Third, opinion in British industry generally had deteriorated.[7]

Cope supported this with the example of the Birmingham Chamber of Commerce, whose members contributed a significant share of British exports: In 1966/67, ninety percent had been in favor of British entry; the proportion, he suggested, was now totally reversed.

Worse still for the FCO, the CBI was thinking of making a statement in June redefining its attitude to UK membership. It was envisaged that this "would involve a distinct watering down of what they said in 1966/67."[8] All of this "seriously disturbed" the FCO official who had met Cope: one of the FCO's most reliable allies on EC entry appeared to be getting cold feet. This had the potential to scupper any new initiatives if it became more widely known. Faced with this situation the FCO went into overdrive first to examine Cope's arguments and evidence, second to see if his views were corroborated by other members of the CBI leadership, and, third, to exert pressure on the CBI about the form of any statement, and even to question the need for a statement.[9] FCO officials could not believe that other leading CBI staff, notably John Davies, the director-general and known supporter of European integration, would have shifted their position so much and a dispute broke out between Cope and John Robinson, one of the leading FCO officials on European integration, over what Davies and others' views were.[10]

It is clear that Davies' views had shifted from 1965–67 when he had put European integration high on to the agenda for the newly created CBI. He told the Foreign Secretary about his concerns on the cost of the CAP and its impact on the cost of living, and that in 1967 business support had been "unconditional" whereas now Britain could not accept what looked like potentially impossible burdens attached to membership.[11] He told another government minister:

[7] TNA FCO30/481, Killick to Brimelow, "The CBI and Europe," 15 May 1969.

[8] Ibid.

[9] TNA FCO30/482, Robinson, handwritten note added to unknown to Killick, 22 May 1969.

[10] Ibid., Robinson, "The CBI and Europe," 16 May 1969, and Robinson to Killick, "The CBI," 22 May 1969.

[11] TNA FCO30/482, "Record of Talks with the CBI at the FCO," 21 May 1969.

It was essential to take account of the facts that the EC countries themselves had made much less progress with the development of the Community than had been expected at the time of our last effort to join; that the British balance of payments problem had proved much more intractable than we had anticipated; and that the cost to us of subscribing to the common agricultural policy, which they had earlier estimated to be of the order of £250 m. per annum, now seemed likely to be even higher.[12]

Davies also complained that the FCO was accusing the CBI of back-tracking on their enthusiasm for EC membership but that this was not the case, it was just that the position had changed:

[the] CBI was now convinced that if they put the question of membership to British industry today it would be answered in the negative. By comparison with 1967, there were serious doubts about the economic advantages of EEC membership. There had been important changes. There was still a strong need to carry industry along as negotiations proceeded . . . . Whilst the CBI did not wish to embarrass the government, since both wished to achieve the same objective, they had to be mindful of their position vis-à-vis their membership.[13]

As in 1961 with the FBI, the CBI leadership was being constrained by the perceived views of the membership. Following "extensive tours of industry in this country," Cope believed that "general opinion in industry was markedly anti-British membership of the EEC" and that "the Midlands were the worst of the lot."[14] However, that business around Birmingham had changed its views so much was a constructed perception. It was based on an informal lunch arranged by Cope.[15] Two of those invited were notorious for their opposition to British entry into the Community and they dominated the discussion. Cope had then asked for a show of hands on the issue and it was this vote that had gone overwhelmingly against UK entry. In contrast, the director of the Birmingham Chamber of Commerce believed that this was unrepresentative of business opinion in the Midlands: A poll, he believed, would show a substantial majority in favor of entry, though with a larger minority against than in 1967. Certainly, the chamber came out in favor of EC entry in February 1970.[16] Misrepresentation of business opinion at this one event had a major impact on the perceptions of the CBI leadership that the business community was losing some of its enthusiasm for EC entry.

Nevertheless, it is clear that there was some vociferous opposition to EC entry from some industrialists, even if they constituted a minority. The CBI published an anodyne statement announcing that the CBI was updating its

---

[12] TNA BT241/2156, POM 345, "Dinner with the CBI," 20 May 1969.
[13] TNA FCO30/482, "Note of the meeting with CBI on 27 May, 1969."
[14] Ibid., "The CBI and Europe," 15 August 1969.
[15] Ibid., Rooke to Robinson, 2 October 1969.
[16] "Chamber still Supports EEC Entry," *Midland Industry and Commerce* (February 1970), 102–5.

1966/67 appraisal, that it was principally concerned with the effect upon British industry and that it would take into account the CAP, the effect on the balance of payments, on the cost of living, wage rates and "other important elements in our economic life."[17] This was sufficiently watered down to appease the FCO and was approved at the CBI Council with little apparent opposition.[18] Yet, when Sir John Hunter, the shipbuilder, suggested at the Council meeting that there should be no acceptance of the principle of entry, the remarks were met with applause from other Council members. Even if there was support in business for Britain joining the EC, it was now conditional and could not be taken for granted.

Attention then turned to the study itself and the tone of CBI staff comments began to be more positive and closer to FCO expectations. Cope now believed that the conclusion of the study would be very similar to 1966 and that the role of the CBI was "leading industry into recognizing once again the considerable long term benefits of membership," but that "this is not proving an easy task" with one CBI Regional Council coming out against entry except on unrealistic terms, while other Regional Councils were more positive but largely because they could see no alternative.[19] The strategy adopted by the CBI leadership, and approved by the FCO, was for the appraisal to be completed in two stages. The first would focus on the strictly industrial implications: illustration of the importance of Europe to British industry, a consideration of developments since 1966 and a section on the possibilities for a European industrial policy, something in which Derek Ezra, the chairman of the committee dealing with the review, was particularly interested and built on earlier interest in technological collaboration.[20] The second part would consider the wider aspects of European integration and their implications for industry and would follow as these aspects became clearer. This potentially more contentious part of the study was drafted by the CBI's Economic Committee, who tried to estimate the effect of the tariff changes, the likely cost of the CAP, the likely impact on monetary policy, and the likely impact on the cost of living.[21]

In the published version of the CBI's report, symbolically called *Britain in Europe* to mark the shift from *Britain and Europe*, the short-term costs of entry on the balance of payments were broadly similar to the government's own estimates once changes in costs announced after *Britain in Europe* was

---

[17] TNA FCO30/482, CBI Council statement, "Britain and Europe," 16 July 1969.

[18] Ibid., Robinson to Brimelow, "The CBI and Europe," 15 July 1969; MRC MSS200/C/1/1/C, C.64.69, CBI Council meeting, 16 July 1969.

[19] TNA FCO30/482, Cope to Marjoribanks, 10 July 1969.

[20] Ibid., Ezra to Marjoribanks, "CBI Study," 28 July 1969. On his interest in industrial policy see Ibid., Cope to Marjoribanks, 10 July 1969. On FCO approval see Ibid., Robinson to Killick, 5 August 1969.

[21] MSS200/C/1/2/E, E.431.69, and thereafter. See also, CBI, *Britain in Europe: A Second Industrial Appraisal* (London, January 1969).

published and differences in methodology were incorporated.[22] However, in two respects the CBI was disappointed with the government document. First, both in Whitehall and at the CBI it was felt that *Britain in Europe* was stronger on its analysis of industrial policy and in particular on technology, with the government underestimating the potential for business collaboration and its impact on growth.[23] The second difference was the approach to the long-term impact of entry. The government made no attempt to quantify the positive long-term dynamic effects. Worse still, it was felt that the government document implied that the achievement of these dynamic effects was dependent on business responding to British membership of the EC – all the government had to do was to negotiate entry – and this was wrong, particularly, given the emphasis business was now placing on industrial policy and its impact on the business landscape:

The European governments must be reminded that the future industrial environment is very much their responsibility and that vigorous action will be required on their part to harmonise the legal, fiscal and financial environment, and the whole gamut of non-tariff barriers to trade and to industrial restructuring – standards, rules and regulations covering safety, health and welfare, legal and accounting practice etc. etc.[24]

Given the positive tone on the benefits of British entry into the EC in *Britain in Europe*, it is not surprising that relations with the FCO improved sharply and were seen by FCO officials to be "close and fruitful," with them getting "all we want on the CBI exercise under the counter" and Derek Ezra praised for having been "extremely helpful" and having "played an influential role as chairman of the CBI's Europe Committee."[25] Equally, it was predictable that certain members of the CBI Council would be highly critical of the report. When he introduced the report to Council in December 1969, Ezra tried to head off opposition by describing "a series of intensive informal consultations" which had taken place.[26] Opinions had been gathered from trade associations, individual firms, trade federations in EFTA and the EC as well as contacts with the EC Commission and the government. There had also been a confidential and informal enquiry of chairmen of over one hundred leading industrial concerns, in both the public and private sector, seeking

[22] MRC MSS200/C/1/2/O, O.15.70, "Britain and the EEC: Government White Paper, and CBI Report 'Britain in Europe' – A Comparison," undated but early 1970. See *Britain and the European Communities: An Economic Assessment* (Cmnd. 4289) (London: HMSO, February 1970).

[23] TNA T312/2882, Williamson to Slater, "CBI Report on 'Britain in Europe'," 1 January 1970; and MRC MSS200/C/1/2/O, O.15.70, "Britain and the EEC: Government White Paper, and CBI Report 'Britain in Europe' – A Comparison," undated but early 1970.

[24] MRC MSS200/C/1/2/O, O.15.70, "Britain and the EEC: Government White Paper, and CBI Report 'Britain in Europe' – A Comparison," undated but early 1970.

[25] TNA FCO30/482, Robinson to Williams, 2 December 1969.

[26] MRC MSS200/C/1/2/C, C.2.70, CBI Council meeting, 17 December 1969.

their views in comparison to those of 1966 and asking for an explanation of any change of opinion. Seventy percent of those chairmen questioned were in favor of entry "if suitable terms could be arrived at," about 20–23 percent were indeterminate and only 7 percent were against on the evidence available. Again to make his case as strong as possible Ezra made clear that the key issue – the cost of entry – was complex and hard to quantify. Assessments of the short-term costs had been made but developments like the French devaluation and the Hague summit made any such calculations unreliable. Therefore, he suggested, "the costs of entry was a matter for negotiation."[27] Ezra was trying to play down the difference between the quantifiable short-term costs and the harder to measure long-term advantages: "one could do no more at present than pose the question of the initial cost."

Those on the CBI Council opposed to British entry were not persuaded, criticizing the report, its assumptions and its authors: The members "were being led by the nose" was how one put it.[28] There was in particular a concern that Britain was no longer able to compete with continental competition, given recent wage inflation in Britain and that the cost of entry would only fuel this wage inflation.[29] In many respects the criticisms were valid: The membership was being led towards a particular conclusion. Nevertheless, despite the debate being "long and controversial," a majority of speakers supported the report and the Council did approve the publication of *Britain in Europe* as a basis for consultation with its membership. The consultation was not, however, to take the form of an open request for members' opinions but was to take place through the CBI Regional Councils and six special meetings around the country.[30]

EXPLAINING DEVELOPMENTS IN BUSINESS OPINION

What is striking about this Council meeting was that there was little attempt to make drafting amendments to the report. Those opposed to the report wanted it edited by someone less pro-European than Ezra to which he responded that if the Council wanted the paper significantly rewritten then a new committee would have to be found to undertake the task.[31] By the end of 1969 there was not only a clearly defined group of industrialists against British entry but the division between those in favor of entry and those against was now distinct: It was no longer a matter of tone between those "in favour, provided" and others "opposed, unless" (see Chapter 5).

---

[27] Ibid.   [28] Ibid., J. S. Holmes.
[29] Ibid., Holmes, M. H. Bulpitt, N. A. Sloan and Sir John Hunter.
[30] MRC MSS200/C/1/2/O, O.1.70, Cope to members of the Overseas Committee and the Europe Steering Committee, 7 January 1970.
[31] MRC MSS200/C/1/2/C, C.2.70, Lord Woolley, CBI Council meeting, 17 December 1969.

Why had business opinion developed in this way and what factors had brought this about? The answer, unsurprisingly, is complex and again reflects the range of angles from which business approached the issue of "going into Europe." The position of small firms remained a potent concern for some, but it seemed that they were divided on the topic rather than opposed outright.[32] At the other extreme there was also divided opinion among large firms. A clear majority of the chairmen of one hundred of the largest British companies may have favored entry, but there was some evidence that these companies were no longer the driving force for British entry that they had been. Lord Robens, the chairman of the National Coal Board and soon to be chairman of Vickers, believed: "Seven or eight years ago, the real British industrial enthusiasts had been the largest and most modern and progressive firms such as ICI. But since then all these firms had looked after their main interest by getting proper manufacturing footholds inside the Common Market. So they were all right in any case."[33] Yet, there were also many large companies still looking to internationalize and found this still a good reason to support British entry, while others viewed British entry as a way of increasing US investment in Britain.[34] Another division within business related to the economic position of Britain. The competitiveness of British business was one concern. Another was the impact on the balance of payments, but this was perceived in different ways: Some were worried about the impact of entry on the balance of payments which had been weak for a number of years – entry might require the government to introduce deflationary policies; others pointed to the recent improvement in the balance of payments which might remove the need for such action. A third anxiety in relation to the economy was the implications for monetary policy and that the drive for economic and monetary union in the EC would shackle government policy to the detriment of British economic performance. The chairman of the CBI's Economic Committee was one businessman exercised by this last issue.[35]

It is also important to stress the importance of perceptions of economic realities rather than the realities themselves. Once more there were many unknowns and uncertainties both about the general impact of membership and also the details of the negotiations. With the overall balance of advantage less certain than in 1966/67 and with these uncertainties, other factors became more decisive. In this context, sentiment had more room to influence business opinion: One businessman at the CBI Council meeting was against

---

[32] Ibid., Holmes and Beldam, chairman of the CBI Committee for the problems of Small Firms, CBI Council meeting, 17 December 1969.

[33] TNA FCO30/482, O'Neill to Robinson, "CBI Attitudes," 13 October 1969.

[34] MRC MSS200/C/1/2/C, C.2.70, Shanks, CBI Council meeting, 17 December 1969.

[35] For example, TNA FCO30/481, Hannay to Petrie, "CBI/UNICE Meeting," 2 April 1969 and attached paper "International Monetary Policy" circulated by Weeks.

entry for "historical and political reasons."[36] Similarly, Cope believed that the reasons for the growth in opposition to UK entry "were not economic or commercial, but in the main more vague and emotional – as he put it, based on considerations like the Queen, sovereignty of parliament, independence of British policy and so on."[37] There was also a leap of faith for those in favor of EC entry given that any expected benefits would only begin to flow in the long term and were not prone to accurate measurement: "Britain's destiny lay in Europe" was how one businessman put it.[38]

There was one further factor which was of growing significance among those in favor of EC entry: It became common to stress the importance of EC industrial policy.[39] Technology policy had remained an important consideration in the thinking of British business since the second application but this had now broadened out into a consideration of other aspects as well. In part, this was an outcome of the major tariff reductions on manufactured goods agreed in the Kennedy Round but it also reflected developments within the Six where factors related to the creation of a European industrial base were beginning to receive closer consideration, notably in relation to taxes and company law and a European capital market. This was part of the European response to Americanization and was an area where the Commission and the Six were more open to UK involvement. Some of these issues are discussed in more depth in Chapters 3 and 11, but the wider aspects are important here.

There were two dimensions to the subject. First, it was felt that British business had something to offer the Six: "Europe would not flourish without Britain."[40] On the other side of the coin, the EC had something important to offer the UK. If the UK was to make effective its potential gains from membership then an active EC industrial policy was seen as crucial. This was made clear in *Britain in Europe*:

Of even greater importance [than the removal of non-tariff barriers] is the need to create a harmonised environment in which industry can operate effectively on a European scale. This we consider essential for several key industries based on the advanced technologies . . . . There is every prospect that even the most advanced and exigent among them can operate profitably in the setting of an enlarged Community throughout which uniform legal, fiscal and financial rules and regulations apply. The enlarged market and uniform rules are hardly less essential for many other industries for whom economies of scale in production, marketing, financing, etc., are of great importance. If Western Europe is to compete effectively in world markets, industrial restructuring from a European, rather than a national, base is essential. British firms

---

[36] MRC MSS200/C/1/2/C, C.2.70, Holmes, CBI Council meeting, 17 December 1969.

[37] TNA FCO30/482, Killick, "The CBI and Europe," 15 August 1969.

[38] MRC MSS200/C/1/2/C, C.2.70, Vinson and Marshall, CBI Council meeting, 17 December 1969, respectively.

[39] Anthony Rowley, "EEC Entry Means More than Tariff Removal," *Midlands Industry and Commerce* (March 1970), 1645.

[40] MRC MSS200/C/1/2/C, C.2.70, Norman, CBI council meeting, 17 December 1969.

through their efforts in recent years in research, development and reorganisation, are now in a strong position to make a substantial contribution to the wider arrangements on which future industrial progress in Europe depends.[41]

The need was for European companies.[42] This required less nationalistic policy in the EC and a climate that encouraged cross-border collaboration and mergers. Here the CBI was fully supportive of the way in which EC industrial policy seemed to be developing; for example the Commission's Aigrain Report proposed European technological collaboration in a number of advanced technology industries. There also needed to be some industrial machinery to encourage transnational collaboration and mergers more generally, plus the creation of common legal, financial and fiscal environments through harmonization of national policies in these areas. British business believed that it was from such fundamental industrial integration that the main benefits of membership would come.[43] Thus by the beginning of 1970 the CBI was keen to see significant steps towards deeper integration in these fields and, with it, the need for a European-level approach to policy in order for truly European business to emerge. In this respect at least the CBI had become Europeanized. The same could be said of much of its membership. The benefit from EC entry raised most often by trade associations in the consultation process on the report was the likelihood of a common industrial environment resulting from harmonization of a range of factors like taxation, standards and company law.[44]

HEADING TOWARDS NEGOTIATIONS AND THE NEGOTIATIONS THEMSELVES

By the end of January 1970 the CBI's leadership was confident that there was a substantial consensus in favor of EC entry. The terms of the negotiations remained important but the CBI "believed that they had educated their membership to consider the issue as being not simply one of whether or not to join the Community, but as a choice between becoming members or remaining permanently outside any large integrated industrial area."[45] The consultation process, which consisted of a questionnaire to trade associations, meetings of all the CBI Regional Councils, the CBI Smaller Firms Council and seven regional conferences, raised little opposition to EC entry. Only sixteen speakers at the regional conferences and three trade associations

---

[41] CBI, *Britain in Europe*, 1.   [42] Ibid., 9–16.

[43] TNA T312/2882, Croft, "Britain and Europe: President's Dinner with the CBI," 28 January 1970.

[44] MRC MSS200/C/1/2/O, O.32.70, "'Britain in Europe' and 'Britain in the World' – Consultations with the Membership," 26 May 1970.

[45] TNA T312/2882, Croft, "Britain and Europe: President's Dinner with the CBI," 28 January 1970.

openly opposed membership and the London Regional Council had voted in favor by a 10:1 majority. Armed with this information a statement was drafted for the CBI Council, which noted that the "consensus" was that *Britain in Europe* had reached the correct conclusions and that negotiations should begin with a view to achieving membership on "suitable terms."[46]

However, behind this broad endorsement the picture was less certain. First, the variety of the comments at the regional conferences made it difficult to reach any clear analysis of opinion.[47] Secondly, the attendances had been disappointing, averaging around fifty. Thirdly, most speeches at them concentrated on the uncertainties or worries, although where votes were taken (Birmingham and Glasgow) there were clear 2:1 majorities in favor of membership. There also remained much concern about the likely increase in the cost of living and its impact on wages and fears about the need for regional policy to offset the exacerbation of regional problems. As Cope summed it up, the case for entry seemed to rest on what the EC would become (with industrial policy) or could become (with British influence over developments): "there seemed little enthusiasm for joining the Community as it was today."[48]

By June when the CBI Council met to discuss the draft statement and the outcome of the consultation exercise much had changed. First, a new Conservative government headed by Ted Heath, the ardent supporter of European integration, as Prime Minister, had been elected and, secondly (and unrelated), Britain had been invited to open negotiations on 30 June about British accession to the EC.[49] This changed context had a number of effects. First, opponents of British entry still voiced their concerns but, as the new director-general of the CBI pointed out, to come out against the statement would suggest that business was against even opening the negotiations to see what might emerge.[50] Secondly, it was nevertheless agreed to amend the wording of the statement from referring to a "consensus" in favor of opening negotiations to the weaker phrase "a substantial balance of opinion." Finally, and related to this, even in the Council meeting attention was shifting towards the arrangements for ensuring that British business was fully involved in the negotiation process.

Both within the CBI leadership and among trade associations there was a belief that good relations which allowed informal and frank discussion of issues already existed with government departments.[51] This boded well for the detailed day-to-day consultations with Whitehall and the UK delegation

[46] MRC MSS200/C/1/2/O, O.41.70, CBI Overseas Committee and the CBI Europe Steering Committee meeting, 28 May 1970.

[47] Ibid., Cope.   [48] Ibid.   [49] Hannay, *Britain's Entry*, 16.

[50] MRC MSS200/C/1/1/C, C.47.70, CBI Council meeting, 24 June 1970.

[51] Ibid., CBI Council meeting, 24 June 1970; and MRC MSS200/C/1/2/O, O.57.70, "Summary Record of a Meeting of Trade Associations (and of Contributions from Member Associations Unable to Attend)," 8 July 1970.

during the negotiations.[52] But there was also a need for a strategic document setting out industry's key recommendations to the government. To this end the CBI submitted two documents to the government prior to the opening of any serious negotiations.[53] Much of their content was predictable and similar to the views of the Association of British Chambers of Commerce (ABCC).[54] Ultimately five issues came to the fore as issues of central concern to the CBI during the negotiations. These were industrial policy, the impact of the costs of entry on the British economy, economic and monetary union, regional policy, and the impact on small firms. At the outset of the negotiations it was industrial policy that was seen as a key area of long-term gain from British entry.[55] The topic remained a central concern throughout the negotiations but was not itself part of the formal negotiations. Instead, as the Community's policy developed, for example on company law (see Chapter 11) and technological collaboration, the CBI examined the proposals.[56] The second concern was that the cost of entry would be such that the balance of payments would deteriorate to such an extent that the government would be forced to introduce deflationary policies, thereby negating the potentially positive impact from membership on Britain's growth performance.[57] The initial burden that would be faced by British business was viewed as a key consideration in judging the terms negotiated.[58]

The third issue had already emerged as a concern of the CBI's Economic Committee. The CBI closely followed the debate over economic and monetary union in the EC that followed the 1969 Hague summit, and which led to the Werner Report and its program to achieve economic and monetary union by 1980.[59] There was an extensive debate in the Six about how it was best to bring about monetary union: Should it be by integration of the economies and coordination of economic policies first, followed by monetary union or

---

[52] Hannay, *Britain's Entry*, 189, Lord, *British Entry*, 122, and Kitzinger, *Diplomacy and Persuasion*, 262.

[53] MRC MSS200/C/1/2/O, O.55.70, "The Negotiations with the EEC: Industry's Recommendations," undated but July/August 1970, and O.81.70, "Entry into the EEC – Cost and Transfer Problems."

[54] "The ABCC's Conference 1971," *Commerce International* (August 1971), 5.

[55] MRC MSS200/C/1/2/O, O.23.70, Elkin to the Europe Steering Committee, 27 April 1970, covering "Industrial Policy in an Enlarged European Community," CNPF–CBI report to the Integration Committee of the CEIF, March 1970, and O.90.70, "Report of the Industrial Working Party of the Europe Steering Committee," 19 November 1970.

[56] MRC MSS200/C/3/COM/25/2; and MRC MSS200/C/1/2/O, O.85.70, Elkin to Europe Steering Committee, 20 October 1970.

[57] Hannay, *Britain's Entry*, 171; and MRC MSS200/C/1/2/O, O.55.70, "The Negotiations with the EEC: Industry's Recommendations," undated but late July/early August 1970.

[58] MRC MSS200/C/1/2/O, O.11.71, CBI staff, "Membership of the European Community. The Economic Implications for Britain," and O.45.71, Europe Steering Committee 26th meeting, 24 March 1971.

[59] Horst Ungerer, *A Concise History of European Monetary Integration: From EPU to EMU* (Westport: Quorum, 1997).

by bringing about monetary union first, which would force economies to coordinate? From the CBI's perspective:

The Commission and the Six are hurrying to an objective which is indeed desirable, but too quickly and by a dangerous road. The CBI dislike, and regard as unrealistic and dangerous, premature European monetary integration and locking of exchange rates. They see.... the risk in this of the UK becoming a depressed area of the Community if our prices get out of line and we could not adjust the exchange rate.[60]

The CBI kept a close eye on developments in this field thereafter.[61]

The possibility of economic and monetary union and its potential consequences on the British economy also increased concerns about the regional impact of UK entry and led to calls for an EC regional policy.[62] Following the consultation process on *Britain in Europe*, it was agreed that the impact on the regions needed to be reviewed, and CBI Scotland embarked on such an exercise.[63] The raw results were not overly encouraging: A positive balance of only 5 percent was found between those who expected sales to increase and those who expected a decline, 26 percent expected a fall in sales in the domestic market, and nearly 20 percent forecast a decrease in sales to the Commonwealth through the loss of Commonwealth preference.[64] Scottish textiles, engineering, and paper were optimistic about the impact of entry, steelmakers were uncertain, while shipbuilders were divided. The need for transport to be reorganized was emphasized as a concern but overall, "it is unlikely that on balance the competitive position of industry in Scotland will suffer from entry."[65] However, fears about the regional impact continued to be voiced in the CBI Regional Councils.[66] The final issue also related to the impact on entry of a particular group of firms, in this case smaller firms. The June CBI Council meeting had specifically referred to keeping the topic under review during the negotiations and, in response, the Smaller Firms Council created a Europe Working Party. Between them, they investigated

---

[60] TNA T312/2882, Slater to Owen, "CBI Recommendations on UK Negotiations with the EEC," 21 September 1970.

[61] MRC MSS200/C/1/2/E, E.26.72, "EEC Economic and Monetary Union," undated; and MRC MSS200/C/3/E/562, O.183.72, "CBI Policy Priorities after the Paris Summit."

[62] MRC MSS200/C/1/2/E, E.180.70, "EEC Economic and Monetary Policy," undated.

[63] MRC MSS200/C/1/2/E, E.298.70, Regional Development Committee, undated; MRC MSS200/C/1/2/R, CBI Scotland, "Survey into the effects of UK entry into the European Economic Community on Industry in Scotland," undated; and MRC MSS200/C/1/2/E, E.153.71, "Scotland and EEC Entry: The Report of a Study Group on the Effects on an Assisted Area of the United Kingdom," March/April 1971.

[64] MRC MSS200/C/1/2/R, CBI Scotland, "Survey into the Effects of UK Entry into the European Economic Community on Industry in Scotland," undated.

[65] MRC MSS200/C/1/2/E, E.153.71, "Scotland and EEC Entry: The Report of a Study Group on the Effects on an Assisted Area of the United Kingdom," March/April 1971, 6.

[66] Ibid., E.542.71, "Regional Development Committee, "UK Entry into the EEC and Regional Policy," undated but November/December 1971.

a range of issues relating to European integration and met their continental counterparts.[67]

These general issues were kept under constant review by business during the negotiations, informed by regular contact with government officials and ministers, though much of the detailed discussions between government and industry was at the level of trade associations.[68] The CBI also strengthened its links with the continent during the period of negotiations. This was not just with their counterpart industrial federations and the umbrella organization UNICE, but also with the Commission itself. Meetings with Commission officials became increasingly common and the CBI leadership believed that they were able to discuss topics with the Commission that the government found hard to do in the context of the negotiations.[69] More than symbolic in this respect was the CBI's decision to open an office in Brussels in January 1971.[70]

While these issues were kept under review, it was only when the terms of the completed negotiations were clear that the wider business community could make a final and informed decision about whether it supported UK entry on the terms negotiated. The terms of the negotiations were released in the government's July 1971 White Paper *The United Kingdom and the European Communities*, and with Parliament not voting on the issue until October, there was time for a further consultative exercise, and both the CBI and ABCC embarked on such an exercise.[71]

Some individual chambers of commerce, like London and Birmingham, issued their own statements of support for the terms set out in the White Paper.[72] In the case of Birmingham, this followed consultation with its 4,164 member companies, of which only eleven responded that they opposed UK entry. The Manchester Chamber of Commerce followed suit soon afterwards.[73] Then, in October, the ABCC issued its opinion that the

---

[67] MRC MSS200/1/1/G, G.277.70, "Minutes of the 'Europe' Working Party of the Smaller Firms Council," 13 October 1970, and G.196.71, "Meeting in Cologne 15/16 July of Representatives of the CBI's Smaller Firms Council with Small Firms Representatives of UNICE," July 1971.

[68] MRC MSS200/C/1/1/C, C.54.70, "Director-General's Report to Council," September 1970; MRC MSS200/C/1/2/O, ES2-5.2, "Notes of a Meeting of the HMG/CBI Joint Europe Group," 9 October 1970, O.93.70, "Overseas Director's Report," November 1970, and O.3.71, Europe Steering Committee, 25th meeting.

[69] MRC MSS200/C/1/1/C, C.77.70, "CBI Work in Connection with Europe," December 1970, C.16.71, "Director-General's Report to Council, March 1971"; and MRC MSS200/C/1/2/O, O.45.71.

[70] CBI, *Annual Report for 1971*, 9.

[71] *The United Kingdom and the European Communities* (Cmnd. 4715) (London: HMSO, July 1971).

[72] London Chamber of Commerce and Industry, *Annual Report for 1971*, 1; "Birmingham Chamber Goes for Europe," *Midland Industry and Commerce* (August 1971), 557.

[73] "Britain and the Common Market," *Monthly Record of the Manchester Chamber of Commerce* (October 1971), 195.

terms of the transition were acceptable, summing up well the case for entry:

Membership of the enlarged Community should lead to much improved efficiency and productivity in the United Kingdom with a higher rate of investment and faster growth in real incomes. It will be essential, however, that everyone engaged in agriculture, commerce and industry makes a great effort to seize the opportunities that will open up, and education will be needed at all levels to ensure that everyone knows what is at stake.

The present rate of investment is clearly not adequate to ensure that British industry is in a position to take advantage of the Common Market. Industry must be continually encouraged and enabled to invest more. It is essential too that the current spate of inflation be brought under control . . . .

The consequences of staying out of the Communities would be grave. Britain would be depriving itself of the opportunity to help formulate EEC policy and of the chance to participate in the Community's decisions which, as the power and the influence of the Community grow, must increasingly affect us. We should also be rejecting the opportunity to share the benefits of a customs union and, in time, an economic and monetary union comprising some 250 million people. It is worth recalling that the OECD has estimated that Britain's growth outside the Community in the next few years will lag substantially behind that of the Six. On the other hand entry promises a rise in living standards . . . .

We recognise that the early years following entry into the EEC might be difficult but, with firm leadership and a full understanding by everyone of the rewards to be won if the challenge is met, we are convinced that the British people will benefit from entry.[74]

This statement says much about attitudes among business leaders to UK entry at this time. Many of the same assumptions and beliefs underpinned the attitude of the CBI leadership. The CBI's Europe Steering Committee met two days after the White Paper was issued and agreed that "the CBI should be firmly committed to entry, and should give a clear lead to the country not only on the economic aspects" and, like the ABCC statement, greater emphasis was placed on the costs of not joining.[75] To this end, Derek Ezra, the chairman of the committee, and Gerry Norman, the chairman of the CBI's Overseas Committee, put their names to a letter by leading businessmen published in *The Times* that emphatically supported British membership.[76] When the CBI Council met, few spoke in opposition to entry: It was believed that an overall majority of CBI members favored entry.[77]

The ensuing consultation with the membership confirmed this position. The Economic Committee, chaired by the more skeptical Sir Hugh Weeks,

---

[74] "The Common Market: Association of British Chambers of Commerce Supports UK Entry," *Monthly Record of the Manchester Chamber of Commerce* (November 1971), 232–4.

[75] MRC MSS200/C/1/2/O, ES 17.1, Europe Steering Committee 28th meeting, 9 July 1971.

[76] "Joining EEC; A Verdict from Industry," letter in *The Times*, 12 July 1971, 13.

[77] MRC MSS200/C/1/1/, C.50.71, CBI Council meeting, 15 July 1971.

raised the most concerns and felt that the balance of payments implications of entry had been underplayed.[78] By contrast, all of the Regional Councils found the terms acceptable and the Smaller Firms Council voted in favor of acceptance of the terms twenty-four to two, with two abstentions.[79] Trade associations appeared to be "looking forward to the opportunities afforded by membership."[80]

Finally, while there was no survey of the membership, the director-general wrote to every individual member asking for them to provide their views.[81] Of the 1,065 letters received, only fifty-five were opposed to entry, thirty-five were neutral and the remaining 975 were classified as in favor of entry.[82] The classifications of some of the letters as positive could be questioned and, more significantly, the tone of many of those in favor was not one of rampant enthusiasm – there was no perceived viable alternative and there were concerns about whether British business would be competitive – but the scale of the majority overwhelms these concerns.[83] There were always going to be firms that would lose out from EC entry and it might have been thought that there would be significantly more than fifty-five responses against entry. Within those fifty-five letters, some companies did emphasize economic factors: There were concerns about the cost of entry and competitiveness, of the loss of Commonwealth preference, of the regional impact and of tax changes (notably from whisky distilleries).[84] The vast majority were small companies but some did export and had experience of operating on the continent. However, the letters also illustrate xenophobia and nationalism bordering on racism and bigotry.[85] Thus, for some of that small proportion of respondents who were opposed to entry, irrational prejudice played an important part in their opinion. No economic case would ever have persuaded them of the value of British membership of the European Community.

Sentiment, gut instinct, and personal opinion were also factors in some of those members who responded in favor of British entry. One firm submitted two responses, one pro and one anti, because the two joint managing

---

[78] MRC MSS200/C/1/2/O, O.105.71, "Consultation with the CBI Membership on the Acceptability of the Terms," 24 August 1971; and MRC MSS200/C/1/2/E, E.290.71, Economic Committee meeting, 2 August 1971.

[79] MRC MSS200/C/1/2/O, O.105.71, "Consultation with the CBI Membership on the Acceptability of the Terms," 24 August 1971.

[80] Ibid.

[81] MRC MSS200/C/3/IA/2/90, director general to members, 6 August 1971.

[82] MRC MSS200/C/1/1/C, C.57.71, CBI Council meeting, 15 September 1971.

[83] For the individual responses see MRC MSS200/C/3/INT/3/23/1–27.

[84] See MRC MSS200/C/3/INT/3/23/1.

[85] Ibid., Robinson, D. Robinson & Co. Ltd., (electrical and electronic control components and systems), 13 August 1971, Managing Director, Helipebs Ltd., 13 August 1971, Managing Director, Whitehead Letterfiles Ltd, 16 August 1971, H. Butterfield, Managing Director, Stanhope Engineers (Bradford) Ltd., 16 August 1971 respectively.

directors had different opinions.[86] However, many emphasized the opportunities that would be available, the costs of not joining and the political argument for entry.[87] To CBI staff the letters revealed "the suspected silent majority" in favor of entry and Derek Ezra was able to tell the Europe Steering Committee that the committee was "obviously reflecting industrial opinion and not leading it."[88]

Given the weight of this silent majority, the outcome of the CBI Council debate in September, which finalized the CBI's response on the negotiations, was a foregone conclusion. There were still some diehard opponents of entry present but only one person directly opposed the issuing of a statement in favor of entry, and he was opposed to entry on political grounds.[89] There were no heated disagreements like those in 1970 when the Council had considered *Britain in Europe* and whether to support the opening of negotiations. The draft statement was rephrased but British business believed that membership of the EC "will be in the best interests of industry, all those who work in it and of the country."[90] As expected, at the end of October, the House of Commons voted in favor of the terms negotiated for entry and Britain finally became a member of the EC on January 1, 1973 along with Ireland and Denmark.

What had happened to the significant levels of opposition that were thought to exist back in 1969 when *Britain in Europe* was being drafted, and which led to FCO officials fretting that the CBI was getting cold feet just as the possibilities of membership were becoming brighter? First, there is little evidence that the growing popularity of EC entry among business was representative of a wider social movement in public opinion. Popular opinion remained mixed about entry.[91] This implies reasons particular to business but again the issues are complex. There was a degree of blind faith shown by some small firms who lacked knowledge but hoped it would be advantageous to the country, if not to themselves.[92] Others highlighted the political dimension, suggesting that without EC entry Britain would become a washed-up

[86] Ibid., D. Dawson, Joint Managing Director, Dawson, McDonald & Dawson Ltd., 23 August 1971, and MRC MSS200/C/3/INT/3/23/5, A. E.Dawson, Joint Managing Director, Dawson, McDonald & Dawson Ltd., 15 August 1971.

[87] MRC MSS200/C/1/1/C, C.57.71, Adamson, CBI Council meeting, 15 September 1971.

[88] MRC MSS200/C/1/2/O, O. 105.71, and O.116.71, Europe Steering Committee 29th meeting, 1 September 1971.

[89] MRC MSS200/C/1/1/C, C.57.71, Berner, CBI Council meeting, 15 September 1971.

[90] "CBI Approves Common Market Entry Terms," *The Times*, 16 September 1971, 19.

[91] Roger Jowell and James Spence, *The Grudging Europeans: A Study of British Attitudes towards the EEC* (London: Social and Community Planning Research, 1975).

[92] MRC MSS200/C/3/INT/3/23/2, D.D. Attwater, Managing Director, Attwater & Sons, R. Z. Watts, Managing Director, Accles and Shelvoke, and H. C. Davis, Autoflow Engineeering; and MRC MSS200/C/3/INT/3/23/3, Bolton's Superheater and Pipe Works, and Brecknell–Redcliffe Electronics.

power, an off-shore island no more important than Iceland.[93] Nevertheless, the majority, and in particular the larger firms, had very explicit economic rationales for entry. For many large firms, UK entry was the culmination of a process of European integration, which the firms had themselves begun through overseas investment earlier in the 1960s (see Chapter 3).[94] For others it was the opportunities offered by deeper integration that appealed: It was not just the opportunity to be involved in the framing of policy but also the prospects offered by EC industrial policy in terms of free capital movement, harmonization of taxation and company law, and technological collaboration, which mattered.

There were also short-term factors. One of the major factors behind this positive tone was the belief that the terms negotiated were better than had been expected. The impact of higher food prices from EC entry on the cost of living was also no longer seen as being so great because world food prices had risen closer to EC levels. In addition, the Conservative government announced that it was going to introduce VAT in any case and so this was no longer a cost of entry. Thirdly, Britain's contribution to the EC budget was graduated over the course of a longer than expected seven-year transition period. While this would give time for industry to adjust to the costs, access to EC markets would be available relatively quickly as industrial tariffs would be reduced by 80 percent within three years and imports of certain raw materials would still be allowed from outside the EC at below the duty levels of the common external tariff.[95] The CBI now felt able to reduce the estimates of the cost of entry from the £400 m. per year forecast in *Britain in Europe* to £100–£200 m. per year over the transition period 1973–1980, rising to £300 m. per year by 1980.[96]

Also, throughout the discussions the costs of not joining came increasingly to the fore both as an argument strengthening the case for entry and as a perception held in business more generally. For many businessmen, there was no viable alternative and therefore little real choice: UK entry into the EC was "no magic cure" to the country's economic problems but the situation was likely to be even harder if the UK remained outside the EC or if it joined later.[97] In this respect, there was a clear resonance with the 1950s when fear of exclusion was a major factor behind business support for the free trade area idea. However, there was one important difference: In the 1950s the

---

[93] MRC MSS200/C/3/INT/3/23/2, P. Hutchings, Group Information Manager, Avon Rubber Group; and MRC MSS200/C/3/INT/3/23/3, Beckman Instruments Ltd., G.E. Bissell, Bower Roebuck, Bowthrope Holdings.

[94] MRC MSS200/C/3/INT/3/23/3, Secretary, Beecham Group Ltd., 13 August 1971, and British Cellophane Ltd., 1 September 1971.

[95] MRC MSS200/C/1/2/O, O.85.71, "An Assessment of the Outcome of the Negotiations by the Europe Steering Committee," 14 July 1971.

[96] "CBI Approves Common Market Entry Terms," *The Times*, 16 September 1971, 19.

[97] MRC MSS200/C/3/INT/3/23/2, D. J. Iddon, Managing Director, Adam Rouilly & Co. Ltd.

Commonwealth was a very clear alternative, in the early 1960s there was EFTA, now there was no viable alternative in the eyes of business.

PREPARING FOR UK ENTRY

With the decision for entry taken by Parliament it was clear that the next and final stage in the process of UK entry had been reached. Attention now focused on the ongoing and continuing developments in the EC and any relevant new proposals emanating from the EC Commission: hence a continued concern with regional policy, tax harmonization, company law harmonization, and economic and monetary union.[98] More significantly, the CBI began to put in place arrangements to deal with this new world. The Europe Steering Committee was wound up and replaced with a new Europe Committee tasked "to coordinate and promote CBI policies in relation to the EEC."[99] Still chaired by Ezra and with some members of the Steering Committee retained, the rest of its members consisted of the chairs of other CBI committees, as shown in Table 8.1. The committee was no longer about formulating policy on Europe in general but was now about ensuring the CBI's understanding of developments in particular areas and ensuring the coordination of any response.

In a similar vein, the CBI President wrote to the Prime Minister stressing the importance of industry and government working together to influence Community developments in Britain's interests.[100] To this end, he asked Heath if the CBI would be able to see government position papers on Community affairs to ensure a consistent approach wherever possible, as the CBI's continental counterparts were afforded this privilege by their governments, and there was considerable sympathy in Whitehall to this request.[101] As a government minister told CBI representatives, it was crucial for all nongovernmental organizations, including the CBI, to maintain the closest contact with the Commission and to ensure a common line in response to have the maximum effect.[102]

One other major task faced the CBI and the wider business community. It no longer had to lead or even create business opinion on Europe but it still had to make sure that business played its part in exploiting the opportunities and overcoming the challenges presented by EC entry. There was a lot of preparation to be done in educating companies about the opportunities

[98] TNA PREM15/1531, Sir John Partidge to Heath, 12 May 1972, covering C38A 72, CBI Europe Committee, "Objectives in Europe," 5 May 1972.

[99] MRC MSS200/C/1/2/O, O.118.71, Adamson to Europe Steering Committee members, 26 October 1971, and O.139.71, "CBI Europe Committee," 1 December 1971.

[100] TNA PREM15/1531, Partidge to Heath, 1 November 1971.

[101] Ibid., Ticknell to Simcock, 26 November 1971, and Gregson to Wright, "HMG/CBI Communications," 16 March 1972.

[102] Ibid., Pakenham to Armstrong, 1 July 1972.

Table 8.1. *CBI Europe Committee Membership*

	CBI Committee Chaired	Company
Derek Ezra	Chair	National Coal Board
Hugh Weeks	Economic	ICFC
Gerry Norman	Overseas	De la Rue
R. S. Sims	Research and Technology	Delta Metal Electronics
W. F. Cartwright	Regional Development	British Steel Corporation
Akun G. Davies	Taxation	Rio Tinto Zinc
Sir Reginald Wilson	Trade practices	Transport Development Group
J. M. Langham	Production	Stone-Platt Industries
Sir David Barritt	Energy	Davy-Ashmore
John Langley	Environmental and Technical Legislation	Imperial Tobacco
R. G. Beldam	Smaller Firms	Beldam Asbestos Co.
J. MacNaughton Sidey	Transport	P&O European Air and Transport
Z. Brierley		Z Brierley Ltd.
Stuart Douglas		British Man-Made Fibres Federation
Sir Patrick Reilly		British-France Bank
J. E. Nash		Samuel Montagu
A. Winegarten		National Farmers' Union
A. H. C. Greenwood		British Aircraft Corporation
E. J. W. Hellmuth		Midland Bank
Andrew Shonfield		Director, Royal Institute for International Affairs
J. L. Lutyens		George Kent Ltd.

Source. MRC MSS200/C/1/2/O, O.139.71, 1 December 1971.

available in Europe and how best to exploit them. Many players had a role in this exercise. The government brought together a collection of case studies of various company strategies on Europe under the title *Preparing for Europe*.[103] Again the wider impact of EC entry was emphasized: "the whole field of a company's operations could be affected by entry."[104] Banks provided guides and conferences for their customers and many such guides were also published, providing material on continental markets and on the European Community.[105] Organizations that had been working for British entry, like the Federal Trust, also played their part.[106]

However, it was the representative organizations of business that did the most in this respect. The journals of the regional chambers of commerce were filled with articles on European markets, Community regulations and policies, advice on investment opportunities and much more. They also organized many conferences, seminars and workshops, publications, briefings, trade fairs, advice on export documentation among other things. For example, the London Chamber of Commerce published an EC flowchart to help smaller firms to plan for entry, which sold over 15,000 copies.[107] Reading lists for businessmen were another favorite.[108] Inevitably, much of the activity was aimed at smaller firms. The CBI did likewise. It produced a series of briefing documents, a checklist for trade associations to help with their preparations and a pamphlet for small firms, as well as many articles in *CBI Review*.[109]

The CBI's big idea was the "Impact Europe" train. This was to be a specially furbished train hired by the CBI to travel the country to bring high quality presentations to the regions in a convenient way over a six-week period.[110] The choice of such an approach was significant. The alternative of a series of regional conferences was rejected as the train was seen as something "unique and dynamic" which would receive national and local publicity, potentially "really waking industry up" to the EC.[111] Despite some hiccups in its preparations, the CBI Impact Europe train started at London Euston on April 27 before traveling 2,750 miles around the country and

---

[103] DTI, *Preparing for Europe* (London, 1972).   [104] Ibid., 1.

[105] National Westminster Bank, *The Common Market and the United Kingdom* (London, 1 September 1970); Derek Prag and E. D. Nicholson, *Businessman's Guide to the Common Market* (London: Pall Mall, 1973); and M. E. Beesley and D. C. Hague (eds.), *Britain in the Common Market: A New Business Opportunity* (London: Longman, 1974).

[106] Federal Trust, *Industry and the Common Market* (London, April 1971).

[107] *Commerce International* (January 1973), 5.

[108] For example, "Steps into Europe," *Midlands Industry and Commerce* (January 1972), 31.

[109] CBI, *Small Firms and the Common Market: Action That Small Firms Should Take* (London, January 1972).

[110] MRC MSS200/C/3/DG2/117, "Paper on EEC Seminars on a CBI train," January 1972.

[111] Ibid., "Paper on EEC Seminars on a CBI train," January 1972, and "Brief on CBI Train for Regional Chairmen Dinner – 19 January 1972."

presenting the seminars in nearly thirty towns and cities.[112] The train itself was divided into exhibition space, a restaurant car, a VIP lounge and four conference areas, where simultaneous seminars could occur for 100 business executives, exhibition space and a restaurant car. In addition to talks by CBI staff, there were three videos, a novel technology at the time, which could also be purchased or hired for later showings.

The impact of the CBI Impact Europe train on the wider business community, much like all the other educative tools and efforts to get industry to prepare for entry, is impossible to discern. Just as there was a diverse range of factors that influenced business opinion, so each individual firm responded to the challenge of EC entry in its own unique way. Nor did this change on January 1, 1973 when Britain became a member of the European Community. Rather this was just the start and much still remained to be done. Nevertheless, the environment in which British business operated after 1973 was different because of European integration, even if, to this day, the deeper integration in the field of industrial policy seen as so important by British business in the 1970s has not yet emerged. Similarly, when the Labour government elected in 1974 called a referendum on British membership for the following year, British companies did not want to see the decision to join reversed and campaigned vigorously and successfully for Britain to stay in the Community. Having taken so long to achieve entry, even if the benefits proved less than had been hoped for, British business was not going to let Britain turn its back on Europe.

CONCLUSION

January 1973 and entry into the EC marked the end of a long march from the 1940s for British business in its desire to build a closer relationship with the EC. In other respects, it was just a staging post on an even longer struggle to adapt to Britain's changing position in the world, in which some aspects of European integration impacted upon British companies prior to membership and others did not for a few more years. Many developments found in earlier periods continued here. The Kennedy Round made it even clearer that for the vast majority of business the appeal of European integration was less about the removal of tariffs and more about a complex range of factors relating to the whole environment in which business operated. Moreover, this impacted upon individual firms in particular ways continuing to make it difficult to make generalizations about the importance of different factors on attitudes to European integration.

---

[112] Ibid., "Brief on CBI Train for Regional Chairmen Dinner – 19 January 1972," and T. F. Otway to CBI Regional Secretaries, "CBI Impact Europe Train – Sales Drive," 28 March 1972.

Having said that, there was the growing emphasis attached to EC industrial policy, covering the harmonization of company law and of taxation as well as technological collaboration, which was a significant development. British business became increasingly adamant that such deeper integration was an essential aspect of the appeal of European integration. There was a clear desire for a truly single market and an expectation that this would be achieved. Looking back from today's perspective, this seems naïve given the lack of harmonization that has been achieved to date, but however naïve, that expectation existed at this time and helps to explain the enthusiasm for the UK's union with the EC. Equally, that expectation was based on faulty perceptions of European integration, again illustrating the importance of the way in which business perceived European integration, or even what it might become, rather than what it actually achieved.

More generally, business opinion in the period from 1968 to 1973 underwent many significant changes. Following the 1967 veto, British business had become increasingly pessimistic about the prospects of entry and began to turn its eyes towards second-best alternatives. These became increasingly popular not only because there was perceived to be little chance of EC entry for the foreseeable future, but also because the EC was itself becoming less appealing as the costs of membership grew and the problems of the British economy increased. It is not surprising given this that even after de Gaulle lost power in France business was ambivalent about EC entry and relations with the pro-EC FCO deteriorated. This, however, proved no more than a wobble and the leaders of the business community were able to exert sufficient influence to ensure that business did still endorse EC membership (on the right terms), although this was partly because attitudes to European integration in the British business community had not shifted as far as business leaders seem to have believed. After this endorsement in 1970, those businessmen opposed to EC entry still had a loud voice but were unable to influence either business opinion or the public stance of business towards European integration in any significant way. In this sense, it was the decisions taken in 1969–70 that were more important than those in 1971. By then the tide was clearly moving inevitably towards membership and the issue changed from deciding whether to join the EC to preparing for entry.

PART III

EUROPEAN INTEGRATION AS MORE THAN TARIFFS

9

Competition Policy

British business' attitude to the development of EC competition policy is an illuminating case, not the least because competition policy has always been seen as essential to the success of European integration. In this respect, it provides a key link between market integration and political integration. As McGowan and Wilks have put it, competition policy is "the first supranational policy" in the European Union.[1] Implemented by Directorate General IV of the Commission and the European Court of Justice since its outset, EC competition policy raises issues about sovereignty and regulation, in addition to business attitudes to restrictive practices and competition policy. Despite this, the subject has received little detailed attention by historians of European integration and a number of preconceptions commonly appear in the existing literature. First, EC competition policy is often presented as breaking with traditional European approaches to competition as part of the process of Americanization, with its roots traced back to the 1890 Sherman Act.[2] Secondly, British entry into the EC in 1973 is often presented as a competitive shock for British business, which showed many signs of an anticompetitive bias.[3] Extending this argument, a counterfactual is developed that earlier entry by Britain would have provided an earlier competitive shock, ignoring the possible influence of Britain on the development of EC competition policy and assuming that the markets of the Six were competitive.

British business was clearly very exercised by competition policy provisions in the Treaty of Rome and Regulation 17, which in 1962 set out how the provisions for competition policy in the treaty were to be implemented. This illustrates the importance attached by business to aspects of European

[1] L. McGowan and S. Wilks, "The First Supranational Policy in the European Union: Competition Policy," *European Journal of Political Research*, Vol. 28, No. 2 (1995), 141–69.

[2] See M. L. Djelic, *Exporting the American Model: The Post-War Transformation of European Business* (Oxford: Oxford University Press, 1998). In contrast, see D. J. Gerber, *Law and Competition in Twentieth Century Europe: Promoting Prometheus* (Oxford: Oxford University Press, 1998).

[3] Stephen Broadberry, *The Productivity Race: British Manufacturing in International Perspective, 1850–1990* (Cambridge: Cambridge University Press, 1997), 293; and Stephen Broadberry and N. F. R. Crafts, "The Post-War Settlement: Not Such a Good Bargain After All," *Business History*, Vol. 40, No. 2 (1998), 74.

integration other than tariff removal. Yet, we need to be careful in jumping to conclusions about the motives for this interest. At other times, British business was worried by European integration acting as a motor for European cartelization, and later on in the 1960s, it favorably compared competition policy in the EC to that in Britain. This chapter will show that the significance attached to this issue by British industry fluctuated over time, was driven by a shifting balance of factors, and reflected a range of opinion within industry. The balance between the role of peak-level business associations and that of individual firms also shifted over time. Finally, the chapter will illustrate that European integration impacted upon British business prior to Britain joining the EC, highlighting the interaction between the domestic business environment and the European one even for non-members of the EC. Before turning attention to business attitudes directly, it is helpful to provide some context. First, this will be provided in terms of the comparative adoption of restrictive business practices in Europe and then, in the next section, in terms of the comparative provision of national competition policies.

RESTRICTIVE PRACTICES AND COMPETITION LAW IN POSTWAR EUROPE

National and international cartels have a long history but it is with the period from the late nineteenth century that cartelization is most associated, and, especially the 1930s, when cartelization is commonly seen to have reached its high point.[4] A commonly quoted figure is that 42 percent of international trade was cartelized in the period 1929–37.[5] Many historical accounts of the development of individual cartels in that period also now exist.[6] British business was as much a party to these restrictive arrangements as companies in other countries with 28–34 percent of Britain's exports and 16 percent of the gross output of British manufacturing affected by international agreements in 1938.[7] Also, in March 1939, the Federation of British Industries (FBI) signed the famous "Düsseldorf Agreement" with the Reichsgruppe Industrie

[4] H. G. Schröter, "Cartelization and Decartelization in Europe, 1870–1995: Rise and Decline of an Economic Institution," *Journal of European Economic History*, Vol. 25, No. 1 (1996), 129–53; and A. Kudō and T. Hara (eds.), *International Cartels in Business History* (Tokyo: University of Tokyo Press, 1992), 1–24.

[5] UN, *International Cartels* (New York: UN, 1947), 2; and J. Rahl, "International Cartels and Their Regulation," in O. Schachter and R. Hellawell (eds.), *Competition in International Business: Law and Policy on Restrictive Practices* (New York: Columbia University Press, 1981), 244–5.

[6] D. Barbezat, "A Price for Every Product, Every Place: The International Steel Export Cartel, 1933–1939," *Business History*, Vol. 33, No. 4 (1991), 68–86; and Clemens Wurm, *Business, Politics and International Relations: Steel, Cotton and International Cartels in British Politics, 1924–1939* (Cambridge: Cambridge University Press, 1993).

[7] H. Mercer, *Constructing a Competitive Order: The Hidden History of British Antitrust Policies* (Cambridge: Cambridge University Press, 1995), 15.

that aimed, among other things, at replacing "destructive competition" with "constructive co-operation" by carving up world trade between Britain and Germany.[8] As Helen Mercer and others have argued, the Second World War strengthened the basis of domestic cartel arrangements in Britain through the increased role of trade associations.[9] Equally, she has shown how the reestablishment of international cartels, which had inevitably broken down during the war, was a central concern of British industrialists' approach to postwar reconstruction.[10] Thus, the FBI argued for the replacement of the "jungle law of unregulated competition" by the "more modern and realistic view" of "planning designed to raise world prosperity by orderly methods."[11] Similarly, the London Chamber of Commerce proposed that, "The outlook which expresses itself in such phrases of economic belligerency as "capturing markets" must be changed to one of good neighbourliness. Competition, both within a nation and internationally, should remain, but should be reduced from a life-to-death struggle to healthy emulation."[12] G. C. Allen suggests that by the end of the 1940s restrictive practices had become "characteristic of a large part, perhaps the greater part of British industry."[13] The best estimate available suggests that 50–60 percent of British manufacturing output was subject to cartel regulation in 1958.[14] Even if the weaknesses in this calculation are acknowledged, it is still clear that restrictive practices (not just cartels it should be noted) were extensive and common within British industry just as the EC was being established.

Nevertheless, while cartelization was common in postwar British industry, there is no comparative context. The existing literature does assume a link between Britain's *absolute* level of cartelization and Britain's *relative* poor economic performance in this period that may not be justified.[15] After all, continental Europe was the center of interwar cartelization.[16] Moreover, it

---

[8] C. C. S. Newton, *Profits of Peace: The Political Economy of Anglo-German Appeasement* (Oxford: Oxford University Press, 1996), 99–101; and R. F. Holland, "The Federation of British Industries and the International Economy 1929–39," *Economic History Review*, 2nd ser., Vol. 34, No. 2 (1981), 287–300.

[9] Mercer, *Constructing*, 23–7 and 63–8; D. Swann, D. O'Brien, P. Maunder and W. S. Howe, *Competition in British Industry: Restrictive Practices Legislation in Theory and Practice* (London: George Allen and Unwin, 1974), 46; and G. C. Allen, *Monopoly and Restrictive Practices* (London: George Allen and Unwin, 1968), 84.

[10] Mercer, *Constructing*, 34 and 64–5.   [11] FBI, *International Trade Policy* (London, 1944).

[12] Quoted in Hexner, *International Cartels*, 158.

[13] G. C. Allen, *The Structure of British Industry* (London: Longmans, 1961), 81.

[14] D. C. Elliott and J. D. Gribbin, "The Abolition of Cartels and Structural Change in the UK," in A. P. Jacquemin and H. W. de Jong (eds.), *Welfare Aspects of Industrial Markets* (Leiden: Martinus Nijhoff, 1977), 353–4.

[15] Stephen Broadberry and Nicholas Crafts, "UK Productivity Performance from 1950 to 1979: A Restatement of the Broadberry–Crafts View," *Economic History Review*, Vol. 56, No. 4 (2003), 718–35.

[16] UN, *International Cartels*, 4.

Table 9.1. Agreements and Collective Arrangements Registered in Certain European Countries, September 1963

Segment of economy	UK[a]	Netherlands	Sweden	Denmark	Norway	Germany
Manufacturing, total	288	496	255	109	118	130
Covering national or regional market			242	79	100	130
Covering local market			13	30	18	0
Handicraft production	i.c.	27	144	190	5	0
Construction	311	27	3	376	7	0
Extractive industries	3		4	1	1	6
Agriculture, forestry and fishing, total	15	6	65	23	46	n.s.
Wholesale trade (including export and import trade)	53	159	43	43	32	2
Retail trade, total	26[b]	24	225	47	89	0
Covering national or regional market	18		85	13	22	
Covering a large town	5		31	3	5	
Covering a small town	2		109	31	62	
Banking, total	n.s.	14	5	136	2	n.s.
Insurance, total	n.s.	22	55	20	9	n.s.
Transportation, total	n.s.	42	29	126	26	n.s.
Public utilities	1		1		1	29932[d]
Professions	1			48	17	0
Other services	n.s.		38	65	9	3
Other horizontal	1[c]		134		0	0

Vertical agreements						
Primary producers with processors	8	i.c.	1	4	12	n.s.
Manufacturers with manufacturers	50	i.c.	28	10	5	n.a.
Manufacturers with distributors	54	i.c.	50	47	22	n.a.
Distributors with distributors	5	i.c.	20	15	16	n.a.
All other vertical	12	i.c.	13	33	21	0
Unclassified		6				
Total collective agreements	828	823	1114	1293	438	30073

Notes: n.s.: not subject to notification; i.c.: included in other classifications; n.a.: number of agreements not available.

[a] Excludes agreements which, though all restrictions have been terminated, are still on the register.

[b] Includes one agreement of unknown territorial scope.

[c] Covers one agreement pertaining to lending, that because of certain peculiarities, became subject to registration.

[d] Consists of registrations of agreements between governmental bodies and public utilities by which the latter are given exclusive rights, etc.

Source: Edwards, Cartelization, 7

was Europe as a whole, not just Britain that was associated with a tradition of private business agreements to protect profits and avoid the full effects of competition.[17] As an Italian industrialist put it: "The agreement 'not to compete' which European big businessmen tended to consider as a highly civilised act, one worthy of a gentleman, something like a treaty of peace, loses all such significance and becomes a 'conspiracy in restraint of trade,' a quite contrary moral concept."[18] This was not just an Italian view.[19] When the Council of Directors of European Industrial Federations (CDEIF) had its first meeting after the war in Paris in the autumn of 1946, the conversation soon turned towards what the British delegate regarded as "a general blessing of cartels."[20]

That cartels existed in postwar Europe is beyond dispute, as has been shown by many authors with regard to West Germany and France.[21] The Netherlands has been called "Europe's cartel paradise."[22] What is less clear is their postwar scale and whether, and if so, when, any demise occurred.[23] Individual estimates and statistics of the extent of cartelization exist, but such calculations are far from reliable and have no consistent basis of formulation.[24] Corwin Edwards carried out the most systematic study available, but even here the figures remain severely limited in their comparative value.[25] All one can say is that domestic cartels remained a numerically widespread phenomenon in much of Western Europe. Table 9.1 sets out

---

[17] R. C. Barnard, "How Good are Your Contracts?," in J. R. Crowley (ed.), *The Antitrust Structure of the European Common Market* (New York: Fordham University Press, 1963), 61.

[18] E. Minoli, "Industry's Views of Trade Regulation in the EEC," in Crowley, *Antitrust Structure*, 48–9.

[19] D. S. Landes, "French Business and the Businessman: A Social and Cultural Analysis," in E. M. Earle (ed.), *Modern France: Problems of the Third and Fourth Republics* (Princeton: Princeton University Press, 1951), 348.

[20] MRC MSS200/F/3/E1/16/24, report of the Paris conference.

[21] H. C. Wallich, *Mainsprings of German Revival* (New Haven: Yale University Press, 1955), 133–41; V. Berghahn, *The Americanisation of West German Industry 1945–1973* (Oxford: Berg, 1986), 101–3; W. C. Baum, *The French Economy and the State* (Princeton: Princeton University Press, 1958), 251–68; H. W. Ehrmann, *Organized Business in France* (Princeton: Princeton University Press, 1957), 368–92; and V. G. Venturini, *Monopolies and Restrictive Trade Practices in France* (Leiden: A. W. Sijthoff, 1971).

[22] Quoted in Wendy Asbeek Brusse and R. T. Griffiths, "Paradise Lost or Paradise Regained? Cartel Policy and Cartel Legislation in the Netherlands," in S. Martin (ed.), *Competition Policies in Europe* (Amsterdam: North-Holland, 1998), 15–39.

[23] Wendy Asbeek Brusse and R. T. Griffiths, "The Incidence of Manufacturing Cartels in Post-War Europe," in C. Morelli (ed.), *Cartels and Market Management in the Post-War World* (Business History Unit, L. S. E. Occasional papers 1997, No. 1), 78–117.

[24] Ehrmann, *Organized Business*, 372 and 375, Baum, *French Economy*, 253.

[25] C. D. Edwards, *Cartelization in Western Europe* (Washington: US State Department, 1964).

Table 9.2. *International Agreements and Collective Arrangements for Which Nationally Reported Information Could be Obtained, September 1963*

UK	20
Sweden	24
Denmark	15
Norway	13
Germany	29

Source: Edwards, *Cartelization*, 21.

Table 9.3. *Breakdown of Parties to Notifications to the EC Commission by Country*

	Total Notifications (%)	
	Forms A, B, and C[a]	Form B1[b]
France	18.7	15.2
W. Germany	25.0	24.6
Italy	9.5	10.3
Belgium	9.0	11.2
Netherlands	8.6	10.9
Luxemburg	1.1	0.8
UK	8.8	10.1
Switzerland	4.4	3.3
Other European third countries	6.4	6.1
US and Canada	6.6	5.8
Other non-European third countries	1.9	1.7

[a] Form A for negative clearances, Form B for exemptions, and Form C for complaints.
[b] Form B1 for notification of simple exclusive-dealing arrangements.
Source: OECD, *Annual Report on Developments in the Field of Restrictive Business Practices* (1965), 38, quoted in McLachlan and Swann, *Competition Policy*, 147.

his findings on domestic cartels and Table 9.2 on registered international cartels.

A second source is notifications to the European Commission in response to the implementation of the EC's policy against restrictive practices. The breakdown of the resulting notification of agreements is set out in Table 9.3. However, it was estimated that only between 5 percent and 50 percent of agreements had been notified and the evidence suggests national differences in underreporting.[26] Given the uncertainties of the data, Britain does not stand out noticeably from the experience of other European countries, that is, Britain does not appear markedly more cartelized than its European competitors.

Equally, British competition law holds up in comparison to that in most of the rest of Western Europe. English law, like that of the USA, operated on a common law basis under which manufacturers could not use the courts to enforce a restrictive agreement. Prior to the implementation of the competition policy in the Treaty of Rome, enforcement of such agreements through the courts remained possible on the continent.[27] Even after the Treaty of Rome, Dutch courts were still enforcing contracts that supported restrictive practices banned under the terms of the treaty.[28] National antitrust legislation in Europe presents a similar picture of weak legislation.[29] This criticism applied to British legislation, the Monopolies and Restrictive Practices Act, 1948, but following the 1956 Restrictive Trade Practices Act, G. C. Allen believed that British legislation was more hostile to restrictive practices than national legislation on the continent.[30] When the Treaty of Rome was signed in March 1957, "there was no member state which had a comprehensive law of a competitive nature and proven effectiveness."[31] West Germany was the first of the Six to introduce a major piece of antitrust legislation in July 1957 but other EC member states only gradually followed suit.[32] Also, passing legislation did not necessarily mean effective implementation: For example, French antitrust legislation has been damned as "an exercise in futility."[33] In comparison to national legislation elsewhere in Europe, British competition policy was at least as strong and, after 1956, definitely stronger than that found in continental countries with the exception of West Germany, both in terms of its legal basis and its implementation.[34]

---

[26] Ibid., 25; and D. L. McLachlan and D. Swann, *Competition Policy in the European Community* (London: Oxford University Press, 1967), 146–8.

[27] A. Chandler, *Scale and Scope: The Dynamics of Industrial Capitalism* (Cambridge, MA: Belknap Press, 1990), 287–8; and W. Friedmann and P. Verloren van Themaat, "International Cartels and Combines," in W. Friedmann (ed.), *Anti-Trust Laws: A Comparative Symposium* (London: Stevens and Sons, 1956), 474–7.

[28] D. G. Goyder, *EEC Competition Law* (Oxford: Clarendon, 1988), 37; and PEP, *Cartel Policy and the Common Market* (London: PEP, 1962), 265–7.

[29] UN, *Economic Survey of Europe in 1949* (Geneva: UN, 1950), 103.

[30] Allen, *Monopoly*, 141.

[31] Goyder, *EEC Competition Law*, 4; and L. Laudati, "The European Commission as Regulator: The Uncertain Pursuit of the Competitive Market," in G. Majone (ed.), *Regulating Europe* (London: Routledge, 1996), 257.

[32] Gerber, *Law and Competition*.

[33] F. Jenny and A. P. Weber, "French Antitrust Legislation: An Exercise in Futility," in Jacquemin and de Jong (eds.), *Welfare Aspects*, 401–33.

[34] For contrasting views of German law here, see Gerber, *Law and Competition*, and A. J. Nicholls, *Freedom with Responsibility: The Social Market Economy in Germany, 1919–1963* (Oxford: Oxford University Press, 1994), 335–7.

MARSHALL AID

In the late 1940s, there was much talk of cartels among European business-men and representatives of British industry were certainly not averse to con-sidering the possibility of cartelization with their continental counterparts. Significantly, however, British business representatives seemed more cautious than others were about taking these activities forward because of concerns about American perceptions. Thus for eighteen months various approaches from French business were received cautiously by the FBI because "their inevitable cartel flavor coupled with the timing vis-à-vis Marshall Aid has made it undesirable to offer them any encouragement."[35] It was not that British industry was against involvement in international agreements but that there was a clear concern about American attitudes to cartelization.[36] Thus, the FBI leadership was interested in being involved in these interna-tional agreements but remained wary that they would turn into cartels.[37] Similarly, at international conferences with the Americans, the British sup-ported their continental counterparts in defending cartels but did not take the lead in this.[38]

Marshall Aid also called for European integration in the form of a cus-toms union. At this stage, European business directly linked the concept of European integration to the need for industrial ententes and business self-government.[39] It was believed that business was better placed to bring about European integration than national governments.[40] As Beutler of the Bunder-sverband der Deutschen Industrie (BDI) told Kipping, the key was to explain to a skeptical USA that reciprocal specialization was the best way of offer-ing cost advantages rather than market fixing arrangements.[41] Cartelization and European integration were viewed as separate but closely related topics

---

[35] MRC MSS200/F/3/S1/21/47, D/6234, "Visit M. Gilbert, President of the Association for Franco-British Economic Expansion 7/4/48."

[36] MRC MSS200/F/3/D3/9/38, Gilbert at the meeting between the FBI and the Assocation for Franco-British economic expansion, 7 April 1948.

[37] MRC MSS200/F/3/E1/16/27, Kipping to Morelli (Italian CGII), 30 December 1948; and MRC MSS200/F/3/D3/6/50, "Short Report on Franco-German Industrial Talks in Dusseldorf on November 8 and 9, 1951."

[38] Neil Rollings and Matthias Kipping, "Private Transnational Governance in the Heyday of the Nation-State: The Council of European Industrial Federations (CEIF)," *Economic History Review*, Vol. 61 (2008), forthcoming.

[39] MRC MSS200/F/3/D3/9/38, Gilbert, at FBI-ABFEE meeting, 7 April 1948; and MRC MSS200/F/3/E1/16/27, "Le Mouvement pour l'Union Douaniere et Economique Europeenne" by Cornil, administrateur delegue de la Federation des Industries belges, 12 April 1949.

[40] MRC MSS200/F/3/E1/16/27, Kipping to Morelli, 30 December 1948; Ibid., "Le Mouvement pour l'Union Douaniere et Economique Europeenne" by Cornil, administrateur delegue de la Federation des Industries belges, 12 April 1949; and FBI, *Annual Report for 1952*, 26.

[41] MRC MSS200/F/3/D3/6/50, "Short report on Franco-German industrial talks in Dusseldorf on November 8 and 9 1951."

at this time by many industrialists. This contrasted sharply with American views about the need for an effective competition policy to ensure that the removal of tariffs was not simply replaced by private barriers to trade.

EUROPEAN COAL AND STEEL COMMUNITY

American desires for an effective competition policy to ensure the success of economic integration are often presented as gaining success with the signing of the Treaty of Paris in April 1951, establishing the European Coal and Steel Community (ECSC). Article 65 provided a general prohibition of restrictive agreements. Even with provision for some exemptions, the mere existence of a general prohibition was significant: Jean Monnet liked to call the treaty "Europe's first antitrust law."[42] This was all the more so given that the coal and steel industries had been among the most cartelized during the interwar period. American influence on the form of the article has been highlighted.[43] Indeed, a large part of the wording of Articles 65 and 66 (Articles 60 and 61 in earlier drafts) was written by Robert Bowie, a Harvard Law School antitrust specialist and General Counsel to the American High Commissioner in Germany, John McCloy, one of Monnet's closest friends.[44] Secondly, there was a terrific struggle involved in getting these articles into the treaty in the face of opposition from both industry and governments: it was one of the main factors extending the negotiations.[45] As business in the Six was largely opposed to the ECSC, often because of the antitrust measures, Djelic has argued that the battle over these articles was "symbolic of the conflict between the two systems of industrial production," that is the American business system and the continental European business system, with this marking a key turning point in the victory of the American system.[46]

In contrast to Djelic's position, the FBI viewed the creation of the ECSC as likely to operate as a cartel against Britain but that there seemed little advantage from British membership.[47] In this view the FBI was largely led by the views of the coal industry and the British Iron and Steel Federation (see

[42] S. Dell, *Trade Blocs and Common Markets* (New York: Alfred Knopf, 1963), 72.

[43] K. Nicolaïdis and R. Vernon, "Competition Policy and Trade Policy in the European Union," in E. Graham and J. D. Richardson (eds.), *Global Competition Policy* (Washington DC: Institute for International Economics, 1997), 275–6.

[44] Djelic, *Exporting*, 151 and 156; and G. Majone, "The Rise of Statutory Regulation in Europe," in Majone, *Regulating Europe*, 50.

[45] J. Gillingham, *Coal, Steel, and the Rebirth of Europe, 1945–1955* (Cambridge: Cambridge University Press, 1991), 228–83; Berghahn, *Americanisation*, 132–54; and Djelic, *Exporting*, 150–7.

[46] Djelic, *Exporting*, 156. See also Venturini, *Monopolies*, 88; and R. Evely, "Cartels and the Coal-Steel Community," *Cartel* No. 3 (1952–53), 84.

[47] Alan McKinlay, H. Mercer and Neil Rollings, "Reluctant Europeans?: The Federation of British Industries and European Integration, 1945–63," *Business History*, Vol. 42, No. 4 (2000), 96–97.

Chapter 4).[48] The operation of the ECSC did little to suggest that the FBI's attitude was misplaced. It was soon clear to contemporaries that, despite any good intentions in the High Authority, restrictive agreements continued to operate widely in the coal and steel industries. As one US executive put it, "The Treaty bans cartels, yet actually there are embodied in it many of the essential features of a cartel."[49] The High Authority itself admitted that it found it very difficult to introduce more competition into the coal and iron and steel industries: Implementation, rather than the wording in the treaty, was crucial.[50] The High Authority tried to work with the industries to bring about gradual change but with limited success.[51] Here the existence of the European GEORG coal cartel, and even more so the steel export cartel, illustrated the High Authority's limitations.[52] What is perhaps most striking here, and in contrast to American concerns, is that British business seems to have remained relatively agnostic and disinterested in the development of the ECSC. The cartel implications of the ECSC and the impact of Articles 65 and 66 were not a central concern for most of British industry in the early 1950s.[53] When there was concern, for example over the steel export cartel, it was agreed not to be too critical in case the British steel industry wanted to become associated with the cartel at a later date, as had happened in the interwar period.[54]

THE TREATY OF ROME, THE FREE TRADE AREA, AND EFTA

By the mid-1950s the issue of restrictive practices and cartels had risen up the agenda of British business. Two developments were responsible for this. First, the UN's Economic and Social Committee (ECOSOC) and later GATT

---

[48] Edmund Dell, *The Schuman Plan and the British Abdication of Leadership in Europe* (Oxford: Oxford University Press, 1995), 219–221; and Ruggero Ranieri, "Inside or Outside the Magic Circle? The Italian and British Steel Industries Face to Face with the Schuman Plan and the European Coal and Steel Community," in Alan S. Milward, Ruggero Ranieri, Frances M. B. Lynch and F. Romero, *The Frontier of National Sovereignty: History and Theory 1945–1992* (London: Routledge, 1993), 117–54.

[49] Quoted in Dell, *Trade Blocs*, 72; and *Proceedings of an International Conference on Control of Restrictive Business Practices* (Glencoe, IL: Free Press, c. 1960), 216.

[50] Dell, *Trade Blocs*, 97; and W. Diebold, *The Schuman Plan: A Study in Economic Co-Operation, 1950–1959* (New York: Praeger, 1959), 355.

[51] Diebold, *Schuman Plan*, 398–401; and H. L. Mason, *The European Steel and Coal Community: Experiment in Supranationalism* (The Hague: Martinus Nijhoff, 1955), 78.

[52] D. Spierenburg and R. Poidevin, *The History of the High Authority of the European Coal and Steel Community: Supranationality in Operation* (London: Weidenfeld and Nicolson, 1994), 265 and 445. For the steel export cartel, see Spierenburg and Poidevin, *History*, 106–8.

[53] See TNA BT258/1384.

[54] TNA FO371/111259–60, various correspondences, 1953–54.

regularly considered international action against restrictive trade practices. Secondly, and more importantly, 1956 had marked the introduction in Britain of the Restrictive Trade Practices Act. The FBI was opposed to an international agreement on international restrictive practices on the grounds that, as the USA and Britain (following the 1956 Act) had stronger domestic legislation, they would be disadvantaged.[55]

Such considerations were also relevant to business in Britain in the negotiations with the Six over the Free Trade Area (FTA), and, at the end of the 1950s, in its initial preference for EFTA over EC membership. The response from the membership to the FBI's 1956 survey on the proposals for a free trade area covering Western Europe is known for the emphasis placed on safeguards and the need for "fair competition" (see Chapter 5). This has usually been associated with a desire for protection and at best a concern with dumping.[56] However, part of the issue related to restrictive business practices and national differences in legislation to deal with them. As the FBI's submission to the government noted:

All barriers other than tariffs which either interfere with the free movement of goods or are discriminatory in effect should receive special scrutiny, including quotas, specification or registration regulations and anomalies in patent and trademark protection.[57]

British industry was worried that in an FTA in which the 1956 British legislation discouraged restrictive practices more in Britain than on the Continent, British companies would be excluded from European cartels (of firms in the EC) but exposed to their unfair competition (and dumping).[58] It was essential therefore that the FTA included provision for dealing with restrictive trade practices to ensure a level playing field, but provision that was not overly restrictive.

In January 1957, the OEEC reported that a free trade area including the Six was feasible, but raised the rules of competition as one of the particular

---

[55] MRC MSS200/F/1/1/192, Grand Council meeting, 20 April 1955; Pilkington, "The Challenge of Competition," *FBI Review*, April 1955, 19–20; and TNA BT11/5616, Consultative Committee for Industry meetings 30 October 1957, 9 December 1957 and 12 December 1958.

[56] Robert Lieber, *British Politics and European Unity: Parties, Elites and Pressure Groups* (Berkeley: University of California Press, 1970), 56–60; and Theodore Bromund, "From Empire to Europe: Material Interests, National Identities, and British Policies towards European Integration, 1956–1963," Ph.D. dissertation, Yale University, 1999, 311–22.

[57] MRC MSS200/F/1/2/84, "British Industry and European Free Trade Area," Hayman to Thorneycroft, 1 November 1956.

[58] TNA BT258/91, McGregor to Robinson, meeting with Sir Hubert Hutchinson, 11 October 1956; TNA BT258/229, Swindlehurst, note of a meeting between the President of the Board of Trade and Sir Raymond Streat, 10 October 1956; MRC MSS200/F/3/D3/5/44, "Economic Integration of Western Europe," BEAMA to FBI, 14 October 1956.

problems to be addressed.[59] The report noted that it would be desirable if the FTA and the Six adopted similar policies and advocated the adoption of a set of principles prohibiting certain practices and a complaints procedure to deal with any remaining practices.[60] However, the signing of the Treaty of Rome by the Six in March 1957 made such a solution difficult, if not impossible. That there should be a strong competition policy in the EC had been proposed from the outset.[61] Articles 85–94 of the treaty set out the rules of competition, covering restrictive practices, abuse of dominant positions, and state aid. Article 85(1) clearly prohibited any practices, which prevented, restricted or distorted competition within the EC. These rules of competition went beyond the competition policy of any of the Six, with the exception of what was to become the new German law. Moreover, officials of the Commission made clear their understanding of the importance of an effective competition policy to the success of the common market.[62]

British industry did not like what it saw. There was a concern that additional European requirements should not be imposed on top of the 1956 Act.[63] There was also dismay that the Treaty of Rome envisaged some measure of central supervision.[64] Additional European regulation of restrictive practices, superimposed on the 1956 Act, was in the eyes of British business not a matter to be covered by any FTA convention. Given the existence of Articles 85–90, this was an impossible position to sustain but when the national industrial federations of the non-Six issued their joint statement in March 1958, they called only for a system for dealing with complaints about restrictive practices.[65] Yet it was this approach, much milder than the Treaty of Rome, that was adopted in the Stockholm Convention and established in the European Free Trade Association. There was no emphasis towards prohibition, no clear machinery for dealing with complaints and

---

[59] The report is in TNA BT11/5552.

[60] For the British government's response, see *A European Free Trade Area* (Cmnd. 72) (London: HMSO, 1957).

[61] Goyder, *EEC Competition Policy*, 21–3; and J. Temple Lang, *The Common Market and Common Law* (Chicago: University of Chicago Press, 1966), 379.

[62] P. Verloren van Themaat, "Rules of Competition and Restrictive Trade Practices," International and Comparative Law Quarterly Supplementary Publication No. 1, *Legal Problems of the EEC and the EFTA* (London: Stevens and Sons, 1961), 76–88; A. Coppé, "The Economic and Political Problems of Integration," in M. G. Schimm and R. O. Everett (eds.), *European Regional Communities: A New Era on the Old Continent* (New York: Oceana, 1962), 3–17.

[63] MRC MSS200/F/3/O5/2/2, Hayman to Eccles, 31 July 1957; and FBI, *European Free Trade Area: A Survey for Industrialists* (London, 1957), 52.

[64] FBI, *European Free Trade Area*, 52–3; and ABCC, FBI and NUM, *A Joint Report on the European Free Trade Area* (London, September 1957), 9.

[65] *Free Trade in Western Europe: A Joint Statement by the Industrial Federations and Employers' Organisations of Austria, Denmark, Norway, Sweden, Switzerland and the United Kingdom* (Paris, 1958), 6–7.

no new powers to supplement national governments' existing legislation.[66] In part, the acceptance of such weak provisions was a consequence of the need to reach agreement quickly – in the first instance it was necessary to concentrate on trade issues.[67] Nevertheless, the outcome was a substantive difference between EFTA and the EC over their rules of competition and British business preferred EFTA in this respect.[68]

British business had a second problem with the Treaty of Rome, the difficulty of interpreting the precise meaning of the provisions in the Treaty of Rome.[69] The EC Commission was urged to provide clarification and British business was not alone in making these requests, with the International Chamber of Commerce (ICC) doing likewise.[70] This was part of a much wider debate on the meaning of the articles in the Treaty of Rome and, in part, was a consequence of the compromises that underpinned the treaty.[71] For all the strong antitrust language of Article 85(1), there were also the exemptions available under Article 85(3). The interpretation of these exemptions was more important than the commitments of Article 85(1) because the extent of exemption would determine how widely the policy would apply.[72] Secondly, the articles were brief and vague such that they were open to almost any interpretation. One commentator noted at the time, "There have been ingenious interpretations from business circles, which could well be defended, that practically every sort of cartel could be allowed under paragraph 3 of Article 85."[73] Differences of opinion among lawyers existed over such key issues as to what constituted an "enterprise" and a "concerted practice" and it was unclear whether prohibition of an agreement invalidated the whole agreement or just the offending section.[74] A considerable legal literature also emerged debating the meaning of the key phrase "likely to affect trade between Member States." This issue was not helped by the problem

---

[66] See A. Martin, "Restrictive Trade Practices in the EFTA," International and Comparative Law Quarterly, *Legal Problems of the EEC and the EFTA* (London: Stevens and Sons, 1961), 89–98; and G. and V. Curzon, "EFTA Experience with Non-Tariff Barriers," in H. Corbet and D. Robertson (eds.), *Europe's Free Trade Area Experiment* (Oxford: Pergamon, 1970), 135–6.

[67] UK Council of the European Movement, *European Industrial Conference* (London: 1958), 73.

[68] C. P. Cottis and J. R. M. Whitehorn, "Some Observations on British Restrictive Practices Legislation," International and Comparative Law Quarterly Supplementary Production No. 2, *Comparative Aspects of Restrictive Trade Practices* (London: Stevens and Sons, 1961), 38–9.

[69] UK Council, *European Industrial Conference*, 73–7.   [70] MRC MSS200/F/3/O2/2/9.

[71] Goyder, *EEC Competition Policy*, 22; "EEC Cartel Policy in the Making," *Common Market* No. 1, (1960–61), 45; and P. Pujade, "The Harmonisation of Conditions of Competition," *Aspects of European Integration: An Anglo–French Symposium* (London: PEP, 1962), 88.

[72] McLachlan and Swann, *Competition Policy*, 452–3.

[73] *Proceedings of an International Conference*, 154.

[74] McLachlan and Swann, *Competition Policy*, 131, and Temple Lang, *Common Market and Common Law*, 469.

of translation: Authorized versions of the treaty existed in French, German, Dutch, and Italian. In the first, the verb "affecter" was used, which simply meant to affect or concern, whereas in the other three versions verbs were used which all meant to affect adversely.

The final issue that was left unclear related to the implementation of the provisions in the Treaty. This led to a furious debate and to completely opposing interpretations being vigorously supported. Again, there were a range of issues[75]:

> To what parts of the economy did the provisions apply?
> What was the relationship between these provisions and national legislation?
> Whether the prohibitions were directly applicable or only to those found by the relevant authority to be in violation?
> Whether the provisions applied immediately or only once the regulations giving effect to the treaty had been issued?

The provisions represented a compromise based on vagueness and uncertainty. There was no clear legal position that flowed from the articles. Loftus E. Becker, an American lawyer who had been legal adviser to the Department of State 1957–1959, summed up the position well: "In view of the great generality of the language used in the appropriate Treaty provisions, the lack of judicial precedents and a very considerable degree of uncertainty as to the application of these Treaty provisions to specific cases, both within the Commission and among national experts who constitute the Consultative Committee – amounting at times to serious disagreements – it is too early to predict what the law will be in this field."[76] If these issues caused so much dispute among the member states the situation for British business was that much harder.

Drawing this section together, three points can be made at this stage. First, British industry was not supportive of the competition provisions of the Treaty of Rome, preferring a weaker policy. This was one element of the case for supporting membership of EFTA over membership of the EC. Secondly, it would be easy, on the basis of this finding, to suggest that British industry had little desire to engage in an active, competitive market. However, we need to be careful here. British industry was not alone in disliking Articles 85 and 86. The same could be said of much of industry in Europe at this time. In addition, one aspect of this disapproval was the dislike of supranational institutions, particularly ones in which British industry felt it

[75] Corwin Edwards, *Control of Cartels and Monopolies: An International Comparison* (New York: Oceana, 1967), 288; and G. J. Linssen, "The Application of Articles 85 and 86 of the Treaty," in Crowley (ed.), *Antitrust Structure*, 31–3.

[76] L. E. Becker, "Vertical Agreements Under the EEC 'Antitrust' Law," in Crowley, *Antitrust Structure*, 89.

would be unfairly disadvantaged, given national differences in competition law, and another was the uncertainty about key aspects of the policy. Thirdly, at this stage, the views of British business were dominated by the peak-level associations, particularly the FBI. It was the leadership of the FBI that formed business opinion in this field and presented it both to the government and to its constituent membership. The position became much more complex in the early 1960s when British business interest in the antitrust provisions of the EC reached their peak.

REGULATION 17

Given the uncertainties about how to interpret Articles 85 and 86 of the Treaty of Rome, it was the implementation of the treaty provisions which would be crucial, first in the form of the regulation to apply the rules, and, secondly, in the operation of policy thereafter by the EC Commission and the case law decisions of the Court of Justice. Article 87 of the Treaty of Rome set out a timetable for drafting regulations to implement Articles 85 and 86 and from this emerged Regulation 17, which came into operation in March 1962. It was this regulation that provided a procedural basis on which competition policy could be implemented and was, therefore, crucial to the development of policy. Again, Regulation 17 came down in favor of the principle of competition and, as such, has been seen to represent a victory once more for pressures to introduce a strong competition policy.[77] But, once more the debate over the form of what became Regulation 17 was fierce and long.[78] Agreement was only reached because of bartering over various policies between member states.[79] Under the regulation, all agreements which it was believed fell within the terms of the rules of competition had to be notified to the Commission with deadlines of November 1, 1962 for existing multilateral agreements and February 1, 1963 for bilateral agreements.

With the advent of Regulation 17 we can see a shift in the network of relationships dealing with EC competition policy. The British government's position was circumscribed in two ways. First, the negotiations on entry were in progress and, secondly, it was impossible for the government to advise on the interpretation of Community law in relation to particular cases: "These are matters which must be left to the firms concerned to decide with the aid of their legal advisers in the light of the exact terms and effects of their own arrangements."[80] Given this vacuum the position of peak-level associations

---

[77] PEP, *Cartel Policy*, 211; and M. Cini and L. McGowan, *Competition Policy in the European Union* (Basingstoke: Macmillan, 1998), 19.

[78] Edwards, *Control*, 289; and Cini and McGowan, *Competition Policy*, 19.

[79] "Commentary," *Cartel*, No. 12 (1962), 1 and 27.

[80] TNA BT258/1590, Lanchin to Birch, 22 October 1964, and Wallace to Lough, 15 November 1962.

became increasingly important and their information networks played a greater role. The FBI had followed developments closely, even before Britain applied for membership of the EC in 1961: When the draft of Regulation 17 appeared in December 1960 the FBI was quick to study it, aware that the rules would affect those British companies with agreements with firms in the Six.[81] The government was told that the draft regulations, "were causing widespread disquiet in British industry" because of the amount of work they would involve and the complex legal issues that they raised.[82] Indeed, they would "handicap any association with the Six." Even allowing for rhetorical license, the rules of competition were an important feature of the Treaty of Rome for British business and, hence, also of its attitude to EC membership. In the FBI's July 1961 policy statement, *British Industry and Europe*, the issue of restrictive practices and the Treaty of Rome's provisions were raised as the first of only three "substantial problems" if Britain was to join the EC, repeating the preference for intergovernmental cooperation over common supranational institutions.[83]

The final version of Regulation 17 was considered closely by the peak-level organizations and the need to bring it to the attention of their memberships was stressed.[84] In the FBI's case, this meant an article in the *FBI Review* that April, followed in the summer by two pamphlets.[85] The first was a summary of the whole Treaty of Rome, the second was *Restrictive Trade Practices and the European Economic Community*, both achieving considerable sales in addition to their free distribution to members.[86] Conferences on the subject were well attended by businessmen and a wide range of legal commentaries on EC competition law were published as well.[87] Such was the attention given by the FBI to the subject that the official responsible, C. P. Cottis, was recognized by government officials as "an expert on the Community law on restrictive practices," and met with DGIV officials of the Commission[88] His range of contacts are clearly illustrated

---

[81] MRC MSS200/F/3/S2/2/12, director-general's supplementary report, December 1960.

[82] TNA BT11/5559, CCI meeting, 26 January 1961.

[83] FBI, *British Industry and Europe* (London, July 1961), 3–4.

[84] MRC MSS200/F/3/S2/2/13, FBI Grand Council meeting, 14 February 1962; GLA MS17558, ABCC European Panel, meeting 13 March 1962, and MS14487/6, ABCC Overseas Committee, meeting, 4 April 1962.

[85] C. P. Cottis, "The Treaty of Rome: Restrictive Practices," *FBI Review* (April 1962), 42–3.

[86] FBI, *The Rome Treaty* (London, 1962); and FBI, *Restrictive Practices and the European Economic Community* (London, 1962).

[87] A. Campbell, *Restrictive Trading Agreements in the Common Market* (London: Stevens and Sons, 1964); "Registration of Agreements," *Birmingham Chamber of Commerce Journal*, (February 1963), 137; GUABRC UGD309/1/5/35A, T. J. Wells (FBI) to J. H. Worlledge, 30 July 1962; and GUABRC UGD258/1/6, Directors' minutes, Alexander, Ferguson & Co. Ltd, 30 May 1962.

[88] TNA BT258/1590, Llewellyn–Smith to Sinclair, 30 September 1964, and "Answers to Questions put by C. P. Cottis to Geritt Linssen," 21 November 1962.

over the issue of whether the February 1963 deadline on notification was to be extended. It was he who rang the Board of Trade to inform them that he had heard in Paris that Robert Marjolin intended proposing a postponement, although much to the FBI's embarrassment this came to nothing (see below).[89] Similarly, after the landmark Consten–Grundig case in the European Court of Justice in 1964 he met with Grundig's lawyer in Germany.[90]

Despite this recognized level of expertise the FBI still misinterpreted EC competition policy in key respects. It became apparent that British industry, and the FBI in particular, in its pamphlet *Restrictive Practices*, had taken too literal view of the wording of the Treaty of Rome and Regulation 17.[91] Its advice on the registration of multilateral agreements was a case where the FBI had to apologize to its members:

> The FBI's advice to members on the registration of agreements with the common market Commission had been based upon an exposition of the rules of competition which had taken the wording of the relevant articles in the registrations at its face value. However, by November 1st, the deadline for registrations of all except two-party agreements, the total number in fact registered was ludicrously small in relation to what might have been expected: moreover, it was known that a fair proportion of this smaller number consisted of registrations by American companies. Other evidence had been received too, that a cavalier attitude was being taken towards the rules of competition in many circles inside the Six.[92]

As an outsider, the FBI believed the Commission when it "let it be known that Europe is no longer the classic home of cartels."[93]

Ultimately, however, with Regulation 17 and the publication of deadlines for notifications, peak-level organizations could only advise. It was the decision of each individual firm whether to register agreements, abandon them, hide them, or adjust them. Many firms were aware of the implications and reviewed any existing agreements.[94] Most of the advice industry received recommended notification.[95] Some firms clearly followed this advice.[96] Others did not. One example is Babcock and Wilcox Ltd., the engineering

---

[89] Ibid., Seaman to Dennehy, "EEC – Notification of Sole Agency Agreements," January 1963.

[90] Ibid., Sinclair to Dennehy, undated, covering a report by Cottis on his visit to Germany and Brussels, 30 November to 4 December 1964.

[91] British Institute of Management, *Management and the European Common Market*, 96; and Lieber, *British Politics*, 100.

[92] MRC MSS200/F/3/S2/2/13, Grand Council meeting, 12 December 1962.

[93] H. W. de Jong, "EEC Competition Policy towards Restrictive Practices," in K. D. George and C. Joll (eds.), *Competition Policy in the UK and EEC* (Cambridge: Cambridge University Press, 1975), 58.

[94] For example, Coats Patons Ltd., see GUABRC UGD199/1/1/8, Directors meeting, 18 October 1962 and GUABRC UGD199/1/1/81, Executive directors meeting, 8 October 1962.

[95] Cottis, "The Treaty of Rome"; and FBI, *Restrictive Practices*.

[96] For example, Standard Motor Co., see MRC MSS226/ST/3/O/EU/5.

company. Originally an offshoot of an American parent, the Babcock and Wilcox Company, by the postwar period the British company had a market-sharing agreement not only with its American counterpart but also with its sister companies throughout Europe.[97] The initial reaction of T. R. Brabazon, the company's assistant secretary to Regulation 17 was straightforward: It was likely that the company's existing market-sharing agreements were prohibited under Article 85 because any sales in another company's territory required the payment of a 5 percent service commission plus a sales commission of 1.5–5 percent. Instead of registering the agreements he urged that all intercompany meetings and minutes should stop mentioning the commission and that instead of paying the commission "each company will pay each other a proper reward to be agreed (which is tacitly understood to be at the same rate) for the use of patent and trademark rights of the local company."[98] Brabazon's goal was to avoid registering any of the company's agreements because registration of even one agreement could "possibly prove an acute embarrassment to Babcock companies in other countries."[99] To this end the company sought the advice of Pierre LePaulle, a French lawyer and expert on the EC, who concurred with the idea of rewriting the agreements, explicitly terminating them but continuing them in practice as before. Brabazon was so concerned that he recommended ensuring that the company's files and invoices were consistent with any changes.[100]

In addition, he sought the advice of friends to see if anyone had "applied himself to the problem of circumventing the Treaty in circumstances similar to ours." He continued in this private and confidential letter written from home to a friend in another company, "I am wondering whether you have thought up any cunning devices for dealing with the situation. We, like other licensors, are most reluctant indeed to impair the picture of territorial exclusivity within Europe in favor of a free-for-all in which all our present associates and licensees can compete with each other."[101] He ended, continuing the conspiratorial tone, by asking his friend to destroy the letter if his company did not face the same problems. Thereafter, Brabazon spent his time in lengthy correspondence with LePaulle on the form of any new agreements and advising existing licensees in Europe not to register their agreements with Babcock and Wilcox Ltd. at that stage.

The problem was knowing what would be acceptable to the Commission and, by September 1962, with the delay in Britain's application to join the EC, the company's management decided to take the matter of new agreements no

---

[97] GUABRC UGD309/1/1, board meetings, 8 November 1955 and 10 June 1958.
[98] GUABRC UGD309/1/5/35A, Brabazon to Reisner, "Treaty of Rome, German Babcock and Wilcox Company," 27 April 1962.
[99] Ibid., Brabazon to Worlledge, 4 May 1962.
[100] Ibid., "Treaty of Rome–Restrictive Practices," by Brabazon, 6 July 1962.
[101] Ibid., Brabazon to Haxby, 5 September 1962.

further for the present because many of the existing agreements were long-standing, often over fifty years old, and there was little desire to renegotiate them. However, within two months the Commission had made clearer its intention to apply Article 85 to exclusive dealerships and the issue had to be opened again. A further meeting with LePaulle convinced Brabazon that he had to cancel the existing agreements and replace them with new ones. However, Deutsche–Babcock and Wilcox–Dampfkessel–Werke, the German sister company, was unwilling to sign the new agreement because it believed that the new agreement still violated Article 85. LePaulle was called in to persuade the Germans to sign but without success. As a result, the new agreements were put off and the old ones continued in existence, unregistered, after the notification date to the Commission. Other companies had already responded to the Treaty of Rome by embarking on a new push to form cartels among European business.[102] Some British companies, like Courtaulds, the textile company, were involved in this reaction to the establishment of the common market.[103] Although the company believed that the EC would have little effect overall, its British market for viscose might suffer. As a result, it investigated the possibility of collective action with its main European competitors to avoid "cut throat prices" but none emerged.[104]

However, that companies did not register their agreements was not always driven by a desire to hide or even extend these agreements. Even in the case of Babcock and Wilcox, one factor was uncertainty and this was also true of many other British companies. While Regulation 17 could be seen as a "milestone," it was still "a complicated, in some degree obscure, legal document."[105] Once more the French translation was badly drafted and with the further translation into English a number of issues remained obscure and the document remained unofficial.[106] However, there were more fundamental problems. "A quite unnecessary amount of confusion and doubt" was the outcome of the regulation simply because no one knew how widely and how severely it would be applied.[107] This doubt could not be removed by

[102] MRC MSS200/F/3/O2/2/16, Tennant to Maudling, 22 January 1959; TNA BT11/5729, CCI meeting, 26 November 1959; and Action Committee for the United States of Europe, *Statements and Declarations of the Action Committee for the United States of Europe 1955–67* (London: Chatham House/PEP, 1969), 53–4.

[103] D. C. Coleman, *Courtaulds: An Economic and Social History* (Oxford: OUP, 1980).

[104] Courtaulds Archive Department, miscellaneous records, "For Information of the Directors of Viscose Division – Policy in Respect of European Integration," 13 December 1960, board papers, memo, 15 February 1961, and "The Development of the Fibre Industry in Europe," by A. H. Wilson, Deputy Chairman, Courtaulds Ltd., 30 May 1961.

[105] W. Snijders, "Application of the Provisions Concerning Competition Up to the End of the Transitional Period," *Common Market*, No. 9 (1969), 191; and McLachlan and Swann, *Competition Policy*, 137.

[106] TNA BT258/1590, Lough to Seaman, 14 November 1962.

[107] Ibid., Kemp to Wallace, 30 November 1962.

the publication of EC Commission guidelines in the absence of a ruling from the Court of Justice.

Added to this uncertainty was confusion about the registration deadline. The FBI heard that the deadline would be extended given that no official copy of a revised version of the proposals arrived in Britain until only three weeks before the original deadline.[108] The UK delegation to the EC could not confirm this because Commission officials had been instructed not to answer questions on the issue.[109] The FBI were then informed by the Community's Information Service in the UK that postponement was "a virtual certainty" but this proved not to be the case.[110] Registration was not a straightforward process either: Each agreement required a separate form, no copies of which existed in London apart from 200 photostats supplied by the Board of Trade, the form was complicated and long, then had to be translated into an approved member language, usually French, copied six times and finally sent to Brussels.[111] Many firms either ran out of time or had little inclination to try to meet the deadline given the difficulties and costs involved and their desire to preserve commercial privacy. It is all the more surprising that 34,500 bilateral notifications were received by the Commission by the February 1, 1963 deadline. The vast majority of these, around 80 percent, were exclusive agency agreements.

Nor was a failure to notify a solely British phenomenon – it was estimated that only between 5 and 50 percent of relevant agreements had been registered. Brabazon believed even 34,500 notifications represented a significant failure to disclose agreements.[112] With only 800 multilateral agreements notified and national differences in the level of notification, the extent to which companies across Europe failed to register was clear.[113] Other circumstantial evidence supports this view. A lawyer for one company reported that his company intended filing 100,000 agreements alone (clearly it did not!) and another American company estimated that it had 27,000 reportable agreements.[114] At a conference in the USA, an audience of the representatives of eighty-one companies and thirteen law firms virtually all, on a show of hands, had relevant agreements in Europe but about two-thirds were dis-

[108] "EEC's Deadline on Restrictive Practices: British Firms Perplexed," *The Guardian*, 11 January 1963.

[109] TNA BT258/1590, Galsworthy to Lough, 9 January 1963.

[110] Ibid., Seaman to Dennehy, "EEC – Notification of Sole Agency Agreements," January 1963.

[111] Ibid.; "FBI Anxiety over EEC Demand," *The Times*, 11 January 1963; and "FBI Concern on EEC Pacts: Registration Date Still in Force?" *Financial Times*, 11 January 1963.

[112] Brabazon, who quoted a figure of 50,000 agreements, still thought the figure low, see GUABRC UGD 309/1/5/35A, Brabazon to Worlledge, 5 April 1963.

[113] "EEC gets Doubtful Response on Restrictive Practices," *The Times*, 1 November 1962, 20; and McLachlan and Swann, *Competition Policy*, 146–8.

[114] Barnard, "How good?" 67; and Edwards, *Control*, 293.

posed to advise not to notify agreements.[115] In addition, despite one million copies of the notification forms being ordered, supplies in France and the Netherlands, as well as London, ran out prior to the deadline.[116] Thus it can only be assumed that even after the introduction of Regulation 17, vast numbers of agreements remained in existence.

THE POLICY IN PRACTICE

Prior to the February 1963 deadline the Commission was optimistic that it was finally on top of the situation and that action would focus on those restrictions that were the most damaging to the EC, that is, horizontal agreements.[117] Unfortunately, this was to become a vain hope as the Commission was swamped by the number of bilateral agreements notified to it. Accordingly, the Commission found itself forced to focus on less damaging and often fairly minor vertical agreements and to soften its implementation of the policy. For the rest of the 1960s the development of competition policy remained slow. Case law developed gradually while DGIV had to concentrate its efforts on drawing up exemptions and giving informal decisions to reduce the number of cases to be considered. A further shift away from per se prohibition emerged in the mid-1960s with the acceptance that a market analysis was required in each case in order to make a decision about the effect of any agreement – knowledge of the terms of any agreement were not enough. Thus it became virtually impossible to predict the validity or not of any agreement, especially as the standards for granting individual exemptions under Article 85(3) were applied flexibly.[118] By the 1970s it was possible to note that not only had EC antitrust policy had little effect but that, "In practice there is a wide gap between the actual provisions of the Treaty and regulations and the practice of the Commission itself."[119]

The issue of competition policy remained an important element of the EC for British business right up to Britain's entry in January 1973. The CBI study, *Britain and Europe*, published in 1966–67, gave full attention to the issue of restrictive practices.[120] The same was true of the CBI's reappraisal of

---

[115] Discussion in Crowley, *Antitrust Structure*, 148–9.

[116] "Take Off for EEC Cartel Policy," *Common Market* No. 3, (1963), 55–6.

[117] Linssen, "Application," 45.

[118] British Mechanical Engineering Confederation, *The EEC and UK Engineering Companies* (London: Engineering, Chemical and Marine Press, 1971), 51.

[119] A. K. Cairncross et al., *Economic Policy for the European Community* (London: Macmillan, 1974), 143–4; and British Mechanical Engineering Confederation, *EEC and UK Engineering Companies*, 51.

[120] CBI, *Britain and Europe, Vol. 1: An Industrial Appraisal* (London, 1966); CBI, *Britain and Europe, Vol. 2: Supporting Papers* (London: 1966), and CBI, *Britain and Europe, Vol. 3: A Programme for Action* (London, 1967).

British membership of the EC in the 1970s.[121] Similarly, the issue appeared regularly in the 1970s as a topic of discussion in business journals and conferences. Indeed, competition policy was one of the aspects often mentioned when it was suggested that European integration meant "more than tariff removal."[122]

Nevertheless, there was a significant change in British industry's attitude to EC competition policy. Although ICI was threatened with action under Article 85 in the late 1960s, most companies were no longer so exercised by the subject.[123] In light of the experience of the slow implementation of the rules of competition, the preference for the devil it knew, existing British policy and the maintenance of national sovereignty, as opposed to the "misty European monster," became harder to sustain as the mists began to disappear and the monster no longer seemed so frightening.[124] EC competition policy was no longer viewed as an obstacle to British entry: "Community law and practice are evolving slowly and organically, and while the system is not one it is suggested that Britain should adopt spontaneously its acceptance does not seem to imply any major obstacle to British entry into the Community."[125] Over time this acceptance of EC competition policy became less grudging.[126]

Indeed, there were reasons for preferring EC policy provision to Britain's. Even in the early 1960s there was some feeling that the EC's regulations were less severe than British legislation and the FBI certainly felt free to use this argument as a means of criticizing the implementation of the 1956 Restrictive Trade Practices Act.[127] This feeling became far stronger after the Labour government introduced the Monopolies and Mergers Act in 1965. British legislation now stood out of line with merger policy in the rest of Europe: None of the member states had legislation to inhibit mergers and the Commission had begun actively to encourage European mergers as a counter to the perceived American challenge. "In common with the EEC Commission and the governments of the EEC countries," it was felt, "the UK government should watch, and where necessary police, the market behavior of large firms, but not seek to control the flexible structure of industry."[128] It was not simply the development of policy in the EC that mattered but also

[121] CBI, *Britain in Europe: A Second Industrial Appraisal* (London, 1969), 7.

[122] A. Rowley, "EEC Entry Means More than Tariff Removal," *Midlands Industry and Commerce*, (March 1970), 164–5; and A. Rowley, "Entry Means More than Tariff Removal," *Commerce International*, (March 1970), 21–2.

[123] See TNA BT241/2285 for papers relating to the ICI case.

[124] "EEC gets Doubtful Response on Restrictive Practices," *The Times*, 1 November 1962, 20.

[125] CBI, *Britain and Europe, Vol. 1*, 22.

[126] CBI, *Britain in Europe*, 7.

[127] MRC MSS200/F/3/S2/21/6, E.49A.62, "Draft Evidence to the Board of Trade Enquiry into the Working of the Restrictive Trade Practices Act 1956," undated but 1962.

[128] MRC MSS200/C/1/1, C.62.66, "UK Anti-Trust Legislation: Reasons for Seeking Changes," September 1966. See also *Britain and Europe, Vol. 1*, 22.

how it compared with domestic policy. Both were changing and it was the relative position that mattered in considering which seemed preferable to British business. Given changes at home and the experience of developments in Europe, one obstacle to British industry's wholehearted support for EC membership was not just removed but turned into a positive virtue.

CONCLUSION

The case of competition policy has highlighted a number of issues relating to British business and European integration. First, it has shown that business perceptions of European integration went beyond consideration of tariffs from the outset. Competition policy was a factor taken into consideration in determining attitudes to European integration as part of the changing business environment. Secondly, attitudes did change over time. In the early years after the war there was a concern about the impact of European integration, through its encouragement of continental European cartels, on unfair competition. By the late 1950s this concern had shifted to the rigor of the proposals in the Treaty of Rome while a decade later EC competition policy was being used as a means of criticizing British merger policy. Not only did attitudes change over time but they also involved weighing up the relative appeal of British and EC policy, while the prospect of applying both rigorously did not appeal. Thirdly, it effectively illuminates the link between market integration and political integration both in terms of the need for an active competition policy to achieve market integration but also in relation to the mixture of political action by peak-level organizations like the FBI/CBI and corporate action at the level of the firm in deciding about notification of agreements. Related to this, the FBI/CBI had an important role not just in advising members but also in exploiting its network of contacts across Western Europe. Fourthly, it illustrated the problems of being outside the EC. EC legislation still affected British companies and they had to adjust their strategies in consequence despite Britain not being a member of the EC and having had no input into the drafting of the policy. For business in the EC interpreting Articles 85 and 86 and Regulation 17 was hard enough given poor translations and uncertainty; for British business outside the EC it was even harder and mistakes were made particularly in translating the policy too literally.[129] The main objective of competition policy in the Community was to bring about market integration, not to foster competition per se. While a competitive system was seen as important, "the rules of competition . . . are not based upon any dogmatic conception of competition" and "competition is not seen as an end and even not as the only way of achieving the

---

[129] TNA BT258/1590, "Answers to Questions put by C. P. Cottis to Geritt Linssen," 21 November 1962.

fundamental purposes of the Community."[130] When a Commission official was asked about the possible case of a British firm trying to operate in the Six requesting that the Commission break up a restrictive practice, he replied, "The Commission may be grateful if the practice was brought to its notice although it may not be enthusiastic to follow it up."[131] British business did not appreciate this at the outset but by 1973 had learned its lesson.

---

[130] F. Spaak and J. Jaeger, "The Rules of Competition within the European Common Market," in Schimm and Everett, *European Regional Communities*, 161.

[131] R. Mussard, "The Regulation of the Restrictive Business Practices under the Common Market Treaty," International and Comparative Law Quarterly, Supplementary Publication No. 4, *Restrictive Practices, Trade Marks and Unfair Competition in the Common Market* (London: Stevens and Sons, 1962), 25.

10

Indirect Taxation

While competition policy has been described as the first supranational policy, taxation is conventionally presented at the other end of the spectrum, as the policy area "most resistant to moves to shift the locus of power to the supranational level."[1] A commitment to tax harmonization as part of European integration therefore represents a clear assault on national sovereignty: Tax harmonization raises key issues about European integration and has been a recurring topic of debate and disagreement throughout the history of European integration. Yet, to date, tax issues have received very limited coverage in historical accounts of European integration.[2] Taxation is also a crucial element of the business environment and one to which firms respond through their corporate strategy and through political lobbying. Typically business has called for a shift in the tax burden from direct to indirect taxation. This is underpinned by a belief that levels of taxation and the balance between direct and indirect taxation have important effects on economic performance. It is unsurprising, therefore, that faced with evidence of declining competitiveness British business should turn to taxation as a perceived cause of this problem. Again, however, despite being "the most prevalent form of intervention in the free production and sale of goods and services" business historians have neglected the topic.[3] Indeed, it is only recently that any sort of mainstream history of taxation has started to emerge.[4] Perhaps one reason for this is the complexity of the subject and the importance of detail. Often there can be agreement within business, for example, on the issue of the overall tax burden or the unpopularity of a particular tax but the particular nature of any reform will impact on individual firms in different ways. This is also relevant

[1] Jeremy Richardson, "Preface," in Claudio Radaelli, *The Politics of Corporate Taxation in the European Union: Knowledge and International Policy Agendas* (London: Routledge, 1997), viii.

[2] An exception is Frances Lynch, "A Tax for Europe: The Introduction of Value Added Tax in France," *Journal of European Integration History*, Vol. 8, No. 2 (1998), 67–87.

[3] PEP, *Growth in the British Economy* (London: Allen and Unwin, 1960), 112.

[4] On modern Britain see Martin Daunton, *Just Taxes: The Politics of Taxation in Britain, 1914–1979* (Cambridge: Cambridge University Press, 2002); and Hugh Pemberton, "A Taxing Task: Combating Britain's Relative Decline in the 1960s," *Twentieth Century British History*, Vol. 12, No. 3 (2001), 354–75.

to tax harmonization at the EC level because while there may be common demands from business across Europe for the principle of tax harmonization, the more contentious issue of around which tax regime to harmonize remains.

All these themes are illustrated in this chapter which begins by considering the issue of taxation in the early postwar years, then moves on to a consideration of the issue in relation to the creation of the EC and the alternative model of the free trade area, before focusing on the issue of value-added tax (VAT), the general indirect sales tax adopted by the EC member states by the mid-1970s.[5] For Britain shifting to a VAT was a major change in indirect taxation because the existing equivalent, purchase tax, was less a source of tax revenue than a tool used to manage the economy – it only applied to a select group of commodities, mainly consumer durables, at relatively high rates which were then adjusted by the government depending on the state of the economy. As a result, if British business was to demand a shift in the incidence of taxation away from direct taxation on income and profits to an indirect tax on sales, then it was impossible to use purchase tax in its existing form because it was not applied generally to all sales. The need was for a more widely based indirect tax. This could be a reformed purchase tax or some other tax. European integration is relevant here because of the decision in the early 1960s for the EC to adopt VAT. If Britain joined the EC it was likely that it would have to adopt VAT. Therefore there was a complex interaction between the national and European levels: domestic tax policy impacted upon business attitudes to European integration and European integration impacted upon attitudes to domestic tax policy. Given the fluctuating expectations about British engagement with the EC with the applications to join in 1961, 1967, and 1970, and de Gaulle's vetoes in 1963 and 1967, this interaction was dynamic and shifting as well.

TAXATION IN THE EARLY POSTWAR YEARS

After the Second World War through the 1950s and into the 1960s there was a degree of consistency in British business views on taxation. Four issues dominated its thinking. First, there was the perennial complaint that the overall burden of taxation was too great, and in particular, this was associated with the cost of providing the Welfare State. As Martin Daunton has noted, "Attitudes to the impact of taxation on incentives and the desirability

---

[5] A value added tax is a tax on the value added at each stage of production and sale, that is, the difference between the price paid for inputs and the price charged for the processed goods. A cascade turnover tax, the main alternative form of indirect taxation used at the time, is applied at every stage in the production and distribution chain. Thus, the tax would be applied a number of times as a good was produced, the more stages of production the greater the number of times the tax was applied.

Table 10.1. *Taxation as a Percentage of GNP*
(1958, Some 1957)

| | Social Security Payments | | |
	Excluded	Included	Difference
W. Germany	23.3	33.3	10.0
France	20.9	30	9.1
Luxemburg	20.3	28.3	8.0
Italy	18.2	27	8.8
Netherlands	19.1	26.6	7.5
Belgium	14.2	20.5	6.3
UK	24.4	28.2	3.8

Source: H. A. Junckersdorff, *International Manual on the European Economic Community* (University of St. Louis Press, 1963), Table 10.2.

of equality were highly contested and stood at the heart of British politics from the late 1950s."[6] To British industrialists the postwar burden of taxation was just too great, reducing incentives to save, incentives to be entrepreneurial and the ability to compete effectively. Table 10.1 illustrates the extent to which this criticism was valid: In terms of general taxation there was some validity compared to the members of the European Community, but this was largely because the Welfare State in Britain was funded out of general taxation rather than direct contributions. Related to this complaint was the second issue, the desire to shift the burden of taxation away from direct taxation and on to indirect taxation and, as it became clearer that the overall tax burden was neither extreme compared to other countries and that a significant reduction was unlikely, so attention increasingly focused on this aspect. The problem was that in Britain there was no general indirect taxation. The key sources of revenue were concentrated on particular commodities – tobacco, alcohol, oil, and motor vehicle duties. The only exception was purchase tax. This had been introduced during the Second World War to reduce consumption of luxury goods, and after the war became one of the key tools of demand management. Its incidence remained limited to certain goods, largely luxuries and consumer durables, and its rates were adjusted regularly to alter demand in the economy in line with the overall state of economic activity.[7] Table 10.2 illustrates the type of commodities liable to purchase tax. It also shows that the rates charged on those goods liable to purchase tax were high, much higher than a general sales tax, but

[6] Daunton, *Just Taxes*, 17.
[7] Alun Davies, "Britain into Europe: The Prospect of Tax Reform," *British Tax Review* (1962), 81–90.

Table 10.2. *Purchase Tax Rates on Various Commodities, June 1948–1973 (Percentage of Price)*

	Apr 9, 1948	Jun 16, 1948	Nov 29, 1948	Apr 20, 1950	Apr 11, 1951	Mar 17, 1952	May 14, 1952	Apr 15, 1953	Jan 6, 1954	Oct 27, 1955	Apr 10, 1957	Apr 16, 1958	Apr 8, 1959	Jul 26, 1961	Apr 10, 1962	Nov 6, 1962	Jan 1, 1963	Jul 21, 1966	Mar 20, 1968	Nov 23, 1968	Jul 20, 1971	Mar 22, 1972
Garments and footwear[a]	33 1/3					33 1/3	25			5				5 1/2	10			11	12 1/2	13 3/4	11 1/4	
Floor coverings	33 1/3							25		30	15		12 1/2	13 3/4	10			11	12 1/2	13 3/4	11 1/4	
Ironmongery	33 1/3							25		30	15		12 1/2	13 3/4	10			11	12 1/2	13 3/4	11 1/4	
Toys	33 1/3							25		30			25	27 1/2	25			27 1/2	33 1/3	36 2/3	30	25
Drugs and medicines	33 1/3							25		30			25	27 1/2	25			27 1/2	33 1/3	36 2/3	30	25
Stationery and office requisites	33 1/3							25		30			25	27 1/2	25			27 1/2	33 1/3	36 2/3	30	25
Bicycles and motor cycles	33 1/3							25		30			25	27 1/2	25			27 1/2	33 1/3	36 2/3	30	25
Motor cars[b]	33 1/3				66 2/3			50		60			50	55	45	25		27 1/2	33 1/3	36 2/3	30	25
Refrigerators	33 1/3				66 2/3			50		60		30	25	27 1/2	25			27 1/2	33 1/3	36 2/3	30	25
Washing machines	33 1/3				66 2/3			50		60		30	25	27 1/2	25			27 1/2	33 1/3	36 2/3	30	25
Vacuum cleaners	33 1/3				66 2/3			50		60		30	25	27 1/2	25			27 1/2	33 1/3	36 2/3	30	25
Radio and television sets	66 2/3	33 1/3						50		60			50	55	45		25	27 1/2	33 1/3	36 2/3	30	25
Office furniture	66 2/3		33 1/3					25		30	15		12 1/2	13 3/4	10			11	12 1/2	13 3/4	11 1/4	
Motor cars[c]	66 2/3			33 1/3	66 2/3			50		60			50	55	45	25		27 1/2	33 1/3	36 2/3	30	25
Electric space and water heaters	100							75	50	60		30	25	27 1/2	25			27 1/2	33 1/3	36 2/3	30	25
Jewellery	100							75	50	60		30	25	27 1/2	25			27 1/2	50	55	45	25
Perfumery and cosmetics	100							75		90		60	50	55	45		25	27 1/2	50	55	45	25

[a] Rates for utility goods pre-1955.
[b] Retail value less than £1280.
[c] Retail value more than £1280.
Source: 64th Report of the Commissioners of Her Majesty's Customs and Excise for the year ended 31 March 1973 (Cmnd. 5482) (HMSO, London, 1973).

also fluctuated regularly. So, for example, the purchase tax on cars never fell below 25 percent and fell from 55 percent to 25 percent between July 1961 and November 1962 before rising again to 27.5 percent in July 1966 and peaking at 36.66 percent in November 1968. Purchase tax rates on the other commodities followed a similar pattern. With the incidence and yield so selective – over a third of the yield came from motor cars in the early 1960s – any shift in the burden of taxation towards indirect taxation would have made the situation even more discriminatory and unstable for those firms whose products were liable to purchase tax. The impact of purchase tax was the third issue and the Federation of British Industries (FBI) had been campaigning for a fundamental reexamination of the tax from the early 1950s.[8] The fourth issue, export incentives, also had implications for purchase tax. British exporters believed that their continental counterparts were unfairly advantaged because of the way in which turnover taxes were levied there. There was a suspicion that such taxes provided some form of incentive to exporters that was not available to British exporters.[9] This was all part of a wider debate about export subsidies and fair competition.[10] Given all these concerns about the tax regime in general and purchase tax in particular, it is unsurprising that British business started to cast its eyes over the Channel to see what it could learn given the growing awareness of better economic performance there.

In relation to the development of European integration, tax issues emerged as points of contention on a regular basis, though it would be hard to discern this from most historical accounts of integration. Immediately after the war, the UN study group on customs unions noted that a lack of harmonization of sales or turnover taxes would be a problem for any customs union, and practical evidence to support this contention could be found in the case of the creation of Benelux, the customs union of Belgium, Netherlands and Luxembourg established in 1949.[11] Similarly, the issue of tax harmonization surfaced shortly after the ECSC came into existence.[12] There were important differences between the French and West German tax systems with higher direct taxation in West Germany and higher indirect taxation in France.

[8] "Purchase Tax Revision," *The Times*, 7 May 1952, 3.

[9] EIU and NABM, *Taxes for Britain: The Impact of the Common Market* (London, 1962), 7.

[10] Neil Rollings and Matthias Kipping, "Private Transnational Governance in the Heyday of the Nation-State: The Council of European Industrial Federations (CEIF)," *Economic History Review*, Vol. 61 (2008), forthcoming.

[11] UN, *Customs Unions* (New York: UN, 1947), 63–4; and James Meade, Hans Liesner and Sidney Wells, *Case Studies in European Economic Union: The Mechanics of Integration* (London: Oxford University Press, 1962), 85–102.

[12] J. Gillingham, *Coal, Steel, and the Rebirth of Europe, 1945–1955* (Cambridge: Cambridge University Press, 1991), 345; Meade, Liesner and Wells, *Case Studies*, 310; Lynch, "Tax for Europe," 82; and D. Spierenburg and R. Poidevin, *The History of the High Authority of the European Coal and Steel Community: Supranationality in Operation* (London: Weidenfield and Nicholson, 1994), 83.

Exports within the ECSC were exempted from turnover taxes (indirect taxation) in the country of origin; instead they were liable to an import levy in the country of destination equal to the turnover tax in the destination country on that product. German exports to France thus faced a larger tax burden than French exports to West Germany: there was meant to be a common market for steel among the member states but imports of steel into France faced an 18 percent import duty while those into Germany only 5–6 percent. The dispute was only resolved by the appointment of a committee to consider the issue. Lincoln Steel, the chairman of the FBI's Overseas Trade Policy Committee, summed up the lessons from this episode for British business: The practical difficulties of implementing the ECSC under a common High Authority were "very great, particularly since there were no common systems of taxation, social security and currency."[13] Even prior to the creation of the European Community, British business was aware that European integration raised potentially contentious issues relating to taxation, especially indirect taxation.

THE CREATION OF THE EUROPEAN COMMUNITY AND THE FREE TRADE AREA PROPOSALS

During the talks from 1955 onwards, which led to the signing of the Treaty of Rome in March 1957, the issue of tax harmonization tended to be subsumed into the wider issue of the harmonization of social charges, such as social security, and wages more generally, an issue on which the French were insistent, in return for opening their markets.[14] The Treaty of Rome included provision for equal pay (Article 119) and the harmonization of indirect taxation (Article 99). However, like competition policy, the meaning of these articles was opaque, and much depended on what followed. With regard to tax harmonization the EC Commission acted speedily with a group of experts reporting in December 1959 that "the maintenance of the diversity of tax systems currently applied in the different member states is prejudicial in character to the good working of the common market and that it is desirable, as well as being anticipated in Art. 99 of the Treaty, to go on towards a harmonisation of the differing legislation relating to turnover taxes."[15] As a result, a few months later, the Neumark Committee, the report of which was

---

[13] MRC MSS200/F/1/1/192, Grand Council meeting, 10 February 1954.
[14] Lise Rye Svartvatn, "In Quest of Time, Protection and Approval: France and the Claims for Social Harmonization in the European Community, 1955–56," *Journal of European Integration History*, Vol. 8, No. 1 (2002), 85–102.
[15] *The EEC Reports on Tax Harmonization, General Introduction to the Reports of Sub-Groups A, B and C* (Amsterdam: International Bureau of Fiscal Documentation, 1963), 13; and Donald Puchala, *Fiscal Harmonisation in the European Communities: National Policies and International Co-operation* (London: Frances Pinter, 1984), 28.

to be so influential in the introduction of VAT, was established to consider the issue of EC tax harmonization.

How did British industry respond to these developments given its own concerns about UK tax policy and about export incentives? Initially the potential impact was obscure and not the focus of attention, but once the possibility of British membership of a free trade area became real, the implications heightened industrialists' concerns about their ability to compete. Businessmen continued to emphasize the burden of taxation under which they operated, to highlight differences in treatment on the continent and to lobby for changes to domestic policy.[16] The FBI's generally positive statement on the proposal to open negotiations over a FTA in November 1956 was typical:

It must be made possible for UK industry to compete on equal terms. In these days when re-equipment and modernisation of plant depends so largely upon ploughing back of profit, the effect of very high taxation has to be compensated by the level of gross profits. Competitive conditions in a Free Trade Area may therefore lead to a progressive decline unless taxation is reduced. British industry must be no worse placed in this respect than its competitors.[17]

Those sectors whose products were liable to purchase tax, such as the car industry, continued to highlight that particular burden as well, as Sir Patrick Hennessy, chairman of Ford's, made clear:

The German motor industry, burdened by a turnover tax of only 6 per cent, increased its sales last year by one-fifth, almost equally in its home market and abroad. In the UK, the intention was that a high rate of purchase tax would divert home sales to export. Not only has it failed in this but it has so reduced the volume of sales in the home market that costs have been increased and the ability to compete in export markets has been thereby impaired. Early and progressive relief is necessary to remove this serious handicap which purchase tax indirectly imposes upon the export effort of the motor industry.[18]

With the possibility of a FTA the FBI actively began to consider the possibility of a general sales tax as an alternative to purchase tax.[19] In making such studies and statements, business was using British involvement in European integration as a new context in which to frame complaints about the British tax regime. Indeed, Norman Kipping, the director-general of the FBI, viewed this as one advantage of involvement with the government over European

---

[16] FBI, *European Free Trade Area: A Survey for Industrialists* (London, 1957), 59.

[17] MRC MSS200/F/1/2/84, "British Industry and the Free Trade Area," sent to Thorneycroft, 1 November 1956.

[18] "Ford Motor Company Limited," *The Times*, 26 March 1957, 16.

[19] MRC MSS200/F/1/1/195, Taxation Committee meetings, 15 January 1957 and 23 October 1957, and Purchase Tax Panel meeting, 15 October 1957.

integration: It offered an opportunity to lobby for domestic reforms, including taxation.[20]

These calls for tax harmonization were very clearly aimed at getting the British government to take action to the benefit of British business rather than in support of tax harmonization per se. British business was aware that tax harmonization would require a significant degree of political integration and supranationalism, even at this early stage of European integration.[21] This helped to distinguish the EC from a FTA and British business did not support such a loss of sovereignty at this stage. The 1957 joint statement by the ABCC, FBI and NUM on the FTA proposals distinguished two types of safeguards: those that related to rules of competition designed to ensure fair trading conditions and those which require "going a great deal further in the direction of a fusion of the economies of the countries concerned than is implied in the EFTA concept," continuing:

These [the latter] relate to those differences in costs in various countries which are the outcome of such factors as taxation, conditions of employment and social welfare charges. The Six have met this problem not merely by a customs union but by a Treaty which intends a thoroughgoing economic union whereby conditions will be deliberately brought about in which many of these factors will in time be harmonised.... Such an equality could only be brought at the price the Six have shown themselves willing to pay, that is by adherence to far-reaching measures of economic integration, and probably also to supranational institutions, such as are contained in the Treaty of Rome. That price must we think be regarded as higher than HM [Her Majesty's] Government or the country at large would wish to pay, and we have no reason to think that industrial opinion would take a different view.[22]

Tax harmonization was, therefore, one of a number of factors which made clear to British business the difference between a FTA and the EC, and that while harmonization was believed desirable, if not essential, to business as a means of improving competitiveness, harmonization only appealed because it was believed that British taxes were higher than those in the Six.

THE FIRST APPLICATION, 1961–1963

Opinion in British business on the idea of tax harmonization remained largely unchanged through the creation of the European Free Trade Association and it was only in the early 1960s that the issue reemerged. It was at that time that interest in tax developments in the EC came to a head. For much of the 1950s, consideration of European integration raised issues about harmonization in general, in which tax harmonization was an element, but from the early

---

[20] MRC MSS200/F/3/D3/5/44, Kipping, draft speech to Grand Council, 9 October 1956.
[21] TNA BT205/17, CCI 40th meeting, 20 October 1955.
[22] TNA CAB134/1862, ES(EI)(57)256, "EFTA. Report by ABCC, FBI and NUM," September 1957, 3–4.

1960s onwards attention came to focus more directly on taxation, and in particular, on indirect taxation. Within the Six, the work of the Neumark Committee from 1960, with its report released in July 1962 and endorsed by the Council of Ministers in November, marked this shift by recommending that the EC should adopt VAT, recently introduced in France, instead of a turnover tax which the other five EC member states used.[23]

The second development was that in July 1961 Harold Macmillan, the Prime Minister, announced that Britain was opening negotiations with the Six, the members of the EC, with a view to applying for membership. Thus, the Neumark Committee's report came out in the middle of the negotiations between Britain and the Six. While the British government was aware that EC membership might have long-term implications for the British tax regime, it was reluctant to embark on tax reform and believed that the issue could be ignored because progress on the issue in the EC was so slow.[24] As Ted Heath, the minister responsible for the negotiations, noted, "I doubt whether there will be much wind blowing over the terrain of taxation for a little while and certainly not enough to try out a kite!"[25] Once a member of the EC, Britain would have the power of veto over EC tax harmonization, like other member states, if required.[26] To government officials, purchase tax was not only consistent with the Treaty of Rome but it was a far more efficient tax than VAT: once in the EC, the aim should be to harmonize indirect taxation around purchase tax.[27] This approach floundered with the adoption by the EC Council of Ministers of the Neumark Committee's recommendation to adopt VAT. Worse, as Britain did not raise tax harmonization at the start of the negotiations as a potential issue, it could not raise it later in the negotiations and was faced with a *fait accompli*, which one Treasury official believed was "so distasteful to us" that Britain should reconsider its prospective membership of the Community.[28] In this one area, even if no other, the government was relieved by de Gaulle's veto in January 1963.

In contrast, British business was less committed to the existing tax regime, with the FBI actively considering tax reform. In 1961, the FBI set up two committees to consider aspects of the tax reform issue. The first considered

[23] *The EEC Reports on Tax Harmonization.*

[24] TNA CUST49/5124 Part 1, Pepper to France, "Special group: six/seven problem," 29 March 1961 and Robinson to White, 7 June 1961; and TNA T312/418, Lucas to Barrow, 4 December 1961.

[25] TNA T312/418, Phelps to Radice, May 1962, and Heath to Sir John Russell, 28 December 1961.

[26] Alan S. Milward, *The United Kingdom and the European Community, Vol. 1: The Rise and Fall of a National Strategy 1945–1963* (London: Frank Cass, 2002), 461; and TNA T312/418, IG(61)143 revised, 8 September 1961.

[27] TNA CUST49/5124 Part 1, Ashford to Cory, 14 February 1962; and TNA T312/418, Hancock to McKean, "The EEC's Plans for Harmonisation of Turnover Taxes by the Common Market Countries," 31 October 1962, and Hancock to Keeble, 24 September 1962.

[28] TNA T312/418, Clark to Widdup, 22 October 1962.

the balance of the fiscal system. Crucially, at its meeting on June 15, 1961, a month prior to the announcement of the government's decision to open negotiations, the committee agreed to concentrate on the viability of extending purchase tax rather than shifting to a continental-style of indirect taxation because the latter would involve large-scale changes to the tax system.[29] However, the FBI's Grand Council refused to approve the report in November because, having now applied to open negotiations on EC membership, entry to the EC would require moves towards harmonizing indirect taxation and, as a result, many of the report's conclusions were regarded as "obsolete."[30]

The second FBI report, by the Working Party on Export Incentives, was more influential. Chaired by Sir Archibald Forbes (see Chapter 4), it was set up in October 1961 to consider whether there was a case for introducing export incentives.[31] In addition to rejecting the use of such incentives, the report recommended that the government should be asked to "make an urgent study of the fiscal system with the object of determining whether the export effort could be assisted by changes in the present pattern of distribution of taxation and in the type and scope of indirect taxes, having due regard to the question of harmonization of the UK tax system with those of the Common Market countries."[32] The committee itself believed that a broader based system of indirect taxation, be it through purchase tax or a turnover tax, or VAT, would act as an incentive to export and that such a change would allow a reduction of direct taxation.

With the prospect of EC membership impinging on the issue of tax reform, the FBI was keen for the government to consider a French-style value-added tax. This was not because the FBI supported the introduction of VAT; it just wanted the subject studied. Actually, the FBI was coming round to the view that a switch from purchase tax to VAT would not be an incentive to exports.[33] Nevertheless, there was a strong conviction on the part of the wider business community and in the general public that adopting continental-style indirect taxation would offer an incentive, psychological if not real, to exports.[34] De Gaulle's veto in January 1963 of Britain's first application had little impact in this respect. With many businessmen continuing to call for reform of indirect taxation, it was politically awkward for the FBI to voice clear opposition to the replacement of purchase tax by a turnover

[29] MRC MSS200/F/1/1/196, Hancock working party meeting, 15 June 1961.

[30] Ibid., Taxation Committee meeting, 12 October 1961 and Taxation Panel meeting, 1 November 1961; TNA T320/51, unknown to Hancock, 28 March 1962.

[31] TNA T320/61, "Report of the Working Party on Export Incentives," February 1962.

[32] Ibid., 34.

[33] FBI, *Value Added Turnover Tax* (London, 1963); TNA T320/53, Armstrong to Sir Gordon Richardson, 10 April 1963.

[34] TNA T320/53, Armstrong to Mitchell, "Reform of the Tax Structure," 8 February 1963; and Sir Edwin Leather to Selwyn Lloyd, 2 May 1962.

or value-added tax. As a result, Sir Norman Kipping, the director-general of the FBI, suggested that the government should announce the establishment of an official study on the subject. Its report might then have a bigger impact on correcting the misapprehensions in public opinion.[35] This suggestion was picked up and from it emerged the government appointed Committee on Turnover Taxation, better known as the Richardson Committee.

Before turning to the work of this committee one further point needs to be made. Although government officials were resistant to business calls for tax reform, it is clear that the parts of the government responsible for tax policy were poorly informed about European integration and related tax harmonization proposals. Often newspapers and other published sources were the basis of information or they were dependent on other parts of government informing them of relevant developments.[36] At times this meant turning to business organizations, for example, using the FBI's *Taxation in Western Europe*, a review of the various tax systems first published for its membership at the time of the FTA proposals and which went through a number of editions.[37] More significantly, it was through the FBI that the Treasury obtained a copy of the draft submission from the Commission to the Council of Ministers on the adoption of VAT.[38] This reliance on business also provided business with greater opportunities to influence tax policy, an area in which business organizations in Britain often have limited impact. The adoption of Kipping's proposal for the Committee on Turnover Taxation is one such example, although it was also proposed at the same time in a report by the National Economic Development Council on *Conditions Favourable to Faster Growth*.[39]

THE RICHARDSON COMMITTEE

The Committee on Turnover Taxation, commonly known as the Richardson Committee after its chairman, Gordon Richardson, later to become Governor of the Bank of England, was appointed in April 1963, "To inquire into the practical effects of the introduction of a form of turnover tax, either in addition to existing taxation, or in substitution either for the purchase tax or for the profits tax or both."[40] Four factors were to be taken into consideration in conducting the inquiry: the development of the economy and

[35] TNA T320/492, Armstrong, "Export Incentives," 22 February 1963.
[36] TNA T312/418, Hancock to Radice, 18 September 1962, and Hancock to McKean, 28 November 1962, added note by Widdup to Clark, 29 November 1962.
[37] Ibid., Harding to Hancock, 20 September 1962 and after, and Phelps to Radice, May 1962. FBI, *Taxation in the Proposed European Free Trade Area* (London, October 1957) was the first edition.
[38] TNA T312/418, Hancock to McKean, 31 October 1962.
[39] NEDC, *Conditions Favourable for Faster Growth* (London: HMSO, 1963).
[40] *Report of the Committee on Turnover Taxation*, (Cmnd. 2300) (London: HMSO, 1964), 7.

the promotion of exports; the fair distribution of the burden of taxation; the maintenance of revenue; and efficiency in tax collection and administration. These terms of reference were crucial. Coming after de Gaulle's veto of Britain's application to join the EC, there was no reference to the implications of EC membership: The committee was asked to consider the specific merits of a turnover tax, in practice VAT, against the existing purchase tax and other taxes, in particular, profits tax. As such, the fact that Britain might have to adopt VAT with EC membership was no longer relevant.

The committee's *Report*, which was published in March 1964, categorically rejected the case for introducing VAT as an alternative to either profits tax or purchase tax, going well beyond the views of contemporary observers.[41] There was an awareness that the *Report* looked like being "another field in which our policy may diverge from that of the Community in the near future and where a further obstacle may be created to our eventual membership."[42] Where does British business fit into this story? First, the Richardson Committee put great emphasis on the views of industry in reaching its conclusion to reject VAT. Crucial here was the belief that businesses, especially in manufacturing, would regard a value-added tax and the profits tax as very different types of taxation and would react differently to them:

A value-added tax would be regarded as a charge or cost and that businesses would aim to recover it in prices, either immediately or in their next review of costs and prices. On the other hand, . . . [companies] did not, or did not directly, take the profits tax (and income tax) into account in prices.[43]

In other words, any attempt to shift the tax burden from profits tax to indirect taxation in the form of VAT would lead to increased prices, making British goods less competitive and possibly setting off a round of wage demands. This view was based on the results of a questionnaire circulated to "the managements of a fairly small number of large businesses."[44] Seventeen business organizations, listed in Table 10.3, were approached, of which three were nationalized industries. Additional responses came from the FBI and the Institute of Chartered Accountants of England and Wales and later from the Gas Council, British Petroleum Company Limited and Esso Petroleum Company Limited. The questionnaire then formed the basis of oral evidence

[41] Douglas Dosser, "The VAT in the UK and the EEC," in Alan Peacock and Francesco Forte, (eds.), *The Political Economy of Taxation* (Oxford: Blackwell, 1981), 118.

[42] TNA T320/226, "Brief for WEU Meeting: The Report of the Richardson Committee and the Harmonisation of Turnover Taxation in the Common Market," note by the Treasury and Customs and Excise, 15 April 1964, and O'Neill to Keeble, 24 March 1964; and TNA T320/49, Pliatzky to McKean, "Harmonisation of Turnover Taxes," 2 October 1963.

[43] *Report of the Committee on Turnover Taxation*, 73.   [44] Ibid., 70.

Table 10.3. *Business Organizations Consulted by the Richardson Committee*

Associated Electrical Industries Limited
Boots Pure Drug Company Limited
The Bowater Paper Corporation Limited
The British Motor Corporation Limited
British Railways Board
The Electricity Council
English Sewing Cotton Company Limited
Ford Motor Company Limited
George Wimpey & Company Limited
Guest, Keen & Nettlefolds, Limited
Imperial Chemical Industries Limited
Marks & Spencer Limited
Pilkington Brothers Limited
Shell International Petroleum Company Limited
Unilever Limited
Vickers Limited

Source: *Report* of the Committee on Turnover Taxation, 70.

presented to the committee by all seventeen organizations plus the FBI and the Gas Council.[45]

Despite this degree of consultation and the additional written representations from a range of trade associations, companies and other business-related organizations, it would seem that the committee oversimplified business attitudes towards VAT. The majority of submissions did not support the introduction of VAT, favoring a broadening of purchase tax with a uniform rate instead. Nevertheless, a closer study of the submissions reveals the complexity of the issue, the diversity of opinion and the contingent nature of many of the views, none of which is evident from the *Report* of the committee. Some views were straightforward and easily explained. The Retail Distributors' Association was in favor of widening purchase tax rather than VAT because purchase tax only related to the wholesale stage of production whereas VAT would involve a large administrative burden for retailers. The National Coal Board did not favor the replacement of profits tax by VAT (or a broader based purchase tax) because they did not earn profits (the removal of profits tax would not ease its tax burden) and energy products were not liable to purchase tax but probably would become liable to a broader based purchase tax or VAT. The Society of Motor Manufacturers and Traders (SMMT), given the burden of purchase tax on motor vehicles, wanted to shift away from the *status quo* towards a broader based form of

---

[45] Ibid., Appendix F and Appendix G.

indirect taxation.[46] Unilever, usually a stalwart supporter of anything that might ease Britain's accession into Europe, took a contrary position here, based on calculating the likely relative tax burdens on its products. If Britain joined the Community it would have to adopt VAT, its submission noted, but "this is no reason to abandon purchase tax now."[47] There were, in other words, a diverse range of starting points for different industries and firms.

There were also inconsistencies and clear disagreements among the submissions on key issues. There were disagreements over the impact of replacing profits tax with VAT. Within the SMMT the majority of members believed that any such shift would be passed on in increased prices and were not in favor of it. The two exceptions to this position were the British Motor Corporation and the Ford Motor Company, both of whom favored the introduction of VAT.[48] More generally, the FBI was clear that if VAT replaced profits tax, companies would pass on the taxation in increased prices. Yet this was questioned by the Association of British Chambers of Commerce submission. Despite being strongly opposed to the introduction of VAT, the ABCC saw the issue as one of degree, not of absolutes: "the degree to which *all* taxes are reflected in prices is governed by the scale of competition and the level of profit margins" (emphasis added).[49]

Context was also important and made the views expressed contingent rather than absolute because they were dependent on other factors. A survey of its members carried out by the Birmingham Chamber of Commerce to inform its 1963 budget submission illustrates this point. Firms which produced consumer durables, who might have been expected to have been in favor of a shift from direct to indirect taxation as it would replace purchase tax on their goods with a wider based indirect tax at a lower rate, were not so because their priority was to ease hire–purchase restrictions, that is, the credit terms they were able to offer to consumers.[50] It was not that they were against the change in taxation per se. Similarly, for both the FBI and the SMMT the rate at which VAT would be charged was an important consideration.[51] There was also the issue of the details about which products

[46] TNA T320/55, "Committee of Inquiry into Turnover Taxation," Retail Distributors' Association, n.d.; TNA T320/54, TT(63)25 part 2, 25 July 1963; and TNA T320/56, "Memorandum for Submission to the Committee on Turnover Taxation," SMMT, August 1963.

[47] TNA T320/54, TT(63)27, Report of the Unilever Study Group on Turnover Taxation, 29 May 1963.

[48] TNA T320/56, "Memorandum for submission to the Committee on Turnover Taxation," SMMT, August 1963, 7–8.

[49] Ibid., E.224.63, FBI, "The Introduction of a Turnover Tax in the UK," 15; and TNA T320/54, ABCC, "Report of the Views of the Tax Panel on a Tax on Added Value," 16 April 1963, 3–4.

[50] "Economic policy," *Birmingham Chamber of Commerce Journal*, No. 62 (January 1963), 29–30.

[51] TNA T320/56, E.224.63, FBI, "The Introduction of a Turnover Tax in the UK," 8–9 and "Memorandum," SMMT, 3–4.

might be exempted and other details remained unclear. After all, although the EC planned to harmonize indirect taxation on VAT, the only system of VAT then operating was in France. Even there, at this stage VAT only applied at the wholesale stage and not at the retail stage as was planned in the EC. As the FBI's submission put it:

> The study in isolation of one aspect of a country's fiscal system – its indirect taxes – is liable to lead to false conclusions about the course which future fiscal policy should in general pursue. Valid conclusions are also difficult to reach because the arguments which might support them are, at best, expressed in terms of probabilities and, at worst, of conflicting possibilities, one of which has to be selected as the most likely in fact to occur.[52]

The FBI may not have been in favor of VAT but it was aware of the complex and contingent nature of any tax change which made it impossible to make definitive pronouncements like the Richardson Committee did.

THE SECOND HALF OF THE 1960s

By the second half of the 1960s the position was changing and with it business attitudes to VAT and tax harmonization. First, a new Labour government was elected in 1964 and introduced a number of new taxes. The National Association of British Manufacturers (as the NUM had renamed itself) had protested in 1962 that the British tax system "resembles nothing so much as a Heath Robinson contraption," but as yet no solution to this problem had been reached beyond adding further "bric-a-brac."[53] The changes since then had only added to this sense of grievance: The CBI complained in 1966, "The fiscal changes of the past two years have greatly intensified dissatisfaction with our system of taxation and the desire for fundamental reform."[54] This created a desire for a thorough review of the tax system: on one hand, EC membership offered a route to starting this process, while on the other, the introduction of VAT, without other alterations, was further piecemeal change.[55] However, opinion did shift towards greater support for VAT, partly as a result of Britain's second application to join the EC, but also because one of the first steps of the Confederation of British Industry (CBI) was to embark on the *Britain and Europe* study. Another factor was a further study of VAT within the National Economic Development Office (NEDO), which worked for the National Economic Development Council. A new NEDO paper argued for the introduction of VAT and a reduction of corporation tax, which had been introduced in 1965 to replace income tax and profits

---

[52] Ibid., E.224.63, FBI, "The Introduction of a Turnover Tax in the UK," 14.

[53] EIU and NABM, *Taxes for Britain: The Impact of the Common Market* (London, 1962), 4.

[54] MRC MSS200/C/3/ECO/16/4, E.343A.66, "Proposed Review of the Fiscal System," 16 August 1966.

[55] Ibid., E/243/66, "President's Notes for the NEDC meeting 15th June 1966."

tax paid by companies. This was closely linked to another paper considering once more the topic of taxation and export incentives.

The CBI's *Britain and Europe* study reflected this growing sense of dissatisfaction with Britain's tax system. Many of its recommendations were predictable: The need for a widening of the tax base and a shift towards greater reliance on indirect taxation were both reiterated. Most significant was the more positive tone adopted towards VAT: It was administratively more cumbersome than purchase tax and would apply to more goods but this was true of any general indirect tax and that as long there was "an immediate and substantial" cut in direct taxation this change should not cause any major difficulty.[56] It concluded: "Entry into the Community could thus imply many changes in British tax legislation in the long term. No real immediate problems of adjustment are apparent. This is, however, an area where it will be particularly important that the implications of possible future membership should be given due weight in the evolution of British policy."[57] The increased possibility of Britain joining the Community, rather than any fundamental shift in view on VAT, was, it would seem, the main factor behind the more positive view towards VAT shown by the CBI compared to the FBI's submission to the Richardson Committee.

Britain and Europe, vol. 1 was then sent to the CBI's membership for comment (see Chapter 7). Hardly any replies referred directly to VAT. A large number did, nonetheless, call for tax harmonization: The only sector where there was little mention of taxation was food and drink.[58] However, it is clear that these demands for tax harmonization built on long-standing perceptions rather than any newfound support for VAT. Tax harmonization was seen to mean a reduction of British taxation and/or a shift towards more indirect taxation (for example, SMMT, British Man-Made Fibres Federation).[59] In other words, British industry faced an unfair tax burden and that this needed to be equitable to that experienced by business in the Six so that British business could compete fairly. It is also clear that uncertainty remained widespread. This was shown by the returns from the questionnaire sent out to 1700 companies as part of the consultation exercise on *Britain and Europe*. One question asked: "Do you on balance see the following as advantages to your company as a result of British membership of an enlarged EEC: har-

[56] CBI, *Britain and Europe, Vol. 1: An Industrial Appraisal* (London, 1966), 20.

[57] Ibid., 21.

[58] The replies can be found in MSS200/C/3/S1/12/11. Trade associations calling for tax harmonisation included the Roll Makers' Association, British Internal Combustion Engine Manufacturers' Association, Covered Conductors Association, Electronic Engineering Association, British Iron and Steel Federation, British Non-Ferrous Metals Association, SMMT, British Man-Made Fibres Federation, Wool Textile Delegation, National Hosiery Manufacturers' Federation, Zip Fastener Manufacturers' Association, Association of Solid Woven Belting Manufacturers, Webbing Manufacturers' Association, British Leather Federation.

[59] MRC MSS200/C/1/2/O and MSS200/C/3/S1/12/11.

monization within an enlarged EEC of policies on: taxation?"[60] Of the 865 responses, 44 percent replied "Yes", 19.9 percent "No", 23.2 percent "Don't know", with the rest either not applicable or rejected. What is significant in these tables is the scale of the "Don't knows." As shown in Table 10.4 all sectors apart from food, drink, and tobacco had such returns at over 20 percent. It might have been expected that large firms would be better informed; however, while the smallest firms have the highest percentage of "Don't knows" at 28.7 percent, this fell to 17.5 percent for firms with 200–499 employees before rising again to 22.3 percent for 500–4,999 employee firms and falling only marginally to 21.1 percent for firms with over 5,000 employees (see Table 10.4). Most significantly, the size of the "Don't knows" was far larger than in any other similar question posed in the questionnaire. This would suggest that not knowing whether tax harmonization would be advantageous was not simply an issue of ignorance but also of uncertainty. It was not clear to many firms whether they would gain or lose because the detailed form of tax harmonization mattered and on this there was little information.

Despite this uncertainty in the business community the CBI presented industry's views in *Britain and Europe, vol. 3* in 1967 as clear and positive towards VAT. "Most of the replies from manufacturing associations," it observed, "favour the adoption of a value-added sales tax, which would put them on equal terms with their EEC competitors over export rebates." It continued, "Early introduction of the value-added tax would in the opinion of many respondents ease the impact of entry and convince the Six of the earnestness of the British approach."[61]

After this clear affirmation of support for the introduction of VAT in 1967 the CBI's statements again became more cautious.[62] In part, this was due to a growing concern that the introduction of VAT would fuel inflationary pressures and also that de Gaulle's second veto once more removed European integration from the equation for the foreseeable future. A third factor was that the CBI awaited the outcome of the NEDO's study of VAT which finally emerged in 1969.[63] In his foreword to that study, Fred Catherwood, the director-general of NEDO made clear his support for the introduction of VAT, as he had to the Richardson Committee as managing director of British Aluminium, but the rest of the report tried to set out the main considerations in deciding on whether to adopt VAT rather than making any firm recommendations. Nevertheless, the report is informative of industry's views because it reported on a questionnaire on the merits of VAT sent to the sectoral Economic Development Councils, bodies consisting of managers,

---

[60] MRC MSS200/C/1/2/O, "CBI Europe Study," attached press release, 7 March 1967, question C (iii)(d)(1).

[61] CBI, *Britain and Europe, Vol. 3: A Programme for Action* (London, 1967), 21.

[62] MRC MSS200/C/1/2/C, C.21A.68, "CBI Statement on Policy on Europe," no date but 1968.

[63] NEDO, *Value Added Tax* (London: HMSO, 1969).

Table 10.4. *Company Response by Sector and by Size of Operation (Number of Employees) to a Question on Tax Harmonization in the 1967 CBI Questionnaire on European Integration*

	Yes	%	No	%	Do Not Know	%	Not Applicable	%	Rejects	%	Total
(A) Sectors											
Mechanical engineering	87	42	43	20.8	51	24.6	19	9.2	7	3.4	207
Electrical engineering	44	48.4	17	18.7	22	24.2	4	4.4	4	4.4	91
Metals and metal manufacture	50	48.4	16	15.5	25	24.3	6	7.8	4	3.9	103
Vehicles	29	52.7	8	14.5	12	21.8	3	5.5	3	5.5	55
Textiles, cloth, footwear	45	41.3	22	20.2	25	22.9	14	12.8	3	2.8	109
Food, drink, tobacco	24	42.9	16	28.6	7	12.5	8	14.3	1	1.8	56
Chemical	25	37.9	21	31.8	14	21.2	4	6.1	2	3	66
Building construction	23	46	9	18	10	20	8	16	0	0	50
Paper and printing	19	42.2	4	8.9	16	35.6	4	8.9	2	4.4	45
Other industries	28	43.1	10	15.4	15	23.1	10	15.4	2	3.1	65
Rejects	7	38.9	6	33.3	4	22.2	0	0	1	5.6	18
Total	381	44	172	19.9	201	23.2	82	9.5	29	3.4	865
(B) Number of employees											
0–199	75	30.4	49	19.8	71	28.7	41	16.6	11	4.5	247
200–499	78	47	31	18.7	29	17.5	23	13.9	5	3	166
500–4999	167	49.6	72	21.4	75	22.3	15	4.5	8	2.4	337
>5000	60	55	20	18.3	23	21.1	2	1.8	4	3.7	109
Rejects	1	16.7	0	0	3	50	1	16.7	1	16.7	6
Total	381	44	172	19.9	201	23.2	82	9.5	29	3.4	865

Note: The question was, "Do you on balance see the following as advantages to your company as a result of British membership of an enlarged EEC: (d) Harmonisation within an enlarged EEC of policies on: (1) taxation."

Source: MRC MSS200/C/1/2/O, attached to letter from Norman to members, 7 March 1967.

trade unionists in an industry with government officials, which discussed the performance of the industry. The responses largely reflected the views of management in each sector and formed an important foundation for the report. There remained support for a shift to indirect taxation and there was now a stronger conviction that all taxation was passed on to consumers in increased prices. More specifically, many of the points about diversity of opinion and the importance of detail made in the submissions to the Richardson Committee were again evident; but this time, they were noted. As the report put it:

On the whole the views expressed about the general desirability, or the special effects, of a VAT were diverse and inconclusive, and there was no unanimity or even a general consensus either in favor of, or against, the introduction of the tax, or about its general industrial and economic impact. Also, the assumptions on which some of the conclusions were reached (for example, on the other tax changes which might be made, or on the levels at which a VAT might be imposed) varied very widely between one industry and another. However, it was clear that there is a very genuine and widespread concern in industry mainly about the complexity of our existing tax arrangements (both direct and indirect), and that at least a part of the intuitive appeal which a VAT seems to possess lies in the belief (even though probably coloured somewhat by the thought that the grass is always greener on the other side of the hill) that it is simple and comprehensive and would enable much of the present tax jungle to be cleared away.[64]

By 1969, therefore, industrial opinion in Britain remained unhappy with the existing tax regime, in particular, demanding a shift towards indirect taxation, but was not sure that VAT offered an appropriate solution to the problem, in large part because of the uncertainty over the detailed introduction. As the Treasurer of the Ford Motor Company noted: "To be in favour of or opposed to the introduction of a VAT system indicates a lack of familiarity with the problem. There are so many possible variations on the VAT, some good, some bad, that the proposed system has to be specified in some considerable detail before admiration or antipathy can be properly expressed."[65] This was particularly the case when the issue of European integration was stripped out of the discussion. Nevertheless, British membership of the EC could not be ignored and, as shown in 1966–67, once this was on the agenda, attitudes towards VAT became more positive. Yet, even here, this remained a balance of opinion and the CBI's comments hid a wide and diverse range of opinion, reflecting not just the implications for each sector of industry but also the differences for individual firms within each sector.

[64] Ibid., 6.
[65] A. L. Kingsholt, "Industrial Implications of a Value–Added Tax," in T. M. Rybczynski (ed.), *The Value-Added Tax: The UK Position and the European Experience* (Oxford: Basil Blackwell, 1969), 63.

This picture was further muddied by the uncertainty about the details of any changes and the resulting different interpretations that emerged.

THE HAGUE SUMMIT TO 1973

After the fall of de Gaulle and the Hague summit in 1969, the likelihood of Britain's membership of the EC increased, and in 1970 negotiations opened once more. Tax harmonization once more played little direct role in the negotiations.[66] Moreover, the Conservatives, who were elected to power in the same year with a commitment to introduce VAT independent of the issue of membership, brought forward the required legislation in 1971 and VAT began to operate in April 1973, only four months after British entry into the EC. In this context it might be expected that tax issues became less important aspects of European integration for British business but this would be misleading. If anything they became more important as the relevance of non-tariff barriers became clearer and EC policy on tax harmonization developed, particularly in the light of the commitment to economic and monetary union, which, it was believed, increased the need for some measure of harmonization of direct taxation.[67]

With regard to VAT, British business continued to exhibit its long-standing ambivalence. For example, uncertainty over the detailed implementation still existed and this continued to matter – what would be the rate, what taxes would VAT replace? Divisions of opinion also remained clear.[68] The CBI itself continued to reflect this lack of consensus. In January 1970 it published its update of the 1966 appraisal *Britain and Europe*, now entitled *Britain in Europe*. In the supporting paper the VAT issue was presented in a clearly positive and unequivocal light:

The argument in favour of the United Kingdom adopting the VAT has been strengthened by recent events. The continuing weakness of the British balance of payments has drawn attention to the need to promote exports in all possible ways. As GATT regulations forbid the rebate of direct taxes, it is submitted that a shift from direct to indirect taxation would benefit exports by permitting the rebate of all indirect taxes incurred on exported goods.

The VAT is the best form of indirect tax to rebate . . . . Also, whereas costs and prices have risen in the countries which have adopted VAT systems, they have not risen as dramatically as some observers forecast in 1966 with the result that this argument

---

[66] Douglas Dosser, "Foreword," in Douglas Dosser, (ed.), *British Taxation and the Common Market: A Volume of Essays* (London: C. Knight, 1973), vii.

[67] Douglas Dosser and S. Han, *Taxes in the EEC and Britain: The Problem of Harmonisation* (London: PEP, 1968), 25; Sir Arnold Francis, "The Taxation Implications of UK Entry into the EEC," *Commerce International* (April 1971), 15–7.

[68] For examples see MRC MSS200/C/3/S1/12/9, Paul Glennie–Smith, British Footwear Manufacturers' Federation, to Whitehorn, 25 November 1969; and MRC MSS200/C/1/2/R, London and South-East Regional Council meeting, 27 January 1970.

propounded by detractors of the tax has been considerably weakened. Thus, the original arguments stated in 1966 in favour of the United Kingdom adopting a VAT have been strengthened by developments which have taken place since then.[69]

The importance of moving Britain's tax regime closer into line with continental practice in order to remove potential fiscal obstacles to entry was also stressed. While the report did raise the issue of the impact of introducing VAT on the cost of living, it concluded by suggesting the possibility of ignoring the issue: The government might introduce VAT irrespective of EC membership and thus any impact would be irrelevant to any assessment of the cost-of-living impact of EC membership.[70] This sleight of hand is indeed what the government was to do in its White Papers on the economic assessment of membership. Here then the CBI seemed clear in its commitment to VAT.

In stark contrast to this position was the report of the CBI's working party on VAT, which was set up just as *Britain in Europe* was being published and reported to the CBI Council in November 1970. It was set up to examine VAT in comparison with other forms of consumption taxation for achieving the CBI's goal of a shift away from direct taxation, and was also asked to take into account the implications of the possibility of UK entry into the EC.[71] The working party concluded, with one dissenter, that it "could not see any advantages in VAT over alternative methods such as the extension of purchase tax and the imposition of specific taxes on certain services."[72] With regard to EC entry the working party concluded that in the long term Britain would have to harmonize with the Community system of VAT but it was difficult to say when this would be and that there were options about the timing and manner of introducing the tax. In other words, in the working party's opinion EC entry made little difference to its conclusions, particularly in the short term. Moreover, in spite of *Britain in Europe* rejecting concerns about the impact of introducing VAT on the cost of living, it would appear that this was a growing concern in business given the increasing fears of inflationary pressures and awareness of the cost of living impact of the Common Agricultural Policy.[73] The CBI's taxation panel, for example, considered the comparative impact of existing consumer expenditure taxes with that of a VAT charged at 10 percent.[74] This effort was flawed and rudimentary but also reflected the problems in estimating the impact of the tax change on the

[69] CBI, *Britain in Europe: A Second Industrial Appraisal* (London, January 1969), appendix H, 58.

[70] Ibid., 8 and 21.

[71] MRC MSS200/C/1/1, C.74.70, CBI Council meeting, 18 November 1970.

[72] Ibid.

[73] MRC MSS200/C/1/2/O, O.32.70, "'Britain in Europe' and 'Britain in the world' – Consultations with the Membership," 26 May 1970, 1.

[74] MRC MSS200/C/1/2/E, E.696A.69, appendix to taxation panel meeting, 10 November 1969.

price of particular commodities: "Retailers' actual mark-ups varied widely from trade to trade and from shop to shop, so the effect of the change on particular prices would vary similarly."[75] A second growing concern in industry with the introduction of VAT was the need for a period of preparation. In other words, the transition period before VAT was introduced needed to be lengthy. This was included in the CBI's recommendations to the government on the EC negotiations following representations from trade associations.[76] Thus, there were still doubts, uncertainties and worries in British industry about the introduction of VAT when the government announced its intention to introduce the tax. Thereafter Customs and Excise embarked on a massive process of consultation with the CBI and various trade associations on the details of the legislation but there was little point discussing the principle of its introduction.[77] Similarly, while the announcement of Britain's intention to introduce VAT was greeted warmly by the Six, the issue now lost its salience to business consideration of British entry into the EC per se, with attention turning to direct taxation in the light of the possibility of economic and monetary union.[78]

CONCLUSION

This chapter has shown how the tax issue is an important and illuminating case study of British industry and European integration. On one hand, taxation was a key element of the business environment, while on the other, the possibility of EC membership was so too, and the two overlapped most obviously in relation to the issue of whether Britain should adopt VAT. At some points the two worked together while in other respects they worked against each other. There was a tension between the broad position of business favoring tax harmonization as a means of reducing its tax burden and of shifting the tax burden to indirect tax for which adopting VAT provided a rationale while those most informed about tax issues were less enthusiastic about the merits of VAT. Perceptions about the state of the tax burden faced by British business were resistant to change. To many businessmen, there seemed an obvious link between their inability to compete and the tax burden they faced and, on the other side of the coin, between continental European economic success and the nature of taxation there. Detailed examination often

---

[75] Dorothy Johnstone, *A Tax Shall be Charged* (London: HMSO, 1975), 106.

[76] MRC MSS200/C/1/2/O, O.55.70, "The Negotiations with the EEC: Industry's Recommendations," no date, 11, and O.57.70, "Summary Record of a Meeting of Trade Associations (and of Contributions from Member Associations Unable to Attend) on Britain in Europe held on 8 July 1970," 2.

[77] For a detailed account see Johnstone, *A Tax*.

[78] David Hannay (ed.), *Britain's Entry into the European Community: Report by Sir Con O'Neill on the Negotiations of 1970–1972* (London: Whitehall in association with Frank Cass, 2000), 131.

questioned this link, but the perception remained. It is this that helps explain the antipathy or contingent attitude towards VAT (though not to tax reform more generally) among the CBI leadership, large company tax specialists, etc., but the wider belief among businessmen that Britain was missing out and wanted tax harmonization. The EC's perceived tax advantages were an enticing mirage: "In taxation," an FBI tax expert told an audience of businessmen in Glasgow in 1963, "the grass on the foreigner's lawn always seems greener than the grass on one's own; only on closer examination one finds that what looked like an immaculate stretch of turf is more like an obstacle course."[79]

A further tension existed between the broad position and the impact of particular tax changes on different firms where assumptions had to be made about the taxes to be replaced and the rates of VAT to be implemented. This did provide some opportunity for the peak-level organizations such as the FBI and CBI to lead business opinion, but the positions adopted by these bodies were fragile and hid an underlying diversity of opinion not just between industries but between firms within the same industry. A prime example here is the car industry, where some firms favored a change to VAT and others did not. Finally, these positions were complex, fluid, relative, and contingent where detail, often unknown, mattered. The issue of tax harmonization highlights a key point, but one often neglected, which was made by Laffan and her fellow authors: Most actors in Europe pursue a wide range of projects, not European integration per se.[80] Taxation, a central part of the business environment, was one of those projects for British business and through analysis of the topic one gets an insight into how European integration impacted on business perceptions of tax issues and how the tax issues impacted on its perceptions of European integration.

[79] MRC MSS200/C/3ECO/16/1, G. L. Walker, "Aspects of Taxation in the UK and EEC," speech to be given at Accountants Hall, Glasgow, 7 March 1963.
[80] B. Laffan, R. O'Donnell, and M. Smith, *Europe's Experimental Union: Rethinking Integration* (London: Routledge, 2000), 8.

11

Company Law and the European Company

One of the most vibrant topics in the social sciences in recent years has been corporate governance. Awareness of the impact of different corporate governance models on economic performance led to much comparative analysis on the "best" corporate governance model.[1] Similarly, it was suggested that globalization would push governments to adopt this "best" model in order to maintain competitiveness. More recently, there has been a tendency to highlight the continuation of distinctive national models in the context of the varieties of capitalism literature.[2] At the heart of this literature lies a distinction between two "types" of corporate governance: the Anglo-Saxon model, a company-based system based on a fiduciary relationship between shareholders and managers, and a continental, or enterprise-based, system, in which stakeholders are more center stage.[3] The impact of European integration on these models has been a fertile ground of study in recent years and with it the emergence of the concept of Europeanization.[4] In applying this concept, attention has shifted from a bottom–up process of the dynamics of European integration to a top–down focus on the effects of EU membership on member states.[5] In this context one area of attention has been the impact of EU directives aimed at company law harmonization to see if the EU is moving to a center ground between these two models of capitalism, or whether one of them is becoming more dominant. As the EU has,

---

[1] C. Mayer, "Corporate Governance, Competition and Performance," *Journal of Law and Society*, Vol. 24, No. 1 (1997), 152–76.

[2] Peter Hall and David Soskice (eds.), *Varieties of Capitalism: The Institutional Foundations of Comparative Advantage* (Oxford: Oxford University Press, 2001); Georg Menz, *Varieties of Capitalism and Europeanization: National Response Strategies to the Single European Market* (Oxford: Oxford University Press, 2005).

[3] M. Albert, *Capitalism v. Capitalism* (New York: Four Walls Eight Windows 1993).

[4] Y. Mény, P. Muller and J. L. Quermonne (eds.), *Adjusting to Europe: The Impact of the European Union on National Institutions and Policies* (London: Routledge, 1996); Georg Menz, "Re-regulating the Single Market: National Varieties of Capitalism and their Responses to Europeanization," *Journal of European Public Policy*, Vol. 10, No. 4 (2003), 532–55; and Lucian Cernat, "The Emerging European Corporate Governance Model: Anglo-Saxon, Continental, or Still the Century of Diversity?" *Journal of European Public Policy*, Vol. 11, No. 1 (2004), 147–66.

[5] Menz, "Re-regulating the Single Market," 534.

in recent years, drafted directives relating to worker representation, a key feature of the continental model, and to takeovers, one of the main aspects of the Anglo-Saxon model, this has been seen as a fruitful area of study.[6]

In this literature, Britain is usually located, unsurprisingly, in the Anglo-Saxon model. However, historians have highlighted fundamental differences between the British model and the American model.[7] Also, it is important to understand the extent to which the British model of corporate governance has moved towards the continental model in the context of attempts to Europeanize company law. More generally, while there have been historical analyses of corporate governance regimes, a historical dimension to the study of Europeanization is still lacking. This chapter marks a first foray into this field as a step to filling this gap. That there is a historical dimension to the subject is clear given that the EC's First Directive in this area was drafted in 1964 and enacted in 1968 and others have followed, yet, to date, the subject has remained in the realm of legal studies.[8] Moreover, the subject was seen as a key aspect of Europe's response to the American challenge in the 1960s so that "Eurochampions," transnational European companies large enough to compete against American multinationals, could emerge. The chapter begins with an account of the problems of developing Eurochampions and the EC policy responses before turning to the response of British business.

"EUROCHAMPIONS"

As was shown in Chapter 3, there was considerable anxiety in Europe about the scale of American foreign direct investment (FDI) in Europe. European companies appeared more willing to join with a non-EC company than a company from another member state. There seemed to be a reluctance to create European transnational companies.[9] National governments found that they had limited powers to stop this influx of US FDI. In facing this

---

[6] Cernat, "Emerging European Corporate Governance Model," 149.

[7] Steven Toms and Mike Wright, "Divergence and Convergence within Anglo-American Corporate Governance Systems: Evidence from the US and UK, 1950–2000," *Business History*, Vol. 47, No. 2 (2005), 267–95.

[8] Frank Wooldridge, *Company Law in the United Kingdom and the European Community: Its Harmonization and Unification* (London: Athlone Press, 1991); and Vanessa Edwards, *EC Company Law* (Oxford: Oxford University Press, 1999).

[9] R. Vernon, "Enterprise and Government in Western Europe," in R. Vernon (ed.), *Big Business and the State: Changing Relations in Western Europe* (London: Macmillan, 1974), 3–24; A. Sampson, *The New Europeans: A Guide to the Workings, Institutions and Character of Contemporary Western Europe* (London: Hodder and Stoughton, 1968), 113; P. Lemaitre and C. Goybet, *Multinational Companies in the EEC: Part A: Whose Gain?* (Chichester: John Wiley, 1984), 4; and J. Hayward, "Introduction: Europe's Endangered Industrial Champions," in J. Hayward (ed.), *Industrial Enterprise and European Integration: From National to International Champions in Western Europe* (Oxford: Oxford University Press, 1995), 1–20.

American challenge, Servan-Schreiber saw the solution in the creation of "Eurochampions" that would be able to compete against US multinationals in certain crucial high technology industries.[10] It was only through this route, he believed, that the technology gap could be closed.[11] These European companies would also play a central part in furthering European integration, both economically and politically.[12]

Few such transnational European companies emerged. Shell and Unilever already existed as Anglo-Dutch companies but they were unique prior to the 1960s.[13] One of the earliest to join them was Agfa–Gevaert in 1964.[14] They were the two major producers of photographic film in continental Europe, one German and one Belgian. Others were Fokker–VFW, Fiat–Citroën and Dunlop–Pirelli and some other firms embarked on joint ventures. An EC Business Co-operation Centre, sometimes referred to as the European Business Marriage Bureau, was created to help European companies find suitable partners in other member states to stimulate the number of such transnational collaborations but with little success.[15] However, far greater obstacles to transnational European mergers were perceived than just the need for some "dating agency" for firms. Legal, fiscal, and psychological barriers in the way of transnational mergers were frequently highlighted as the crux of the problem. This "kaleidoscope" of different national systems and attitudes constituted a major set of obstacles for the transnational integration of European industry.[16] Goldmark noted, "It is not enough to establish a common market without creating the necessary economic and legal framework within which it can function."[17] Servan-Schreiber saw action in this field as

[10] J. J. Servan-Schreiber, *The American Challenge* (London: Hamish Hamilton, 1968).

[11] See Christopher Layton, *European Advanced Technology: A Programme for Integration* (London: George Allen and Unwin, 1969); Roger Williams, *European Technology: The Politics of Collaboration* (London: Croom Helm, 1973).

[12] C. Kindleberger, "European Integration and the International Corporation," *Columbia Journal of World Business* (Winter 1966), 65; Christopher Layton, *Cross-Frontier Mergers in Europe: How Governments Can Help?* (Bath: Bath University Press, 1971), 10–11; and Werner Feld, *Transnational Business Collaboration among Common Market Countries: Its Implications for Political Integration* (New York: Praeger, 1970).

[13] G. Jones, *Renewing Unilever: Transformation and Tradition* (Oxford: Oxford University Press, 2005).

[14] On Agfa–Gevaert see G. Devos, "Agfa–Gevaert and Belgian Multinational Enterprise" in G. Jones and H. G. Schröter (eds.), *The Rise of Multinationals in Continental Europe* (Aldershot: Edward Elgar 1993), 201–12. For other cases, see Feld, *Transnational Business Collaboration*, 34–40.

[15] TNA FCO70/143, correspondence from 1973; and "Why Europe Needs an IRC of its Own," *The Times*, 22 April 1970, 27.

[16] M. Stewart, "Transnational Enterprise: The European Challenge," *Columbia Journal of World Business* (July–August 1972), 6.

[17] Francis Goldmark, "Europe Catches the Merger Fever," *Columbia Journal of World Business*, Vol. 4, No. 2 (1969), 51.

the foremost priority.[18] Only after these obstacles had been removed would European-owned corporations of sufficient scale to compete with American multinationals emerge and the technology gap be closed.

The Treaty of Rome made clear the need for companies to be free to establish themselves in any member state, just like individuals, (Article 58) while Article 54 gave the EC powers to introduce measures to harmonize company law. In addition, Article 220 called on member states to negotiate with each other over the mutual recognition of firms, the ability for firms to transfer their registered office from one country to another and the possibility of mergers between firms in two different member states. Thus there were two strands to company law harmonization. The first was the harmonization of national company laws or rather, as it worked out in practice, the piecemeal harmonization of parts of company law. Action in this field, based on Article 54, led to quite philosophical discussions about what constituted a company given national differences in the legal definition. The first directive here was proposed by the Commission in 1964 and was accepted by the Council of Ministers in 1968. It dealt with disclosure, validity in law of the engagements entered into by a company and nullity of the company.[19] Britain had no input into this directive as it was drafted, negotiated and came into operation prior to British accession and some aspects of the directive have caused particular difficulties as it involved concepts alien to British company law.[20] Four further draft directives were issued between 1970 and 1972. These dealt with the formation of public limited companies, mergers, annual accounts, and company board structure respectively.

The second strand was the idea of the European Company or, to give its proper title, Societas Europaea (SE). The latter was to be a completely new entity, additional to existing national company law provision; the idea being that a "European company" would be able to operate in all the member states subject to uniform rules.[21] In particular, this was hoped to deal with two issues. First, it was impossible for a company to move its corporate headquarters between member states without liquidating the original company and incorporating a new one, with all the administrative and fiscal costs that this would involve. Secondly, although there were examples of

---

[18] Servan-Schreiber, *American Challenge*, 119.

[19] E. Stein, *Harmonization of European Company Laws* (Indianapolis: Bobbs-Merrill, 1971), 195–312.

[20] Edwards, *EC Company Law*, 16.

[21] H. C. Ficker, "Company Law within the EEC," in G. W. Keeton and S. N. Frommel (eds.), *British Industry and European Law* (London: Macmillan, 1974), 36–43; P. Sanders, "Structure and Progress of the European Company," in C. Schmitthoff (ed.), *The Harmonisation of European Company Law* (London: UK National Committee of Comparative Law, 1973), 83–100; D. Thompson, *The Proposal for a European Company* (London: PEP, 1969); and S. D. Cheris and E. R. Fischer, "The European Company: Its Promise and Problems," *Stanford Journal of International Studies*, No. 6 (1971), 113–45.

transnational "mergers" between companies in member states, these were not true mergers but usually entailed complex arrangements involving holding companies and separate legal structures, as happened with Agfa–Gevaert. Again, existing national company laws had no provision for transnational mergers: it was legally impossible for two companies in two different member states to merge. With a European Company statute in place, it was believed, companies could decide to opt for this structure or stay based on national legislation. This idea had first been broached in the Council of Europe in 1949, but became more widely discussed a decade later with such a proposal emerging concurrently in France and from Professor Sanders, from the Netherlands.[22] An international congress was held the following year, 1960, to consider the issue further and concluded that a common European form of trading company was required. However, little progress was made until 1965, when the French government called on the Community to establish a form of European company which, it was argued, would help European firms to cope with increased competition from American companies.[23] The French proposal was for a uniform law to be enacted by each member state. However, the Commission argued that this would not deal with the issue of transferring a company from one member state to another, nor allow transnational mergers and so they opted for the more ambitious idea of a separate supranational piece of legislation. Sanders was accordingly asked to produce a draft statute with the help of others, a task completed in December 1966. After further discussion four issues stood out on which further advice was required:

(a) the degree of supranationality;
(b) the kind of persons entitled to form a European company, under what conditions, and what the minimum capital should be;
(c) the method of dealing with employer participation; and
(d) the inclusion of the Italian system of registered shares.

These remained key issues but nevertheless a revised draft statute was submitted to the Council of Ministers in 1970, to be replaced by a further revised version in 1975. Despite renewed interest in the 1980s, it was not until 2001 that the SE concept was finally enacted and became a reality in 2004.[24]

---

[22] R. Fornasier, "Toward a European Company," *Columbia Journal of World Business* (September–October 1969), 54; and C. Schmitthoff "The Role of the Multinational Enterprise in an Enlarged European Community," in M. E. Bathurst, K. R. Simmonds, N. March Hunnings and J. Welch (eds.), *Legal Problems of an Enlarged European Community* (London: Stevens & Sons, 1972), 224.

[23] Thompson, *Proposal*, 10.

[24] E. Werlauff, *SE – The Law of the European Company* (Copenhagen: DJF Publishing, 2003), and C. T. da Costa and A. de M. Bilreiro, *The European Company Statute* (The Hague: Kluwer, 2003).

Many at the time thought that fiscal barriers to transnational European corporations were greater than the legal barriers.[25] Although there was no mention of direct taxation in the Treaty of Rome, the EC Commission signaled its interest in the reform of direct taxes as early as 1959 and the 1960 Neumark Committee was appointed to consider this as well as indirect taxation.[26] Following the committee's report in 1963, the Commission issued a program for the harmonization of direct taxes in 1967. Its main objectives were to facilitate the free movement of capital, remove fiscal barriers to company mergers and to establish uniform depreciation rates – the focus was on company taxation. Following this in January 1969 the Commission issued two draft directives, one relating to the tax aspects of international company mergers, the other on the tax treatment of parent and subsidiary companies and two years later, two further draft directives, one on the common tax arrangements with regard to transfer payments between parent companies and subsidiaries, and the other on mergers, the splitting of companies, and the transfer of assets. There were two tax issues in this respect. First, there was the tax liability in establishing the merger. This raised complex issues about capital gains tax, which applied to transnational mergers but did not apply in the same way to mergers between companies in the same country. Secondly, the taxation of a transnational company's operations thereafter raised the issue of double taxation in particular. That the two draft directives issued on direct taxation both related to the ease of operation of European transnational companies shows the priority which was accorded to this issue.[27] Harmonization of direct taxation was also relevant to the proposals for the achievement of economic and monetary union by 1980 made by the Werner Committee in 1970.[28] The Council of Ministers' resolution specifically called for more rapid fiscal harmonization, which was increasingly seen as integral to the EC's development beyond a customs union.[29] However, in practice, progress remained slow.

THE RESPONSE OF BRITISH BUSINESS

Although there had been few major European mergers, there was a fear that British firms would in the future have to compete against not only American

[25] Servan-Schreiber, *American Challenge*, 119; Layton, *Cross-Frontier Mergers*, 12.

[26] A. Jiménez, *Towards Corporate Tax Harmonization in the European Community: An Institutional and Procedural Analysis* (London: Kluwer, 1999), 107.

[27] G. Brosio, "National Tax Hindrances to Crossborder Concentration in the European Economic Community," *Harvard International Law Journal*, Vol. 11, No. 2 (1970), 311–57; and Cheris and Fischer, "European Company," 115–27.

[28] Werner Committee, "Report to the Council and the Commission on the Realization by Stages of Economic and Monetary Union in the Community," *Bulletin of the European Communities* (Supplement) 11 (1970).

[29] Donald Puchala, *Fiscal Harmonisation in the European Communities: National Policies and International Co-operation* (London: Frances Pinter, 1984), 24–25.

companies established in Europe but also continental European groups. This was a theme that the Prime Minister, Harold Wilson, had raised in 1967, and which underpinned his call for a European Technology Community.[30] Just as the idea of creating Eurochampions could improve the competitiveness of European industry and stimulate political integration, so the same lessons, Wilson believed, could be drawn for Britain. Wilson was driven by two considerations: first, improving the competitiveness of British industry, which was seen to be due to the inability to operate on a similar scale to US firms because of the limited size of the domestic market, and, secondly, as a means of showing the potential benefits of Britain joining the EC.[31] Wilson launched his idea at a keynote speech at the Guildhall in November 1966. A year later, he returned to the theme as the centerpiece of his speech:

The message that must go out tonight from Guildhall is that while negotiations for British entry must inevitably take some time, the widening of the technological gap will not wait for negotiating timetables.

We have decided therefore that a new impetus must now be given towards creating the basis for a European technology, which is a categorical imperative for all of us. . . . Negotiations and the new drive for a European technology must go ahead too, through a realisation that greater competitiveness requires production – and research – in larger scale units. . . . If we, Europe, are to be fully competitive, we have to think more and more of mergers on a European scale, proceeding from working arrangements and bilateral agreements to a more truly multilateral approach. This will mean not only an acceptance of broader horizons for our new industrial pattern, it will mean devising machinery to forward this process.

Next, the Board of Trade are prepared as a matter of urgency, jointly with industry now to examine and prepare the steps necessary to bring our domestic arrangements in the field of patents, monopolies and restrictive practices, and company law into line with the requirements of a wider economic integration in conformity with the principles of the Treaty of Rome.[32]

The recognition of the need to harmonize policies, including company law harmonization, was significant: This remained a topical issue from this date into the 1970s.

This represented a marked change in attitude: Previously the only issue in this area given any attention in Britain related to freedom of establishment.[33] There was no consideration of company law harmonization by

---

[30] TNA FCO70/1, Hancock to Bell, 27 March 1967.

[31] John W. Young, "Technological Co-operation in Wilson's Strategy for EEC entry," in Oliver Daddow (ed.), *Harold Wilson and European Integration: Britain's Second Application to Join the EEC* (London: Frank Cass, 2003), 95–114; Layton, *European Advanced Technology*.

[32] TNA FCO70/1 contains a copy of the speech made on 13 November 1967.

[33] P. Leleux, "Companies, Investment and Taxation in the European Economic Community," in K. Diplock (ed.), *Legal Problems of the European Economic Community and the European Free Trade Association* (London: British Institute of International and Comparative

industry during the first application to join the EC in the early 1960s. The CBI's 1966 appraisal of the situation, *Britain and Europe vol. 1*, devoted only two paragraphs to the topic, simply reporting that a number of draft directives and conventions for company law harmonization were in preparation but that the problems were formidable and progress was likely to be slow.[34] Reference was also made to the Community's consideration of a new legal entity, the European Company. The second paragraph explained why the CBI was so relaxed about the topic: While some changes to company law in Britain would be necessitated by Community membership, there was not likely to be any unification of law before Britain would be able to participate in them and that it was unlikely that any changes would cause any major difficulties nor require any special attention during the negotiations. Despite the CBI's involvement in discussions about the European Technology Community with the government, *Britain and Europe vol. 3*, published in July 1967, made no mention of the topic in the program for action, only referring to company law harmonization in the part on consultations with industry and here only to repeat that the difficulties were formidable because of differences between the member states.[35]

Within the Six, there was initially little support for action in this field, particularly in the form of a European company, from business. It feared that any measures would bring together the worst features of each national system and, with the help of expert lawyers and accountants, companies were able to establish subsidiaries where they wanted and, indeed, exploit these national differences in company law to their own advantage.[36] However, by 1967, UNICE, the representative body of business in the Six, and the International Chamber of Commerce had both pronounced themselves to be in favor of the proposal as long as certain details, in particular worker participation and tax questions, could be resolved.[37]

British business held similar views by this time: A number of large companies came out in favor of the idea. Following Wilson's Guildhall speech the CBI had exploratory talks with the government. In December, a group of representatives from ICI, Shell, Unilever, Lloyds Bank Europe Ltd., Courtaulds, Dunlop, Reed Paper Group, Rio Tinto Zinc, and Forte met to consider the

Law, 1961), 23–44; and "The Treaty of Rome: Establishment and Services," *FBI Review* (September 1962), 31–33.

[34] CBI, *Britain and Europe, Vol. 1: An Industrial Appraisal* (London, 1966), 22.

[35] CBI, *Britain and Europe, Vol. 3: A Programme for Action* (London, 1967), 21.

[36] Stein, *Harmonization*, 431–2; Thompson, *Proposal*, 9, and D. Thompson, "The Creation of a European Company," *International and Comparative Law Quarterly* No. 17, (1968), 184; M. Vasseur, "A Company of European Type," *Journal of Business Law* (1964), 359.

[37] Fornasier, "Toward a European Company," 54; and P. Sanders, "The European Company," *Journal of Business Law* (1968), 185.

possible advantages that might follow from an ability to create a European company.[38] Six advantages were noted:

(a) the facilitation of international mergers and joint ventures;
(b) the advantage of operating under a common statute instead of six different national laws;
(c) the greater freedom afforded in the raising of capital;
(d) the "stilling" of national prejudice against foreign competition;
(e) the impetus which would be given to the harmonization of national laws; and
(f) the assistance which small and medium-sized companies would derive from a common form company.

These views were communicated to government officials but little further happened, although the representatives were formally constituted as a working party of the CBI's Company Law Committee, and the CBI and some large British companies were also involved in the ICC's study of the subject.[39] Throughout the period, the CBI was reactive to Community initiatives in this field. Indeed, the CBI's Company Law Committee did not meet between June 1969 and February 1971.[40]

However, one of the reasons why the committee did not meet was that a working group of the committee, the EEC working group on company law, was created to deal with these issues. Among the six members were representatives from Esso, Dunlop, British Insulated Callender's Cables, and Shell.[41] Similarly, in 1971 an ad hoc working party of the committee was appointed to consider the European Company Statute.[42] From such analysis, the CBI's 1970 report, *Britain in Europe*, gave much more attention to the subject than did its predecessor and summed up the balance of issues:

The absence of a common legal environment has not prevented a large number of companies from becoming international in their investment and production as well as marketing. It is perfectly possible in today's circumstances to set up a branch or subsidiary for manufacturing or marketing purposes, or to effect takeovers in any west European country. . . .

There are significant legal disparities, which make it difficult, expensive, and indeed daunting to establish collaboration across a border. For the industrial giants the difficulties may not be insuperable. For others they frequently are.

---

[38] MRC MSS200/C/1/1/G, G.250.68, "Background Note for Company Law Committee – Present State of Work on the "European Company" and Transnational Corporations," no date but June/July 1968.

[39] Ibid., and G.258.68, meeting of the Company Law Committee, 10 July 1968.

[40] MRC MSS200/C/1/1/G, G.18.71, 13 January 1971.

[41] MRC MSS200/C/3/COM/3/4, G.191.70, meeting of the working group, 22 July 1970, and G.192.70, "Text of Note by European Secretariat," undated, membership list attached.

[42] MRC MSS200/C/1/1/G, G.285.71, "Consideration of the Draft Statute for a European Company – Paper 1," CBI Company Affairs Directorate, December 1971.

There is little dispute about the necessity for cross-frontier collaboration by European industry at all levels for general economic benefit. We believe that the creation of a common legal environment would be one of the simplest and most effective methods of securing this. . . .

It is of course impossible to tell to what extent a common legal environment would stimulate cross-border collaboration. . . .

We are encouraged by the fact that work is being done within the EEC to find a solution to the problem of creating an acceptable formula for a European Company. . . . However, progress to date is slow.

In our view, a solution must speedily be found if a positive industrial policy is to be achieved in Europe.[43]

Turning support for the principle of a common legal environment into practice was not as simple as *Britain in Europe* suggested, particularly as it was unclear what input British industry would have into the creation of this environment: For those companies wishing to operate in the Community, the draft directives mattered whether Britain joined the Community or not.[44] It was believed that company law harmonization was unlikely to be an issue during the negotiations for entry, but it was hoped that the negotiations would provide an opportunity to make British views known.[45]

With the publication of the draft European company statute and of four directives on company law harmonization within a short space of time, discussion in this field became far more frequent and the workload far heavier. The CBI Company Affairs Directorate found it hard to keep abreast of developments despite a wide network of contacts.[46] The CBI often had to commission its own translations of the directives, which were adequate for most purposes but were freer in translation and less reliable than a proper legal document.[47] These unofficial documents would usually be replaced by government translations but even these had to be treated with reserve because of concerns about their accuracy.[48] Some months later, an official Community translation would become available. These official translations often ran out of stock for considerable periods of time.[49] As well trying to remain informed of developments, much time was also spent on educating the wider membership about the implications of the draft directives and statute. As one businessman wrote in 1972, "I had not realised the legal implications of EEC

---

[43] CBI, *Britain in Europe: A Second Industrial Appraisal* (London, January 1970), 14.

[44] CBI, *Britain in Europe*, 7.

[45] MRC MSS200/C/1/1/G, G.168.70, "Company Law in the EEC" by Butt, 26 June 1970.

[46] MRC MSS200/C/3/COM/3/2, "EEC Company Law Harmonisation," Gray to Savidge, 16 February 1972.

[47] Ibid., G.7.73, "Introduction," by the Company Affairs Directorate, undated but early 1973.

[48] MRC MSS200/C/3/COM/3/2, AWPE73/9, Butler to members of the Advisory Working Party on Europe, 15 February 1973.

[49] Ibid.; and MRC MSS200/C/3/COM/3/3, Hussey to Jones (Molins Ltd), 7 February 1973, Jones to Hussey, 9 February 1973, and Hussey to Jones, 19 February 1973.

entry for companies in this country. Gathering from what many of the industrialists present said, neither had they."[50] Even an international company on the scale of ICI asked the CBI for copies of the draft directives.[51] Accordingly, the CBI published a series of "briefs" "to inform members generally of developments in the Community about which they may have heard but of which they may have little or no detailed knowledge."[52] These included company law harmonization.

What particularly exercised the CBI, however, was a fear that British views would be discounted in the consideration of these draft directives. The CBI held discussions with its counterparts in UNICE and approached the Commission directly but feared that the government would not be interested in pushing the CBI's views until Britain's application for accession to the Community had been accepted.[53] The discussions with UNICE and the Permanent Conference of the Chambers of Commerce of the EEC were particularly helpful because they provided insights on the divisions within the Six on the draft legislation and as to whether opposition to a particular proposal was likely to be forthcoming.[54] This was important because there were concerns about all of the directives: It was argued that British company law was significantly different from that on the continent, and, in particular, that British company law allowed companies more freedom than was often envisaged in the draft directives, in which provision was often mandatory and rigid.[55] However, it was the fifth directive, dealing with two-tier boards that caused the greatest concern. The same could be said of this aspect of the European company statute. British business felt uneasy about this but was particularly concerned if this incorporated provision for the sensitive issue of worker participation. There were other "objectionable" elements in the draft directive to which British business were likely to be "especially allergic": the exclusive nature of the membership of the two boards, the liabilities of directors, the treatment of nonvoting shares, and the provisions relating to the appropriation of profits.[56] The expectation had been that movement in this area would be slow and did not, therefore, need to be incorporated in the negotiations over British entry. The rush of directives and the draft European Company Statute during the period of negotiations created much work for the CBI's Company

[50] MRC MSS200/C/3/COM/3/2, Webb to Hussey, 13 January 1972.

[51] Ibid., Flint to Gray, 13 December 1971.

[52] MRC MSS200/C/3/COM/3/4, G.25.71, "Company Law in the EEC," undated.

[53] Ibid.

[54] MRC MSS200/C/3/COM/3/3, Felgate to Gray, 10 June 1972 and Hussey to Holman, 15 March 1973.

[55] Ibid., "Harmonisation of Company Law," Brown to members of the Advisory Working Party on Europe, 16 April 1973; and MRC MSS200/C/3/COM/3/2, "EEC Directives," 8 May 1972, and Risaik (Secretary, Dunlop) to Grey, 16 June 1972.

[56] MRC MSS200/C/1/1/G, G.184.72, Gray to members of the Company Affairs Committee, 1 June 1972; and MRC MSS200/C/3/COM/3/2, note by Sir John Nicholson, undated.

Affairs Directorate and for the Confederation's various committees covering this area.[57] Ironically, having been excluded from the negotiations, much of this work was driven by the fear that the directives would be put in place prior to British membership without British business having a full input into the drafting process. This required not only general positions to be taken but also detailed comments on each article of the directives and statute, each of which was long and complex. Yet often this had to be done on the basis of unofficial translations. In the end, British industry did have a considerable input into the final form of the directives and the draft fifth directive has never been ratified. As a result, while it remains an important aspect of British industry's views on European integration, its significance was not so much the topic itself but that the Community was deepening integration in this area just as negotiations for membership were taking place.

Similarly, the idea of the European Company did appeal to British industry but the lack of it was an obstacle to transnational mergers rather than a complete barrier to British companies joining with continental European counterparts. Surveys of business opinion at the time agreed with the CBI's view that these legal obstacles did not prevent the creation of European transnational corporations: These obstacles made life harder but they could be overcome.[58] Few company executives said that they planned to adopt the proposed European Company statute in practice and one executive thought the whole exercise a waste of time.[59] Ultimately, it was unclear what impact company law harmonization would have in stimulating economic integration: It seemed that it ought to be important but whether it was in reality was less clear.

The CBI was also aware that company law harmonization could not progress far without action to harmonize corporate taxation.[60] Business now began to examine this subject more closely, emphasizing the impact of differences in direct taxation within the Community.[61] It was increasingly realized that differences in tax regimes could be a key obstacle to the emergence of "European" companies, an important consideration given that the idea of such companies was put forward by many large British companies as a factor in favor of British membership of the EC.[62] Like company law

---

[57] See MRC MSS200/C/3/COM/3/4–7.

[58] R. Mazzolini, *European Transnational Concentrations: Top Management's Perspective on the Obstacles to Corporate Unions in the European Economic Community* (London: McGraw Hill, 1974); C. de Houghton, *Cross-Channel Collaboration* (London: PEP, c. 1967).

[59] Mazzolini, *European Transnational Concentrations*, 35–7; and Jack N. Behrman, *National Interests and the Multinational Enterprise: Tensions among the North Atlantic Countries*, (Hemel-Hempstead: Prentice-Hall, 1970), 166.

[60] MRC MSS200/C/3/COM/3/2, Gray to Brown, 25 July 1972.

[61] For example, TNA BT241/2156, Brown to Hughes, 22 July 1969, reporting on a conversation with A. F. Young, chairman of Redland Holdings Limited.

[62] TNA BT241/2156, Hughes, 23 July 1969; Roland Gribben, "Opportunities for British Industry," *Commerce International* (January 1973), 22.

harmonization, the CBI regarded corporate taxation as a "slow burner" where early action was unlikely: The plan of action in *Britain and Europe vol. 3* made no mention of direct taxation apart from the perennial demand for a shift from direct to indirect taxation.[63] Again, like company law harmonization, the CBI gave greater attention to the topic in 1970 and wrote about it in a similar fashion to the section on company law harmonization:

Whilst fiscal differences do not prohibit collaboration or rationalisation they can and indeed do have a significant distorting effect. . . .

We recognise that the difficulties to be overcome before a common fiscal environment can be achieved are very considerable. . . .

If governments can be persuaded to accept the arguments for European cross-border collaboration, and the need for a large and undistorted market – both of which we believe to be fundamentally necessary to the economic strength and survival of Europe – it follows that they must be persuaded of the need for fiscal policies to support this.[64]

However, like company law harmonization, contemporary surveys of business opinion suggested that while businessmen saw tax differences as real difficulties, they were surmountable. Mazzolini carried out the most extensive survey of businessmen at the time.[65] He interviewed over 150 leading executives working in Europe. From these interviews he concluded, "The juridical impossibility of merging is not fundamental. Other legal structures are available, which (from the management point of view) give results similar to the *de jure* merger. Fiscally, the most important stumbling block is operating taxes . . . as opposed to taxes concerning the set-up of the concentration."[66] The most serious problems in these respects, he argued, were managers' exaggerated perceptions of these difficulties. This related to a wider issue, which was often highlighted by commentators at the time as the most serious obstacle to the emergence of European transnational companies, that is, sociopsychological differences.[67] These could take a variety of forms from consumer tastes to language differences. However, the most important was the field of human relations within the enterprise. These are always key aspects in any merger but were seen as even more significant in transnational mergers.[68] In particular, Mazzolini found that for many of his interviewees the most serious difficulties for transnational tie-ups lay in four areas: managerial resistance to change, the perceived threat involved,

---

[63] CBI, *Britain and Europe, Vol. 1*, 20; and *Britain and Europe, Vol. 3*, 8–9.

[64] CBI, *Britain in Europe*, 16.

[65] Mazzolini, *European Transnational Concentrations*; Brosio, "National Tax Hindrances," 349.

[66] Mazzolini, *European Transnational Concentrations*, x.

[67] Ibid., 107–61; Feld, *Transnational Business Collaboration*, 40–2; and C. Tugendhat, *The Multinationals* (Harmondsworth: Pelican, 1973), 111.

[68] Tugendhat, *Multinationals*, 107.

nationalism, and misconceptions.[69] Put the other way, for these obstacles to be surmounted those companies involved in any transnational linkage had to show goodwill and trust one's partners.[70] There was little that policy harmonization could do to resolve these aspects of European transnational mergers.

A CASE STUDY: THE DUNLOP–PIRELLI MERGER

In March 1970, Dunlop and Pirelli jointly announced their plan to form a union of equals between the two companies.[71] The detailed proposals were approved by the respective shareholders just before the end of the year and the union came into being. With a combined turnover of £940 m. Dunlop–Pirelli became the largest European tire producer and came close to matching Firestone as the world's second largest tire manufacturer. Six reasons were put forward for the union: a marriage of equals which would retain the two groups' domestic identities but challenge the US giants; to improve the research program; a complementary geographical spread of plants; benefits of diversification; the organizational structures and management practice were already similar so the benefits of union could be easily realized; and to undertake future strategy more boldly – "we can now have a European tyre marketing strategy," for example.[72]

There was a range of possible models to follow in terms of the union's organizational structure. In addition to long-standing transnational companies like Shell and Unilever there were also the more recent linkups such as Agfa–Gevaert, with cross-holding of shares, similar to Shell; VFW–Fokker, where a new central company was created; the R & D collaboration of lorry manufacturers MAN–Saviem; the proposed tie-up between Fiat and Citroën, based on stock purchases; and the common joint subsidiary model adopted by Panavia to produce the Tornado aircraft.[73] The structure adopted in the Dunlop–Pirelli case was closest to the Agfa–Gevaert model and involved each group taking a share (between 40 and 49 percent) in the other group's activities, the specific level determined by the desire to ensure an equality between the holdings, with the parent boards remaining in place. An outline structure of the cross holdings is set out in Figure 11.1.

What does this case illustrate about the various barriers to the creation of Eurochampions?[74] First, the UK government (both Labour and

---

[69] Mazzolini, *European Transnational Concentrations*, 132.

[70] De Houghton, *Cross-Channel Collaboration*, 21.

[71] "Dunlop and Pirelli in Big Link-up," *The Times*, 3 March 1970, 19.

[72] "Dunlop–Pirelli – A Union for Expansion," *Rubber Journal* (April 1970), 41; and Stewart, "Transnational Enterprise," 6.

[73] Mazzolini, *European Transnational Concentrations*, 22–6; and Feld, *Transnational Business Collaboration*, 34–8.

[74] The Dunlop archives for this period are not available and so this is based on government records, CBI records and the contemporary press and trade journals.

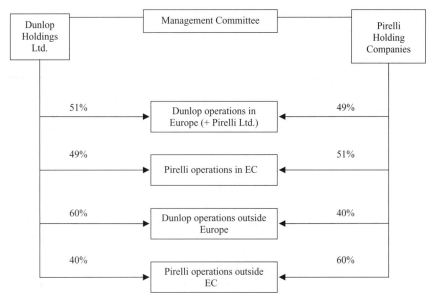

Figure 11.1. Outline structure of the Dunlop–Pirelli cross holdings.
Source: C Layton, *Cross-Frontier Mergers in Europe: How Governments Help?* (Bath University Press, Bath, 1971), p 29.

Conservative) supported the idea and so did not take steps to prevent it. On the contrary, ministers made positive statements about the value of the union and saw the union as an appropriate and helpful development.[75] This was particularly relevant at a time when Britain was negotiating accession to the EC.[76] More than this, government officials did their best to help find solutions to particular difficulties faced by the two groups: The government was informed in June 1969 that the two groups hoped to join forces and from that date officials in a range of departments gave advice and considered ways of fine-tuning legislation to make transnational mergers easier.[77] Just because the government was supportive does not mean, however, that government policies had no impact on the form of the union. One of the first concerns of Dunlop was to avoid having to register the linkup under the Restrictive Practices Act 1956 as it was not a full merger.[78] On the other hand, not

[75] TNA BT344/66, "Proposed Transaction involving Dunlop Company Ltd and Pirelli Group," unsigned and undated but 1969, 9–10; TNA T295/635, "Dunlop/Pirelli," Littler to Hudson, 11 February 1970.

[76] TNA BT344/66, "Dunlop/Pirelli," Littler to Hudson, 21 January 1970; and TNA BT344/67, "Note of a Meeting Held in the Secretary's Office," Smith, 13 November 1972.

[77] TNA T295/635, France to Allen, 16 June 1969, and "Tax Problems for International and Holding Companies," Walker to Littler, 5 January 1970.

[78] TNA BT344/66, "Dunlop/Pirelli Merger," Davies, 25 July 1969.

being a full merger removed any exchange control considerations.[79] A second concern was the legal obstacles. The idea of a European company was not seen to be of any use in this case as the existing companies continued in existence.[80] There remained a number of legal obstacles, however, relating to Italian law and to shareholder interests. Again, with hindsight, these were not insurmountable problems but they still delayed the creation of a suitable structure: It had originally been hoped to announce the proposed union in September 1969 but this only happened six months later.[81] Another cause of delay was the tax issues raised by the union and one where the groups needed further assistance from the government. In the long term, Dunlop felt that double taxation was more important than any other financial issue: The union increased Dunlop's tax liabilities by about 3 percent.[82] However, without help from the government the capital gains involved in the merger would have resulted in an insuperable tax burden, estimated at £10–12 m.[83] The Inland Revenue gave advice on reducing the tax burden and it was even proposed to revise the Finance Bill to help further.[84] All together, the talks behind the union took two years and it was estimated that it cost Dunlop and Pirelli of the order of £1.5 m. each to overcome all the legal and fiscal obstacles.[85] Clearly, in this case, these were not insurmountable barriers, but it is clear that the structure of the resulting union was heavily influenced by the solutions to the obstacles that had to be overcome: The outcome was not necessarily the most efficient structure. It is impossible to know but it is likely that such barriers would have been a deterrent to other such European transnational mergers or unions. "A barbed wire entanglement" was how Reay Geddes, the chairman of Dunlop, described the process.[86]

However, there were also sociopsychological difficulties that emerged once the union began to operate. Even during the negotiations, Dunlop found that it may have undervalued Pirelli and had to try to find extra funding to ensure a position of equality.[87] This not only showed the problems in making such arrangements but was also of relevance because Dunlop was already heavily geared and had insufficient cash flow to finance its existing

---

[79] "Dunlop–Pirelli – The Unknown Factors," *Financial Times*, 16 December 1970.

[80] MRC MSS200/C/1/1/G, G.34.71, "CBI/Dunlop Working Lunch," 26 January 1971.

[81] Ibid.; and TNA BT344/66, "Dunlop/Pirelli," Morley, 16 September 1969.

[82] MRC MSS200/C/1/1/G, G.34.71, "CBI/Dunlop Working Lunch," 26 January 1971; and Stewart, "Transnational Enterprise," 6.

[83] TNA T295/635, "D: P," note by Geddes, 16 July 1969; TNA FCO70/1, "Domestic Taxation and EEC," Snelling, 11 June 1969; and "Dunlop–Pirelli – The Unknown Factors," *Financial Times*, 16 December 1970.

[84] TNA BT344/66, "Dunlop/Pirelli," Littler, 21 January 1970; and TNA T295/635, "International Mergers – Taxation Consequences: Dunlop/Pirelli," France to Dowler, 2 October 1969.

[85] "Investment Reforms Will Take Time," *The Times*, 26 October 1971, 28.

[86] Quoted in Stewart, "Transnational Enterprise," 9.

[87] TNA BT344/67, "Dunlop–Pirelli Merger. Brief for Mr John Davis," 29 October 1970.

expansion program.[88] As a result, when the Italian economy started to have problems and large wage increases for the Pirelli workforce in Italy followed, Dunlop was unable to cope with the consequent level of losses and had to protect itself from further losses.[89] Serious talk of a divorce followed in 1973 and despite a renewed commitment from both sides to the union, the tie-up was formally abandoned in 1981.[90] The financial exposure of Dunlop was itself part of a wider malaise in the union based on the continuing separation of the two groups.[91] Given this, and that the union was very much driven through on the personal friendship of Geddes and Leopoldo Pirelli, the coordinating committees at the top of the organization had a crucial role to play in ensuring the effective running of the union. However, it appeared that this coordination was not effective.[92] Stopford and Turner's view of the Dunlop–Pirelli union was damning: "a classic case of how the search for a European solution, born in the euphoria of the early 1970s, was both mismanaged and ill-judged as a response to the emerging conditions of global competition."[93] There is an element of validity to these criticisms as it is clear that the two companies made some important mistakes in creating the union. On the other hand, there were significant costs involved in bringing the union about and, while these may not have been insurmountable, it does help to throw light on why so few such transnational mergers occurred.

CONCLUSION

The Dunlop–Pirelli case does provide some understanding why such efforts were made to harmonize company law, create a new European company, and harmonize direct taxation. These were all obstacles which could be overcome but which increased the financial costs and the time involved in bringing about such transnational collaboration. These were off-putting. However, it is equally clear that there were many other problems at least as important about which legislation could do nothing and why business was ambivalent about the impact of some of these measures. The principle of a European company, in particular, was appealing to British business given that it had so many large companies compared to the Six and that such legislation would offer the opportunity to operate freely in any of the member states if Britain joined the EC. However, with discussion of draft legislation

---

[88] TNA T295/635, "D: P," Littler to Hudson, July 1969.

[89] See the government–Dunlop correspondence in TNA BT344/67.

[90] Mazzolini, *European Transnational Concentrations*, 102; and "Tireless Efforts to Make a Difficult Marriage Work," *The Times*, 28 June 1973.

[91] TNA BT344/67, "Dunlop: Don't Mix your Tyres – Especially if One Has a Puncture," *Sunday Times*, undated.

[92] Ibid.; and TNA BT344/67, "Dunlop–Pirelli," by Potter, 8 November 1972.

[93] J. Stopford and L. Turner, *Britain and the Multinationals* (Chichester: John Wiley, 1985), 86.

occurring without British input, the practice was less appealing: Britain was likely to be party to implementing the legislation without it taking into consideration British practice. The idea of worker participation on joint boards of a company was integral to this draft legislation but was anathema to British business and contrary to the traditions of British company law and the British model of corporate governance. It was believed British business would be "allergic" to such a system. As in the case of indirect tax harmonization there was a distinction between agreeing to harmonize and then deciding about the appropriate model around which to harmonize. Given the different governance traditions, this was never going to be easy but there was never any hint from business leaders that these were grounds for not joining the EC. Rather, much like the difficulties that company law harmonization was meant to overcome, these were one of the unpleasant but surmountable costs of entry.

The wider message to be drawn from this case relates to Europeanization. It is sometimes helpful to think about European integration as a top–down process rather than just a bottom–up process. However, what is most helpful is to think of this as a two-way process in which the two forces interact with each other. On the one hand, economic forces of integration have led firms to become more European in their investment plans and corporate strategies and this has created a pressure for political integration. On the other, political integration in the form of company law harmonization and direct tax harmonization reduces the costs of such firm-led integration. This is not a simple or straightforward process. As shown in Chapter 3 in the case of ICI and other British multinationals, economic integration may remove the urgency for political integration, and, as shown here, the political integration cannot deal with sociopsychological barriers but there is a dialectic process at work here. These issues are elaborated in Chapter 12.

Conclusion

In one of the most oft-cited metaphors for describing the study of European integration, Donald Puchala used the well-known story of the blind men and the elephant. Each blind man touched a different part of the elephant and reached their own conclusions about what the elephant looked like; all of course wrong.[1] All describe different and important features of what constitutes an elephant without being able to grasp the whole. The study of the history of European integration has been slightly different. For many years the field has been dominated by diplomatic historians, all of whom it could be said pored over the same part of an elephant and ignored the rest of the animal. It is significant in this respect that "Despite its growth in recent years, European integration history is still a relatively small research field which does not yet play a major role in contemporary history more generally and is not particularly well connected to social science research on the EU."[2] The most obvious exception to this criticism would be Alan Milward whose works have been more widely influential but whose constant clarion call has been for histories of European integration to move beyond the realms of diplomatic history.[3] This book has responded to that call: Readers may dispute how important the part of the elephant analyzed here is, but it would be hard for them to disagree that it is a part of the elephant and a part about which remarkably little is known. This is remarkable because European integration is a boom field with a vast and ever-expanding literature, and few would deny that business has been a key recipient of the gains from European integration and might, therefore, have an interest in how it has developed. It is equally remarkable that European integration continues to be overlooked in so many mainstream social scientific and historical treatments of topics, which, it is clear, have been touched by the experience of European integration. Here are two examples – picked because in other

---

[1] Donald Puchala, 'Of Blind Men, Elephants, and European Integration," *Journal of Common Market Studies*, Vol. 10, No. 3 (1972), 267–84.

[2] Wolfram Kaiser, 'From State to Society? The Historiography of European Integration," in M. Cini and Angela Bourne (eds.), *Palgrave Advances in European Union Studies* (Basingstoke: Palgrave, 2006), 191.

[3] Most recently in Alan S. Milward, *Politics and Economics in the History of the European Union* (Abingdon: Routledge, 2005), x.

respects these two books are exemplary models and have been rightly highly influential in their fields. The first is Crafts and Toniolo's *Economic Growth in Europe since 1945*.[4] This provides a set of accounts of national growth experiences since 1945, but only a few mention the impact of European integration. The second example is Whittington and Mayer's *The European Corporation*, which traces the development of large corporations in Britain, France, and Germany since the Second World War, but does not consider the role of European integration or indeed specify what is meant by "European" apart from studying corporations in three major European states.[5]

MAIN FINDINGS

What then is the contribution of this book in these circumstances? Let us begin with its main findings before considering some of the wider issues raised by these findings and finally setting out some thoughts for a future agenda of work in this area. First, trading issues relating to tariffs, preferences and protection were a central consideration for business in influencing its perceptions of, and response to, European integration. However, from the outset this was only part of the story. From the 1950s onwards, foreign direct investment became an increasingly important response from British firms to European integration, and this was the case whether Britain was part of the EC or not. That this wave of investment into Western Europe began in the 1950s, even if not on a large scale, suggests that British business was not as slow to foresee the opportunities offered by European integration as has been conventionally presented. This wave of investment also illustrates the growing internationalization of production and the tensions that this began to create between business and national governments in relation to European integration. British business believed the way to improve its performance and hence that of the economy was by allowing firms to internationalize by whatever means appropriate to maintain firms' competitiveness, be it by exporting, foreign direct investment, joint ventures or whatever. In contrast, the economic departments of the government were fixated on the balance of payments and exports. Added to that one of the Labour government's economic advisers in the 1960s was Nicholas Kaldor, renowned for his interest in export-led growth.

However, it has also been shown that simply widening the focus to cover overseas investment as well as exports is still inadequate as a guide to business perceptions of European integration. It has been demonstrated that from the outset of European integration business was aware that there was

---

[4] N. F. R. Crafts and Gianni Toniolo (ed.), *Economic Growth in Europe since 1945* (Cambridge: Cambridge University Press, 1996).

[5] Richard Whittington and Michael Mayer, *The European Corporation: Strategy, Structure, and Social Science* (Oxford: Oxford University Press, 2000).

a political dimension and that this was one aspect that clearly distinguished the European Community from proposals for a free trade area. Thus there was a keen interest in all activities which were judged to have a significant effect on the business environment – competition policy, taxation, and company law are the topics examined here, but there are many other examples, such as standardization.[6] It is only by incorporating these aspects that it becomes possible to understand why certain sectors of the economy supported British involvement in European integration when the contemporary economic assessments of the impact of such integration pointed to losses. This encompassing view of European integration was also important politically because business, through its representative associations, used the case of the EC, with its higher growth rates, to criticize British policy by comparison. This provided a new lever with which to exert pressure on government to reform policy in favor of business interests, for example, over indirect taxation and merger policy. Adopting such a comparative perspective meant that any British business attitudes to European integration were always relative, contingent, and potentially shifting, rather than absolute and fixed in support or opposition to European integration. Details mattered as small changes, for example, in tax rates or in the types of agreements covered by EC competition policy, could have significant impacts on these comparisons. Details also mattered when it came to issues of harmonization. One of the ways in which European integration appealed to British business was the prospect of a "level playing field," a phrase still often used by business in relation to EU-level policies. The appeal of such a concept in principle did not, however, deal with achieving harmonization in practice, where the crucial issue was which model around which to harmonize. This was particularly critical in the British case because of the prospect of entry at various times during the 1960s but without any input into the relevant discussions in the EC.

As a consequence of the importance attached to these details and the range of factors involved, business opinion on European integration always reflected a balance of a range of opinions where differences existed not just between industries but also between firms within the same industry, depending on the weight given by each firm to the various relevant factors. In addition, business often had to provide its opinion when lacking the requisite information on these details. Uncertainty and conditionality were, therefore, common features of business opinion on European integration, hence the emphasis placed on safeguards. In addition, this uncertainty provided opportunities for business leaders, in the form of the peak-level associations, to create business opinion. This happened in two ways. The first was through education of the membership: Members were led towards the desired

[6] See Michelle Egan, *Constructing a European Market: Standards, Regulation, and Governance* (Oxford: Oxford University Press, 2001).

conclusion – support for greater integration – by the provision of documents with a pro-EC slant as the starting point for consultation with the membership, as happened in 1966 and 1970. Secondly, business leaders were also able to manipulate the responses in ways that the leaders thought appropriate, as Sir Norman Kipping did with the returns to the 1956 survey on the free trade area. However, the leadership was not always able or willing to do this and, as in 1969, could be pulled in different directions by the membership and by government.

Two further findings are relevant here. One is the confirmation of the need to go beyond peak-level business organizations when trying to discern business opinion. It is inevitable that such bodies have been the starting point for much work on business and European integration, but it is important to acknowledge that there are clear limits to how representative they have been. It is an oversimplification to take the pronouncements of these organizations as the summation of business opinion rising from below. It is necessary to study business opinion at all levels, from the firm to the peak level because of the complexity of the factors involved in the creation of business attitudes to European integration. The second point is that many analyses of European integration, particularly the historiography, adopt a very traditional model of policy-making. This model presents government as unitary, distinct from society, and hierarchical, justifying a focus on diplomatic history, in the British case on the Foreign Office, and downplaying the role of other actors, including business. Typifying this approach, Kaiser concludes, "The business associations only influenced the governmental decision-making process where the government itself was unclear as to the future course of European policy such as in the final phase of the FTA negotiations."[7] However, in recent years it has become increasingly common to reject this type of view of policy-making and apply models based around notions of governance.[8] In these models, central government is fragmented, has permeable boundaries, and is characterized by policy networks. A governance approach seems more helpful here given the way in which business played a role in policy-making. This was not just in times of governmental uncertainty but reflected the strength of the networks that business had on

---

[7] Wolfram Kaiser, *Using Europe, Abusing the Europeans: Britain and European Integration, 1945–63* (Basingstoke: Macmillan, 1996), p. 89.

[8] R. A. W. Rhodes, *Understanding Governance: Policy Networks, Governance, Reflexivity and Accountability* (Buckingham: Open University Press, 1997); R. A. W. Rhodes (ed.), *Transforming British Government Volumes 1 and 2* (Basingstoke: Palgrave, 2000) and the other products of the ESRC Whitehall Programme. For applications to this period see Rodney Lowe and Neil Rollings, "Modernising Britain, 1957–1964: A Classic Case of Centralisation and Fragmentation?" in Rhodes (ed), *Transforming Vol. 1*; Astrid Ringe and Neil Rollings, "Responding to Relative Decline: The Creation of the National Economic Development Council," *Economic History Review*, Vol. 53, No. 2 (2000), 331–53; and Hugh Pemberton, *Policy Learning and British Governance in the 1960s* (Basingstoke: Palgrave, 2004).

the continent and which allowed business organizations access to information unavailable to the government. Illustrative here is the envious comment made by one government official to another in 1958:

I enclose a copy of a note which I have just received from the FBI; it is a record made by their French representative of a round-table discussion held in Paris on April 23rd and 24th at which he was present. I have not copied the long and impressive list of names attached to the note but they include a pretty fair selection of leading figures from the Six and the Coal and Steel Community. I have not discovered how the FBI's French representative – the only person outside the Six and their institutions – came to be present.[9]

But, again, this relationship was not stable and did not operate solely through the peak-level organizations. In the early 1960s prior to Britain's first application to join the EC, the FBI and the ABCC felt constrained by their commitment to EFTA and the business–government relationship shifted to one centered around individual representatives of large companies. What needs to be recognized is that this was a two-way relationship where business and government interacted and were dependent on each other as part of the policy process.

These findings are drawn from the experience of British business. In some respects the British case is special given that it was on the edge of European integration for so long. Nevertheless, many of the findings apply to business in other member states, although the nature of business–government relations differed somewhat given institutional and cultural differences. Studies are already beginning to move below the peak-level business organizations as one sign of a wider recognition of these issues.[10] Nevertheless, much still remains to be done. In particular, there is a need for more comparative work and to move away from national studies such as this one. One way of taking this forward would be to study a single multinational from this perspective, analyzing its corporate and political actions in each market and relating this to its European strategy. This is as valid for American multinationals coming to Europe as it would be of European multinationals. However, this is not a straightforward task. Firms rarely discussed European integration directly in the 1950s and 1960s. Many hours were spent as part of this study examining the records of various companies for relatively scant return. For future studies there is a need for a different approach, which is to "Europeanize" business history more generally, as explained below. This requires business historians to consider the various ways in which the business environment has been influenced by European integration and all the various activities

---

[9] TNA FO371/134501, Golt to Wilson, 9 May 1958, and Gore–Booth note, 16 May 1958.
[10] Marine Moguen-Toursel (ed.), *Firm Strategies and Public Policy in Integrated Europe (1950–1980): Confrontation and Learning of Economic Actors* (Brussels: P. I. E. Peter Lang, 2007).

that firms have undertaken in relation to European integration. This is not a simple or quick task.

WIDER LESSONS

Drawing on these findings four points can be made. As has already been mentioned, contemporary historians need to be more alert to the European dimension in their studies. There are just too many national histories of the period since 1945 that either ignore the topic of European integration completely or, at best, deal with it in a single separate chapter. Similarly, too many histories of European integration are isolated from wider developments. What is required is a "Europeanization" of contemporary history. Europeanization is very much a buzzword in European integration studies currently and like all buzzwords has been applied in multiple settings with multiple meanings.[11] Europeanization does not mean the simple top–down influence of European institutions on national governments, business, and other actors. Nor does it mean that European integration or European institutions explain everything. Instead, it is interactive, bringing domestic politics into the process of European integration: "it closes the loop between domestic politics, integration, and the domestic political systems responsible for integration in the first place" is how it has recently been described.[12] It reflects upon the interaction between top–down forces and bottom–up forces relating to European integration. At its simplest it means to think about the ways in which European integration has become part of the political landscape, adding an extra layer of complexity and interaction to the political process. As Radaelli has put it, "Domestic actors often have discretion to use Europe in different ways." This is just what business did, using that discretion to present Europe as an alternative model to Britain at certain points, as a framework in which British policy should be drawn up at other points and also to be criticized as well.

However, to date, Europeanization has really only been applied to politics and the political. It needs to be applied more widely in order to understand the multitude of interactions that exist in society and in the economy and which are related to European integration. This relates not only to the economy and society at a macro-level, but also to firms and individuals at a micro-level. It is crucial to remember that as Brigid Laffan and her coauthors have noted, "most political, social, and, economic agents in Europe

---

[11] J. Olsen, "The Many Faces of Europeanization," *Journal of Common Market Studies*, Vol. 40, No. 5 (2002), 921–52; Maria Green Cowles, James Caporaso and Thomas Riise (eds.), *Transforming Europe: Europeanization and Domestic Change* (Ithaca: Cornell University Press, 2001) and K. Featherstone and C. Radaelli (eds.), *The Politics of Europeanization* (Oxford: Oxford University Press, 2003).

[12] Claudio Radaelli, "Europeanization: Solution or Problem?" in Cini and Bourne (eds.), *Palgrave Advances*, 58.

pursue a wide range of political, social, economic, and cultural projects, not the project of European integration per se. A remarkable feature of the European integration project is the manner in which it has been grafted on to other projects."[13] Equally, it could be added that other projects have been grafted on to European integration. Adopting this perspective moves the study of European integration into the mainstream of all social science and historical disciplines, adding new insights to them. That this study found such a perspective helpful in considering the formative years of European integration is itself instructive, given the extent to which European integration has developed since then.

The second lesson also draws on the notion of interaction. As set out in Chapter 1, there have been two dominant paradigms for considering European integration: one economic, the other political. The former focuses narrowly on the economic gains of integration associated with the creation of a single market, the latter on the political processes and institutions. However, as shown here, the two are not separate processes but inextricably linked. Business appreciated this link in adopting an encompassing view of European integration that was not simply about tariffs but about political integration as well. As Polanyi made clear, the market is not natural but itself a construct dependent on political and legal processes to create and regulate it.[14] Separating the two, in the way that economists and political scientists have done, results in a partial and distorted view of the process of integration. A political economy of European integration seems the obvious starting point in this respect but even this may not go far enough in emphasizing the interaction between political and economic integration.[15] Perhaps one way forward, from a business perspective, would be to think about environments and landscapes as this encompasses economic, political and societal aspects without distinction.[16]

The third point relates more specifically to the study of business. Individual firms, and business more generally, play a fundamental role in these interactions. Yet again, consideration of the role of business tends to be separated. On one hand, management scientists and business historians have tended

[13] B. Laffan, R. O'Donnell and M. Smith, *Europe's Experimental Union: Rethinking Integration* (London: Routledge, 2000), 8.

[14] Karl Polanyi, *The Great Transformation: The Political and Economic Origins of Our Time* (Boston: Beacon Press, 1944). In relation to European integration, see Peter Kapteyn, *The Stateless Market: The European Dilemma of Integration and Civilization* (London: Routledge, 1993).

[15] Erik Jones and Amy Verdun, "Introduction," in Erik Jones and Amy Verdun (eds.), *The Political Economy of European Integration: Theory and Analysis* (London: Routledge, 2005), 1–10.

[16] See G. Federico and J. Foreman-Peck, "Industrial Policies in Europe: Introduction," in J. Foreman-Peck and G. Federico (eds.), *European Industrial Policy: The Twentieth Century Experience* (Oxford: Oxford University Press, 1999), 4.

to consider corporate strategy in response to European integration where the business environment is taken as the given to which firms react. On the other, political scientists are devoting increasing amounts of time and energy to the political role of business in European integration; more and more this means corporate lobbying by individual firms as well as the more traditional interest in business interest groups.[17] Here business is clearly not reacting to its environment but acting to influence it. Yet there is remarkably little dialogue between these two literatures. To adapt Hirschman's famous model of action, management scientists and business historians have concentrated on exit and loyalty in the form of corporate strategy, whereas political scientists have focused on voice.[18] All three need to be considered together as part of a fuller picture of corporate perceptions and responses to European integration. Political action needs to be incorporated as part of corporate strategy.[19] In this respect, it is well known that multinational enterprises are market makers but relatively little study has been given to the extent to which they are not "institution-takers" but have "actively constructed new environments, including institutional infrastructures."[20]

Currently, this should be pushing on an open door for management scientists and business historians because political scientists and political economists are becoming increasingly interested in firms as actors. There is an increasing awareness of the significance of firms but that these remained "the biggest 'black box' in our analysis."[21] Perhaps most significant here have been the efforts of Hall and Soskice to build on earlier institutional

[17] Robert Bennett, "The Impact of European Economic Integration on Business Associations: The UK Case," *West European Politics*, Vol. 20, No. 3 (1997), 61–90; Pieter Bouwen, "Corporate Lobbying in the European Union: The Logic of Access" *Journal of European Public Policy*, Vol. 9, No. 3 (2002), 365–90; David Coen, "The Evolution of the Large Firm as a Political Actor in the European Union," *Journal of European Public Policy*, Vol. 4, No. 1 (1997), 91–108; Justin Greenwood and Mark Aspinwall (eds.), *Collective Action in the European Union: Interests and the New Politics of Associability* (London: Routledge, 1998); Sonia Mazey and Jeremy Richardson (eds.), *Lobbying in the European Community* (Oxford: Oxford University Press, 1993); and R. H. Pedler and M. P. C. M. van Schendelen (eds.), *Lobbying the European Union: Companies, Trade Associations and Issue Groups* (Aldershot: Dartmouth, 1994).

[18] Albert Hirschman, *Exit, Voice and Loyalty: Responses to Decline in Firms, Organizations, and States* (Cambridge MA: Harvard University Press, 1970).

[19] Amy Hillman, Asghar Zardhooki and Leonard Bierman, "Corporate Political Strategies and Firm Performance: Indications of Firm-specific Benefits from Personal Service in the US Government," *Strategic Management Journal*, Vol. 20, No. 1 (1999), 68. See also David Vogel, "The Study of Business and Politics," *California Management Review*, Vol. 38, No. 3 (1996), 146–65.

[20] Bob Hancké, *Large Firms and Institutional Change: Industrial Renewal and Economic Restructuring in France*, (Oxford: Oxford University Press, 2002), 199.

[21] Neil Fligstein and Alec Stone Sweet, "Institutionalising the Treaty of Rome," in Alec Stone Sweet, Wayne Sandholtz and Neil Fligstein (eds.), *The Institutionalization of Europe* (Oxford: Oxford University Press, 2001), 33.

models with their "varieties of capitalism" approach. Their aim is "to bring firms back into the center of the analysis of comparative capitalism": it is to present "a firm-centered political economy that regards companies as the crucial actors in a capitalist economy."[22] As such, it is a clear corrective to the previous exclusive focus on the role of the state in economic development.[23] Given the expertise of business historians in understanding firms, they are ideally placed to engage in this new interest.

These lessons, if adopted, present an ambitious and extensive agenda across the social sciences. This agenda places business historians in a prime position to be at the center of these developments. It will only happen if they become Europeanized. This book has made a start in raising these issues but it is only a start. Few deny some role for business in the story of European integration but much of that story still remains to be told.

[22] Peter Hall and David Soskice, "An Introduction to Varieties of Capitalism," in Peter Hall and David Soskice (eds.), *Varieties of Capitalism: The Institutional Foundations of Comparative Advantage* (Oxford: Oxford University Press, 2001), 4 and 6. For their precursors, see J. Rogers Hollingsworth and Robert Boyer (eds.), *Contemporary Capitalism: The Embeddedness of Institutions* (Cambridge: Cambridge University Press, 1997); and Peter Hall, 'The Political Economy of Europe in an Era of Interdependence," in Herbert Kitschelt, Peter Lange, Gary Marks and John Stephens (eds.), *Continuity and Change in Contemporary Capitalism* (Cambridge: Cambridge University Press, 1999), 162.

[23] Vivien A. Schmidt, *The Futures of European Capitalism* (Oxford: Oxford University Press), 110–11; Hancké, *Large Firms*.

Index